THE

ESSENTIAL

WALLERSTEIN

Also by Immanuel Wallerstein

Utopistics: Historical Choices of the Twenty-first Century

After Liberalism

THE
ESSENTIAL
WALLERSTEIN

IMMANUEL WALLERSTEIN

THE NEW PRESS   NEW YORK

Published in the United States by The New Press, New York, 2000
Distributed by W. W. Norton & Company, Inc., New York

Pages xiii–xiv constitute an extension of this copyright page.

LIBRARY OF CONGRESS CATALOGING-IN-PUBLICATION DATA

Wallerstein, Immanuel Maurice, 1930–
    The Essential Wallerstein / Immanuel Wallerstein.
        p.   cm.
    ISBN 1-56584-585-4 (hc.)
    ISBN 1-56584-593-5 (pbk.)
    Included bibliographical references and index.
    1. Economic history.   2. Capitalism.   3. Wallerstein, Immanuel
Maurice, 1930–   . I. Title.
    HC51.W29   2000
    330.1—dc21   99-35781

The New Press as established in 1990 as a not-for-profit alternative to the large, commercial publishing houses currently dominating the book publishing industry. The New Press operates in the public interest rather than for private gain, and is committed to publishing, in innovative ways, works of educational, cultural, and community value that are often deemed insufficiently profitable.

The New Press
450 West 41st Street, 6th Floor
New York, NY 10036

www.thenewpress.com

Printed in Canada

9 8 7 6 5 4 3

To the memory of
and in honor of the legacy of
Terence K. Hopkins

Contents

—Preface

I dedicated my most important and influential work, *The Modern World-System*, Volume I, to TKH, in acknowledgment of the continuing influence of Terence K. Hopkins on my work. In 1974, I was remembering the previous twenty years. But there were another two decades of friendship and collaboration after that. And now that he is gone, I wish to say that he is not gone, and that he left a legacy which those who knew him well continue to cherish.

In a reader that brings together my writings over some thirty years, there are many other acknowledgments I need to make publicly. I am a product, educationally, of Columbia College and its general education program, and of the graduate Department of Sociology at Columbia, probably the single most influential locus of world sociology in the 1950s and dedicated to the exposition of structuralism-functionalism. My efforts to synthesize knowledge from many arenas is surely in the general education tradition of Columbia College. My relationship to the graduate program in sociology is more complex. I essentially am, and was from the beginning, a heretic in terms of that mode of social science. But I learned a great deal from having to grapple with what was then an orthodoxy and which was always an intellectually serious endeavor, and no doubt I bear the marks of its training.

At Columbia, there were many professors (some of them later colleagues) whom I recall as intellectually exciting and therefore influential: Mark Van Doren for his wisdom and his puckish insolence, Paul Tillich for his efforts to elucidate the links between moral choice and intellectual issues, C. Wright Mills for his intellectual panache and willingness to buck the tide, Robert S. Lynd for the seriousness of his lifelong political commitment, and Daniel Bell who has always forced me to develop strong arguments in order to defend my political differences with him.

Then, there are the colleagues, in the sense of age-peers who shared my intellectual quest and with whom (in addition to Hopkins) I have argued, debated, and discussed over the past thirty years. There are the three with whom I made up "The Gang of Four"—Samir Amin, Giovanni Arrighi, and Gunder Frank. We wrote two books together, and have attended countless colloquia together. I used to say that I agreed with each of them 80% of the way. In recent years, this percentage has gone down for Gunder Frank. But they have all been intellectual and personal companions. I hesitate to start making a list of all the others with whom I have worked, but minimally I should list the following with whom I have collaborated extensively: the late Otto Kreye in Germany, Etienne Balibar in France, Pablo González Casanova in Mexico, and Anouar Abdel-Malek in Egypt/France.

As for my students at Columbia, McGill, and Binghamton, they have been an endless source of stimulation to me, and the ultimate reward of being a professor. Again, the list is very long, and I will restrict myself to thanking the four of them (no longer students) who gave me their sober and sobering advice on what to include in this volume: Wally Goldfrank, Bill Martin, Richard Lee, and Georgi Derluguian.

And first and not least, I express my gratitude to Beatrice, who has stayed the course for me at many a crucial moment and has almost always given me good advice, of which I have taken less than I should. I promise to reform.

—Permissions

1. "Ethnicity and National Integration in West Africa": *Cahiers d'études africaines*, No. 3, October 1960, 129–39.
2. "Fanon and the Revolutionary Class": *The Capitalist World-Economy* (Cambridge: Cambridge University Press, 1979), 250–68.
3. "Radical Intellectuals in a Liberal Society": Immanuel Wallerstein and Paul Starr, eds., *University Crisis Reader*, New York: Random House, 1971, II, 471–77.
4. "Africa in a Capitalist World": *Issue*, III, 3, Fall 1973, 1–11.
5. "The Rise and Future Demise of the World Capitalist": *Comparative Studies in Society & History*, XVI, 4, September 1974, 387–415. Reprinted with the permission of Cambridge University Press.
6. "Modernization: Requiescat in Pace": L. Coser & O. Larsen, eds., *The Uses of Controversy in Sociology*. New York: Free Press, 1976, 131–35. Copyright © 1976 by the Free Press, a Division of Simon & Schuster. Reprinted with permission of the publisher.
7. "Societal Development, or Development of the World-System?": *International Sociology*, I, 1, March 1986, 3–17.
8. "World-Systems Analysis": A. Giddens & J. Turner, eds., *Social Theory Today*. Cambridge: Polity Press, 1987, 309–24.
9. "Hold the Tiller Firm": *Comparative Civilization Review*, 30, Spring 1994, 72–80.
10. "Time and Duration": *Thesis Eleven*, No. 54, August 1998, 79–87.
11. "What Are We Bounding, and Whom, When We Bound Social Research?": *Social Research*, LXII, 4, Winter 1995, 839–56.
12. "Social Science and the Quest for a Just Society": *American Journal of Sociology*, CII, 5, March 1997, 1241–57.
13. "Long Waves as Capitalist Process": *Review*, VII, 4, Spring 1984, 559–75.
14. "Commodity Chains in the World-Economy Prior to 1800": *Review*, X, !, Summer 1986, 157–70.
15. "Households as an Institution of the World-Economy": J. Sprey, ed., *Fashioning Family Theory: New Approaches*. Newbury Park, CA: Sage, 1990, 34–50.

16. "The Three Instances of Hegemony in the History of the Capitalist World-Economy": *International Journal of Comparative Sociology*, XXIV, 1–2, January–April 1983, 100–08.

17. "Culture as the Ideological Battleground of the Modern World-System": *Hitotsubashi Journal of Social Studies*, XXI, 1, August 1989, 5–22.

18. "The Construction of Peoplehood": *Sociological Forum*, II, 2, Spring 1987, 373–88.

19. "Does India Exist?": *Unthinking Social Science*, Cambridge: Polity, 1991, 130–34.

20. "Class Formation in the Capitalist World-Economy": *Politics and Society*, V, 3, 1975, 367–75.

21. "The Bourgeois(ie) as Concept and Reality": *New Left Review*, No. 167, January–February 1988, 91–106.

22. "The Ideological Tensions of Capitalism": J. Smith, et al., eds., *Racism, Sexism, and the World-System*. New York: Greenwood Press, 1988, 3–9.

23. "1968, Revolution in the World-System": *Theory and Society*, XVIII, 4, July 1989, 431–49.

24. "Social Science and the Communist Interlude": *Polish Sociological Review*, No. 1, 1997, 3–12.

25. "America and the World": *Theory and Society*, XXI, 1, February 1992, 1–28.

26. "The Agonies of Liberalism": *New Left Review*, No. 204, March–April 1994, 3–17.

27. "Peace, Stability, and Legitimacy": G. Lundestad, ed., *The Fall of Great Powers: Peace, Stability, and Legitimacy*. Oslo: Scandinavian University Press, 1994, 331–49.

28. "The End of What Modernity?": *Theory and Society*, XXIV, 4, August 1995, 471–88.

—Introduction

My intellectual biography is one long quest for an adequate explanation of contemporary reality that I and others might act upon. This quest is both intellectual and political—I have always felt it could not be one without being at the same time the other—for myself or for anyone.

I suppose I began this quest when I was in high school in New York City during the Second World War. My family was politically conscious, and world affairs were always discussed in our home. The fight against Nazism and fascism was of primary concern to us long before Pearl Harbor. We were also very conscious of the great split in the global left at the time, that between the Second and Third Internationals. Even in the muted atmosphere of wartime unity, the issues that divided the two Internationals were salient, and they were reflected for me at a local level by the political differences between New York's Liberal and American Labor parties. When I entered Columbia College in 1947, the most vibrant political organization on campus during my freshman year was the American Veterans Committee (AVC). Although I was too young to have been a veteran, I attended the public meetings of the AVC, and saw it torn apart (and destroyed) by this same split.

My own reaction to these debates was complicated. The Social-Democrats convinced me of almost everything in their critique of the Communists: the evils of Stalinism and terror, the unprincipled swervings of the party line, the *langue de bois*. At the same time, however, the Communists convinced me of almost everything they said about the Social-Democrats—about their chronic caving in to Western nationalisms, the incredible weakness of their opposition to capitalist polarization, and their lack of serious militancy concerning racial injustice.

Politically, this created dilemmas with which I have had to wrestle ever since. Intellectually, it turned me to a set of questions that I have developed in my writings over the years: the nature of what I came to call the antisystemic movements, and how their activities were structured by systemic constraints from which they were never able fully to release themselves. In short, I began to historicize these movements, not only in order to understand how they came to do the things they did but also the better to formulate the political options that were truly available in the present.

The early postwar years of 1945–50 were heady days when all seemed possible. They ended for me (and for many others) with the war in Korea. Suddenly, the influence of anti-Communism was overwhelming, and McCarthyism began to flourish in the United States. I served in the U.S. Army from 1951–53, and when I returned to Columbia I decided to write my master's thesis on McCarthyism as a phenomenon of American political culture. I drew on Wright Mills's distinction in *New Men of Labor* between sophisticated conservatives and the practical right, to argue that McCarthyism was a program of the practical right, only marginally concerned with Communists and in fact directed primarily against the sophisticated conservatives. It was a well-received essay, widely cited at the time. It confirmed my sense that I should consider myself, in the language of the 1950s, a "political sociologist."

I decided nonetheless not to make American politics my prime area of intellectual concern. Since my high school years, I had a keen interest in the non-European world. I followed events in modern India in particular, and had read much of Gandhi and Nehru. In 1951, I was involved in an international youth congress, where I met many delegates from Africa who were older than I and already held important political positions in their countries. In 1952, another youth congress was held in Dakar, Senegal. Suddenly I found myself amidst the turmoil of what would soon be the independence movements (in this case of French West Africa).

I decided to make Africa the focus of my intellectual concerns and solidarity efforts. Because I spoke French, and had contacts, I became one of the few scholars who studied Africa across the European linguistic barriers. In 1955, I obtained a Ford Foundation African Fellowship to study in Africa and write a dissertation on the Gold Coast (Ghana) and the Ivory Coast in terms of the role voluntary associations played in the rise of the nationalist movements in the two countries. I had now become an Africa scholar, an intellectual role I would continue to play for two decades. I wrote many books and articles on African themes and issues, and in 1973 I became president of the (U.S.) African Studies Association. Over a twenty-year period, I managed to travel all over Africa, to perhaps three-quarters of the separate states.

If my intellectual quest led me early on away from the familiar grounds of my own country to contemporary Africa—still a colonized continent when I first visited and began to study it—it was because I had a gut feeling in the 1950s that the most important thing happening in the twentieth century was the struggle to overcome the control by the West of the rest of the world. Today we call this a concern with North–South relations, or with core–periphery relations, or with Eurocentrism.

It has to be said that, in the 1950s and indeed for a long time thereafter, my assessment of what was most important was not widely shared. For most people, what some called the cold war between democracy and totalitarianism and others called the struggle between the bourgeoisie and the proletariat (all of these terms being rather narrowly defined) was (and indeed for many remains) the central defining issue of our time. My quest was therefore an upward battle not only against a wide consensus in the political and scholarly worlds but against the concepts deriving from this dominant view that I had myself internalized. Africa is no longer the empirical locus of my work, but I credit my African studies with opening my eyes both to the burning political issues of the contemporary world and to the scholarly questions of how to analyze the history of the modern world-system. It was Africa that was responsible for challenging the more stultifying parts of my education.

I initially thought that the academic and political debates were merely over the empirical analysis of contemporary reality, but I soon became aware that the very tools of analysis were themselves to be questioned. The ones I had been taught seemed to me to circumscribe our empirical analyses and distort our interpretations. Slowly, over some twenty years, my views evolved, until by the 1970s I began to say that I was trying to look at the world from a perspective that I called "world-systems analysis." This involved two major intellectual decisions. The first was that the choice of the "unit of analysis" was crucial, and that the only plausible unit of analysis was a "world-system," or more generally, an "historical social system."

The second intellectual decision was to discard the so-called *Methodenstreit* that undergirded and divided all of modern social science—that between idiographic humanism and nomothetic science—a totally false debate. Instead of choosing sides, which all and sundry insistently adjured me to do, I became convinced—at first instinctively and later in more reasoned ways—that all analysis, if it were to grapple seriously with the description and explanation of the real world, had to be simultaneously historic and systemic.

The case for these two basic premises of my work—the world-system as a unit of analysis, and the insistence that all social science must be simultaneously historic and systemic—will be found in the essays in this volume. Neither premise was popular or greeted with enthusiasm when I first argued them. The first premise became my scholarly trademark, and has had the greatest impact. Once I presented more fully the case for the world-system as a unit of analysis, most notably in volume one of *The Modern World-System* and secondly in the essay reproduced here as number 5, both of which were published in 1974, more people responded favorably. Some were completely convinced; others merely conceded that the argument had to be taken seriously. Those who disputed it most vigorously often did not argue against it on empirical grounds (in terms of its factual correctness) but on epistemological grounds (because it was not a so-called falsifiable proposition).

I thus discovered that it would not be enough to argue for a different description of the real world. The crucial battle was over how we could know which description was in fact true, or truer, or more plausible, or more useful than another. I had to fight the epistemological battles in order that I and others be permitted to proceed with our analyses of social processes as integrated, complex wholes. The essays in part two of this volume show how I increasingly turned my attention to these epistemological arguments and the ways in which they implied different visions of social reality.

I found all of this empirically fruitful as well. I discovered that these two premises allowed me to reinterpret many old debates and collect new and important kinds of data that did indeed, in my view, illuminate contemporary reality. In particular, this revised way of looking at social reality clarified the historical choices involved in constructing the existing world-system as well as those that we shall have to make in the near future as we construct its successor world-system (or systems). World-systems analysis allowed me to range widely in terms of concrete issues, but always in such a way that the pieces might fit together at the end of the exercise. It is not that world-systems analysis enabled me to "discover the truth." It is rather that it enabled me to make what I considered to be plausible interpretations of social reality in ways that I believe are more useful for all of us in making political and moral decisions. It is also that it enabled me to distinguish between long-lasting structures and those momentary expressions of reality that we so regularly reify into fashionable theories. The enormous recent furor concerning so-called "globalization" is an example of the latter.

I concentrated my energy on the description of the historical functioning and development of the modern world-system, which I insisted was a capitalist world-economy. I sought to describe its institutional pillars, its historical origin, and the reasons why I thought it had entered into a period of systemic crisis and therefore of chaotic transition to some new order. Part three of this book contains analytic descriptions of the major institutional structures of this capitalist world-economy—the Kondratieff cycles, the commodity chains, the income-pooling households, the interstate system and its hegemonic cycles, and the geoculture—as well as a detailed critique of both national development and developmentalism as an explanatory model (modernization theory).

The term "world-system" often evokes assumptions of equilibrium and consensus. These are the furthest things from my mind. Indeed the most interesting thing about systems is how all have deep cleavages, which they seek to limit by institutionalizing them. Georg Simmel, Lewis Coser, and Max Gluckman all argued this long ago. However, it is equally true that systems never succeed entirely in eliminating their internal conflicts, or even in keeping them from taking violent forms. This understanding remains the major legacy we have from the work of Karl Marx.

Further, as we have come collectively to know quite clearly in the last few decades, there exist more than one cleavage in any historical system. I therefore began to spend energy trying to analyze which were the major cleavages in the modern world-system, how they differed from and related to one another, and how each limited the effects of the others. These are the themes of part four, an effort to parse out what I think of as the five major cleavages of our modern world: race, nation, class, ethnicity, and gender.

Finally, I turn to the question that ultimately concerns us all most: what to do. I have called part five "Resistance, Hope, and Deception." These three words describe for me the story of the antisystemic movements of the modern world-system. I try to relate the story of these movements to the larger geopolitical scheme, as well as to the political concepts we have evolved to describe both our realities and our aspirations.

I had originally conceived this book with these four sections only. I added a first section of earlier writings (prior to 1974, the date of the publication of *The Modern World-System*, volume one), primarily about Africa and to a lesser extent about the modern university, at the insistence of several of my friends. Since I believe that one cannot understand or evaluate any author without taking into account the context in which he/she wrote, and in particular against what he/she was writing, I was grateful for this suggestion.

Part one of this book thus shows how I made my way towards the elaboration of the position I came to call world-systems analysis. I struggled with what might be meant by ethnicity. I tried to make sense of the exciting and influential writings of Frantz Fanon. I tried to draw conclusions from 1968 about the correct political stance for "radical intellectuals in a liberal society." And I tried to fit my early concern with Africa into my later turn to the study of the modern world-system as a whole and to the questions of the structures of knowledge.

As I have continued to read, observe, analyze, and write, I have come to recognize the recurring and underlying themes of my intellectual venture, what are for me the most difficult questions to elucidate. Four stand out. The first is clearly the weight to give to the universal strivings we all allow ourselves to invent as opposed to the claims of the particular valuations on which we all insist. It is easy to consider one's own views to be expressions of the universal and the views of others as so many expressions of multiple particulars. But if self-centered universalism is Scylla, Charybdis is self-centered difference, the claim that every social expression, every scholarly argument, every perception of the world is equally valid or useful or virtuous, and that there are neither intellectual nor moral distinctions worth making. Both positions negate the possibility of collectively analyzing, appreciating, and approaching a maximally rational, maximally democratic world.

The second persistent issue is the relationship between the real world and our perception of it. Hardly new, this has been central to the debates of recent decades. My own position is quite clear. There exists a real world, and it is the object of our scholarly observations. Else, why would we bother writing about it? In any case, we all live in this real world every day and are thoroughly aware that we must take it into account in everything we do. If we fail to do this, we are seen as psychotic. On the other hand, it is equally clear to me that we perceive this real world as through a pair of glasses, and that the cut of their lenses largely determines what we think we see. That reality is socially constructed seems to me self-evident, provided we remember that its construction is truly social—that is, collective and not individual.

Clearly, to insist simultaneously that a real world exists *and* that we can only view it through a sort of social spectacles creates a dilemma for the serious scholar. It requires constant reflection on how our vision is distorted, and how we can improve the quality of our perception. But each reflection on ourselves is itself subject to the same contradiction. It is this dilemma that has pushed me to make epistemological issues central to my analyses.

The third recurring theme, again not a new one, has been the relationship of intellectual analysis to political action—the ancient question of theory and praxis. I have already said that I personally see no conflict. Quite the contrary! But once again, I think of this as a problem of extremes to avoid. On the one side lies the false claim of disinterestedness so widely mouthed as the presumed indicator of scientificity. On the other side is submission by the scholar to some authority—of the state or of a party—on the grounds of political loyalty. It seems to me that it is the duty of the scholar to be subversive of received truths, and that this subversion can be socially useful only if it reflects a serious attempt to engage with and understand the real world as best we can.

The final theme is how to account for in a single analysis the facts that the world has enduring structures *and* that it is constantly changing. This is of course a second epistemological question, and one to which I have given much attention from the beginning. Most of us tend to speak either in the form of more or less timeless truths or in the form of descriptions of unique situations. But no situation can truly be described as unique, since the words with which we describe it are categories that necessarily presume features common to some larger group, and hence to some continuing structure that appears to be stable. At the same time, of course, no truth holds forever, because the world is inevitably and eternally changing. Rather, we must work with temporarily useful structures/categories that bear within them the processes by which they are transformed into other structures/categories.

I believe that I have been fairly consistent in my views over the time I have been writing. Still, I have to acknowledge that there were three turning points in my political and intellectual development. The first, as

I have already indicated, was my struggle with the issues that have plagued the left for most of its organizational history—the rift between the Second and Third Internationals. The second was my encounter with Africa and with national liberation movements. This enabled me to put the debates of the Internationals into their proper context, as essentially European debates that ignored the fundamental and ongoing polarization of the capitalist world-economy. And the third was the world revolution of 1968, which I experienced directly at Columbia University, and which helped expunge from my thinking both the lingering illusions of liberalism and a rosy view of the antisystemic movements. It sobered me up.

Inevitably, my views evolved in some important respects. This did not happen unaided. I acknowledge a continuing intellectual debt to Marx, Freud, Schumpeter, and Karl Polanyi. Among those I have known personally and read extensively, the three that have had the most impact in modifying my line of argument (as opposed to deepening a parallel line of argument) have been Frantz Fanon, Fernand Braudel, and Ilya Prigogine (in that chronological order). Fanon represented for me the expression of the insistence by those disenfranchised by the modern world-system that they have a voice, a vision, and a claim not merely to justice but to intellectual valuation. Braudel more than anyone else made me conscious of the central importance of the social construction of time and space and its impact on our analyses. And Prigogine forced me to face the implications of a world in which certainties did not exist—but knowledge still did. The reader will no doubt perceive how these three thinkers have changed the shape of my arguments. (I discuss them directly in essays 2 and 10.)

World-systems analysis, as I argue in essay 9, is not a theory but a protest against neglected issues and deceptive epistemologies. It is a call for intellectual change, indeed for "unthinking" the premises of nineteenth-century social science, as I say in the title of one of my books. It is an intellectual task that is and has to be a political task as well, because—I insist—the search for the true and the search for the good is but a single quest. If we are to move forward to a world that is substantively rational, in Max Weber's usage of this term, we can neglect neither the intellectual nor the political challenges. And neither can we separate these from each other. We can only struggle uneasily with both challenges simultaneously, and push forward as best we can.

Part One

En Route to World-Systems Analysis

1—Ethnicity and National Integration in West Africa

This article was the direct result of my encounter with contemporary African reality, in particular in Ghana and the Ivory Coast, where I had done research on my doctoral dissertation. I was initially puzzled about the fact that there seemed to be simultaneously a strong nationalist movement and a flourishing of what were called "tribal associations," and that quite often the same people seemed to be involved in both. To understand this, I had to reframe "tribalism" as "ethnicity"—one of the first usages of this term, I believe—and to see the rise of ethnicity not as a contradiction to the rise of nationalism but as a parallel process in the development of the modern world.

M any writers on West Africa, whether academic or popular, assert that there is currently a conflict between tribalism and nationalism which threatens the stability of the new West African nations. In fact, the relationship between tribalism and nationalism is complex. Although ethnicity (tribalism) is in some respects dysfunctional for national integration (a prime objective of nationalist movements), it is also in some respects functional. Discussion of the presumed conflict might be clarified by discussing this hypothesis in some detail. Before doing so, it should be noted that we deliberately use the term ethnicity in preference to tribalism, and we shall preface our remarks by carefully defining our use of the term ethnicity.

In a traditional, rural setting, an individual is a member first of all of a family and then of a tribe.[1] The demands the tribe makes on him vary with the complexity of the tribal system of government,[2] as does the degree to which family and tribal loyalties are distinct. To a large extent, however, family and tribal loyalties support each other harmoniously.

Under colonial rule, the social change brought about by European administrators and the process of urbanization has led to widespread shifts of loyalty. This process has been called "detribalization." Writers speaking of tribal loyalty often confuse three separate phenomena which it would be useful to distinguish: loyalty to the family; loyalty to the tribal

3

community; and loyalty to the tribal government, or chief.[3] Often what a writer means by detribalization is simply a decline in chiefly authority. It does not necessarily follow that an individual who is no longer loyal to his chief has rejected as well the tribe as a community to which he owes certain duties and from which he expects a certain security.[4]

It may be objected that West Africans do not make a distinction between the tribal government and the tribal community. This is perhaps true in the rural areas but they do when they reach the city. For in the city they find that there are new sources of power and prestige which, for many persons, are more rewarding than the tribal government. Hence they tend to lose some of their respect for the authority of the chief. The tribe, however, still can play a useful, if partially new, function as an ethnic group. The *Gemeinschaft*-like community to which the individual belongs may no longer be exactly the same group as before; the methods of government are different; the role in the national structure is different. This community, however, bears sufficient resemblance to the rural, traditional "tribe" that often the same term is used. In this discussion, however, we shall use "tribe" for the group in the rural areas, and ethnic group for the one in the towns.

Some writers have challenged the very existence of detribalization. Rouch, for example, says he finds instead "supertribalization" among the Zabrama and other immigrants to Ghana.[5] For as Mitchell has commented of another part of Africa: "People in rural areas are apt to take their tribe for granted, but when they come to the town their tribal membership assumes new importance."[6] This is, however, a false debate. We shall see that quite often the group from which the individual is "detribalized" (that is, the tribe to whose chief he no longer pays the same fealty) is not necessarily the same group into which he is "supertribalized" (that is, the ethnic group to which he feels strong bonds of attachment in the urban context).

Membership in an ethnic group is a matter of social definition, an interplay of the self-definition of members and the definition of other groups. The ethnic group seems to need a minimum size to function effectively, and hence to achieve social definition.[7] Now it may be that an individual who defined himself as being of a certain tribe in a rural area find no others from his village in the city. He may simply redefine himself as a member of a new and larger group.[8] This group would normally correspond to some logical geographical or linguistic unit, but it may never have existed as a social entity before this act.

Indeed, this kind of redefinition is quite common. Two actions give such redefinition performance and status. One is official government sanction, in the form of census categories,[9] or the recognition of "town chiefs"; the other is the formation of ethnic (tribal) associations which are described more accurately by the French term, *association d'originaires.* These associations are the principal form of ethnic (tribal) "government"[10] in West African towns today.

Some of these ethnic associations use clearly territorial bases of defining membership, despite the fact that they may consider their relationship with traditional chiefs as their *raison d'être.* For example, in the Ivory Coast, Amon d'Aby has described the process as follows:

> One of the most curious phenomena noted in the Ivory Coast immediately after Independence was the marked tendency of indigenous elites to create regional associations.
>
> Inhabitants of an administrative district or of several combined were grouped in these associations. Their purpose was no longer that of organizing sports and other recreational activities as the prewar apolitical structures. It was rather to facilitate progress in their areas. The associations tried to foster the collaboration of the young educated generations with the older generations represented by their customary chiefs who still held on to antiquated concepts and outdated policies.[11]

It should be observed that the administrative units in question (les cercles) are the creation of the colonial government, and have no necessary relationship to traditional groupings. Such ethnic associations, formed around nontraditional administrative units, are found throughout West Africa.[12] A presumably classic example of the significance of tribalism in West African affairs is the role which traditional Yoruba-Ibo rivalry has played in Nigeria politics. Yet, Dr. S. O. Biobaku has pointed out that the very use of the term "Yoruba" to refer to various peoples in Western Nigeria resulted largely from the influence of the Anglican mission in Abeokuta in the 19th century. The standard "Yoruba" language evolved by the mission was the new unifying factor. Hodgkin remarks:

> "Everyone recognizes that the notion of 'being a Nigerian' is a new kind of conception. But it would seem that the notion of 'being a Yoruba' is not very much older."[13]

Sometimes, the definition of the ethnic group may even be said to derive from a common occupation — indeed, even dress — rather than from a common language or traditional polity. For example, an Accra man often tends to designate all men (or at least all merchants) coming from savannah areas as "Hausamen", although many are not Hausa, as defined in traditional Hausa areas.[14] Similarly the Abidjan resident may designate these same men as Dioula.[15] Such designations may originate in error, but many individuals from savannah areas take advantage of this confusion to merge themselves into this grouping. They go, for example to live in the *Sabon Zongo* (the Hausa residential area), and even often adopt Islam, to aid the assimilation.[16] They do so because, scorned by the dominant ethnic group of the town, they find security within a relatively stronger group (Hausa in Accra, Dioula in Abidjan, Bambara in Thiès), with whom they feel some broad cultural affinity. Indeed, assimilation to this stronger group may represent considerable advance in the prestige-scale for the individual.[17]

Thus we see that ethnic groups are defined in terms that are not necessarily traditional but are rather a function of the urban social situation. By ethnicity, we mean the feeling of loyalty to this new ethnic group of the towns. Epstein has urged us to distinguish between two senses of what he calls "tribalism": the intratribal, which is the "persistence of, or continued attachment to, tribal custom," and tribalism within the social structure, which is the "persistence of loyalties and values, which stem from a particular form of social organization."[18] This corresponds to the distinction we made above between loyalty to tribal government and loyalty to the tribal community. In using the term ethnicity, we are referring to this latter kind of loyalty. This distinction cannot be rigid. Individuals in West Africa move back and forth between city and rural area. Different loyalties may be activated in different contexts. But more and more, with increasing urbanization, loyalty to the ethnic community is coming to supersede loyalty to the tribal community and government. It is the relationship of this new ethnic loyalty to the emergent nation-state that we intend to explore here.

There are four principal ways in which ethnicity serves to aid national integration. First, ethnic groups tend to assume some of the functions of the extended family and hence they diminish the importance of kinship roles; second, ethnic groups serve as a mechanism of resocialization; third, ethnic groups help keep the class structure fluid, and so prevent the emergence of castes; fourth, ethnic groups serve as an outlet for political tensions.

First, in a modern nation-state, loyalties to ethnic groups interfere less with national integration than loyalties to the extended family. It is obvious that particularistic loyalties run counter to the most efficient allocation of occupational and political roles in a state. Such particularistic loyalties cannot be entirely eliminated. Medium-sized groups based on such loyalties perform certain functions—of furnishing social and psychological security—which cannot yet in West Africa be performed either by the government or by the nuclear family. In the towns, the ethnic group is to some extent replacing the extended family in performing these functions.

The role of the ethnic group in providing food and shelter to the unemployed, marriage and burial expenses, assistance in locating a job has been widely noted.[19] West African governments are not yet in a position to offer a really effective network of such services, because of lack of resources and personnel. Yet if these services would not be provided, widespread social unrest could be expected.

It is perhaps even more important that ethnic associations counter the isolation and anomy that uprooted rural immigrants feel in the city. Thus Balandier has noted that in Brazzaville the early emergence of ethnic associations tends to indicate a high degree of uprootedness among the ethnic group, which tends to be found particularly in small minorities.[20]

But from the point of view of national integration is the ethnic group really more functional than the extended family? In the sense that the ethnic group, by extending the extended family, dilutes it, the answer is yes. The ties are particularistic and diffuse, but less so and less strong than in the case of kinship groups. Furthermore, such a development provides a precedent for the principle of association on a nonkinship basis. It can be seen perhaps as a self-liquidating phase on the road to the emergence of the nuclear family.[21] Thus, it can be said with Parsons, that ethnic groups "constitute a focus of security beyond the family unit which is in some respects less dysfunctional for the society than community solidarity would be."[22]

The second function suggested was that of resocialization. The problem of instructing large numbers of persons in new normative patterns is a key one for nations undergoing rapid social change. There are few institutions which can perform this task. The formal educational system is limited in that it is a long-range process with small impact on the contemporary adult population. In addition, universal free education, though the objective of all West African governments at the present time, is not yet a reality in any of these countries. The occupational system only touches a small proportion of the population, and a certain amount of resocialization is a prerequisite to entry into it. The government is limited in services as well as in access to the individuals involved (short of totalitarian measures). The family is in many ways a bulwark of resistance to change.

The ethnic groups, touching almost all the urban population, can then be said to be a major means of resocialization. They aid this process in three ways. The ethnic group offers the individual a wide network of persons, often of very varying skills and positions, who are under some obligation to retrain him and guide him in the ways of urban life.

By means of ethnic contacts, the individual is recruited into many non-ethnic nationalist groupings. Apter found evidence of this is Ghana, where he observed a remarkable number of classificatory brothers and other relatives working together in the same party, kinship thus providing a "reliable organizational core in the nationalist movement."[23] Birmingham and Jahoda similarly suggest the hypothesis that kinship (read, ethnic) links mediated Ghana political affiliation.[24]

And lastly, members of the ethnic group seek to raise the status of the whole group, which in turn makes it more possible for the individual members to have the mobility and social contact which will speed the process of resocialization.[25]

The third function is the maintenance of a fluid class system. There is in West Africa, as there has been historically in the United States, some correlation between ethnic groups and social class, particularly at the lower rungs of the social ladder. Certain occupations are often reserved for certain ethnic groups.[26] This occurs very obviously because of the use of ethnic ties to obtain jobs and learn skills.

It would seem then that ethnicity contributes to rigid stratification. But this view neglects the normative context. One of the major values of contemporary West African nations is that of equality. Individuals may feel helpless to try to achieve this goal by their own efforts. Groups are less reticent, and as we mentioned before, its members usually seek to raise the status of the group. The continued expansion of the exchange economy means continued possibility of social mobility. As long as social mobility continues, this combination of belief in equality and the existence of ethnic groups striving to achieve it for themselves works to minimize any tendency towards caste-formation. This is crucial to obtain the allocation of roles within the occupational system on the basis of achievement, which is necessary for a modern economy. Thus, this is a self-reinforcing system wherein occupational mobility contributes to economic expansion, which contributes to urban migration, which contributes to the formation of ethnic associations and then to group upward mobility, which makes possible individual occupational mobility.

The fourth function we suggested was the ethnic groups serve as an outlet for political tensions. The process of creating a nation and legitimating new institutions gives rise to many tensions, especially when leaders cannot fulfill promises made. Gluckman's phrase, the "frailty in authority,"[27] is particularly applicable for new nations not yet secure in the loyalty of their citizens. We observed before that ethnic groups offered social security because the government could not. Perhaps we might add that this arrangement would be desirable during a transitional period, even were it not necessary. If the state is involved in too large a proportion of the social action of the individual, it will be burdened by concentrated pressure and demands which it may not be able to meet. It may not yet have the underlying diffuse confidence of the population it would need to survive the non-fulfillment of these demands.[28] It may therefore be of some benefit to divert expectations from the state to other social groups.

The existence of ethnic groups performing "an important scapegoat function as targets for displaced aggression"[29] may permit individuals to challenge persons rather than the authority of the office these persons occupy. Complaints about the nationalist party in power are transformed into complaints about the ethnic group or groups presumably in power. This is a common phenomenon of West African politics, and as Gluckman suggests:

> "These rebellions, so far from destroying the established social order [read, new national governments] work so that they even support this order. They resolve the conflicts which the frailty in authority creates."[30]

Thus, in rejecting the men, they implicitly accept the system. Ethnic rivalries become rivalries for political power in a nontribal setting.

The dysfunctional aspects of ethnicity for national integration are obvious. They are basically two. The first is that ethnic groups are still particularistic in their orientation and diffuse in their obligations, even if they are less so than the extended family. The ethnic roles are insufficiently segregated from the occupational and political roles because of the extensiveness of the ethnic group. Hence we have the resulting familiar problems of nepotism and corruption.

The second problem, and one which worries African political leaders more, is separatism, which in various guises is a pervasive tendency in West Africa today.[31] Separatist moves may arise out of a dispute between élite elements over the direction of change. Or they may result from the scarcity of resources which causes the "richer" region to wish to contract out of the nation (e.g., Ashanti in Ghana, the Western Region in Nigeria, the Ivory Coast in the ex-federation of French West Africa). In either case, but especially the latter, appeals to ethnic sentiment can be made the primary weapon of the separatists.

In assessing the seriousness of ethnicity as dysfunctional, we must remember that ethnic roles are not the only ones West Africans play. They are increasingly bound up in other institutional networks which cut across ethnic lines. Furthermore, the situation may vary according to the number and size of ethnic groupings. A multiplicity of small groups is less worrisome, as Coleman reminds us, than those situations where there is one large, culturally strong group.[32]

The most important mechanism to reduce the conflict between ethnicity and national integration is the nationalist party. Almost all of the West African countries have seen the emergence of a single party which has led the nationalist struggle, is now in power, and dominates the local political scene.[33]

In the struggle against colonial rule, these parties forged a unity of Africans as Africans. To the extent that the party structure is well articulated (as, say, in Guinea) and is effective, both in terms of large-scale program and patronage, the party does much to contain separatist tendencies.

Linguistic integration can also contribute, and here European languages are important. It is significant that one of the Ghana government's first steps after independence was to reduce the number of years in which primary schooling would be in the vernacular. Instruction in English now begins in the second year. We might mention, too, that Islam and Christianity both play a role in reducing centrifugal tendencies.

Lastly, there is the current attempt to endow pan-Africanism with the emotional aura of anticolonialism, the attempt to make Unity as much a slogan as Independence. Even if the objective of unity is not realized, it serves as a counterweight to ethnic separatism that may be very effective.

Thus we see that ethnicity plays a complex role in the contemporary West African scene. It illustrates the more general function of intermediate groups intercalated between the individual and the state, long ago discussed by Durkheim.[34] It points at the same time to the difficulties of maintaining both consensus and unity if these intermediate groups exist.[35]

NOTES

1. A tribe is what Murdock calls a community, and he notes: "The community and the nuclear family are the only social groups that are genuinely universal. They occur in every known human society . . ." (G. Murdock, *Social Structure*, New York, Macmillan, 1949, p. 79.)

2. Statements on the typologies of tribal organizations in Africa are to be found in: M. Fortes and E. Evans-Pritchard, ed., *African Political Systems*, Oxford, 1940; — J. Middleton and D. Tait, *Tribes without Rulers*, London, 1958; — D. Forde, "The Conditions of Social Development in West Africa," in *Civilisations*, III, No. 4, 1953, pp. 472–476.

3. We shall not discuss further the role of the family in West Africa today. We note here that it would be an oversimplification to suggest that family ties have drastically declined in the urban areas. In any case, the strength of family ties can vary independently of the strenth of tribal ties.

4. There are, to be sure, cases where the two loyalties decline together, and there is consequently severe anomy. Failure to distinguish this case from one in which primarily loyalty to the chief alone diminishes can result in much confusion. See this comment by Mercier in which he tries to clarify this confusion: "It is among this minority [the seasonal workers] that one can really speak of detribalization in the sense of a total degradation of the role of the former social cadres. We have seen, on the contrary, that among the permanent population, kinship structures and ethnic affiliation played a considerable role." (P. Mercier, "Aspects de la société africaine dans l'agglomération dakaroise: groupes familiaux et unités de voisinage," p. 39, in P. Mercier et al, "L'Agglomération Dakaroise," in *Études sénégalaises*, No. 5, 1954.)

5. J. Rouch, "Migrations au Ghana," in *Journal de la Société des Africanistes*, XXVI, No. 1/2, 1956, pp. 163–164.

6. J. C. Mitchell, "Africans in Industrial Towns in Northern Rhodesia," in *H.R.H. The Duke of Edingburgh's Study Conference*, No. 1, p. 5.

7. Mercier observes: "One should also note that the smaller the size of an ethnic group in a town, the greater the importance of just being related to someone when closer kinship ties do not exist." (*Op. cit.*, p. 22.)

8. In Dakar, Mercier notes: "A certain number of people, obviously of Lebou origin, . . . called themselves Wolof, proof of the crisis of the old Lebou identity." (*Op. cit.*, p. 17.)

9. For example, G. Lasserre writes: "L'habitude est prise à Libreville de recenser ensemble Togolais et Dahoméens sous l'appellation dé 'Popo'." (*Libreville*, Paris, Armand Colin, 1958, p. 207.)

   Epstein notes a similar phenomenon in the Northern Rhodesian Copperbelt towns, where one of the major ethnic groups, sanctioned by custom and by census, is the Nyasalanders. Nyasaland is a British-created territorial unit, but people from the Henga, Tonga, Tumbuka, and other tribes are by common consent grouped together as Nyasalanders. (A. L. Epstein, *Politics in an Urban African Community*, Manchester, Manchester University Press, 1958, p. 236.)

10. By government we mean here the mechanism whereby the norms and goals of the group are defined. There may or may not be an effective, formal structure to enforce these norms.

11. F. Amon d'Aby, *La Côte d'Ivoire dans la cité africaine*, Paris, Larose, 1952, p. 36.

12. Similar phenomena were reported in other areas undergoing rapid social change. Lewis reports the growth in Somalia of a "tribalism founded on territorial ties [in] place of clanship," at least among the southern groups (I.M. Lewis, "Modern Political Movements in Somaliland, I", in *Africa* XXVIII, July 1958, p. 259). In the South Pacific, Mead observes: "Commentators on native life shook their heads, remarking that these natives were quite incapable of ever organizing beyond the narrowest tribal borders, overlooking the fact that terms like 'Solomons', 'Sepiks' or 'Manus', when applied to Rabaul, blanketed many tribal differences." (M. Mead, *New Lives for Old*, New York, Morrow, 1956, p. 79.)

    The article by Max Gluckman, which appeared since this paper was delivered, makes the same point for British Central Africa. Cf. "Tribalism in British Central Africa", in *Cahiers d'Études Africaines*, I, janv. 1960, pp. 55-70.

13. T. Hodgkin, "Letter to Dr. Biobaku," in *Odù*, No. 4, 1957, p. 42.

14. Rouch, *op. cit.*, p. 58.

15. A. Kobben, "Le planteur noir," in *Études éburnéennes*, V, 1956, p. 154.

16. The religious conversion is often very temporary. N'Goma observes: "Islam doesn't survive well the move of Moslem families from city to country. It has been observed that the city-dweller who returns to his original group often resumes the worship of the earth and of ancestral spirits." (A. N'Goma, "L'Islam noir," in T. Monod, ed., *Le Monde noir, Présence africaine*, No. 8-9, p. 324.) The motive for the original conversion may in part explain this rapid reconversion.

17. G. Savonnet observes in Thiès, Sénégal: "The name Bambara is generally used to designate Sudanese (even if they are Khassonke, Sarakolle, or even Mossi). They were eager to accept this designation as the Bambara (as previously they did that of Wolof), since it was considered to be a race more advanced than their own." ("La Ville de Thiès," in *Études sénégalaises*, No. 6, 1955, p. 149.)

18. Epstein, *op. cit.*, p. 231.

19. Mercier notes: "There are many in the current crises of unemployment who cannot survive in the city without the help of their family. This becomes a sort of spontaneous unemployment insurance program." (*Op. cit.*, p. 26.)

    See also *passim*, K. A. Busia. *Report on a Social Survey of Sekondi-Takoradi, Accra, Government Printer, 1950*; I. Acquah, *Accra Survey*, London, University of London Press, 1958; O. Dollfus, "Conakry en 1951-1952. Etude humaine et économique," in *Études guinéennes*, X-XI, 1952, pp. 3-111; J. Lombard, "Cotonou, ville africaine," in *Études dahoméennes*, X, 1953.

20. G. Balandier, *Sociologie des Brazzavilles noires*, Paris, Armand Colin, 1955, p. 122.

21. Forde suggests that "This multiplicity of association, which is characteristic of the Westernisation procedure, is likely to preclude the functional persistence of tribal organisations as autonomous units in the economic or political sphere." (*Op. cit.*, p. 485.)

22. T. Parsons, *The Social System*, Glencoe, Free Press, 1951, p. 188.

23. D. Apter, *The Gold Coast in Transition*, Princeton, Princeton University Press, 1955, p. 127.

24. W. B. Birmingham and G. Jahoda, "A Pre-Election Survey in a Semi-Literate Society," in *Public Opinion Quarterly*, XIX, Summer, 1955, p. 152.

25. Glick explains the role of Chinese ethnic groups in Chinese assimilation into Hawaiian society in just these terms. (C. Glick, "The Relationship between Position and Status in the Assimilation of Chinese in Hawaii," in *American Journal of Sociology*, XLVII, September, 1952, pp. 667–679.)

26. P. Mercier, "Aspects des problèmes de stratification sociale dans l'Ouest Africain," in *Cahiers internationaux de sociologie*, XVII, 1954, pp. 47–55; Lombard, *op. cit.*, pp. 57–59.

27. M. Gluckman, *Custom and Conflict in Africa*, Oxford, Basil Blackwell, 1955, ch. 2.

28. Unless, of course, it compensates for lack of legitimation by increase of force as a mechanism of social control, which is the method used in Communist countries.

29. Parsons, *op. cit.*, p. 188.

30. Gluckman, *op. cit.*, p. 28.

31. Separatism, of course, arises as a problem only after a concept of a nation is created and at least partially internalized by a large number of the citizens.

32. J. S. Coleman, "The Character and Viability of African Political Systems," in W. Goldschmidt, ed., *The United States and Africa*, New York, The American Assembly, 1958, pp. 44–46.

33. There is normally room for only one truly nationalist party in a new nation. Other parties in West Africa countries, when they exist, tend to be formed on more particularistic (ethnic, religious, regional) bases.

34. E. Durkheim, *The Division of Labor in Society*, Glencoe, Free Presss, 1947, p. 28.

35. See the discussion of this problem in S. M. Lipset, "Political Sociology," in R. K. Merton, L. Broom, L. S. Cottrell, Jr., eds., *Sociology Today*, New York, Basic Books, 1959.

2—Fanon and the Revolutionary Class

Frantz Fanon was the target of endless criticism, not merely from defenders of the status quo but from orthodox Old Left thinkers who saw in him the spokesperson of adventurist, anarchist tendencies within the left. In a sense, this was an old argument, and quite acute in the 1950s. In the post-1968 atmosphere, the debate has not gone away but it has been muted and less acerbic. I felt it necessary to elucidate Fanon's position which seemed to me more on the mark than that of his critics.

PREFACE TO AN ARTICLE

This article is the continuation of a conversation. I knew Frantz Fanon at two moments of his life, and had long conversations with him. The first time was in the summer of 1960, when he was full of life and passion. It was in Accra and he was serving as the representative of the Provisional Government of the Algerian Republic, responsible for links to the government of Ghana and secondarily to other governments and movements in Black Africa. The second time was in the fall of 1961 when he was dying of leukemia in a hospital in Washington, DC, dying but still full of life and passion. He had just written *Les damnés de la terre*, a book composed with speed during the remission he had between his first and second (fatal) bout of illness, written speedily out of fear he might not complete it.

In this second period, Fanon had developed an intense curiosity about the United States, where he found himself. He wanted to know what made America tick and what were the prospects for revolution, particularly among the Blacks. At one moment of our conversation, referring to I no longer remember what, he suddenly said angrily: "Vous américains, vous n'êtes pas prêts à vous dialoguer. Vous vous monologuez toujours." I have always remembered this admonition, though it was not directed at me personally.

In the 1970s, the USA is happily no longer the all-powerful hegemonic power she was in 1961, a reality that had twisted the conscious-

14

ness of all Americans. Perhaps the moment has come when the United States, and most particularly the American left, can enter into a dialogue with their comrades in the struggle elsewhere. Fanon believed that the function of critical intelligence is to illuminate and make rational the work of militants. It is in this spirit that I should like to consider his views on class consciousness and revolutionary movements.

*   *   *

The failure of voluntarist revolution and ideas [in the 1960s] has discredited the writers associated with them. But it should not obscure the genuine defects of the Marxist analysis which prevailed in the 1950s and to which Fanon drew attention.   E. J. HOBSBAWM (1973, p.6)

If Marx was not a Marxist, then Fanon surely was not a Fanonist. Fanonism, if I seize the essence of the now countless pejorative (and even some favorable) references to it, is said to be a belief that peasants are more revolutionary than urban workers, that the lumpenproletariat is more revolutionary than the proletariat, that the national bourgeoisie of the Third World is always hopeless, that violence is always purgative, and not only intellectuals but even cadres cannot be relied upon to make the revolution, without spontaneous explosions from the base. While each of these contentions can be backed up by numerous quotations from Fanon, and each reflects a partial truth which he stated, their combinations as "Fanonism" seems to me to miss the whole point of what Fanon was arguing.

A discussion of "Fanonism" uncovers all the issues of revolutionary strategy and political tactics. The passion of the intellectual debate is an expression of political divisions *on the left*. I shall therefore ignore the occasional dyspeptic and usually ill-informed critic on the right and limit this discussion to those supporters and critics who share with Fanon a basic rejection of contemporary inequalities and oppression and a willingness to engage in militant action to change the world.

If one reads the set of such articles and books, one finds oneself amidst what the French call a "dialogue of the deaf." The same words recur throughout—bourgeoisie, proletariat, peasantry, lumpenproletariat—but the nature of these concepts and the empirical realities they are supposed to reflect, seem to be drawn from different universes, only occasionally intertwined. I should like to untangle this skein, in order to get at the nub of the issue. In order to do this, I shall review both the nature of the criticisms of "Fanonism" in the light of what I believe Fanon's views were, and also whom I believe Fanon was attacking and why some of these people are counterattacking. It is only with this underbrush cleared away that I think we can begin seriously a dialogue on the left appropriate for the 1970s.

The degree of the confusion can be seen by noticing the disparity in the answers to the question most authors seem to ask: was Fanon a Marxist? The affirmative camp includes a variety of critics. Enrica Collotti-Pischel argued: "The Marxist element in Fanon is quite large" (1962, p. 830). She felt that "Fanon and Mao Tse-Tung are really on the same line, along with Ho Chi Minh, Castro and other leaders of the anticolonial revolution" (1962, p. 837). Fredj Stambouli agreed: "Fanon's approach . . . remains in the tradition of Marxist-Leninist interpretation" (1967, p. 523). So did Tony Martin: "but he was Marxist in the sense that Lenin or Castro or Mao are Marxist" (1970, p. 385). E. J. Hobsbawm put it more cautiously: "Fanon is incomprehensible outside the context of Marxism and the international communist movement" (1973, p. 6). And Adolfo Gilly should probably be counted in the same group: "He was not a Marxist. But he was approaching Marxism through the same essential door [used in Marx's analyses of historical events, a concern with what the masses do and say and think]" (1965, p. 2).

But, on the other side, Nguyen Nghe saw him as an "individualist intellectual" (1962, p. 27) and implied he was a "Trotskyist" (1963, p. 28). Similarly, Imre Marton accused Fanon of a "subjectivist interpretation" (1965, 8/9, p. 56), reflecting "the illusion of the petty bourgeoisie" (1965, 8/9, p. 59). For Jack Woddis, like Régis Debray and Herbert Marcuse, Fanon used "the slogans of anarchism," an ideology that is "an expression of the viewpoint of the petty bourgeoisie" (1972, p. 402). Renate Zahar seemed to be answering Enrica Collotti-Pischel when she said: "Nonetheless, the analogy between the ideas of Fanon and the Chinese and Cuban theories of the anticolonialist revolution is quite superficial . . ." (1970, p. 100). The most recent and most negative evaluation was that of Azinna Nwafor who called upon readers to "vigorously combat the erroneous formulation of Fanon on the role of social class in the African revolution," contrasting these misconceptions with "a concrete and correct analysis, adoption of appropriate practical measures of which Cabral already serves as a rich source and unerring guide" (1975, p. 27). Peter Worsley by contrast saw considerable overlap in the views of Fanon and Cabral (1972).

The last twist is that of Dennis Forsythe who said that Worsley's characterization of Fanon as a Marxist is "misleading," though Fanon is also not an "anti-Marxist." For Forsythe, "the divergent tendencies in Fanon's theorizing from Marxism analysis," divergencies could also "be detected in the work of Mao T'se-Tung. Che Guevara and Regis Debray . . . constitute an advance on Marxian analysis as far as the Third World is concerned" (1970, p. 4). Forsythe concluded that the "Third World finds itself and speaks to itself through the voice of Fanon, just as Marx spoke up for the impoverished urban masses in the European context" (1970, p. 10).

What is it that those authors who consider Fanon "un-Marxist" complain of? It is surely not his emphasis on the legitimate place of violence in the revolutionary process. Indeed, his "Marxist" critics seem to go out of their way to make it clear they appreciate this part of Fanon's arguments, even if they demur on some nuances. (See Nguyen Nghe 1962, pp. 23–6: Marton 1965, 7, pp. 39–46; Woddis 1972, pp. 25–30, although Woddis insists that "armed struggle" should only be seen as one type of a wider category, "political struggle.")

What they object to, rather, is his view of the politics of the various classes in the "colonial world." This is a crucial issue, for it has implications about "class alliances" within and across frontiers. Let us review each of the four key class terms used by Fanon: proletariat, lumpenproletariat, peasantry, and bourgeoisie.

The phrase of Fanon that shocked the most, and was meant to shock the most, was this:

> It has been pointed out repeatedly that, in colonial territories, the proletariat is the core of the colonized people most pampered by the colonial regime. The embryonic proletariat of the towns is relatively privileged. In capitalist countries, the proletariat has nothing to lose; it has everything to win in the long run. In colonized countries the proletariat has everything to lose.   (1961, p. 84)

From around the world, they snapped back. The Vietnamese communist, Nguyen Nghe, retorted:

The working class in the colonies does not constitute class in the sense that Fanon means, that is, one pampered by the settlers; it is privileged in the revolutionary sense of the word, by the fact that it is in the best position to observe first-hand the mechanisms of exploitation, to conceive the road to the future for the whole of society. (1962, p. 31)

For the Hungarian communist, Imre Marton, ". . . even in simplifying social realities in the extreme, we may still conclude that it is impossible to place on the same plane the proletariat and the national bourgeoisie . . . [The proletariat] is a class subjected to exploitation by foreign capital, but also by national capital" (1965, 8/9, p. 52). And the British Marxist, Jack Woddis, faults Fanon on the simple accuracy of his "incredible claim" that African workers under colonialism were pampered:

All the available facts and statistics, which Fanon either ignored or of which he was not even aware (and if it was the latter, it was totally irresponsible for him to make such sweeping statements without even bothering to find out what were the real facts) completely refute Fanon's claim. Nearly all official and semi-official reports are compelled to admit that under colonial rule the African worker, being 'pampered,' had to put up with deplorable conditions. Low paid, ill-clad, ill-housed, ill-fed, undernourished, diseased—this was too often the condition of the typical African worker. (1972, p. 108)

One wonders can Fanon and these authors be talking about the same people? A closer look reveals they are not quite. Who is then included in this proletariat which Fanon says has everything to lose?

It is made up in fact of that fraction of the colonized people which is necessary and indispensable for the proper functioning of the colonial machine: street-car conductors, taxi-drivers, miners, dockers, interpreters, male-nurses, etc. These are the elements who constitute the most faithful clientele of the nationalist parties and who by the privileged place they occupy in the colonial system constitute the 'bourgeois' fraction of the colonized people. (1961, p. 84)

One additional quote will more clearly identify this "pampered" proletariat of Fanon who are but a "bourgeois" fraction:

The great error, the congenital vice of the majority of political parties in the underdeveloped regions has been to follow the classic schema of appealing first of all to the most conscious elements: the proletariat of the towns, the artisans and the civil servants, that is, to an infinitesimal part of the population *who scarcely came to more than one per cent.* (1961, p. 84; italics added)

Is this proletariat, who *along with the civil servants and the artisans* are less than one per cent, the "typical African worker" of whom Woddis was talking? Clearly not, for Woddis says that Fanon's argument "fails to take account of the peculiar class structure of Africa where, during the colonial period in which Fanon pretends the workers enjoyed a special luxury, the overwhelming majority of workers were *casual, unskilled migrant labourers or seasonal workers in agriculture*" (1972, p. 102; italics added). Did Fanon then fail to notice this group of whom Woddis talks? Not at all, but as we shall see, he called them lumpenproletarians and peasants. We will come to the question later of which terminology is more useful. Here I limit myself to pointing out that, by a semantic confusion, Woddis is attacking a straw man.

Nguyen Nghe's critique is more discriminating:

> [The Fanonian conception involves] to begin with the error of placing in the same class the dockers and the miners with the interpreters and the male-nurses. The former constitute the true proletariat, the industrial working class (in the colonies, we must also locate here the workers on large plantations): the latter form part of the petty-bourgeoisie, also a revolutionary class, but with less resolution and follow-through.   (1962, p. 30)

Since Nguyen Nghe just previously cited Truong Chinh, "theoretician of the Vietnamese revolution," as saying that the four classes that "make up the people" and "constitute the forces of revolution" are "the working class, the class of peasant workers, the petty-bourgeoisie, and the national bourgeoisie," we must note that Nguyen Nghe is speaking of still a different group from both Fanon and Woddis, for his "industrial working class" includes workers on large plantations ("peasants" in Fanon's usage) but excludes "interpreters and male-nurses." The latter become petty bourgeois, "also revolutionary but with less resolution and follow-through." But once again, is there not an element of word juggling here? Nguyen Nghe's less resolute "petty-bourgeois" and Fanon's unreliable "proletarians" seem to be at the very least, overlapping categories.

If we move to a discussion of the lumpenproletariat, the debate becomes perhaps clearer. Neither Nguyen Nghe nor Marton really discussed the lumpenproletariat. But in Woddis's attack on Fanon, they played a central role. Woddis, relying on Marx, made the quite correct point that for Marx the lumpenproletariat served mainly as "the bribed tool of reactionary intrigue" although, on occasion, it could play a positive role. "But as a class, or rather sub-class, it would only be *swept* into movement by the proletariat at a time of revolution; it could certainly not initiate or lead a revolution" (1972, p. 80). What Woddis did *not* do is tell us who exactly are the lumpenproletarians and what their relationship is with the "casual, unskilled migrant labourers" he included in the proletariat. It seems that for Woddis the actual lumpenproletariat is limited to "the real *déclassés*" (1972, p. 82) or, on the very same page, "the declassed and criminal elements." If declassed is supposed to refer to those who have shifted *downward* in life style as a result of changed class location of the adult, and not merely to uprooted migrants from country to city, one wonders if there are *any* declassed elements in Africa today, or even in the Third World generally. One certainly wonders if there are many.

This is not the group in any case Peter Worsley thought of when he read Fanon:

> It is a great mistake to think of them statically, as constituting a separate category — lumpenproletarians — sharply marked off from the peasants as if they were really a fixed and consolidated social class, firstly, because they are ex-peasants, anyhow, and secondly, because they are essentially *people in process*. The are *becoming* townsmen — eventually, they hope, a part of the settled, employed urban working-class population. But they are a long way from being absorbed and accepted into urban society. They are outcasts, marginal men, travelers between two social worlds, occupants of a limbo to which most of us would think hell preferable, but which for them represents a great improvement in many respects upon the village life they have abandoned.
>
> (1969, pp. 42–3)

A more sophisticated skepticism about the lumpenproletariat has been expressed by Robin Cohen and David Michael whose attack was directed less against Fanon than what they called "an identifiable 'Fanonist tradition' [that] has been established by Peter Worsley, Oscar Lewis, Peter Gutkind, and others" (1973, p. 32). The complaint of Cohen and Michael about the "Fanonists," but one that might equally be made about Woddis, was that they assumed the marginality of the lumpenproletariat, whereas:

> The lumpenproletariat is much less alienated from the neo-colonial economy than the Fanonists imply. Many of them, indeed, have an important stake in the system and live, like parasites, off the productive labour of others — whether it

be through dependence on the income of employed kin, through theft or through the provision of services like prostitution.   (1973, p. 36)

Furthermore, Cohen and Michael believed that the very category may be a dubious researcher's taxonomy which groups together as "street people" such varied types as "beggars, religious ascetics and prophets, the physically disabled and insane" plus another whole segment of the population among whom ". . . distinctions need to be drawn between those who are de-employed, those who are intermittently employed, those who have given up all hope of securing employment, those who still seek jobs and those who have accommodated themselves to a socially disapproved livelihood as thieves, pimps or prostitutes" (1973, pp. 37-8). These are helpful precisions for a discussion of political tactics. For the moment, we simply note that this makes clear that Fanon was indeed talking of a far larger social category than Woddis suggested.

It is about the peasantry that we find Fanon's second shock-quote:

> It is quite clear that, in colonial countries, the peasantry alone is revolutionary. It has nothing to lose and everything to gain. The peasant, the declassed person, the starving person is the exploited person who discovers soonest that violence alone pays. For him, there is no compromise, no possibility of coming to terms.   (1961, p. 46)

Nguyen Nghe was struck by the vigor of the affirmation. He called on us "simultaneously to capture the profound truth of Fanon's affirmation, to appreciate the inestimable support of the peasant masses for the revolution"—and to see where Fanon went wrong. "The peasant, *by himself*, can never attain revolutionary consciousness; it is the militant coming *from the towns* who will discern patiently the most capable elements among the poor peasants, educate them, organize them, and it is thus only after a long period of political work that one can mobilize the peasantry" (1962, p. 29; italics added). The peasantry *alone* is revolutionary! The peasant, by himself, can *never* attain revolutionary consciousness! We are amidst a confrontation of the Algerian and Vietnamese experiences, of the failure to create a revolutionary party and the success. Nguyen Nghe continued:

> The poor peasant may be a patriot and die heroically gun in hand, but *if he remains a peasant*, he will not be able to lead the revolutionary move-

ment . . . The Vietnamese People's Army is made up 90% of peasants but the revolutionary leadership *has not defined itself* as a peasant leadership, and the leaders seek to inculcate in the militants an ideology that is not peasant, but proletarian. (1962, p. 31; italics added)

Nguyen Nghe went further. He suggested that the success *and the limits* of the *Chinese* experience depended precisely on the role the peasantry played in it:

Even far-off Yenan received messages and men continuously from Shanghai located several thousand kilometers away; without his osmosis Yenan would have become the refuge of a mere sect, cut off from historical experience, destined sooner or later to disappear . . .

It is probable that certain negative aspects of the Chinese revolution are due to too strong a peasant imprint, to too long a stay in the countryside of many leaders and militants. (1962, pp. 32–3)

Once again, who are the peasants? Nguyen Nghe sometimes talked of peasants, sometimes of *poor* peasants. Woddis said that "one should not ignore that the peasantry is, in general, based on the petty ownership of the means of production." But he then proceeded to tell us:

The peasantry is really not one homogeneous class. If one can imagine, for example, a tube of toothpaste open at both ends and being squeezed in the middle, one has to an extent a picture of what happens to the peasantry. From an army of smallholders *a mass of poor and often landless peasants* is squeezed out at the bottom, while a small stratum of rich peasants employing wage labour emerges at the top. In other words, the peasantry is in a stage of break-up into three distinct strata with largely different interests. *In fact, the poor landless peasant often ends up as the wage labourer* exploited by the rich peasant. (1972, pp. 59–60; italics added)

It should be clear that Fanon's starving peasant is scarcely Woddis's rich peasant. He is quite probably Woddis's "poor and often landless" peasant who, as Woddis notes, often ends up as the "wage labourer," in short, as a proletarian. Remember Nguyen Nghe also specifically cited wage workers on plantations as proletarians. So Fanon's peasants turn out to be Nguyen and Woddis's proletarians, or almost.

Let us look finally at the fourth major class-category, the bourgeoisie. The plot thickens. For in many ways we are coming to the key question for which the debate about the working classes serves as camouflage. What does Fanon say of the bourgeoisie?

> The national bourgeoisie which comes to power at the end of the colonial re-
> gime is an underdeveloped bourgeoisie. Its economic strength is almost non-
> existent and in any case incommensurate with that of the metropolitan
> bourgeoisie it hopes to replace . . . The university graduates and merchants
> who make up the most enlightened fraction of the new state are noteworthy by
> their paucity, their concentration in the capital city, and the kind of activities in
> which they engage: trafficking (*négoce*), farming, the liberal professions.
> Among this national bourgeoisie one finds neither industrialists nor financiers.
> The national bourgeoisie of underdeveloped countries is not involved in pro-
> duction, invention, construction, labor. It is completely routed towards
> intermediary-type activities . . . In the colonial system, a bourgeoisie that
> accumulates capital is an impossibility.   (1962, p. 114)

Thus, incapable of fulfilling the historic role of a bourgeoisie, it must be
combatted because the national bourgeoisie "is good for nothing" (1961,
p. 132).

The condemnation is global. And it is this unwillingness to find *any*
virtue in the national bourgeoisie that seems to exasperate most of his
critics. Imre Marton chastised Fanon for concentrating exclusively on
the relations of the national bourgeoisie with "imperialist forces." He
forgot, says Marton, the existence of a socialist bloc which has the consequence, for *some* countries, of including the national bourgeoisie
". . . under the pressure of the popular masses . . . to conduct in international affairs a meaningfully anti-imperialist policy and at home a
policy which, to various degrees, takes into consideration certain political and economic aspirations of the popular masses" (1965, 8/9, p. 51).
Woddis repeated the same theme: "But it is equally true that the very
existence of a socialist system provides new possibilities for the national
bourgeoisie to secure help in building its independent economy and in
lessening its dependence on imperialism, all in this very process to come
into conflict with the imperialist powers" (1972, p. 95).

Amady Ali Dieng, agreeing with Marton, added that Fanon had neglected the "generally accepted" distinction in Marxist writings between
the national bourgeoisie "which exploit an internal market whose interests are opposed to those of imperialism," and a "bureaucratic and comprador bourgeoisie . . . whose interests are closely linked to those of
imperialism." Apparently fearing this distinction might however serve to
classify in the camp of the people some of Africa's most reactionary politicians, Dieng quickly added a footnote. "This conception [of a national

bourgeoisie] excludes the Ivory Coast rural bourgeoisie from the ranks of the national bourgeoisie for they are based on the cultivation of coffee and cocoa and thus have their interests tied to imperialism by virtue of the fact that their market lies outside the Ivory Coast" (1967, p. 26). But, since there is scarcely a "bourgeois" anywhere in Africa who is not involved in cash crops or other enterprises linked directly to a *world* market, once we exclude the Ivory Coast rural bourgeoisie we should have to exclude many others, and we would end up with a nearly empty category. At which point, would not Dieng's "bureaucratic and comprador bourgeoisie" in fact heavily overlap with Fanon's national bourgeoisie?

As we have moved through the class categories we have noted semantic confusion after semantic confusion. How strange! Is Fanon so difficult to read? It is true his style was "literary" and far from "precise." It is true that he reveled in rhetorical flourish. But the texts are neither abstract nor abstruse. They are filled with concrete referents and earthly descriptions. It should not have been so difficult to seize the essence — unless one didn't want to.

Whom was Fanon attacking? We must put him in his context. He wrote his major work in 1961 in the seventh year of the Algerian war of national liberation. Independence was in sight. The previous year, in 1960, fifteen African states had become independent, in large part, as Fanon well knew, in the wake of the Algerian struggle. In the summer of 1960, the Congo "collapsed," and the counterrevolution in Africa showed its teeth. Fanon was in the Congo as a representative of the Algerian provisional government at the height of the first crisis and futilely sought to rally the independent African states behind Lumumba. Lumumba's murder must have been announced just as he began to write *The Wretched of the Earth*.

Furthermore, the Algerians had fought a long war, with only belated and begrudging support from the French Communist Party and the USSR. they had little reason to be grateful to Imre Marton's "socialist camp."

Finally, it is indeed historically true for Algeria that the urban proletariat had made revolutionary noise more than it had engaged in action, and that the revolution did begin in the rural areas, "spontaneously" (that is, outside the established organizational structures, and against them).

Fanon found the Algerian revolution an island of health in a sea of neocolonial governments in Africa whose reality he saw clearly far earlier than most observers. While much of the world left was celebrating the advent of the single-party states in Africa, Fanon cried out: "The single party is the modern form of the dictatorship of the bourgeoisie, without mask, without make-up, unscrupulous, cynical" (1961, p. 124).

Burned by Europe, and twice shy. There, too, is another issue full of emotion. It is no accident that Fanon, the Martinican, educated in France, struggling for Algeria, should have become the hero of the Black Panther Party in the United States and other Black militants. Eldridge Cleaver wrote that *The Wretched of the Earth* became "known among the militants of the black liberation movement in America as 'the Bible'" (1967, p. 18). Huey Newton said they read Fanon, Mao, and Che (1963, p. 111). Stambouli defended Fanon's "haste . . . to abandon European models" by pointing to "the inadequacy of these models for the reality of ex-colonial countries" (1967, p. 528). Collotti-Pischel defended Fanon's attack on the inadequacy of the *action* of the European left:

> It is difficult today for a European Marxist to contest, in good faith, the truth of Fanon's thesis that, in the struggle of colonial peoples for independence development, the European masses have in every way sinned by absenteeism and impotence . . . when they "did into directly align themselves in colonial questions with our common oppressors (*padroni*)." (1962, p. 857–8).

For Imre Marton on the contrary, the models of Europe, like the action of the European left, were quite adequate: "Fanon detaches the internal conditions of the countries of the Third World from the general laws governing our epoch . . . What is merely a specific form becomes for Fanon a specific content, in opposition to socialism as it has been realized in the socialist countries" (1965, 8/9, p. 60). Surprisingly, Nguyen Nghe went further in this regard. He charged Fanon with a "refusal of modern values" which condemned the Third World countries to "stay in their rut":

> We cannot begin history over, as Fanon claims. We fit ourselves into the currents of history, or rather we must figure out how to do so. However much we hate imperialism, the primary duty, for an Asian or an African, is to recognize that for the last three centuries, it is Europe that has been in the avant-garde of history. Europe has placed in the arena of history at least two values which had been lacking for many Asian and African countries; two values which go to-

gether, even if at certain moments or in certain places they were not necessarily linked: the renewal of productive forces, and democracy.   (1963, p. 34)

Nguyen Nghe's charge that Fanon wished to begin history over is quite off the mark. It is simply that Fanon had a more acerbic view of Europe's accomplishments. "This Europe which never ceased talking about Man, never ceased proclaiming that she was concerned only about Man, we know today with what sufferings humanity has paid for each of the victories of its spirit" (1961, p. 239). But in any case what concerned Fanon was less the past than the future. "Remember, comrades, the European game is finished forever; we must find something else" (1961, p. 239). If Africa wants to imitate Europe,

> . . . then let us confide the destinies of our countries to Europeans. They will know how to do better than the most gifted among us.
>
> But we wish that humanity advance one small bit, . . . we must invent, we must discover . . .
>
> *For Europe, for ourselves and for humanity,* comrades, we must grow a new skin, develop new concepts, try to create a new man.
>
> (1961, p. 242; italics added)

It is precisely on the questions of class structure in the world-system, and the class alliances that are essential for a revolution, that Fanon looked for "a new skin," and "new concepts." Far from rejecting European thought, in which he was deeply embedded himself, he took the title of his book from the *Internationale*, and he took his starting point from the *Communist Manifesto*: "Workers of the world unite! You have nothing to lose but your chains." He simply said, let us look again to see who has how many chains, and which are the groups who, having the fewest privileges, may be the most ready to become a "revolutionary class." The old labels are old skins, which do not correspond *fully* with contemporary reality.

Fanon did not offer us the finished analysis. He issued the clarion call for this analysis. Marie Peinbam, it seems to me, caught this point exactly: "Fanon was not analysing a revolution; he was trying to sustain one, and to create others . . . Fanon's hypothesis about the spontaneously revolutionary peasantry, far from being an appraisal of a particular situation, was a rallying idea, a myth, a symbol of committed action" (1973, pp. 441, 444). This is why Stambouli could say about Fanon's conception of the role of the peasantry that it aroused the most criticism and that it was the part of his argument that was "perhaps the least understood" (1967, p. 526).

The key tactical issue is how the sides line up in the world struggle, and Fanon was in this matter skeptical of certain received truths. In 1961, his arguments seemed more heretical than they do in the 1970s after so many ideological landmarks have been called into question by the profound split in the world communist movement.

Enrica Collotti-Pischel isolated clearly on the key theoretical issue of what may be called the Leninist heritage about which Fanon was raising questions:

> In substance the origin of the colonial problematic within the Comintern was two-fold. On the one hand there were the political and even more generally human consequences of the Leninist thesis of the world struggle against imperialism, the indispensable unity of the proletarian and colonial revolutionary struggle, the denunciation of the acceptance of colonial oppression on the part of the majority of European social-democrats. On the other hand, there were the whole set of arguments that resulted from the extension to the colonies of concepts elaborated by Marxists primarily in order to take a position on the problem of the *national* questions and which were characterized, at least initially, by factors typically growing out of the particular situation of the problems of national minorities in Europe, that is, out of the heritage of the disintegration of European multinational states.　　　　(1962, pp. 840–1)

The solution to this problematic was the "theory of revolution in two stages," a bourgeois-democratic stage followed by a socialist stage, each stage implying a different class alliance.

In effect, various of his critics are attacking Fanon for assuming that the first stage must necessarily go astray, that it can and must be "skipped." Whereas, say they, it cannot be skipped and will only go astray if adventurist neglect of the primacy of the proletariat undermines the ability of the working classes to check the bourgeoisie *while collaborating with it*, and thereby, in Woddis's phrase, "complete the aim of national liberation" (1972, p. 113), or as Nguyen Nghe argued:

> Endowing armed struggle with absolute metaphysical value leads Fanon to neglect another aspect of the revolutionary struggle, which was not even discussed in his book, the problem of the union of social classes, of different social strata for national independence and, once peace has been restored, for the building of a new society.　　　　(1963, p. 28)

Perhaps the most credible criticism along this line has been made by Basil Davidson who argued that in the one place other than Algeria where Fanon applied his own theories, his judgment was shown to be mistaken. This was in Angola where Fanon was an early strong supporter of the UPA of Holden Roberto against the MPLA of Agostinho Neto.

> The proof of Fanon's error, or of the error of the conclusion which others drew from what he preached or was thought to preach, may be seen most easily of all in the experience of Angola. The almost completely unprepared rising of the Kongo people in March 1961 was very "Fanonist" in conception, but it led to disaster, whereas the progress of the Angolan national movement under MPLA leadership, very "non-Fanonist" in this context, has led to continual expansion and success. (Davidson 1972, p. 10)

This is no doubt a strong argument, to which can best be replied what the most generous of Fanon's sharp critics, Nguyen Nghe, had to say: "If Frantz Fanon were still alive, how many things might he have still learned, in the light of the Algerian experience?" (1963, p. 26). And, one might add, in the light of everything that has happened since Nguyen Nghe wrote?

What is it that we can learn, in the light of Fanon's critique of the inadequacies of revolutionary theory of the 1950s, plus the concrete experience of the 1960s? One thing, I think, is that the trinity of terms which we have to describe the "working class" or the "poor"—proletariat, peasantry, and lumpenproletariat—are in many ways misleading because of connotations that may be said to describe the realities of nineteenth-century Europe (and even that?), but not really correspond with the twentieth-century world.

Peasantry is a term that groups together proletarians and bourgeois, and assumes a kind of socio-geographic separateness of country and city which precisely has been breaking down. Lumpenproletarian is simply a Marxian euphemism for what the bourgeoisie once called the "dangerous classes" and breeds confusion.

I would think the most useful distinctions to make is first of all between proletarians and semiproletarians, that is between those who derive their *life*-income from wage labor and those who, in their life-income, receive one part from wage labor and one part from other sources such as access to usufruct of primary production; doles from family, the state, or the public; and theft. Such a distinction will make it clear why Tony Martin is correct in saying that, for Fanon, "the lumpen-proletariat is but an urban extension of the peasantry" (1970, p. 389). It is because the semiproletarians, in most cases and especially in the peripheral countries of the world-economy, are indeed obliged to move back and forth over their lifetime from urban to rural areas in order to eke out the non-wage segment of their *life*-income.

Once one makes the distinction between the proletariat and the semi-proletariat, it is easy to see how Fanon's ideas can be applied to the "advanced capitalist countries" as well as to the Third World, as Worsley did: "the notion of the 'Third World' refers to a set of *relationships*, not to a set of *countries*. It also points to the special misery of peasantry, *lumpenproletariat*, and to the broad division between the White 'Lords of Human Kind' and the 'Natives' of the earth whether these be in Harlem or in Hong Kong" (1972, p. 220). It is in this context that we can understand the formulation of Eldridge Cleaver: "In both the Mother Country and the Black Colony, the working class is the right wing of the proletariat and the lumpenproletariat is the left wing . . . We definitely have a major contradiction between the working class and the lumpen-proletariat." (Cited in Worsley 1972, p. 222.)

The historic process of capitalism is that of proletarianization. It is far from being completed, if it ever will be. In this process, those who are only semi-employed during their working life must scrounge to survive. They are at once more desperate and more mobile than the permanently employed, however much the latter are exploited. It seems difficult not to agree that the semiproletarians are indeed the "wretched of the earth," and that they are the most likely group to engage spontaneously in violence.

It is curious that Fanon ever should have been attacked for a supposed belief in the unremitting virtues of spontaneity. The chapter on spontaneity after all is entitled "The grandeur *and the weaknesses* of spontaneity." It is in this chapter that he says "The leaders of the insurrection come to see that even very large-scale *jacqueries* need to be brought under control and oriented. These leaders are led to renounce the movement as a mere *jacquerie* and therefore transform it into a revolutionary war" (1961, p. 102). Fanon is neither denying the need for revolutionary *organization* (quite the contrary) nor denying the importance of ideological commitment. He is assessing which groups are most likely to be willing to take the first and hardest steps in a revolution, the serious beginnings. Those who wait for the "right moment" risk waiting for Godot.

Fanon did not therefore endorse any and all forms of violence. His language is quite clear in this matter: "The impetuous wolf who wanted to devour everything, the sudden gust of wind which was going to bring about an authentic revolution risks, if the struggle takes long, and it does take long, becoming unrecognizable. The colonized continually run the risk of allowing themselves to be disarmed by some minor concession" (1961, p. 105). This is why political organization and ideological clarity are imperative. But nonetheless, said Fanon, it is from the mass of semi-proletarians that the militants are likely to be drawn.

There is another distinction to be drawn in our map of class relationships, one within the proletariat proper. It is that between those proletarians who live at or near the level of minimum subsistence adequate for this maintenance and reproduction and little else and those wage workers who receive a substantial income permitting a "bourgeois" style of life but which they spend more or less as they earn it. This group is frequently called "petty bourgeois," a term Fanon tends to avoid. The key fact to note is the absence of a secure property base for this style of life and therefore the risk for an individual of losing the high income, the reward for skill *and conformity*.

This "labor aristocracy" (if one can stretch one's image of Lenin's term to cover not merely skilled workers but cadres, technicians, and professionals) are in a "social contract" with the true bourgeoisie, in which their collective individual remunerations are the political counterpart of their essential conservatism. This "social contract" works both ways. When any particular segment is threatened with exclusion from advantages or not admitted to it, it will become "militant" in its demands. In the colonial countries, these are the "bourgeois fraction" of whom Fanon wrote and whose intentions and actions are "leaders of nationalist movements" he denounced.

Was Fanon then against a "revolution in two states"? It all depends on the interpretation. Collotti-Pischel noted that Mao Tse-Tung accepted this formula, but she added:

The fundamental difference between the position of Mao and that of Stalin was precisely in this different sense of the function of dialectic in the historical process: . . . the national-bourgeois phase in Mao is significantly more transitory and provisional than in Stalin. What mattered was not the development of the phase, but its overcoming.   (1962, p. 847)

As for Fanon, his answer was no less clear: "The theoretical question posed about underdeveloped countries over the last fifty years, to wit, can the bourgeois phase be skipped or not, must be resolved at the level of revolutionary action and not by thinking about it" (1961, p. 131). Is this so wrong?

Rereading Fanon in the light of the history of revolutionary movements in the twentieth century should lead us *away from* polemics and into a closer analysis of the realities of class structures. The fetish of terminology often blinds us to the evolution of the phenomena they are supported to capture. Fanon suspected strongly that the more benefits strata drew from an existing unequal system, the more prudent they would be in their political activity. He pushed us to look for who would take what risks and then asked us to build a movement out of such a revolutionary class. Have the history of the years since he wrote disproved this instinct? I fail to see how and where.

REFERENCES

Cleaver, Eldridge. 1967. *Post-prison Writings and Speeches.* New York: Vintage Ramparts.

Cohen, Robin and David Michael. 1973. 'The Revolutionary Potential of the African Lumpenproletariat: A Skeptical View.' *Bulletin of the Institute of Development Studies,* 5 (October), 31–42

Collotti-Pischel, Enrica, 1962. ' "Fanonismo" e "questione coloniale." ' *Problemi del socialismo,* 5, 834–64.

Davidson, Basil. 1972. Review of T. Museveni *et al., Essays in the Liberation of Southern Africa,* and K. W. Grundy, *Guerilla Struggle in Africa. Anti-Apartheid News* (September), 10.

Dieng, Amady Ali. 1967. 'Les damnés de la terre et les problèmes d'Afrique noire', *Présence africaine,* 62 (2), 15–30.

Fanon, Frantz. 1961. *Les damnés de la terre,* Cahiers libres 27–8: Ed. Maspéro. (The English translation is frequently careless and misleading, particularly when dealing with the nuances of precisely the controversial concepts discussed in this paper. I have therefore made all my own translations.)

Forsythe, Dennis. 1970. 'Frantz Fanon: Black Theoretician'. *The Black Scholar,* 1 (March), 2–10.

Gilly, Adolfo. 1965. 'Introduction.' In Frantz Fanon, *Studies in a Dying Colonialism,* pp. 1–21. New York: Monthly Review Press.

Hobsbawm, E. J. 1973. 'Passionate Witness'. Review of Irene L. Gendzier, *Frantz Fanon: A Critical Study. The New York Review of Books.* 22 February, pp. 6–10.

Martin, Tony. 1970. 'Rescuing Fanon from the Critics.' *African Studies Review,* 13 (December), 381–99.

Marton, Imre. 1965. 'A propos des thèses de Fanon.' *Action* (revue théorique et politique du Parti Communiste Martiniquais), 7 (2), 39–55; 8/9 (3/4), 45–66.

Newton, Huey P. *Revolutionary Suicide.* New York: Harcourt, Brace, Jovanovich.

Nghe, Nguyen. 1963. 'Frantz Fanon et les problèmes de l'indépendance.' *La Pensée,* 107 (February), 23–30.

Nwafor, Azinna. 1975. 'Imperialism and Revolution in Africa.' *Monthly Review.* 26 (April), 18–32.

Perinbam, B. Marie. 1973. 'Fanon and the Revolutionary Peasantry—The Algerian Case.' *The Journal of Modern African Studies,* 11 (September), 427–45.

Stambouli, Fredj. 1967. 'Frantz Fanon face aux problèmes de la décolonisation et de la construction nationale.' *Revue de l'Institut de Sociologie,* 2/3, 519–34.

Woddis, Jack. 1972. *New Theories of Revolution.* New York: International Publishers.

Worsley, Peter. 1969. 'Frantz Fanon: Evolution of a Revolutionary—Revolutionary Theories.' *Monthly Review* 21 (May), 30–49.

——1972. 'Frantz Fanon and the "Lumpenproletariat."' *Socialist Register,* pp. 193–230.

Zahar, Renate. 1970. *L'oeuvre de Frantz Fanon,* Petite collection Maspéro 57. Paris: Maspéro.

3—Radical Intellectuals in a Liberal Society

Paul Starr and I were both involved in the 1968 uprising at Columbia, he as a student reporter for the *Spectator*, and I as the co-chair of the Ad Hoc Faculty Group that sought to mediate the conflict. Two years later, we decided to assemble and publish a collection of the documents that had been produced by the multiple conflicts on U.S. campuses, which we published as the two-volume *University Crisis Reader*. We each then wrote an essay at the end of the book, stating our intellectual/political positions vis-à-vis what I would later call the Revolution of 1968. I thought it most important to talk about the limits and the possibilities of being a radical intellectual in a liberal society.

The student movement of the 1960s has revitalized the left in American life as a serious political force. Its success, however, has posed a serious dilemma for intellectuals on the left, one they did not have to face when the strength of the left was at a low point in the 1950s. It is the traditional moral dilemma of the radical intellectual in a liberal society: how does he reconcile participating in a movement for political change with an ongoing involvement in the occupational networks of the existing society, especially in a society that seeks to mute his radicalism with a carrot rather than a stick, or at least with the carrot first.

This revolt by young people has also been, in many ways, intellectually liberating for the entire American left. It liberated the left from the cramping fears instilled in them by the anti-Stalinism of the Cold War period. Analyses bearing the terminology and methodology of leftist thought have become intellectually respectable once again, at least in the academy. The pieties of the Cold War era have become points of view rather than unquestioned truths. Furthermore, not only has leftist ideology become respectable once again but leftist political action is now viewed as meaningful. During the Cold War era, even those who remained leftist in thought tended to retreat into inactivity and a sense of hopelessness in the face of the seeming futility of leftist political action. Then young people came along who were not burdened with guilt for the errors of previous decades, who were not weary from battles fought and lost, who were naive still in their faith and optimism, and they breathed new life into the American left and even inspired those "over thirty."

Their revolt liberated the left from the cramping effects of the Stalinist style which had pervaded the remaining corners of the American left. The students denounced the bureaucratic ways of Soviet society as base imitations of American society. They reasserted earlier visions of democracy and socialism. By so doing, they made the American socialist movement, perhaps for the first time, an *indigenous* American political movement, a quality essential to longer-term political survival and eventual success, and one whose absence had been sorely felt in previous decades.

I say this despite the romanticizing of Mao and Ho and Che by student radicals, an activity which has more the flavor of *épater les bourgeois* than the sense of serious subordination to these foreign heroes. I say this, too, despite the putative steps toward re-Stalinization made by some segments of the New Left, which are noticeable in some of the recent writings included in this book. The indigenization of socialism will survive, while the restalinized groups will crumble. Destalinization has also been liberating for those over thirty because it has helped to restore their willingness to participate in a political movement and to reinfuse them with some political courage.

This revitalization of the American led by a spontaneous movement—largely of students raised in a "youth culture"—has created two dangers for the left. The first is that the left may tend to see the virtues but not the limitations of spontaneity. The second is that the left may tend to appreciate the need to differentiate itself from and struggle against the liberal center, and not the need to form alliances, when appropriate, with the liberal center in a struggle against the true right.

Spontaneity has had three guises in recent years in the United States: intellectual debunking, militant collective action, and personal liberation. The intellectual debunking may be found throughout this book. It essentially has two themes. One is the assertion that various concepts of liberalism—for example, "value-neutrality" or "access to education on the basis of performance"—are not self-evident truths. They are expressions of the ideology of particular groups in a particular system. They cannot be accepted, uncritically and at face value, by those of the left, but must be assessed in terms of their contemporary social function. The second theme of intellectual debunking is the demonstration that, even in terms of their own values, liberal institutions often fail to play the game as they insist others should play it: the universities' links to government intelligence, and their cooperation with the selective service in ways that threaten the autonomy of the university. This has struck responsive chords in those of the liberal center as well as in those of the left. This is natural, as the former are merely honest liberals trying to preserve their system of values against the inroads of the right. It is probably true, it would have been far less likely that liberals of the center would have raised these issues, and almost certain that had they done so anyway, they would not have succeeded. The reemergence of the American left made it possible to end, for example, classified defense research at American universities.

The second form of spontaneity has been militant collective action, the most important form of which has been confrontation tactics in the universities. This has been the least popular form of spontaneity with the liberal center. Yet there is no question that it has been an important factor in the relative successes of the left. The sit-ins, the obstructions, the disruptions have made the universities face the issues in ways that intellectual debunking alone could never achieve. And once the issues were forced on the universities in this way, they made significant concessions to the demands of the left. At the very least, the universities have been led to approximate more closely their own liberal ideology of autonomy from the state. They have also been led to reconsider their relationship with surrounding communities, especially in urban areas, to take seriously the charge of institutional racism, and to begin implementing some democratization of their internal governance structures. All these are serious gains that should not be underestimated: furthermore, it must be admitted that they were won largely as a result of confrontation tactics.

The third form of spontaneity has been personal liberation—from personal appearance to music to sex to drugs. Albeit the least political of the forms of spontaneity, personal liberation in many ways created the atmosphere in which the other two could flourish. The movement for personal liberation has broken the cycle of socialization by which society prevented the growth of left ideology, and action among the young. Thus, those critics on the right, such as Stanton Evans, who claim that the permissiveness of the liberal center paved the way for the student movement, have an element of truth in their analyses.

If the three forms of spontaneity in the student movement have had positive effects, they also harbor the seeds of self-destruction. The student revolt can destroy the very American left they have rebuilt, and clearly some segments of it are moving in that direction.

Spontaneity is crucial in revolutionary action. But it also has pitfalls, as Frantz Fanon argued so cogently in *The Wretched of the Earth*. Let us look at the pitfalls of each form of spontaneity in the current situation. Each involved pushing a good thing too far for fear of backsliding.

Debunking is essential to clear away the cobwebs of deception. But if it is persisted in when there are few cobwebs left to clear, then it must invent them in order to have some to clear away. This is witch-hunting, and the most recent debates within the left show dangerous signs of this malady. Fear of success, and fear of co-optation, led to a frenetic desire for purity, to a paranoiac fear of infiltration which becomes self-fulfilling, and to a casuistical concern with past peccadilloes and future dangers.

Militant collective action is necessary to counter the systematic violence of entrenched authority, and to shake up the timorous inertia of parlor pinks. But militant collective action is serious political activity and can only be undertaken when one has serious strength. While an element of political strength is self-confidence, it is only one element. If one neglects to make sober calculations of one's real strength and moves too far in advance of it, repression and disaster are the result. Action then becomes adventurism, motivated by fear of collective and personal cowardice. This grievous tendency toward miscalculation is appearing again, as it so often has in the history of left movements, in the modern industrial world. The trouble with adventurist sects is that they not only destroy themselves—this would not be a trouble but a blessing—but that they bring others down in their wake.

Personal liberation is necessary to free the inner psyche from the social controls instilled in it by the dominant social system. It leads us back to using our primordial energies in the service of our values without fear of the frowns of those who are paid to frown. Here the danger is easy to see. Out of a fear of *embourgeoisement*, we can pursue the wisps of perpetual heterodoxy until we have in fact copped out of the central struggle.

Witch-hunting, adventurism, and the cop-out are the dangers. They are often seen clearly by one or another on the left. What is less often seen clearly is that they derive from one common cause: overreaction to disillusionment with the liberal center. The American left—having subordinated itself to an alliance with the liberal center since the New Deal era, and having been ill rewarded by the center when the center moved rightward during the Cold War era—has been sorely tempted to turn against the liberal center and to see in it nothing but one face of the Janus of modern capitalism. This was the famous and ill-fated strategy of the German Communists in 1932 when they denounced the "social fascism" of the liberals and social democrats.

There is a third way, however, for the American left to relate to the liberal center. It does not need to subordinate itself as a junior partner to the liberal center, nor to fail to make meaningful distinctions among liberalism, conservatism, and racism, different ideologies each, reflecting the needs and concerns of different social groups at particular moments of time.

The first need for the American left is intellectual clarification of the ways in which American and world society can and will transform itself into a socialist society. The left, no doubt, has a sociological perspective that is different from that of the liberal center. It also has the outlines of a theory of historical change that is distinct from that of liberalism, which explains why, even when their ultimate objectives seem to converge, radicals seldom agree with liberals on the efficacy of their methods of promoting change. The left is far from having a clearly developed social theory that can account for the continued resiliency of the existing world social system, and clearly indicate the modalities of transforming it.

There is much hard intellectual work to be done by the left. This intellectual work will never be done well if it is isolated from praxis, from involvement in a political movement and political action. But neither will it be done well if it is isolated from the pressures of competing intellectual ideas in the mainstream of intellectual debate, which in America is still located in the university. That the university should flourish is as crucial to the future prospects of the American left as the growth of a strong political movement.

It cannot, of course, be just any university, any more than it can be just any political movement. It cannot be a liberal university that refuses to admit its biases and continues to pretend that what is only its ideology should be considered to be universal truth. It can, however, indeed must be, a university that is open to many streams of thought, self-avowed, competing. It can, and must be, both politicized and open. I join Professor C. B. MacPherson, in his presidential address to the Canadian Association of University Teachers, in believing that our slogan must be "From the liberal to the critical university."

In such a university men of the left will have a place along with others. If such left intellectuals remain *engagé*, not only intellectually but within living political movements, they can draw sustenance from and give vitality to these political movements.

They can then operate, within a liberal society, in a way effectively to affect the liberal center, to push it leftward, to force it to be conscious of the real social choices, to appeal to its conscience and to its self-interest. The American left, under such circumstances, could ally itself with the liberal center when it was profitable, and combat it when it was necessary.

I have not spoken of the problem of the "third world" movements. But, *mutatis mutandis*, the problem the left faces concerning them is similar in many ways to those concerning the liberal center. These movements are left in orientation because they are emanations of oppressed ethnic groups. But they contain many conservative elements because of their need for group unity. The left must learn to support these movements and unite with them when appropriate, but also dissociate itself from them when their conservative elements gain control. This is a delicate and difficult task, and one which requires both knowledge and empathy to do well. But it can in fact be done.

Above all, the radical intellectual must operate with the passionate calm of one for whom the revolution is not a battle of a day, a year, or a decade, but one of centuries. And yet he must do this without fatalistic optimism. The revolution is only inevitable because people make it so. The student revolt has in many ways restored the possibilities for the radical intellectual to rise to his task and find his appropriate place in the movement. The dilemma of activism versus thought, of full-time revolutionary activity versus co-option is false. The radical must operate in both arenas at once. He must break down some, but not all, of the barriers between them. He must participate in the movement, yet also reflect upon it. He must defend the university, but also criticize it. He must encourage spontaneity and protect it, yet also save himself and others from being drowned in it.

4—Africa in a Capitalist World

In 1972–73, I was president of the African Studies Association. I had already written *The Modern World-System*, but it had not yet appeared. I thought it important to use my presidential address to resume and restructure what I had been saying about contemporary Africa within the new perspective I had evolved. The two words, Africa and capitalism, had not been used in the same article too often in the 1950s and 1960s. I wished to insist that we had to view Africa as an intrinsic part of the capitalist world in which we were living.

African studies has gone through three well-known phases as a field of study. Up until 1950 or thereabouts, those studying Africa—they were not yet called Africanists—tended to concentrate almost exclusively on the capturing (or recapturing) of a description of Africa eternal. Launcelot the ethnographer in search of a holy grail of the past that was written in the present tense and was undefiled by contact and uncorrupted by civilization. What was once a myth is now a fairy tale and it would be silly to waste time telling each other the obvious truth that fairy tales are modes of the social control and the education of children.

We then moved collectively into a second phase in which we recognized that there was an African present, and consequently that there was an African past. Thus began the great division of the field of studies which has been so obvious to anyone attending meetings of such organizations as the African Studies Association. There were those who studied what was happening now. They usually called themselves political scientists or economists or sociologists, but some masqueraded under other denominations ranging from architectural planner to urban anthropologist to demographer. There arose a second group who studied what happened before. They usually called themselves historians or archaeologists but they, too, had their aliases: art historian, student of cosmologies, linguist. The two groups maintained a friendly cohabitation under the house of African studies but scarcely could they be said to have had an intimate relationship.

This separation of the present and the past was as artificial and as mythical as the previous collapsing of past and present into one continuing eternity. It was no doubt a great advance in that it permitted some concrete empirical work rooted in concrete historical circumstances to proceed, but it was not satisfying. Those concerned with the present came to realize that much of their scholarship was really a sort of second-hand journalism. And those concerned with the past began to feel that their efforts to prove to non-Africanists that Africa too had splendid kings ultimately proved no more than that naive prejudice was naive. It provided, however, no true answer to the very large questions of Africa's position in the great "rendez-vous de donner et de recevoir"[1] of world cultures. If one wished to say that Africa's economic and technological weakness of today was somehow balanced in a world scale by Africa's glories of yesteryear, there would have to be some clearer, more detailed analysis of the process of evolution from the one to the other.

The logical consequence of this collective discomfort was almost self-evident. Those concerned with the present began looking backwards into the historical past, albeit gingerly. And those concerned with the past began to ask whether the conquest of Africa by Europe in the late nineteenth century marked as sharp an historical discontinuity as they had assumed. So we have J.F. Ade Ajayi addressing the International Congress of African Historians in 1965 on the theme, "The continuity of African institutions under colonialism."[2] Today it is scarcely credible that in 1965 the very title seemed somewhat daring—a measure of how far we have come in the past few years.

Ajayi said then:

> [Historians] should consider the story of how individually or collectively Africans are trying to master the new forces that have descended on them, how and why a man gets himself baptised a Christian, sends his children to school, comes to terms with modern technology by buying a lorry and learning to drive it, and yet insists that the lorry is not just a mechanical device but has a force whose control properly belongs to the god of iron and whose emblems and charms are therefore displayed in the lorry. I find such a man more typical—and more cheering—than the frustrated, paralysed, helpless African portrayed in the theory of disruption.[3]

One historian who was doing what Ajayi called for was Terence Ranger, the organizer of the Congress in Dar es Salaam at which Ajayi spoke. Ranger published soon thereafter a two-part article in the *Jour-

nal of African History entitled "Connexions between 'Primary Resistance' Movements and Modern Mass Nationalism in East and Central Africa."[4] Ranger asserted that so-called primary resistances, far from being reactionary or backward-looking, looked into the future in the same way as did later nationalist movements. He further argued that the two sets of movements were not merely similar but historically connected.

It was not long before these arguments were attacked by Donald Denoon and Adam Kuper as "ideological history," one that "has adopted the political philosophy of current African nationalism, and has used it to inform the study of African history." What is more, said Denoon and Kuper: "The African historian should be committed to writing the truth, rather than the politic half-truth."[5]

Strong rhetoric, but what is the truth? What is the truth now, and what will it be tomorrow? Who defines it today, and who tomorrow? Who indeed is truly dedicated to the truth, and whose interest does which truth serve? I raise of course the questions of the social bases of knowledge. But I do not wish to stop there. Rather I wish to move on from there to suggesting some conceptual bases for the knowledge of the social reality of Africa.

In 1971, Bernard Magubane published an article in *Current Anthropology* which was an attack on the indices used in studying social change in Africa. In particular, he singled out the work of A.L. Epstein and Clyde Mitchell about Northern Rhodesia as foci for his argument. As is the custom of this journal, the paper was submitted to a large number of scholars for comment, and the article was published simultaneously with the comments and a reply to the comments.[6]

The heart of Magubane's critique was that the categories used by Epstein and Mitchell in their analyses were "extremely superficial and at best ethnocentric," and that they lacked "historical perspective."[7] Magubane's explanation of this was that Epstein and Mitchell reflected their social role:

> As men who basically accepted the "civilizing mission" of imperialism their analyses rationalized and attempted to improve the imperial system. The result was a divided effort at social analysis and propaganda which produced a hodgepodge of eclectic and mechanistic formulations.[8]

The commentators were scarcely gentle with Magubane. Epstein accused Magubane of "dissipating his talents in knocking down the men of straw he himself has set up."[9] Mitchell charged him with the "shoddiest kind of criticism . . . *argumentum ad hominem* . . ." He concluded:

> The pity of it is that all he has to offer is destructive and ill-considered comments on the work of others who, for better or for worse, but *nonetheless in good faith,* have faced the challenge and discipline of research of this kind.[10] (Italics added)

While Epstein and Mitchell denounced ad hominem arguments, various of the other commentators offered just such arguments in defense of Epstein and Mitchell. A.J.F. Köbben suggested that to understand Magubane's attitude, "one would need the concerted efforts of the anthropologist, the historian, and the psychologist, and a lot of empathy, if not compassion."[11] Satish Saberwal observed in milder tones that:

> The chiding that Mitchell and Epstein get at Magubane's hand is, in part, the penalty that pioneers often have to pay.[12]

Simon D. Messing reminded us of the German saying: "Undank ist der Welten Lohn."[13] Van den Berghe accused Magubane of "ideologically inspired innuendo," and called him "not even intellectually honest."[14] Philip Mayer asserted merely:

> [Magubane's] own "existential" situation is . . . of some relevance, especially as such a single-minded onslaught on "colonial anthropology" seems almost anachronistic in 1970.[15]

In his reply, Magubane observed with sharpness:

> The importance of my critique of "pluralist" writings like Van den Berghe's and of works like that of Epstein, Mayer, Mitchell, etc. derives not from their intrinsic worth, but rather from the near universal acceptance of their conclusions among certain scholars. What we are faced with in the field of African studies is an accumulation of studies that are theoretically false and have congealed into a steadfast intellectual reality. It is revealing but at the same time sad that of those people who replied to my article, only the three "Third World" commentators understood clearly what I was talking about, whereas the rest could only partially agree or were completely impervious to what I was saying. This is a reflection of the fundamental issue of our time: those who stand for a particular order in the world are unwilling to accept challenges to that order. Persuading such people to see that their ideas must be abandoned is like asking those in power to give up their privileges.[16]

Lest we think that such a vitriolic exchange is exceptional, let us return for a moment to Denoon and Kuper's broadside against Ranger and
what they termed the "Dar es Salaam school" of historiography. These
"nationalist historians," said Denoon and Kuper, might well be regarded
"as providing pie in the past rather than an understanding of present
problems."[17] In his reply, Ranger had a footnote that reads:

> One day, perhaps, if interest should survive that long, a scholar will be able to
> investigate what connections there are between the fact that Denoon and Ku-
> per are both young South African exiles recently working in Makerere and the
> methods and assumptions of their critique of Dar es Salaam historians. I would
> venture some speculations on this myself were it not for the fact that their own
> attempt to situate me in my environment serves as a ludicrous warning of the
> dangers of such an exercise.[18]

No speculation was therefore offered, but Ranger concluded his article with this sentence:

> I am sure that [Denoon and Kuper] will find it easier to serve the goddess of
> disinterested history when they are not working under the pressure of the pro-
> found if obscure forces which impelled their trenchant but totally misleading
> attack on the historians of Dar es Salaam.[19]

In turn, Denoon and Kuper showed no shyness in their rejoinder:

> Finally, Professor Ranger's mention of our South African backgrounds and his
> reference to the "profound if obscure forces" which motivated our critique
> may have puzzled some readers. Is he suggesting a secret subsidy from the
> Communist Party or the CIA? Or darkly hinting at the emergence of a sinister
> Pretoria school of African historiography? Our own view is that far from mak-
> ing any such unworthy imputation, this was Professor Ranger's way of saying
> he could not imagine any good reason for criticizing his school.[20]

The vehemence of feeling is not unfamiliar to those who have followed recent scholarly debates in African studies, although some may
feel as did R.H. Tawney when he commented on H.R. Trevor-Roper's
criticism of his work: "An erring colleague is not an Amalekite to be smit-
ten hip and thigh."[21] What is to the point, however, is to see if there are
underlying themes that would give coherence and unity to a large number of different debates on seemingly different topics. I shall therefore
rapidly survey what it is I think Magubane and his critics are arguing
about, the nub of the issue between Denoon and Kuper on one side and

Ranger on the other, and what is at issue in the somewhat more restrained debate that J.D. Fage and C.C. Wrigley recently engaged in about "slavery and the slave trade." For I think there is a common intellectual issue threaded through these and other debates, overlain of course by some strongly-felt moral, and political issues, and I believe that we can collectively make sense out of the debates only if we bring this underlying issue to the fore.

Note first of all that Magubane's article is about "indices used in the study of social change in colonial Africa." One of his opening suggestions was that "a total historical analysis of social change would, as a matter of course, take into account (various) stages in 'acculturation'."[22] He proceeded to outline three. In each of which the response of Africans to the dominant forces in the colonial situation was different. He noted, in terms virtually identical to those of Ajayi:

> In fact the history of the colonial situation, as opposed to its economics, its politics, its sociology, and its psychology, is in large measure a history of the variety of African responses to the new situation, a history of the ways Africans came to terms with a new set of forces, the ways they accommodated, resisted, or escaped.[23]

To the charge of neglect of these considerations, Magubane's critics shouted "foul." I take one response as typical. Clyde Mitchell said: "Epstein's whole book is about the way in which Africans were organizing to change the status quo from 1932 to 1953."[24]

It is worth listening to Magubane's counterattack in his reply at some length:

> Therefore my point in this article was not that Epstein in his book *Politics in an Urban African Community* did not deal with trade unions, but that he gave the wrong kind of explanation as to the source of these movements. To understand African nationalism and give it a correct historical interpretation, one must understand its dual nature. White settlement is a colonialist force in its own right (territorial colonialism) whose ultimate interest is its preservation in the territory it has occupied. The conflict that arose between Africans and white settlers stemmed from the antagonistic confrontation between white colonizing community *qua* community and the African people *qua* people. When the Africans were introduced into mining and secondary industry, the problem was compounded by class factors. Therefore African nationalism combines the dynamics of national liberation and class struggle. The failure of elite integrationist politics and the beginning of the armed struggle testify to this dual

nature. What is the nature of the relation between the two aspects of African nationalism in southern Africa? The comments by Epstein. Mitchell, and Van den Berghe avoid this issue.[25]

Permit me to reformulate this debate into two very fundamental issues: those of time-scope and space-scope. We are not involved in a simplified debate about the relevance of history. Both sides acknowledged this. What they disagreed about was the "correct historical interpretation." They have not even disagreed about the fact that some kind of structural and behavioral change was occurring under colonial rule, although Magubane charged that the others "have tended to take [the colonial situation] for granted, or to assume that its general characteristics are known."[26] But Magubane insisted there are temporal stages within the colonial period—what might be paraphrased as the period of conquest, the period of "acquiescence" (Magubane's phrase), and the period of national liberation. He argued that by neglecting this periodization, Epstein, Mitchell *et. al.* were in fact talking exclusively about the middle period. This was of course their privilege, and was a relatively minor peccadillo. What is at issue is the assertion that by this absence of explicit periodization (perhaps in the very innards of their own intellectual processes) they could not interpret meaningfully the data which they collected in a technically impeccable manner.

Nor is this all. The second issue is that of space-scope. Magubane said that the conflict was that of a "white colonizing community *qua* community and the African people *qua* people." He talked of the dual nature of African nationalism: it is, he asserted, both "national liberation and class struggle." But Epstein too spoke of growing national consciousness. He too spoke of the union as uniting workers along class lines. Thus, was not Magubane unfair? To Epstein, he was setting up "straw men."

To make sense of this, we must draw out the implicit frameworks of the authors. For Epstein and Mitchell, the geographical frame of analysis was Northern Rhodesia. To the extent that they made use of stratification categories (tribe, class, etc.) these were for them categories of this territorial unit. For Magubane, although he did not say so explicitly, the use of these boundaries distorted the data and made no operational sense. How can a movement be simultaneously one of "national liberation" and one of "class struggle," if the unit of analysis is not larger than the colonial territory — at the very minimum that of the imperial political framework, and more reasonably, as I shall soon argue, that of the world-economy.

Let us now turn to the debate about the so-called Dar es Salaam school of historiography. Here Denoon and Kuper were quite explicit about the issue of time-scope and space-scope. They made it the heart of the debate. Although in many ways I would assimilate[27] their position on the essential underlying issue with that of Epstein and Mitchell, they took the initiative in this debate, seeming to invert the sides by accusing Ranger (whose position I would assimilate to that of Magubane) of provinciality of time and scope.

Denoon and Kuper started their analysis of citing Ranger as depicting in 1965 the likely intellectual debate of the future in these terms: "The Africanist historian . . . will increasingly find his main adversaries not in the discredited colonial school but in the radical pessimists."[28] that is, men who employ what Ranger called "Fanonesque analysis." Denoon and Kuper said of this categorization by Ranger:

> In this confrontation Professor Ranger takes the side of the Africanist by which is meant the historian whose concerns include the study of nationalism. In practice the frequent use of the term *African* is likely to mislead, since the recommended focus for historians is not the whole continent but African activity within national boundaries and generally for a national purpose. The analysis repudiates not only a Fanonesque view, but also any view involving generalization on a scale larger than that of nation — whether a world view, an imperial view or a continental approach. The recommended approach, then, is African nationalist.[29]

Thus, the issue of space-scope is at the forefront of the critique.

Ranger, however, flatly denied the correctness of this perception of his position:

> I do not believe . . . that a historian should concentrate on African activity within national boundaries. To extract such a view from my work cannot be achieved without a dexterity which comes close to manipulation.[30]

Rather, Ranger asserted his position to be quite different:

> The historian "must insist that nationalism is a live subject" — not the *only* subject, not the most *important* subject, but a live subject. So far from being con-

cerned to argue that *all* African historical studies should in some sense be nationalist I was concerned to urge that nationalism should still be studied.[31]

So is there then no argument? Is it all a misunderstanding? Not quite. It turns out on closer analysis that the debate over space-scope is a bit of a front for a more real debate about time-scope. Much of the debate centers around the contents of two books of essays about Tanzania, one edited by I.M. Kimambo and A.J. Temu and the other by A.D. Roberts.[32] Denoon and Kuper took these volumes as the quintessential products of the group they were attacking. Denoon and Kuper cited the Introduction to *A History of Tanzania* in which Professors Kimambo and Temu wrote:

There has been no attempt to deal with colonial administrative structures. This is because our main interest has been on the African himself.[33]

To which Denoon and Kuper responded:

Historians of political development within colonial dependencies, in any part of the world, would be rightly appalled at such a self-imposed limitation.[34]

Denoon and Kuper pointed out that Ranger had challenged previous writers for having regarded certain new African institutions — specifically African independent churches — as "an abnormality, almost a disease."[35] This was, they said, "a straw-man's thesis"[36] — shades of Epstein attacking Magubane. To pursue the parallelism of the two debates, Denoon and Kuper taxed their opponents with disparaging the enthnographers:

Finally, the members of the school show a certain shyness about using the works of the anthropologists who worked in Tanganyika during the colonial period. The social anthropologists were the main group of scholars active in colonial Africa; they worked in the vernaculars; and they published accounts of East African societies and social movements over many years. Not only are their enthnographies invaluable historical documents, but their interpretations would often be suggestive for the historian. The reason for this neglect appears to be the association of anthropology with colonialism.[37]

But how is all this a debate about time-scope? This surfaces clearly in the debate about pre-colonial East Africa. Denoon and Kuper asserted that the authors writing various local histories in the Roberts volume had failed to prove their generalizations, that in the editor's own chapter, "there is a sense of straining to find . . . 'roots of nationalism.'"[38] They cited J.E.G. Sutton's chapter in the Kimambo-Temu volume in which he began with a banality that the Tanzanian nation "is the product of a long historical process stretching back hundreds, even thousands of years"[39] and snidely commented that Sutton "does not in practice attempt to Tanzanianize the australopithecines."[40]

What was all of this leading to? Two statements: one of shock, and one of assertion. The one of shock reads:

> Perhaps this [previous quote] may be regarded as a recognition that a full continuity of large-scale anti-colonial sentiment is not always to be found. At all events, [Lonsdale's] Dar es Salaam colleagues — Gwassa, Iliffe and Temu — appear still to be convinced of the existence of a "missing link" between resistance and TANU nationalism in Tanzania, while Roberts would like to push back the roots of resistance on a national scale well into the nineteenth century.[41]

And the assertion:

> Scholars who regard the outside world's interventions in Africa as having achieved more than nationalism, and who consider that colonialism has been replaced very frequently by neo-colonialism, are not likely to be convinced by the implication that colonial policy was of scant significance even during the colonial years.[42]

But was this the implication these writers wanted to have drawn? Ranger said it missed the point:

> What most of the contributions to a *A History of Tanzania* do stress is African initiative, African choice and African adaptation . . . But there are two things which it is very important to make plain. This first is that to stress African agency is by no means to stress African heroism or efficiency; the second is that a common concern with what Africans did and how they affected their history can lead to a most un-common and varied set of conclusions. The inquiry into African agency is not the resting point which defines a school, but the beginning point out of which all sorts of major differences will arise.[43]

What distinguishes in the end Denoon and Kuper's analysis from the ones they criticize is the emphasis placed on the analysis of the colonial era. Denoon and Kuper argued that because of a "nationalist" political perspective, Ranger *et al* ignored some concrete and specific features of colonial administration in favor of mythological "connexions." Ranger argued rather that to understand African behavior in that period required situating it in a longer time-scale of historical development, the exact bounds of which Ranger did not pursue in this debate.

To demonstrate that this debate is not merely one about how to interpret the colonial period, let us turn to the argument about slavery and the slave trade. John Fage entitled his article "Slavery and the Slave Trade in the Context of West African History."[44] The title itself suggests the space-scope. As for the time-scope his summary depicted it as covering "especially . . . the period from the fifteenth to the nineteenth century." We shall see however that this was not in fact his time-scope, since his analysis involved going further back in time.

Fage started by rejecting both the thesis that slavery was a flourishing institution in West Africa prior to European intrusion and the thesis that it was purely exogenously imposed. And basing himself largely on Philip Curtin,[45] he also rejected the idea that slave-trading in West Africa had "a disastrous effect on its population."[46] Rather, he put forward a different interpretation which he summarized as follows:

> [E]conomic and commercial slavery and slave-trading were not natural features of West African society, but . . . developed, along with the growth of states, as a form of labour mobilization to meet the needs of a growing system of foreign trade in which, initially, the demand for slaves as trade goods were relatively insignificant. What might be termed a "slave economy" was generally established in the Western and Central Sudan by about the fourteenth century at least, and had certainly spread to the coasts around the Senegal and in Lower Guinea by the fifteenth century. The European demand for slaves in the Americas, which reached its peak from about 1650 to about 1850, accentuated and expanded the internal growth of both slavery and the slave trade. But this was essentially only one respect of a very wide process of economic and political development and social change in West Africa.[47]

To argue this position, Fage had to start by undermining the attack on Fage's previous statement by Walter Rodney, whose evidence Fage acknowledged to be crucially relevant.[48] Fage discounted Rodney's finding of the absence of a slave work-force in West Africa prior to the arrival of European slave-traders as true perhaps for the Upper Guinea Coast but not for either the Lower Guinea Coast or the interior. Fage's essential explanation was that the area that Rodney studied was atypical, essentially because it "was an economically little-developed and backward region."[49]

For the other areas, Fage contended the picture was very different:

> In general, we can be confident that what the Portuguese sought to do in Lower Guinea from about 1480 was to profit by imposing themselves (as later they would do in East Africa and Asia) on already existing patterns of trade, and that they from there organized kingdoms in which the idea of foreign trade, carried on under royal control and in accordance with state policy by established merchant classes or guilds, was already well established. Such a system involved the use of slaves—and an appreciation of their economic value—in a number of ways: as cultivators of crops for market on the estates of kings or nobles; as miners, or as artisans in craft workshops, as carriers on the trade routes; and even as traders themselves; as soldiers, retainers, servants, officials even, in the employ of kings or principal men in the kingdom.[50]

Did nothing then change for Fage in West Africa when the Europeans came in the fifteenth century? It's not entirely clear. Fage said that:

> [The] slave trade . . . in West Africa . . . was part of a sustained process of economic and social development. Probably because, by and large, in West Africa land was always more abundant than labour, the institution of slavery played an essential role in its development; without it there were really few effective means of mobilizing labour for the economic and political needs of the state . . .

> On the whole it is probably true to say the operation of the slave trade may have tended to integrate, strengthen and develop unitary, territorial political authority, but to weaken or destroy more segmentary societies. Whether this was good or evil may be a nice point: historically it may be seen as purposive and perhaps as more or less inevitable.[51]

The picture thus that we have from Fage is that there existed some long historical process which began at some unspecified point prior to the fifteenth century in which the European intrusion was merely one of a series of factors which contributed to this "inevitable" and "purposive" evolution. When the Europeans finally conquered West Africa, this was merely one more step in this process:

> The steps taken by Europeans against the slave trade and slavery therefore hastened the day when, in their own economic interest they thought it necessary first to conquer the West African kingdoms, and then to continue the process, initiated by African kings and entrepreneurs, of conquering the segmentary societies and absorbing them into unitary political structures.[52]

We see then clearly that for Fage a meaningful unit of analysis is West Africa from prior to the fifteenth century to the present in which the principal dynamic of social organization and transformation is "state-building."

How different had been Rodney's article. First notice the title: "African slavery and other forms of social oppression on the Upper Guinea Coast in the context of the Atlantic slave-trade." The context (that is, the space-scope) was not "West Africa" but the "Atlantic slave-trade," which was in fact shorthand for the European world-economy. Rodney saw this period as one in which "African society became geared to serve the capitalist system,"[53] — that is, the *world* capitalist system. He said:

> Historically, the initiative came from Europe. It was the European commercial system which expanded to embrace the various levels of African barter economy, and to assign to them specific roles in global production. This meant the accumulation of capital from trading in Africa, and above all the purchase of slaves and their employment in the New World.[54]

Thus, the period 1600–1800 is far from being a middle period in a continuing West African historical pattern as Fage envisaged it; for Rodney it was "the first stage of the colonial domination of Africa by Europeans,"[55] a "protocolonial" period[56] — hence part of a world-historical pattern.

C.C. Wrigley entered into this debate, saying very correctly:

> [Fage's radical reassessment of the Atlantic slave-trade] brings near to the surface certain theoretical assumptions which I believe to be embedded in a large part of recent African historiography . . . [57]

And the assumption that Wrigley was most concerned about bringing to the fore is that slavery and the slave-trade are a necessary condition of the "political development" of West Africa, an inevitable aspect of state-formation.[58] As Wrigley noted, this stands Rodney on his head:

> Hitherto, a historian who was at pains to establish that Africans were enslaving one another before the first caravels dropped anchor off their coasts would have been immediately identifiable as a "colonialist"; he would be manifestly seeking to denigrate the African people and to saddle them with part of the blame for the ensuing calamity of the Atlantic trade. Fage, however, is unmistakably congratulating West Africans on having achieved the institution of slavery without European help.[59]

This, continued Wrigley, was "historicism," taking "classificatory types, formulated in the first place for their heuristic value" and translating them into "developmental stages, conceived as having real existence and arranged in a hierarchy which is both chronological and qualitative."[60] Such historicism is ethnocentric and condemns Africans "to limp painfully in the footsteps of Europe."[61] Note here an interesting paradox. It is suggested that the consequence of using West African space-scope, as did Fage, can lead to conclusions that are Europocentric. It is equally implied that using a European space-scope (taking Europe in the 17th and 18th centuries to include at least parts of West Africa), as did Rodney, can lead to conclusions that place in appropriate perspective what Ranger calls "African agency."

How then do we proceed? In his most recent book, *How Europe Underdeveloped Africa*, Rodney devoted Chapter Two to "how Africa developed before the coming of the Europeans up to the fifteenth century." He gave an explanation that is in the tradition of a recent French literature about the "African mode of production." I myself do not find this part of Rodney's exposition very satisfying. Nor as a matter of fact do I get the impression that Rodney himself does. For he concluded the chapter with a reflection which I endorse entirely:

> One of the paradoxes in studying this early period of African history is that it cannot be fully comprehended without first deepening our knowledge of the world at large, and yet the true picture of the complexities of the development of man and society can only be drawn after intensive study of the long-neglected African continent.[62]

This then is how I think we must proceed. To understand Africa, we must reconceptualize world history. And for the scholarly world to effectuate such a conceptualization, we as Africanists must do our share by doing our work within such a perspective. I am not calling for intellectual supermen. I am merely asking that we wear a new pair of glasses, and that we wear these new glasses in the very process of grinding them. This a hard task, but not a new one, since this is the only way in which man has ever invented the new truths that caught up his new realities and yet simultaneously criticized these new realities in the light of human potentialities.

One key aspect to the process of reconceptualization is to bring to the fore our implicit theories. And this means specifying time-scope and space-scope and justifying our choices. At the same conference in Dar es

Salaam at which Ajayi made his appeal to study the continuities of African institutions under colonialism, Ivan Hrbek gave an unfortunately neglected paper entitled "Towards a periodisation of African history."[63]

Hrbek attacked the relevance of conventional Europo-centric periodizations of Africa, including those of Marxist dogmatists like Endre Sik.[64] He suggested various landmarks or watersheds, working backwards. The most recent was that of the 1960s — the achievement of independence by many states. The second however was not 1884–1885 but rather the moment of "integration of African societies into the sphere of world economy and later world politics."[65] He dated this, with some reservations, as the first decade of the twentieth century. Farther back, he hesitated to give a continent-wide date. Although he would have liked to distinguish what he called "contact zones" and "isolated zones" at that point in time, he pointed out that during the period 1805–1820 there were a large number of major happenings in both zones. He listed the jihad of Osman dan Fodio; the rise of the Zulu under Chaka; the eclipse of Bunyoro and the rise of Buganda; the foundation of modern Egypt under Muhammed Ali; the unification of the Imerina on Madagascar under Radama I; the rise of Omani hegemony on the East African coast under Sayyid Said. According to Hrbek what makes these six instances parallel is that they all "pointed in one direction: the growth of a unified and highly centralized state with an absolute monarch unrestricted in his power by any freely elected council."[66] This was also the moment of the abolition of the slave trade, and although Hrbek dismissed any connection, I am not so sure that he was correct in doing so.

Going further back, Hrbek indicated some skepticism about the conventional belief that the fifteenth or sixteenth century marked a turning point.

> [S]ometimes exaggerated assertions as to the far-reaching consequences of the slave trade are pronounced. In fact the coming of the Europeans and the start of the slave-trade were a direct influence only in coastal regions and their immediate hinterlands . . . In the "isolated" zones African societies continued their independent development without any extracontinental influence. . . .[67]

Finally, Hrbek argued a still earlier turning point — somewhere between the first and fifth centuries A.D.

> . . . when iron working was already known in large parts of Africa and when the introduction of new food-plants [from South-East Asia] enabled the Bantu and also the West African ethnic groups to occupy the forested areas . . .[68]

I outline Hrbek's dates not to defend them but to indicate how different they are from more conventional dating, as suggested not only by many standard texts but by such a critic of these texts as Rodney: that is, pre-1500, 1500–1885, 1885–1960.

A second analyst who came up with dates with some similarities to those of Hrbek is Samir Amin who suggested the following: a *pre-mercantilist period* going back into history and going up to 1600; a *mercantilist* period going from 1600–1800; *completed integration into the capitalist system* (the nineteenth century to the present).[69]

But, you will say, is it so important whether we date a shift at 1500 or 1600, at 1885 or the first decade of the twentieth century? Do we have any tools of historical measurement that are so fine? And what practical consequence can such a seemingly esoteric debate have? The answer is of course that our measures are gross and we should not pretend otherwise. But the debate is not esoteric because behind it lies the issue not of the years, but of the conceptual apparatus we have used to come up with one set of dates or another. And this is not merely important: it is all-determining.

To make sense of African history, we must have a theory of human society. If we go back to the year 1000 or thereabouts, our knowledge of what was going on in Africa is far more sparse than any of us would like. We know there were great migrations. We know that in various places there were state-apparatuses. We know that in some places there was long-distance trade. But we do not know too much—in part because we have not really looked for the answers—about the geographical bounds of the various divisions of labor in Africa. No doubt there were many mini-systems, largely or entirely self-sufficient. But how many worlds were there—that is, arenas in which there were systematic sustained exchanges of essential goods? And even more difficult, how many of these took the form of a world-empire—that is, a single division of labor with a single overall political structure; and how many took the form of a world-economy—that is, a single division of labor with multiple political systems? We know that historically the first world-economy to overcome the basic instability of this systemic form and therefore survive over a long period of time is the capitalist world-economy which originated as a European world economy in the sixteenth century. But we also know that the course of human history has seen the passing existence of many world-economies, some of which disintegrated and others of which became transformed into world-empires.

Take for example Mali. At its height was it a world-empire or part of a larger world-economy that included parts of the Maghreb as well as areas in the forest zone to the south, within which the state of Mali was only one of many political systems? I suspect the latter is true for at least part of the time, but the hard research remains to be done. Instead of writing epicycles around an evolutionary theory of a "feudal" stage of social development by talking first of an "Asiatic mode of production" and then of an "African mode of production," don't we have to undertake a fundamental reassessment of all the varieties of redistributive modes of production, all of which seem to require some kind of political channel of redistribution and all of which seem to inhibit progress in technological productivity because of the absence of a market towards which production is oriented?

What we learn about Mali may enable us to explain intelligently for the first time Carolingian Europe. I am not calling for a systematic comparison. We are not yet at the stage. For we do not even yet have a systematic categorization of the parameters of each, using terms that are at least translatable one to the other. For almost all our work has started from political definitions of space-scope which has prevented us from systematically analyzing social systems—divisions of labor (that is, economic entities)—which may or may not have a single political framework.

If now we turn to a slightly later point in time, something did change in the sixteenth century—not in Africa, but in the world. In the sixteenth century there emerged a European world-economy centered on a combination of Atlantic and Baltic trade which included geographically within its division of labor an area including northwestern Europe, the Christian Mediterranean, northeastern Europe (but not Russia) and Hispanic America. The mode of production was capitalist. Though the genesis of this structure can be dated about 1450, it is only with the Treaty of Cateau Cambrésis in 1559 that the possibility that this world-economy would go the way of all previous ones—transformation into a world-empire or disintegration—was definitely eliminated. And thus it was at this point that the capitalist mode of production (which can exist only within that structure known as a world-economy) could be said to have become the mode of production of this system, therefore determining the social relations of *all* sectors of this world-economy.

Why such a capitalist world-economy should have arisen in Europe and not elsewhere (say, China) is an interesting question. Why it should have arisen at this point of historical time is too. I have tried to speak to these questions elsewhere and it is not to the point of this discussion to dwell on them. We must look rather to the consequences.[70]

A capitalist world-economy is based on a division of labor between its core, its semiperiphery, and its periphery in such a way that there is unequal exchange between the sectors but dependence of all the sectors, both economically and politically, on the continuance of this unequal exchange. One of the many consequences of this system is found in state-structure, the peripheral states being weakened and the core states strengthened by the ongoing process of exchange. A second of the consequences is that each sector develops different modes of labor control, consonant with the principle that highest relative wages are paid in the core sectors and lowest relative wages in the periphery. This is why at this moment in time there emerged in eastern Europe the so-called (and misnamed) "second serfdom" and the *encomienda* system in Hispanic America. Both are forms of coerced cash-crop labor on estates producing for a capitalist world-market.[71]

In addition, in the Americas plantation slavery was developed. Plantation slavery is a form of capitalist wage-labor (labor offered for sale as a commodity on a market) in which the state intervenes to guarantee a low current wage (the cost of subsistence). However there is an additional cost; that of the purchase of the slave. If the slave is "produced" within the world-economy, his real cost is not merely the sales price but the opportunity cost (of failing to use his labor under other wage conditions at presumably a higher level of productivity). As Marc Bloch suggested a long time ago, under these conditions slaves are too expensive[72]—that is, they do not produce enough surplus to compensate for their real cost.

The *only* way to render plantation slavery economically feasible in a capitalist system is to eliminate the opportunity cost, which means that the slaves must be recruited outside the world-economy. In that case, the opportunity cost is borne by some other system and is a matter of indifference to the purchasers. This would change of course if one totally exhausted the supplier and there were no replacement on similar terms. But historically this had not yet occurred at the moment the slave-trade ended.

Trade with an external arena of a world-economy is fundamentally different from trade within the world-economy between the core and peripheral sectors. We can see this if we compare trade in the sixteenth century between western Europe and Poland on the one hand and between western Europe and Russia on the other, or during the same period of time trade between Spain and Hispanic America on the one hand and Portugal and the Indian Ocean area on the other.[73]

There are three visible differences. First, trade within the world-economy is trade in essentials, without which the world-economy could not continue to survive. It involves a significant transfer of surplus, given that a world-economy is based on a capitalist mode of production. It is trade that responds to the world-market of the world-economy. Trade of two world-systems, each external to the other, involves what was called in the sixteenth century the "rich trades." In more precise terms, we can say such trade involves the exchange of products that both sellers define as of very low value but that both buyers define as of high value. This is not capitalist exchange, and is in fact dispensable exchange. There is profit to be made by long-distance traders but this is precisely the kind of profit made by such traders over thousands of years of such trade—a profit based on high price discrepancies due to rarity of the product at the place of consumption and oversupply of the product at the place of production.

Second, trade within a capitalist world-economy weakens the state-structure of a peripheral country involved in it. The steady decline of the power of the Polish king from about 1500 to 1800 is a clear case in point. Trade in external arenas does not weaken and probably strengthens the state-structures of the trading partners. One can point to the increase of the strength of sultans in Malaysia at this same period.

Third, trade within a capitalist world-economy weakens the role of the indigenous commercial bourgeoisie in the periphery. Trade with an external arena strengthens the role of the indigenous bourgeoisie.

Thus far, as you will see, I have assiduously avoided discussing where European trade with West Africa in what Amin called the *mercantilist* period (1600–1800) fits into this picture. The reason is that the answer is not as clear-cut as we would like it. It is evident that this trade between Europe and West Africa meets the description of trade in the external arena on the last two grounds. It strengthens various state-structures in West Africa, and it strengthened the role of the indigenous commercial bourgeoisie. But can it be said to have been luxury trade, and even more can it be said to have been trade that did not involve a substantial transfer of surplus?

One piece of evidence that it could be so described is deductive in nature. Were it not so, were West Africa part of the periphery of the European world-economy, then the cost of slaves in the Western Hemisphere would have had to bear the opportunity cost of their physical loss to West Africa, and that, presumably, would have made them too expensive in the economics of the total economy to be used. And used they were, extensively, as we know. The loss of course to West Africa was very real.[74]

But this could be taken to be circular reasoning. Let me therefore speak directly to the two descriptive features: was the slave-trade of items each seller valued low? And was there no significant transfer of surplus?

The answer is, I believe, that the situation evolved. Victorino Magathães Godinho gave some detailed accounts of the nature of the trade between Portuguese and Africans at a whole series of points along the West African coast down to Angola in the sixteenth century. It seems clear that the main items traded at that time for slaves were brass and copper bracelets ('manillas'), various size trays, barrels of conches, kerchiefs, skullcaps, and some uncut cloth.[75] I do not believe it would be inaccurate to say that this was an exchange of items each seller valued low for what they each valued high. Nor do I think it inaccurate to say that at this point a cessation for any reason would not have upset the respective economies fundamentally, and consequently would have had few implications for the social organization of the respective social systems despite the fact that for Europeans the trade was most profitable,[76] as long distance trade usually is.

This seems to be less the case as we go forward in time. But how much less? Christopher Fyfe's textbook account seems ambivalent. On the one hand he noted that as of the seventeenth century, firearms became a major import. And firearms might be said to be an essential product. Indeed, he said that by the end of the eighteenth century, "there were factories in England [in Birmingham] turning out special arms for the African trade . . ."[77] And thus he implied that such trade was a regular part of the European division of labor. On the other hand, he called the remaining imports (other than firearms) "luxuries rather than necessities; they merely supplemented local manufactures with imports of superior quality."[78] Still, he observed further: "As manufactured goods were imported increasingly, local industry needed to suffer"[79] — a feature we would associate with a process of peripheralization. We thus have an ambiguous set of characteristics describing this trade. Fyfe's own summary points to the argument of evolution over time:

> So, though foreign imports tended to be luxury goods, and the country still remained self-supporting in essentials, as the demands for imports grew steadily, the area was increasingly tied to the economies of countries overseas.[80]

I believe some of this ambiguity dissipates if one goes carefully through Rodney's detailed analysis of "The Nature of Afro-European Commerce."[81] Rodney divided European exports with West Africa into five categories: metal, cloth, alcoholic beverages, weapons, and "a miscellany of baubles, bangles, and beads."[82]

Of the last category, he said: "For both Europeans and Africans, the numerous items of trumpery were placed at the bottom of the scale of values."[83] This would indicate that the trade was not then trade in items disparately valued. He cited *Purchas his Pilrimes* as saying that such items could buy nothing but food-stuff. There are two things to say about this analysis. First, it is contradicted by the evidence of Godinho which I cited just above. Second, even insofar as trumpery were traded for foodstuffs only, Europeans thought they were getting a wild bargain. Rodney himself cited John Ogilby's statement in his 1670 work that the Africans "do not set a high rate upon the best of their commodities."[84] — in which case the Europeans were buying items they valued high but the seller valued low.

On firearms, the one item that might be deemed "essential" trade, Rodney cautioned against giving them too much significance. First of all, he noted that it was a phenomenon that particularly grew in importance in "the later part of the eighteenth century."[85] Second, he suggested that the import of firearms had marginal social consequences:

> It would be attractive to set this category of goods apart as the main stimulus to slaving, on the grounds that guns were used to capture slaves to buy more guns to capture more slaves. If they added a new dimension to military techniques, then they would also have been decisive in relations among the Africans themselves, but in reality their importance was narrowly circumscribed in the period under discussion. European firearms made an impact at a very late date, the first period of Hispano-Portuguese slave trading, for example, had little or nothing to do with the import of firearms. Furthermore, while it is true that coastal residents had by the end of the eighteenth century re-armed themselves with European weapons, the same did not apply to the inhabitants of the interior: and nevertheless it was the Mande-Fula combination in the hinterland which extended domination over coastal tribes, demonstrating clearly that European firearms did not automatically influence the African balance of power.[86]

Rodney was similarly skeptical about the importance of alcoholic beverages. He then reminded us that ordinarily Europeans were required to offer assortments of items for sale, and that European traders often practiced "rooming"—that is, replacement of more expensive items by cheaper ones.

"Rooming" was possible "because the Africans themselves were neither knowledgeable about the price of each European product nor concerned about that factor,"[87] which is another way of saying that the price of the exchange was not determined by the world-market. Rodney used as part of his explanation of how this could be so Polonyi's argument that while the Europeans were working within the framework of a capitalist conception of the economic process, the Africans were operating on a system of "gainless barter." Rodney observed:

> In Polanyi's opinion . . . it was the European system which adjusted to the African. Evidence taken from Upper Guinea helps to substantiate as well as to modify this interpretation.[88]

The modifications Rodney seemed to suggest were that adjustment was in fact "mutual;" that "historically, the initiative came from Europe;" and that over time "African society became geared to serve the capitalist system."[89]

Where are we then? I would summarize the situation as follows. From

1450 to circa 1750, West Africa was in the external arena of the European world-economy and not part of its periphery; that up to 1750 the bulk of the trade could be considered as "rich trades;" and thus that up to that point the two social systems were separate.

However, 1750–1760 or thereabouts marked a major turning point in the European world-economy. It marked the end of the century-long depression which had so exacerbated the mercantilist conflicts between the Netherlands, England, and France. It marked the inception of England's "industrial revolution" which would have contradictory impacts on West Africa.

In the first place, the industrial revolution expanded enormously the demand for sugar and cotton production in the Western Hemisphere, which in turn expanded the demand for slaves. This accelerated demand had to be paid for at a higher price, including the sale of firearms. This in turn led to an atmosphere propitious to the creation of large state-structures—in West Africa, and elsewhere in Africa and the world external to the European world-economy. Thus we see the great spurt that Hrbek observed in Africa in state-building from 1805–1820.

Meanwhile in Europe, England finally definitely eliminated France as a rival for economic hegemony in the Napoleonic Wars—the culmination of two centuries of relative French decline. This then opened the European world-economy as of 1815 to global expansion, for the new scale of European production required a world-wide market of purchase and sale. It was at this point in time that Africa, the Middle East, Asia, and Oceania began to be systemically incorporated into the new single global capitalist system, in almost all cases as part of the periphery.

Once West Africa was part of the periphery and not the external arena, however, slavery was too costly. For slave-trading meant paying an ever higher purchase cost plus now a real diminution in the system's economic productivity (by removal of manpower from a region). Of all countries, Britain had the most to gain from a proper functioning of the capitalist world-economy, so it took the lead in abolishing the slave-trade and substituting "legitimate trade"—that is, encouraging the production by Africans of cash-crops (for example, palm oil) for the world market.

But once incorporated into the periphery, the African state-structures became a threat to the easy flow of unequal exchange. As long as England had world hegemony, it seemed less costly to keep them in check and/or deal with them than to conquer them. However, Britain's hegemony came to be threatened in the world capitalist system—a phenomenon we can date as beginning approximately in 1873, the moment when the constraints of world-wide effective demand created a system-wide depression which in many ways lasted into the beginning of the twentieth century. Among other consequences, this threat to hegemony took the neo-mercantilist form of "preemptive" colonization[90]—to wit, the scramble for Africa, which had the additional advantage of eliminating all strong state-structures in the African periphery.

We are arguing, then, that as of 1750 began a process of steady incorporation of Africa into the capitalist world-economy whose first stage was that of informal empire and whose second stage was that of colonial rule. We must now turn to stage three—decolonization, which can be seen as the completion of this historic process.

As long as the demands made on Africa by the other parts of the world-economy were limited—Africa as producer or Africa as consumer—a colonial system was adequate to the political overseeing of these demands. A small investment in bureaucratic superstructure (including armies) was sufficient to ensure that the most lucrative mines were mined, and that enough cash-crop production was arranged to bear the administrative overhead of colonialism. It was not entire fiction (though it was stated in pious self-exculpating terminology) that colonies were not necessarily profitable exercises, and that a major problem was to make sure that they were "self-financing" and not a drain on the metropolitan treasury.

That is to say, they may not have been profitable—or at least *very* profitable—from the perspective of the metropolitan country as an entity. Colonies of course could be very profitable to individual entrepreneurs or firms, including and even especially to the white settlers. But to make them really profitable, money had to be invested that would have the effect of greatly expanding the rate of productivity and the size of the salaried work-force (the latter being crucial in their capacity as consumers).

For increased investment to result in higher productivity and sufficient distribution to create a minimal local market, indirect rule was the most efficient mode. For only Africans could easily get Africans truly to increase their productivity, and for that these new managers would have to be rewarded. Furthermore, the rewards themselves had the effect of creating the new local markets. And thus by the simple principle that higher quantity at lower rates of profit can equal greater overall profit, the economic expansion of the post–Second World War period in Africa has magnified the economic transfer of surplus from the African periphery to the center far beyond anything that occurred in colonial rule.

To be sure, the fact that first the United States, then West Germany, and latterly the Soviet Union wanted access to these peripheral areas was a consideration that speeded up decolonization—but I now believe this factor was less important than I and many others previously thought. Even without that pressure, decolonization made sense, for the independent governments of Africa are far more efficacious "indirect rulers" than the *obas* and *mwamis* of the colonial era.

And the process towards industrialization in Africa, far from countering this trend, has been part of the same picture. I agree entirely with Samir Amin's summary of this situation:

> With industrialization it is the internal market which begins to provide the primary impetus for growth, even though this market is a distorted one. However in this . . . phase the export trade retains its earlier structure (export of primary goods). It is on the import side that a structural modification is noticeable. Imported industrial goods and food products replace manufactured consumption goods (the appearance of food imports in countries which are still primarily agricultural reflects the distortion in the allocation of resources). . . . From this moment on, the aggravation of the contradictions inherent in [this phase is] characterized by a new, but still unequal, international division of labor in which the periphery becomes the exporter of "classical" industrial products (thereby leaving to the center the benefits of specialization within the more modern industries), and the importer of food surpluses from advanced-capitalist agriculture. The establishment of runaway industries in the Far East is indicative of this new tendency of the system. It is by no means impossible that Africa will rapidly begin taking part in this new international division of labor. . . .[91]

With this in mind, one can be somewhat pessimistic about the ability of a so-called radical African regime to buck the system, as I have been in one recent paper.[92] One can be stern about the validity of any of these regimes calling itself a socialist regime, as I have been in another.[93] I would not want anyone to conclude therefore that I think that Africans or the rest of us are helpless before a juggernaut of economic givens.

For by processes that have often been elucidated, economic givens make possible certain political thrusts. And seen as political thrusts, many efforts can be justified even if they fall far short of their ostensible objectives. For example, Amin concluded his analysis by an unusual defense of *ujamaa*. He did not say it would transform either Tanzania or the African continent. He argued rather that there was a *de facto* convergence of interests in contemporary Africa between the "marginalized masses, the urban proletariat, and impoverished and half-proletarianized poor peasantry." The key political problem for those who seek change is to maintain this alliance. He deduced consequently:

> [Any] development of production based on profit [that is, individual profit — I.W.] (particularly agrarian capitalism) which puts this alliance into question will prove negative in the long run, even if in the short run it facilitates the rapid growth of production.[94]

Any further discussion of the linkage not only between a policy of *ujamaa* but between the future role of the national liberation movements in southern Africa and the modes of world political confrontation within the framework of the capitalist world-economy would be long to develop, and I shall not do it here.

Let me return instead to the fundamental thrust of our argument. Africa is today part of a single world-system, the capitalist world-system, and its present structures and processes cannot be understood unless they are situated within the social framework that is governing them. Furthermore, this capitalist world-system has not emerged full bloom out of nowhere but rather has been the framework of African life—albeit in a perhaps thinner way than today—for about two centuries. Prior to that, African world-systems were non-capitalist systems. They related as external arenas to specific other world-systems, including in one case the European capitalist world-economy.

To understand this earlier period is in many ways far more difficult than to understand the present, or we shall have to sharpen our understanding of social systems to do it. We shall have to rework our knowledge of world historical data (as well as expand it) in order to analyze coherently how pre-capitalist economies functioned, which will—I believe—open many doors for us. Africans have proudly asserted in recent years that they have as much to offer as anyone in the *rendez-vous de donner et de recevoir* of world cultures. Equally, we as Africanists—and Africans first among the Africanists—must be ready to participate in the *rendez-vous de donner et de recevoir* of collective knowledge about a social world whose coherence and cohesion is ever more evident as the praxis of world transformation forces us to see it, to face up to it, and to make our moral choices within it.

NOTES

1. I believe the phrase is that of Léopold-Sédar Senghor, but I cannot locate it. In any case, the sentiment is elaborated in the essay by Chelkh Hamidou Kane. "Comme si nous nous étions donné rendez-vous." *Esprit*, n.2. 29. No. 229 (Oct 1961): 375–387.
2. J. F. Ajayi. "The Continuity of African Institutions under Colonialism," in T. O. Ranger, ed. *Emerging Themes of African History* (Nairobi East African Publishing House, 1968), pp. 189–200.
3. Ajayi, "Continuity," p. 200.
4. T. O. Ranger. "Connexions between 'Primary Resistance' Movements and Modern Mass Nationalism in East and Central Africa," *Journal of African History*, IX. 3:437–453: IX. 4:631–641.
5. Donald Denoon and Adam Kuper. "Nationalist Historians in Search of a Nation. The New Historiography in Dar es Salaam." *African Affairs*, 69, 277 (Oct 1970):348 (hereafter cited as "Nationalist Historians").
6. Bernard Magubane. "A Critical Look at Indices Used in the Study of Social Change in Colonial Africa." *Current Anthropology*, XII, 4–5 (Oct–Dec 1971): 419–431. It is followed by "Comments" (pp. 431–439) and a "Reply" (pp. 439–445).
7. Magubane, "A Critical Look," pp. 430–442.
8. Magubane, "A Critical Look," p. 430.
9. Epstein, "Comments on Magubane, A Critical Look," p. 432.
10. "Comments on Magubane, A Critical Look," p. 436.
11. Köbben, "Comments on Magubane, A Critical Look," p. 433.
12. Saberwal, "Comments on Magubane, A Critical Look," p. 438.
13. Messing, "Comments on Magubane, A Critical Look," p. 438.
14. Van den Berghe, "Comments on Magubane, A Critical Look," p. 438.
15. Mayer, "Comments on Magubane, A Critical Look," p. 433.
16. Magubane, "Reply," p. 439.
17. Denoon and Kuper, "Nationalist Historians," p. 347.
18. Terence Ranger, "The 'New Historiography' in Dar es Salaam: An Answer," *African Affairs*. 70. 278. Jan. 1971, p. 55 (hereafter cited as "An Answer").
19. Ranger, "An Answer," p. 61.
20. Donald Denoon and Adam Kuper, "The New Historiography in Dar es Salaam: A Rejoinder." *African Affairs*, 70, 280. July 1971, p. 288 (hereafter cited as "A Responder").
21. R. H. Tawney, "Postscript to the Rise of the Gentry," in E. N. Carus-Wilson, ed., *Essays in Economic History*, Volume I (London: Edw. Arnold, 1954), p. 214.
22. Magubane, "A Critical Look," p. 419.

23. Magubane, "A Critical Look," p. 420.

24. Mitchell, "Comments on Magubane, A Critical Look," p. 436.

25. Magubane, "Reply," p. 441.

26. Magubane, "A Critical Look," p. 419.

27. When I say I "assimilate" one man's position to another, I do not mean that either endorses the arguments of the other in their respective articles but simply that in treating three debates successively, I see the same underlying issue recurring and wish to identify sides A and B in each.

28. Terence Ranger, "Introduction" to Ranger, ed., *Emerging Themes of African History*, p. xxi and cited in Denoon and Kuper, "Nationalist Historians," p. 331.

29. Denoon and Kuper, "Nationalist Historians," p. 331.

30. Ranger, "An Answer," p. 51.

31. Ranger, "An Answer," p. 52.

32. I. N. Kimambo and A. J. Temu, eds., *A History of Tanzania* (Nairobi East African Publishing House, 1969); A. D. Roberts ed., *Tanzania Before 1900* (Nairobi: East African Publishing House,l 1968).

33. Cited in Denoon and Kuper, "Nationalist Historians," p. 335.

34. Cited in Denoon and Kuper, "Nationalist Historians," p. 335.

35. T. Ranger, *The African Churches of Tanzania*, Historical Association of Tanzania Paper No. 5 (Nairobi: East African Publishing House, n.d.), p. 4. Cited in Denoon and Kuper, "National Historians," p. 336.

36. Denoon and Kuper, "Nationalist Historians," p. 336.

37. Denoon and Kuper, "Nationalist Historians," p. 337. Ranger responded by talking of "Denoon and Kuper's fantasies about our lack of interest in mission sources and our contempt for anthropology." "An Answer." p. 54.

38. Denoon and Kuper, "Nationalist Historians," p. 341.

39. J. E. G. Sutton, "The Peopling of Tanzania," in Kimambo and Temu, p. 1, cited in Denoon and Kuper, "Nationalist Historians," p. 342.

40. Denoon and Kuper, "Nationalist Historians," p. 342.

41. Denoon and Kuper, "Nationalist Historians," p. 346.

42. Denoon and Kuper, "Nationalist Historians," p. 347.

43. Ranger, "An Answer," p. 59.

44. J. D. Fage, "Slavery and the Slave Trade in West African History," *Journal of African History*, X, 3. (1969): 393–404 (hereafter cited as "Slavery").

45. Philip D. Curtin. *The Dimensions of the Atlantic Slave Trade* (Madison, Wisconsin: University of Wisconsin Press, 1969), cited in Fage, "Slavery," p. 398.

46. Fage, "Slavery," p. 403.

47. Fage, "Slavery," p. 404.

48. "In default of evidence of the relation between the existence of an external demand for slaves and of slavery and an internal trade in slaves for the West African Sudan, we must turn to the Guinea area, where commonly the first truly external traders were the European seatraders, who first arrived on the coasts in the fifteenth century. The evidence for Upper Guinea, from the Gambia to modern Liberia, has been analysed by Dr. Walter Rodney," Fage, "Slavery," p. 395. Fage's footnote reference is to Walter Rodney, "African Slavery and Other Forms of Social Oppression on the Upper Guinea Coast in the Context of the Atlantic Slave-Trade." *Journal of African History*, VII. 3 (1966): 431–443 Since Fage's article appeared, Rodney's monograph has come out. Walter Rodney, *A History of the Upper Guinea Coast, 1545–1800* (Oxford: Clarendon, 1970).

49. Fage, "Slavery," p. 397.

50. Fage, "Slavery," p. 398.
51. Fage, "Slavery," pp. 400, 402.
52. Fage, "Slavery," p. 403.
53. Rodney, *History of the Upper Guinea Coast*, p. 199.
54. Rodney, *History of the Upper Guinea Coast*, p. 199.
55. Walter Rodney, *West Africa and the Atlantic Slave-Trade*, Historical Association of Tanzania Paper No. 2 (Nairobi: African Publishing House, 1967), p. 21.
56. Rodney, *History of the Upper Guinea Coast*, p. 118.
57. C. C. Wrigley, "Historicism in Africa: Slavery and State Formation." *African Affairs*, 70. 279 (April 1971): 113 (hereafter cited as "Historicism").
58. Wrigley, "Historicism," p. 117.
59. Wrigley, "Historicism," p. 116.
60. Wrigley, "Historicism," p. 121.
61. Wrigley, "Historicism," p. 124.
62. Walter Rodney, *How Europe Underdeveloped Africa* (London: Bogle-L'Ouverture Publications, 1972), p. 80.
63. Ivan Hrbek. "Towards a Periodisation of African History," in Ranger, ed., *Emerging Themes of African History*, pp. 37–52 (hereafter cited as "Periodisation").
64. See Hrbek, "Periodisation, pp. 38–42.
65. Hrbek, "Periodisation," p. 45.
66. Hrbek, "Periodisation," p. 48.
67. Hrbek, "Periodisation," p. 49.
68. Hrbek, "Periodisation," p. 51.
69. See Samir Amin, "Sous-développement et dépendance en Afrique noire contemporaine." *Partisans*, No. 64, (mars-avril 1972): 3–34.
70. All the statements in this paragraph are dealt with in great detail in my *The Modern World-System: Capitalist Agriculture and the Origins of the European World-Economy in the Sixteenth Century* (New York: Academic Press, 1974).
71. I elaborate this argument in "The Rise and Future Demise of the World Capitalist System. Concepts for Comparative Analysis," *Comparative Studies in Society and History* (XVI, 4, 1974 (ch. 5 this volume)).
72. "Experience has proved it: of all forms of breeding, that of human cattle is one of the hardest. If slavery is to pay when applied to large-scale enterprises, there must be plenty of cheap human flesh on the market. You can only get it by war or slave-raiding. So a society can hardly base much of its economy on domesticated human beings unless it has at hand feebler societies to defeat or raid." Marc Bloch, "The Rise of Dependent Cultivation and Seignorial Institutions," in *Cambridge Economic History of Europe*, I.M.M. Postan, ed., *The Agrarian Life of the Middle Ages*, 2nd ed., (Cambridge: at the University Press, 1966), p. 247.
73. See my *The Modern World-System*, ch. VI.
74. See Rodney: "It is obvious that because of the Atlantic slave-trade people could not lead their ordinary lives. The majority of the population of West Africa lived by farming, and agriculture must have suffered during that period. In the first place, the loss of so many people represented a loss of labour in the fields. In the second place, those who were left behind had little reason to plant crops which they might never be around to reap. At the end of the eighteenth century, one of the arguments used by Europeans who wanted to abolish the Atlantic slave-trade was that abolition would allow the Africans to work and produce other commodities which Europeans could buy. They pointed out that as long as the Atlantic slave-trade continued people found it extremely difficult to carry on worthwhile activities." *West Africa and the Atlantic Slave-Trade*, p. 16.

75. Vitorino Magalhães Godinho, *Os Descubrimentos e a Economia Mundial*, Volume 2 (Lisboa: Ed. Arcadia, 1965), esp. pp. 528, 532.

76. The Venetian Cadamasto was told in 1455 that voyages to Guinea yielded a return of between six and ten times the outlay . . . Elsewhere [in West Africa] the Portuguese gathered less dazzling but still substantial riches. A.F.C. Ryder, "Portuguese and Dutch in West Africa before 1800," in J.F. Ade Ajayi and Ian Espie, eds. *A Thousand Years of West African History* (Ibadan, Nigeria: Ibadan University Press, 1965), pp. 220, 222.

77. Christopher Fyfe. "West African Trade, A. D. 1000–1800," in Ajayi and Espie, eds., *A Thousand Years of West African Trade*, p. 248 (hereafter cited as "West African Trade").

78. Fyfe, "West African Trade," p. 249.

79. Fyfe, "West African Trade," p. 249.

80. Fyfe, "West African Trade," p. 252.

81. Rodney, *History of the Upper Guinea Coast*, ch. VII.

82. Rodney, *History of the Upper Guinea Coast*, p. 172.

83. Rodney, *History of the Upper Guinea Coast*, p. 172.

84. Rodney, *History of the Upper Guinea Coast*, p. 172.

85. Rodney, *History of the Upper Guinea Coast*, p. 176.

86. Rodney, *History of the Upper Guinea Coast*, p. 177.

87. Rodney, *History of the Upper Guinea Coast*, pp. 188–189.

88. Rodney, *History of the Upper Guinea Coast*, p. 192.

89. Rodney, *History of the Upper Guinea Coast*, p. 199.

90. See my "The Colonial Era in Africa: Changes in the Social Structure," in L. H. Gann and Peter Duignan, eds., *Colonialism in Africa, 1870–1960*, Vol. II. *The History and Politics of Colonialism, 1914–1960* (Cambridge: at the University Press, 1970), pp. 399–421.

91. Amin Samir, "Traditional Phases in Sub-Saharan Africa," *Monthly Review*, 25, 5 (Oct. 1973) pp. 54–55 (hereafter cited as "Transitional Phases").

92. See "The Range of Choice: Constraints on the Policies of Governments of Contemporary African Independent States" in Michael F. Lotchie, Ed., *The State of the Nations* (University of California Press, 1971), pp. 19–33.

93. See "Dependence in an Interdependent World: The Limited Possibilities of Transformation Within the Capitalist World-Economy," *African Studies Review*, 17, 1 (Apr. 1974), 1–26.

94. Amin, "Transitional Phases," p. 56.

Part Two

WORLD-SYSTEMS
ANALYSIS AND
SOCIAL SCIENCE

5—The Rise and Future Demise of the World Capitalist System: Concepts for Comparative Analysis

This article, which was written in 1972 and appeared in 1974 at the same time as Volume I of *The Modern World-System*, is my first attempt to explain what I meant by a "unit of analysis," and thereby both to lay out the main theoretical premises of world-systems analysis and to indicate the intellectual views that I wished to contest. It has become the "classic" essay in the sense that it has been the most widely reproduced and widely cited of all my articles, and is often the only piece some students have read of me.

T he growth within the capitalist world-economy of the industrial sector of production, the so-called "industrial revolution," was accompanied by a very strong current of thought which defined this change as both a process of organic development and of progress. There were those who considered these economic developments and the concomitant changes in social organization to be some penultimate stage of world development whose final working-out was but a matter of time. These included such diverse thinkers as Saint-Simon, Comte, Hegel, Weber, Durkheim. And then there were the critics, most notably Marx, who argued, if you will, that the nineteenth-century present was only an antepenultimate stage of development, that the capitalist world was to know a cataclysmic political revolution which would then lead in the fullness of time to a final societal form, in this case the classless society.

One of the great strengths of Marxism was that, being an oppositional and hence critical doctrine, it called attention not merely to the contradictions of the system but to those of its ideologists, by appealing to the empirical evidence of historical reality which unmasked the irrelevancy of the models proposed for the explanation of the social world. The Marxist critics saw in abstracted models concrete rationalization, and they argued their case fundamentally by pointing to the failure of their opponents to analyze the social whole. As Lukacs put it, "it is not the primacy of economic motives in historical explanation that constitutes the decisive difference between Marxism and bourgeois thought, but the point of view of totality."[1]

In the mid-twentieth century, the dominant theory of development in the core countries of the capitalist world-economy has added little to the theorizing of the nineteenth-century progenitors of this mode of analysis, except to quantify the models and to abstract them still further, by adding epicyclical codas to the models in order to account for ever further deviations from empirical expectations.

What is wrong with such models has been shown many times over, and from many standpoints. I cite only one critic, a non-Marxist, Robert Nisbet, whose very cogent reflections on what he calls the "Western theory of development" concludes with this summary:

> [We] turn to history and only to history if what we are seeking are the actual causes, sources, and conditions of overt changes of patterns and structures in society. Conventional wisdom to the contrary in modern social theory, we shall not find the explanation of change in those studies which are abstracted from history; whether these be studies of small groups in the social laboratory, group dynamics generally, staged experiments in social interaction, or mathematical analyses of so-called social systems. Nor will we find the sources of change in contemporary revivals of the comparative method with its ascending staircase of cultural similarities and differences plucked from all space and time.[2]

Shall we then turn to the critical schools, in particular Marxism, to give us a better account of social reality? In principle yes; in practice there are many different, often contradictory, versions extant of "Marxism." But what is more fundamental is the fact that in many countries Marxism is now the official state doctrine. Marxism is no longer exclusively an oppositional doctrine as it was in the nineteenth century.

The social fate of official doctrines is that they suffer a constant social pressure towards dogmatism and apologia, difficult although by no means impossible to counteract, and that they thereby often fall into the same intellectual dead-end of ahistorical model-building. Here the critique of Fernand Braudel is most pertinent:

> Marxism is a whole collection of models. . . . I shall protest . . . , more or less, not against the model, but rather against the use to which people have thought themselves entitled to put it. The genius of Marx, the secret of his en-

during power, lies in his having been the first to construct true social models, starting out from the long term (*la longue durée*). These models have been fixed permanently in their simplicity; they have been given the force of law and they have been treated as ready-made, automatic explanations, applicable in all places to all societies. . . . In this way has the creative power of the most powerful social analysis of the last century been shackled. It will be able to regain its strength and vitality only in the long term.[3]

Nothing illustrates the distortions of ahistorical models of social change better than the dilemmas to which the concept of stages gives rise. If we are to deal with social transformations over long historical time (Braudel's "the long term"), and if we are to give an explanation of both continuity and transformation, then we must logically divide the long term into segments in order to observe the structural changes from time A to time B. These segments are, however, not discrete but continuous in reality; ergo they are "stages" in the "development" of a social structure, a development which we determine however not *a priori* but *a posteriori*. That is, we cannot predict the future concretely, but we can predict the past.

The crucial issue when comparing "stages" is to determine the units of which the "stages" are synchronic portraits (or "ideal types," if you will). And the fundamental error of ahistorical social science (including ahistorical versions of Marxism) is to reify parts of the totality into such units and then to compare these reified structures.

For example, we may take modes of disposition of agricultural production, and term them subsistence-cropping and cash-cropping. We may then see these as entities which are "stages" of a development. We may talk about decisions of groups of peasants to shift from one to the other. We may describe other partial entities, such as states, as having within them two separate "economies," each based on a different mode of disposition of agricultural production. If we take each of these successive steps, all of which are false steps, we will end up with the misleading concept of the "dual economy" as have many liberal economists dealing with the so-called underdeveloped countries of the world. Still worse, we may reify a misreading of British history into a set of universal "stages" as Rostow does.

Marxist scholars have often fallen into exactly the same trap. If we take modes of payment of agricultural labor and contrast a "feudal" mode wherein the laborer is permitted to retain for subsistence a part of his agricultural production with a "capitalist" mode wherein the same laborer turns over the totality of his production to the landowner, receiving part of it back in the form of wages, we may then see these two modes as "stages" of a development. We may talk of the interests of "feudal" landowners in preventing the conversion of their mode of payment to a system of wages. We may then explain the fact that in the twentieth century a partial entity, say a state in Latin America, has not yet industrialized as the consequence of its being dominated by such landlords. If we take each of these successive steps, all of which are false steps, we will end up with the misleading concept of a "state dominated by feudal elements," as though such a thing could possibly exist in a capitalist world-economy. But, as Andre Gunder Frank has clearly spelled out, such a myth dominated for a long time "traditional Marxist" thought in Latin America.[4]

Not only does the misidentification of the entities to be compared lead us into false concepts, but it creates a non-problem: can stages be skipped? This question is only logically meaningful if we have "stages" that "co-exist" within a single empirical framework. If within a capitalist world-economy, we define one state as feudal, a second as capitalist, and a third as socialist, then and only then can we pose the question: can a country "skip" from the feudal stage to the socialist stage of national development without "passing through capitalism"?

But if there is no such thing as "national development" (if by that we mean a natural history), and if the proper entity of comparison is the world-system, then the problem of stage-skipping is nonsense. If a stage can be skipped, it isn't a stage. And we know this *a posteriori*.

If we are to talk of stages, then—and we should talk of stages—it must be stages of social systems, that is, of totalities. And the only totalities that exist or have historically existed are mini-systems and world-systems, and in the nineteenth and twentieth centuries there has been only one world-system in existence, the capitalist world-economy.

We take the defining characteristic of a social system to be the existence within it of a division of labor, such that the various sectors or areas are dependent upon economic exchange with others for the smooth and continuous provisioning of the needs of the area. Such economic exchange can clearly exist without a common political structure and even more obviously without sharing the same culture.

A mini-system is an entity that has within it a complete division of labor, and a single cultural framework. Such systems are found only in very simple agricultural or hunting and gathering societies. Such mini-systems no longer exist in the world. Furthermore, there were fewer in the past than is often asserted, since any such system that became tied to an empire by the payment of tribute as "protection costs"[5] ceased by that fact to be a "system," no longer having a self-contained division of labor. For such an area, the payment of tribute marked a shift, in Polanyi's language, from being a reciprocal economy to participating in a larger redistributive economy.[6]

Leaving aside the now defunct mini-systems, the only kind of social system is a world-system, which we define quite simply as a unit with a single division of labor and multiple cultural systems. It follows logically that there can, however, be two varieties of such world-systems, one with a common political system and one without. We shall designate these respectively as world-empires and world-economies.

It turns out empirically that world-economies have historically been unstable structures leading either towards disintegration or conquest by one group and hence transformation into a world-empire. Examples of such world-empires emerging from world-economies are the so-called great civilizations of pre-modern times, such as China, Egypt, Rome (each at appropriate periods of its history). On the other hand, the so-called nineteenth-century empires, such as Great Britain or France, were not world-empires at all, but nation-states with colonial appendages operating within the framework of a world-economy.

World-empires were basically redistributive in economic form. No doubt they bred clusters of merchants who engaged in economic exchange (primarily long-distance trade), but such clusters, however large, were a minor part of the total economy and not fundamentally determinative of its fate. Such long-distance trade tended to be, as Polanyi argues, "administered trade" and not market trade, utilizing "ports of trade."

It was only with the emergence of the modern world-economy in sixteenth-century Europe that we saw the full development and economic predominance of market trade. This was the system called capitalism. Capitalism and a world-economy (that is, a single division of labor but multiple polities and cultures) are obverse sides of the same coin. One does not cause the other. We are merely defining the same indivisible phenomenon by different characteristics.

How and why it came about that this particular European world-economy of the sixteenth century did not become transformed into a redistributive world-empire but developed definitively as a capitalist world-economy I have explained elsewhere.[7] The genesis of this world-historical turning-point is marginal to the issues under discussion in this paper, which is rather what conceptual apparatus one brings to bear on the analysis of developments within the framework of precisely such a capitalist world-economy.

Let us therefore turn to the capitalist world-economy. We shall seek to deal with two pseudo-problems, created by the trap of not analyzing totalities: the so-called persistence of feudal forms, and the so-called creation of socialist systems. In doing this, we shall offer an alternative model with which to engage in comparative analysis, one rooted in the historically specific totality which is the world capitalist economy. We hope to demonstrate thereby that to be historically specific is not to fail to be analytically universal. On the contrary, the only road to nomothetic propositions is through the historically concrete, just as in cosmology the only road to a theory of the laws governing the universe is through the concrete analysis of the historical evolution of this same universe.[8]

On the "feudalism" debate, we take as a starting-point Frank's concept of "the development of underdevelopment," that is, the view that the economic structures of contemporary underdeveloped countries is not the form which a "traditional" society takes upon contact with "developed" societies, not an earlier stage in the "transition" to industrialization. It is, rather, the result of being involved in this world-economy as a peripheral, raw material producing area, or as Frank puts it for Chile, "underdevelopment . . . is the necessary product of four centuries of capitalism itself."[9]

This formulation runs counter to a large body of writing concerning the underdeveloped countries that was produced in the period 1950–70, a literature which sought the factors that explained "development" within non-systems such as "states" or "cultures" and, once having presumably discovered these factors, urged their reproduction in underdeveloped areas as the road to salvation.[10]

Frank's theory also runs counter, as we have already noted, to the received orthodox version of Marxism that had long dominated Marxist parties and intellectual circles, for example in Latin America. This older "Marxist" view of Latin America as a set of feudal societies in a more or less pre-bourgeois stage of development has fallen before the critiques of Frank and many others as well as before the political reality symbolized by the Cuban revolution and all its many consequences. Recent analysis in Latin America has centered instead around the concept of "dependence."[11]

However, recently Ernesto Laclau has made an attack on Frank which, while accepting the critique of dualist doctrines, refuses to accept the categorization of Latin American states as capitalist. Instead Laclau asserts that "the world capitalist system . . . includes, *at the level of its definition*, various modes of production." He accuses Frank of confusing the two concepts of the "capitalist mode of production" and "participation in a world capitalist economic system."[12]

Of course, if it's a matter of definition, then there can be no argument. But then the polemic is scarcely useful since it is reduced to a question of semantics. Furthermore, Laclau insists that the definition is not his but that of Marx, which is more debatable. Rosa Luxemburg put her finger on a key element in Marx's ambiguity or inconsistency in this particular debate, the ambiguity which enables both Frank and Laclau to trace their thoughts to Marx:

> Admittedly, Marx dealt in detail with the process of appropriating noncapitalist means of production [N.B., Luxemburg is referring to primary products produced in peripheral areas under conditions of coerced labor — I.W.] as well as with the transformation of the peasants into a capitalist proletariat. Chapter XXIV of *Capital*, Vol. 1, is devoted to describing the origin of the English proletariat, of the capitalistic agricultural tenant class and of industrial capital, with particular emphasis on the looting of colonial countries by European capital. Yet we must bear in mind that all this is treated solely with a view to so-called primitive accumulation. For Marx, these processes are incidental, illustrating merely the genesis of capital, its first appearance in the world; they are, as it were, travails by which the capitalist mode of production emerges from a feudal society. As soon as he comes to analyze the capitalist process of production and circulation, he reaffirms the universal and exclusive

domination of capitalist production [N.B., that is, production based on wage labor — I.W.].[13]

There is, after all, a substantive issue in this debate. It is in fact the same substantive issue that underlay the debate between Maurice Dobb and Paul Sweezy in the early 1950s about the "transition from feudalism to capitalism" that occurred in early modern Europe.[14] The substantive issue, in my view, concerns the appropriate unit of analysis for the purpose of comparison. Basically, although neither Sweezy nor Frank is quite explicit on this point, and though Dobb and Laclau can both point to texts of Marx that seem clearly to indicate that they more faithfully follow Marx's argument, I believe both Sweezy and Frank better follow the spirit of Marx if not his letter[15] and that, leaving Marx quite out of the picture, they bring us nearer to an understanding of what actually happened and is happening than their opponents.

What is the picture, both analytical and historical, that Laclau constructs? The heart of the problem revolves around the existence of free labor as the defining characteristic of a capitalist mode of production:

> The fundamental economic relationship of capitalism is constituted by the *free* [italics mine] labourer's sale of his labour-power, whose necessary precondition is the loss by the direct producer of ownership of the means of production. . . .
>
> If we now confront Frank's affirmation that the socio-economic complexes of Latin America have been capitalist since the Conquest Period . . . with the currently available empirical evidence, we must conclude that the 'capitalist' thesis is indefensible. In regions with dense indigenous populations — Mexico, Peru, Bolivia, or Guatemala—the direct producers were not despoiled of their ownership of the means of production, while extra-economic coercion to maximize various systems of labour service . . . was progressively intensified. In the plantations of the West Indies, the economy was based on a mode of production constituted by slave labour, while in the mining areas there developed disguised forms of slavery and other types of forced labour which bore not the slightest resemblance to the formation of a capitalist proletariat.[16]

There in a nutshell it is. Western Europe, at least England from the late seventeenth century on, had primarily landless, wage-earning laborers. In Latin America, then and to some extent still now, laborers were not proletarians, but slaves or "serfs." If proletariat, then capitalism. Of course. To be sure. But is England, or Mexico, or the West Indies a unit of analysis? Does each have a separate "mode of production"? Or is the unit (for the sixteenth–eighteenth centuries) the European world-economy, including England *and* Mexico, in which case what was the "mode of production" of this world-economy?

Before we argue our response to this question, let us turn to quite another debate, one between Mao Tse-Tung and Liu Shao-Chi in the 1960s concerning whether or not the Chinese People's Republic was a "socialist state." This is a debate that has a long background in the evolving thought of Marxist parties.

Marx, as has been often noted, said virtually nothing about the post-revolutionary political process. Engels spoke quite late in his writings of the "dictatorship of the proletariat." It was left to Lenin to elaborate a theory about such a "dictatorship," in his pamphlet *State and Revolution*, published in the last stages before the Bolshevik takeover of Russia, that is, in August 1917. The coming to power of the Bolsheviks led to a considerable debate as to the nature of the regime that had been established. Eventually a theoretical distinction emerged in Soviet thought between "socialism" and "communism" as two stages in historical development, one realizable in the present and one only in the future. In 1936 Stalin proclaimed that the U.S.S.R. had become a socialist (but not yet a communist) state. Thus we now had firmly established *three* stages after bourgeois rule: a post-revolutionary government, a socialist state, and eventually communism. When, after the Second World War, various regimes dominated by the Communist Party were established in various east European states, these regimes were proclaimed to be "peoples' democracies," a new name then given to the post-revolutionary stage one. At later points, some of these countries, for example Czechoslovakia, asserted they had passed into stage two, that of becoming a socialist republic.

In 1961, the 22nd Congress of the CPSU invented a fourth stage, in between the former second and third stages: that of a socialist state which had become a "state of the whole people," a stage it was contended the U.S.S.R. had at that point reached. The programme of the Congress asserted that "the state as an organization of the entire people will survive until the complete victory of communism."[17] One of its commentators defines the "intrinsic substance (and) chief distinctive feature" of this stage: "The state of the whole people is the first state in the world with no class struggle to contend with and, hence, with no class domination and no suppression."[18]

One of the earliest signs of a major disagreement in the 1950s between the Communist Party of the Soviet Union and the Chinese Communist Party was a theoretical debate that revolved around the question of the "gradual transition to Communism." Basically, the CPSU argued that different socialist states would proceed separately in effectuating such a transition whereas the CCP argued that all socialist states would proceed simultaneously.

As we can see, this last form of the debate about "stages" implicitly raised the issue of the unit of analysis, for in effect the CCP was arguing that "communism" was a characteristic not of nation-states but of the world-economy as a whole. This debate was transposed onto the internal Chinese scene by the ideological debate, now known to have deep and long-standing roots, that gave rise eventually to the Cultural Revolution.

One of the corollaries of these debates about "stages" was whether or not the class struggle continued in post-revolutionary states prior to the achievement of communism. The 22nd Congress of the CPSU in 1961 had argued that the U.S.S.R. had become a state without an internal class struggle, there were no longer existing antagonistic classes within it. Without speaking of the U.S.S.R., Mao Tse-Tung in 1957 had asserted of China:

> The class struggle is by no means over. . . . It will continue to be long and tortuous, and at times will even become very acute. . . . Marxists are still a minority among the entire population as well as among the intellectuals. Therefore, Marxism must still develop through struggle. . . . Such struggles will never end. This is the law of development of truth and, naturally, of Marxism as well.[19]

If such struggles *never* end, then many of the facile generalizations about "stages" which "socialist" states are presumed to go through are thrown into question.

During the Cultural Revolution, it was asserted that Mao's report "On the Correct Handling of Contradiction Among The People" cited above, as well as one other, "entirely repudiated the 'theory of the dying out of the class struggle' advocated by Liu Shao-Chi. . . ."[20] Specifically, Mao argued that "the elimination of the system of ownership by the exploiting classes through socialist transformation is not equal to the disappearance of struggle in the political and ideological spheres."[21]

Indeed, this is the logic of a *cultural* revolution. Mao is asserting that even if there is the achievement of *political* power (dictatorship of the proletariat) and *economic* transformation (abolition of private ownership of the means of production), the revolution is still far from complete. Revolution is not an event but a process. This process Mao calls "socialist society"—in my view a somewhat confusing choice of words, but no matter—and "socialist society covers a fairly long historical period."[22] Furthermore, "there are classes and class struggle throughout the period of socialist society."[23] The Tenth Plenum of the 8th Central Committee of the CCP, meeting from September 24–7, 1962, in endorsing Mao's views, omitted the phrase "socialist society" and talked instead of "the historical period of proletarian revolution and proletarian dictatorship, . . . the historical period of transition from capitalism to communism," which it said "will last scores of years or even longer" and during which "there is class struggle between the proletariat and the bourgeosie and struggle between the socialist road and the capitalist road."[24]

We do not have directly Liu's counter-arguments. We might however take as an expression of the alternative position a recent analysis published in the U.S.S.R. on the relationship of the socialist system and world development. There it is asserted that at some unspecified point after the Second World War, "socialism outgrew the bounds of one country and became a world system. . . ."[25] It is further argued that: "Capitalism, emerging in the 16th century, became a world economic system only in the 19th century. It took the bourgeois revolutions 300 years to put an end to the power of the feudal elite. It took socialism 30 or 40 years to generate the forces for a new world system."[26] Finally, this book speaks of "capitalism's international division of labor"[27] and "international socialist co-operation of labor"[28] as two separate phenomena, drawing from this counterposition the policy conclusion: "Socialist unity has suffered a serious setback from the divisive course being pursued by the incumbent leadership of the Chinese People's Republic," and attributes this to "the great-power chauvinism of Mao Tse-Tung and his group."[29]

Note well the contrast between these two positions. Mao Tse-Tung is arguing for reviewing "socialist society" as process rather than structure. Like Frank and Sweezy, and once again implicitly rather than explicitly, he is taking the world-system rather than the nation-state as the unit of analysis. The analysis by U.S.S.R. scholars by contrast specifically argues the existence of *two* world-systems with two divisions of labor existing side by side, although the socialist system is acknowledged to be "divided." If divided politically, is it united economically? Hardly, one would think; in which case what is the substructural base to argue the existence of the system? Is it merely a moral imperative? And are then the Soviet scholars defending their concepts on the basis of Kantian metaphysics?

Let us see now if we can reinterpret the issues developed in these two debates within the framework of a general set of concepts that could be used to analyze the functioning of world-systems, and particularly of the historically specific capitalist world-economy that has existed for about four or five centuries now.

We must start with how one demonstrates the existence of a single division of labor. We can regard a division of labor as a grid which is substantially interdependent. Economic actors operate on some assumption (obviously seldom clear to any individual actor) that the totality of their essential needs—of sustenance, protection, and pleasure—will be met over a reasonable time-span by a combination of their own productive activities and exchange in some form. The smallest grid that would substantially meet the expectations of the overwhelming majority of actors within those boundaries constitutes a single division of labor.

The reason why a small farming community whose only significant link to outsiders is the payment of annual tribute does not constitute such a single division of labor is that the assumptions of persons living in it concerning the provision of protection involve an "exchange" with other parts of the world-empire.

This concept of a grid of exchange relationships assumes, however, a distinction between *essential* exchanges and what might be called "luxury" exchanges. This is to be sure a distinction rooted in the social perceptions of the actors and hence in both their social organization and their culture. These perceptions can change. But this distinction is crucial if we are not to fall into the trap of identifying *every* exchange-activity as evidence of the existence of a system. Members of a system (a mini-system or a world-system) can be linked in limited exchanges with elements located outside the system, in the "external arena" of the system.

The form of such an exchange is very limited. Elements of the two systems can engage in an exchange of preciosities. That is, each can export to the other what is in *its* system socially defined as worth little in return for the import of what in its system is defined as worth much. This is not a mere pedantic definitional exercise, as the exchange of preciosities *between* world-systems can be extremely important in the historical evolution of a given world-system. The reason why this is so important is that in an exchange of preciosities, the importer is "reaping a windfall" and not obtaining a profit. Both exchange-partners can reap windfalls simultaneously but only one can obtain maximum profit, since the exchange of surplus-value within a system is a zero-sum game.

We are, as you see, coming to the essential feature of a capitalist world-economy, which is production for sale in a market in which the object is to realize the maximum profit. In such a system production is constantly expanded as long as further production is profitable, and men constantly innovate new ways of producing things that will expand the profit margin. The classical economists tried to argue that such production for the market was somehow the "natural" state of man. But the combined writings of the anthropologists and the Marxists left few in doubt that such a mode of production (these days called "capitalism") was only one of several possible modes.

Since, however, the intellectual debate between the liberals and the Marxists took place in the era of the industrial revolution, there has tended to be a *de facto* confusion between industrialism and capitalism. This left the liberals after 1945 in the dilemma of explaining how a presumably non-capitalist society, the U.S.S.R., had industrialized. The most sophisticated response has been to conceive of "liberal capitalism" and "socialism" as two variants of an "industrial society," two variants destined to "converge." This argument has been trenchantly expounded by Raymond Aron.[30] But the same confusion left the Marxists, including Marx, with the problem of explaining what was the mode of production that predominated in Europe from the sixteenth to the eighteenth centuries, that is before the industrial revolution. Essentially, most Marxists have talked of a "transitional" stage, which is in fact a blurry non-concept with no operational indicators. This dilemma is heightened if the unit of analysis used is the state, in which case one has to explain why the transition has occurred at different rates and times in different countries.[31]

Marx himself handled this by drawing a distinction between "merchant capitalism" and "industrial capitalism." This I believe is unfortunate terminology, since it leads to such conclusions as that of Maurice Dobb who says of this "transitional" period:

> But why speak of this as a stage of capitalism at all? The workers were generally not proletarianized: that is, they were not separated from the instruments of production, nor even in many cases from occupation of a plot of land. Production was scattered and decentralized and not concentrated. *The capitalist was still predominantly a merchant* who did not control production directly and did not impose his own discipline upon the work of artisan-craftsmen, who both laboured as individual (or family) units and retained a considerable measure of independence (if a dwindling one).[32]

One might well say: why indeed? Especially if one remembers how much emphasis Dobb places a few pages earlier on capitalism as a mode of *production* — how then can the capitalist be primarily a merchant? — on the concentration of such ownership in the hands of a few, and on the fact that capitalism is not synonymous with private ownership, capitalism being different from a system in which the owners are "small peasant producers or artisan-producers." Dobb argues that a defining feature of private ownership under capitalism is that some are "obliged to [work for those that own] since [they own] nothing and [have] no access to means of production [and hence] have no other means of livelihood."[33] Given this contradiction, the answer Dobb gives to his own question is in my view very weak: "While it is true that at this date the situation was transitional, and capital-to-wage-labour relations were still immaturely developed, the latter were already beginning to assume their characteristic features."[34]

If capitalism is a mode of production, production for profit in a market, then we ought, I should have thought, to look to whether or not such production was or was not occurring. It turns out in fact that it was, and in a very substantial form. Most of this production, however, was not industrial production. What was happening in Europe from the sixteenth to the eighteenth centuries is that over a large geographical area going from Poland in the northeast westwards and southwards throughout Europe and including large parts of the Western Hemisphere as well, there grew up a world-economy with a single division of labor within which there was a world market, for which men produced largely agricultural products for sale and profit. I would think the simplest thing to do would be to call this agricultural capitalism.

This then resolves the problems incurred by using the pervasiveness of *wage*-labor as a defining characteristic of capitalism. An individual is no less a capitalist exploiting labor because the state assists him to pay his laborers low wages (including wages in kind) and denies these laborers the right to change employment. Slavery and so-called "second serf-dom" are not to be regarded as anomalies in a capitalist system. Rather the so-called serf in Poland or the Indian on a Spanish *encomienda* in New Spain in this sixteenth-century world-economy were working for the landlords who "paid" them (however euphemistic this term) for cash-crop production. This is a relationship in which labor-power is a commodity (how could it ever be more so than under slavery?), quite different from the relationship of a feudal serf to his lord in eleventh-century Burgundy, where the economy was not oriented to a world market, and where labor-power was (therefore?) in no sense bought or sold.

Capitalism thus means labor as a commodity to be sure. But in the era of agricultural capitalism, wage-labor is only one of the modes in which labor is recruited and recompensed in the labor market. Slavery, coerced cash-crop production (my name for the so-called second feudalism), share-cropping, and tenancy are all alternative modes. It would be too long to develop here the conditions under which differing regions of the world-economy tend to specialize in different agricultural products. I have done this elsewhere.[35]

What we must notice now is that this specialization occurs in specific and differing geographic regions of the world-economy. This regional specification comes about by the attempts of actors in the market to avoid the normal operation of the market whenever it does not maximize their profit. The attempts of these actors to use non-market devices to ensure short-run profits makes them turn to the political entities which have in fact power to affect the market—the nation-states. (Again, why at this stage they could not have turned to city-states would take us into a long discursus, but it has to do with the state of military and shipping technology, the need of the European land-mass to expand overseas in the fifteenth century if it was to maintain the level of income of the various aristocracies, combined with the state of political disintegration to which Europe had fallen in the Middle Ages.)

In any case, the local capitalist classes — cash-crop landowners (often, even usually, nobility) and merchants — turned to the state, not only to liberate them from non-market constraints (as traditionally emphasized by liberal historiography) but to create new constraints on the new market, the market of the European world-economy.

By a series of accidents — historical, ecological, geographic — northwest Europe was better situated in the sixteenth century to diversify its agricultural specialization and add to it certain industries (such as textiles, shipbuilding, and metal wares) than were other parts of Europe. Northwest Europe emerged as the core area of this world-economy, specializing in agricultural production of higher skill levels, which favored (again for reasons too complex to develop) tenancy and wage-labor as the modes of labor control. Eastern Europe and the Western Hemisphere became peripheral areas specializing in export of grains, bullion, wood, cotton, sugar — all of which favored the use of slavery and coerced cash-crop labor as the modes of labor control. Mediterranean Europe emerged as the semi-peripheral area of this world-economy specializing in high-cost industrial products (for example, silks) and credit and specie transactions, which had as a consequence in the agricultural arena share-cropping as the mode of labor control and little export to other areas.

The three structural positions in a world-economy — core, periphery, and semi-periphery — had become stabilized by about 1640. How certain areas became one and not the other is a long story.[36] The key fact is that given slightly different starting-points, the interests of various local groups converged in northwest Europe, leading to the development of strong state mechanisms, and diverged sharply in the peripheral areas, leading to very weak ones. Once we get a difference in the strength of the state-machineries, we get the operation of "unequal exchange"[37] which is enforced by strong states on weak ones, by core states on peripheral areas. Thus capitalism involves not only appropriation of surplus-value by an owner from a laborer, but an appropriation of surplus of the whole world-economy by core areas. And this was as true in the stage of agricultural capitalism as it is in the stage of industrial capitalism.

In the early Middle Ages, there was, to be sure, trade. But it was largely either "local," in a region that we might call the "extended" manor, or "long-distance," primarily of luxury goods. There was no exchange of "bulk" goods, of "staples" across intermediate-size areas, and hence no production for such markets. Later on in the Middle Ages, world-economies may be said to have come into existence, one centering on Venice, a second on the cities of Flanders and the Hanse. For various reasons, these structures were hurt by the retractions (economic, demographic, and ecological) of the period 1300–1450. It is only with the creating of a *European* division of labor after 1450 that capitalism found firm roots.

Capitalism was from the beginning an affair of the world-economy and not of nation-states. It is a misreading of the situation to claim that it is only in the twentieth century that capitalism has become "worldwide," although this claim is frequently made in various writings, particularly by Marxists. Typical of this line of argument is Charles Bettelheim's response to Arghiri Emmanuel's discussion of unequal exchange:

> The tendency of the capitalist mode of production to become worldwide is manifested not only through the constitution of a group of national economics forming a complex and hierarchical structure, including an imperialist pole and a dominated one, and not only through the antagonistic relations that develop between the different "national economies" and the different states, but also through the constant "transcending" of "national limits" by big capital (the formation of "international big capital," "world firms," etc. . . . .).[38]

The whole tone of these remarks ignores the fact that capital has never allowed its aspirations to be determined by national boundaries in a capitalist world-economy, and that the creation of "national" barriers — generically, mercantilism — has historically been a defensive mechanism of capitalists located in states which are one level below the high point of strength in the system. Such was the case of England vis-à-vis the Netherlands in 1660–1715, France vis-à-vis England in 1715–1815, Germany vis-à-vis Britain in the nineteenth century, the Soviet Union vis-à-vis the U.S. in the twentieth. In the process a large number of countries create national economic barriers whose consequences often last beyond their initial objectives. At this later point in the process the very same capitalists who pressed their national governments to impose the restrictions now find these restrictions constraining. This is not an "internationaliza-tion" of "national" capital. This is simply a new political demand by cer-tain sectors of the capitalist classes who have at all points in time sought to maximize their profits within the real economic market, that of the world-economy.

If this is so, then what meaning does it have to talk of structural posi-tions within this economy and identify states as being in one of these po-sitions? And why talk of three positions, inserting that of "semi-periphery" in between the widely-used concepts of core and periphery? The state-machineries of the core states were strengthened to meet the needs of capitalist landowners and their merchant allies. But that does not mean that these state-machineries were manipulable puppets. Obvi-ously any organization, once created, has a certain autonomy from those who pressed it into existence for two reasons. It creates a stratum of offi-cials whose own careers and interests are furthered by the continued strengthening of the organization itself, however the interests of its capi-talist backers may vary. Kings and bureaucrats wanted to stay in power and increase their personal gain constantly. Secondly, in the process of creating the strong state in the first place, certain "constitutional" com-promises had to be made with other forces within the state-boundaries and these institutionalized compromises limit, as they are designed to do, the freedom of maneuver of the managers of the state-machinery. The formula of the state as "executive committee of the ruling class" is only valid, therefore, if one bears in mind that executive committees are never mere reflections of the wills of their constituents, as anyone who has ever participated in any organization knows well.

The strengthening of the state-machineries in core areas has as its di-rect counterpart the decline of the state-machineries in peripheral areas. The decline of the Polish monarchy in the sixteenth and seventeenth centuries is a striking example of this phenomenon.[39] There are two rea-sons for this. In peripheral countries, the interests of the capitalist land-owners lie in an opposite direction from those of the local commercial bourgeoisie. Their interests lie in maintaining an open economy to maxi-mize their profit from world-market trade (no restrictions in exports and access to lower-cost industrial products from core countries) and in elimination of the commercial bourgeoisie in favor of outside merchants (who pose no local political threat). Thus, in terms of the state, the coalition which strengthened it in core countries was precisely absent.

The second reason, which has become ever more operative over the history of the modern world-system, is that the strength of the state-machinery in core states is a function of the weakness of other state-machineries. Hence intervention of outsiders via war, subversion, and diplomacy is the lot of peripheral states.

All this seems very obvious. I repeat it only in order to make clear two points. One cannot reasonably explain the strength of various state-machineries at specific moments of the history of the modern world-system primarily in terms of a genetic-cultural line of argumentation, but rather in terms of the structural role a country plays in the world-economy at that moment in time. To be sure, the initial eligibility for a particular role is often decided by an accidental edge a particular country has, and the "accident" of which one is talking is no doubt located in part in past history, in part in current geography. But once this relatively minor accident is given, it is the operations of the world-market forces which accentuate the differences, institutionalize them, and make them impossible to surmount over the short run.

The second point we wish to make about the structural differences of core and periphery is that they are not comprehensible unless we realize that there is a third structural position: that of the semi-periphery. This is not the result merely of establishing arbitrary cutting-points on a continuum of characteristics. Our logic is not merely inductive, sensing the presence of a third category from a comparison of indicator curves. It is also deductive. The semi-periphery is needed to make a capitalist world-economy run smoothly. Both kinds of world-system, the world-empire with a redistributive economy and the world-economy with a capitalist market economy, involve markedly unequal distribution of rewards. Thus, logically, there is immediately posed the question of how it is possible politically for such a system to persist. Why do not the majority who are exploited simply overwhelm the minority who draw disproportionate benefits? The most rapid glance at the historic record shows that these world-systems have been faced rather rarely by fundamental system-wide insurrection. While internal discontent has been eternal, it has usually taken quite long before the accumulation of the erosion of power has led to the decline of a world-system, and as often as not, an external force has been a major factor in this decline.

There have been three major mechanisms that have enabled world-systems to retain relative political stability (not in terms of the particular groups who will play the leading roles in the system, but in terms of systemic survival itself). One obviously is the concentration of military strength in the hands of dominant forces. The modalities of this obviously vary with the technology, and there are, to be sure, political prerequisites for such a concentration, but nonetheless sheer force is no doubt a central consideration.

A second mechanism is the pervasiveness of an ideological commitment to the system as a whole. I do not mean what has often been termed the "legitimation" of a system, because that term has been used to imply that the lower strata of a system feel some affinity with or loyalty towards the rulers, and I doubt that this has ever been a significant factor in the survival of world-systems. I mean rather the degree to which the staff or cadres of the system (and I leave this term deliberately vague) feel that their own well-being is wrapped up in the survival of the system as such and the competence of its leaders. It is this staff which not only propagates the myths; it is they who believe them.

But neither force nor the ideological commitment of the staff would suffice were it not for the division of the majority into a larger lower stratum and a smaller middle stratum. Both the revolutionary call for polarization as a strategy of change and the liberal encomium to consensus as the basis of the liberal polity reflect this proposition. The import is far wider than its use in the analysis of contemporary political problems suggests. It is the normal condition of either kind of world-system to have a three-layered structure. When and if this ceases to be the case, the world-system disintegrates.

In a world-empire, the middle stratum is in fact accorded the role of maintaining the marginally-desirable long-distance luxury trade, while the upper stratum concentrates its resources on controlling the military machinery which can collect the tribute, the crucial mode of redistributing surplus. By providing, however, for an access to a limited portion of the surplus to urbanized elements who alone, in pre-modern societies, could contribute political cohesiveness to isolated clusters of primary producers, the upper stratum effectively buys off the potential leadership of co-ordinated revolt. And by denying access to political rights for this commercial-urban middle stratum, it makes them constantly vulnerable to confiscatory measures whenever their economic profits become sufficiently swollen so that they might begin to create for themselves military strength.

In a world-economy, such "cultural" stratification is not so simple, because the absence of a single political system means the concentration of economic roles vertically rather than horizontally throughout the system. The solution then is to have three *kinds* of states, with pressures for cultural homogenization within each of them—thus, besides the upper stratum of core-states and the lower stratum of peripheral states, there is a middle stratum of semi-peripheral ones.

This semi-periphery is then assigned as it were a specific economic role, but the reason is less economic than political. That is to say, one might make a good case that the world-economy as an economy would function every bit as well without a semi-periphery. But it would be far less *politically* stable, for it would mean a polarized world-system. The existence of the third category means precisely that the upper stratum is not faced with the *unified* opposition of all the others because the *middle* stratum is both exploited and exploiter. It follows that the specific economic role is not all that important, and has thus changed through the various historical stages of the modern world-system. We shall discuss these changes shortly.

Where then does class analysis fit in all of this? And what in such a formulation are nations, nationalities, peoples, ethnic groups? First of all, without arguing the point now,[40] I would contend that all these latter terms denote variants of a single phenomenon which I will term "ethno-nations."

Both classes and ethnic groups, or status-groups, or ethno-nations are phenomena of world-economies and much of the enormous confusion that has surrounded the concrete analysis of their functioning can be attributed quite simply to the fact that they have been analyzed as though they existed within the nation-states of this world-economy, instead of within the world-economy as a whole. This has been a Procrustean bed instead.

The range of economic activities being far wider in the core than in the periphery, the range of syndical interest groups is far wider there.[41]

Thus, it has been widely observed that there does not exist in many parts of the world today a proletariat of the kind which exists in, say, Europe or North America. But this is a confusing way to state the observation. Industrial activity being disproportionately concentrated in certain parts of the world-economy, industrial wage-workers are to be found principally in certain geographic regions. Their interests as a syndical group are determined by their collective relationship to the world-economy. Their ability to influence the political functioning of this world-economy is shaped by the fact that they command larger percentages of the population in one sovereign entity than another. The form their organizations take have, in large part, been governed too by these political boundaries. The same might be said about industrial capitalists. Class analysis is perfectly capable of accounting for the political position of, let us say, French skilled workers if we look at their structural position and interests in the world-economy. Similarly with ethno-nations. The meaning of ethnic consciousness in a core area is considerably different from that of ethnic consciousness in a peripheral area precisely because of the different class position such ethnic groups have in the world-economy.[42]

Political struggles of ethno-nations or segments of classes within national boundaries of course are the daily bread and butter of local politics. But their significance of consequences can only be fruitfully analyzed if one spells out the implications of their organizational activity or political demands for the functioning of the world-economy. This also incidentally makes possible more rational assessments of these politics in terms of some set of evaluative criteria such as "left" and "right."

The functioning then of a capitalist world-economy requires that groups pursue their economic interests within a single world market while seeking to distort this market for their benefit by organizing to exert influence on states, some of which are far more powerful than others but none of which controls the world-market in its entirety. Of course, we shall find on closer inspection that there are periods where one state is relatively quite powerful and other periods where power is more diffuse and contested, permitting weaker states broader ranges of action. We can talk then of the relative tightness or looseness of the world system as an important variable and seek to analyze why this dimension tends to be cyclical in nature, as it seems to have been for several hundred years.

We are now in a position to look at the historical evolution of this

capitalist world-economy itself and analyze the degree to which it is fruitful to talk of distinct stages in its evolution as a system. The emergence of
the European world-economy in the "long" sixteenth century (1450–
1640) was made possible by an historical conjuncture: on those long-
term trends which were the culmination of what has been sometimes
described as the "crisis of feudalism" was superimposed a more immediate cyclical crisis plus climatic changes, all of which created a dilemma
that could only be resolved by a geographic expansion of the division of
labor. Furthermore, the balance of inter-system forces was such as to
make this realizable. Thus a geographic expansion did take place in conjunction with a demographic expansion and an upward price rise.

The remarkable thing was not that a European world-economy was
thereby created, but that it survived the Hapsburg attempt to transform
it into a world-empire, an attempt seriously pursued by Charles V. The
Spanish attempt to absorb the whole failed because the rapid economic-
demographic-technological burst forward of the preceding century
made the whole enterprise too expensive for the imperial base to sustain,
especially given many structural insufficiencies in Castilian economic
development. Spain could afford neither the bureaucracy nor the army
that was necessary to the enterprise, and in the event went bankrupt, as
did the French monarchs making a similar albeit even less plausible attempt.

Once the Hapsburg dream of world-empire was over—and in 1557 it
was over forever—the capitalist world-economy was an established system that became almost impossible to unbalance. It quickly reached an
equilibrium point in its relations with other world-systems: the Ottoman
and Russian world-empires, the Indian Ocean proto-world-economy.
Each of the states or potential states within the European world-
economy was quickly in the race to bureaucratize, to raise a standing
army, to homogenize its culture, to diversify its economic activities. By
1640, those in northwest Europe had succeeded in establishing themselves as the core-states: Spain and the northern Italian city-states declined into being semi-peripheral; northeastern Europe and Iberian
America had become the periphery. At this point, those in semi-
peripheral status had reached it by virtue of decline from a former more
pre-eminent status.

It was the system-wide recession of 1650–1730 that consolidated the

European world-economy and opened stage two of the modern world-economy. For the recession forced retrenchment, and the decline in relative surplus allowed room for only one core-state to survive. The mode of struggle was mercantilism, which was a device of partial insulation and withdrawal from the world market of *large* areas themselves hierarchically constructed—that is, empires within the world-economy (which is quite different from world-empires). In this struggle England first ousted the Netherlands from its commercial primacy and then resisted successfully France's attempt to catch up. As England began to speed up the process of industrialization after 1760, there was one last attempt of those capitalist forces located in France to break the imminent British hegemony. This attempt was expressed first in the French Revolution's replacement of the cadres of the regime and then in Napoleon's continental blockade. But it failed.

Stage three of the capitalist world-economy begins then, a stage of industrial rather than of agricultural capitalism. Henceforth, industrial production is no longer a minor aspect of the world market but comprises an ever larger percentage of world gross production—and even more important, of the world gross surplus. This involves a whole series of consequences for the world-system.

First of all, it led to the further geographic expansion of the European world-economy to include now the whole of the globe. This was in part the result of its technological feasibility both in terms of improved military firepower and improved shipping facilities which made regular trade sufficiently inexpensive to be viable. But, in addition, industrial production *required* access to raw materials of a nature and in a quantity such that the needs could not be supplied within the former boundaries. At first, however, the search for new markets was not a primary consideration in the geographic expansion since the new markets were more readily available within the old boundaries, as we shall see.

The geographic expansion of the European world-economy meant the elimination of other world-systems as well as the absorption of the remaining mini-systems. The most important world-system up to then outside of the European world-economy, Russia, entered in semi-peripheral status, the consequence of the strength of its state-machinery (including its army) and the degree of industrialization already achieved in the eighteenth century. The independences in the Latin American countries did nothing to change their peripheral status. They merely eliminated the last vestiges of Spain's semi-peripheral role and ended pockets of non-involvement in the world-economy in the interior of Latin America. Asia and Africa were absorbed into the periphery in the nineteenth century, although Japan, because of the combination of the strength of its state-machinery, the poverty of its resource base (which led to a certain disinterest on the part of world capitalist forces), and its geographic remoteness from the core areas, was able quickly to graduate into semi-peripheral status.

The absorption of Africa as part of the periphery meant the end of slavery world-wide for two reasons. First of all, the manpower that was used as slaves was now needed for cash-crop production in Africa itself, whereas in the eighteenth century Europeans had sought to *discourage* just such cash-crop production.[43] In the second place, once Africa was part of the periphery and not the external arena, slavery was no longer economic. To understand this, we must appreciate the economics of slavery. Slaves receiving the lowest conceivable reward for their labor are the least productive form of labor and have the shortest life span, both because of under-nourishment and maltreatment and because of lowered psychic resistance to death. Furthermore, if recruited from areas surrounding their workplace the escape rate is too high. Hence, there must be a high transport cost for a product of low productivity. This makes economic sense only if the purchase price is virtually nil. In capitalist market trade, purchase always has a real cost. It is only in long-distance trade, the exchange of preciosities, that the purchase price can be in the social system of the purchaser virtually nil. Such was the slave-trade. Slaves were bought at low immediate cost (the production cost of the items actually exchanged) and none of the usual invisible costs. That is to say, the fact that removing a man from West Africa lowered the productive potential of the region was of *zero* cost to the European world-economy since these areas were not part of the division of labor. Of course, had the slave trade totally denuded Africa of all possibilities of furnishing further slaves, then a real cost to Europe would have commenced. But that point was never historically reached. Once, however, Africa was part of the periphery, then the real cost of a slave in terms of the production of surplus in the world-economy went up to such a point that it became far more economical to use wage-labor, even on sugar or cotton plantations, which is precisely what transpired in the nineteenth-century Caribbean and other slave-labor regions.

The creation of vast new areas as the periphery of the expanded world-economy made possible a shift in the role of some other areas. Specifically, both the United States and Germany (as it came into being) combined formerly peripheral and semi-peripheral regions. The manufacturing sector in each was able to gain political ascendancy, as the peripheral subregions became less economically crucial to the world-economy. Mercantilism now became the major tool of semi-peripheral countries seeking to become core countries, thus still performing a function analogous to that of the mercantilist drives of the late seventeenth and eighteenth centuries in England and France. To be sure, the struggle of semi-peripheral countries to "industrialize" varied in the degree to which it succeeded in the period before the First World War: all the way in the United States, only partially in Germany, not at all in Russia.

The internal structure of core-states also changed fundamentally under industrial capitalism. For a core area, industrialism involved divesting itself of substantially all agricultural activities (except that in the twentieth century further mechanization was to create a new form of working the land that was so highly mechanized as to warrant the appellation industrial). Thus whereas, in the period 1700–40, England not only was Europe's leading industrial exporter but was also Europe's leading agricultural exporter—this was at a high point in the economy-wide recession—by 1900, less than 10 percent of England's population were engaged in agricultural pursuits.

At first under industrial capitalism, the core exchanged manufactured products against the periphery's agricultural products—hence, Britain from 1815 to 1873 as the "workshop of the world." Even to those semi-peripheral countries that had some manufacture (France, Germany, Belgium, the U.S.), Britain in this period supplied about half their needs in manufactured goods. As, however, the mercantilist practices of this later group both cut Britain off from outlets and even created competition for Britain in sales to peripheral areas, a competition which led to the late nineteenth-century "scramble for Africa," the world division of labor was reallocated to ensure a new special role for the core: less the provision of the manufactures, more the provision of the machines to make the manufactures as well as the provision of the infra-structure (especially, in this period, railroads).

The rise of manufacturing created for the first time under capitalism a large-scale urban proletariat. And in consequence for the first time there arose what Michels has called the "anti-capitalist mass spirit,"[44] which was translated into concrete organizational forms (trade-unions, socialist parties). This development intruded a new factor as threatening to the stability of the states and of the capitalist forces now so securely in control of them as the earlier centrifugal thrusts of regional anti-capitalist landed elements had been in the seventeenth century.

At the same time that the bourgeoisies of the core countries were faced by this threat to the internal stability of their state structures, they were simultaneously faced with the economic crisis of the latter third of the nineteenth century resulting from the more rapid increase of agricultural production (and indeed of light manufactures) than the expansion of a potential market for these goods. Some of the surplus would have to be redistributed to someone to allow these goods to be bought and the economic machinery to return to smooth operation. By expanding the purchasing power of the industrial proletariat of the core countries, the world-economy was unburdened simultaneously of two problems: the bottleneck of demand, and the unsettling "class conflict" of the core states—hence, the social liberalism or welfare-state ideology that arose just at that point in time.

The First World War was, as men of the time observed, the end of an era; and the Russian Revolution of October 1917 the beginning of a new one—our stage four. This stage was, to be sure, a stage of revolutionary turmoil but it also was, in a seeming paradox, the stage of the *consolidation* of the industrial capitalist world-economy. The Russian Revolution was essentially that of a semi-peripheral country whose internal balance of forces had been such that as of the late nineteenth century it began on a decline towards a peripheral status. This was the result of the marked penetration of foreign capital into the industrial sector which was on its way to eliminating all indigenous capitalist forces, the resistance to the mechanization of the agricultural sector, the decline of relative military power (as evidenced by the defeat by the Japanese in 1905). The Revolution brought to power a group of state-managers who reversed each one of these trends by using the classic technique of mercantilist semi-withdrawal from the world-economy. In the process of doing this, the now U.S.S.R. mobilized considerable popular support, especially in the urban sector. At the end of the Second World War, Russia was reinstated as a very strong member of the semi-periphery and could begin to seek full core status.

Meanwhile, the decline of Britain which dates from 1873 was confirmed and its hegemonic role was assumed by the United States. While the U.S. thus rose, Germany fell further behind as a result of its military defeat. Various German attempts in the 1920s to find new industrial outlets in the Middle East and South America were unsuccessful in the face of the U.S. thrust combined with Britain's continuing relative strength. Germany's thrust of desperation to recoup lost ground took the noxious and unsuccessful form of Nazism.

It was the Second World War that enabled the United States for a brief period (1945–65) to attain the same level of primacy as Britain had in the first part of the nineteenth century. United States growth in this period was spectacular and created a great need for expanded market outlets. The Cold War closure denied not only the U.S.S.R. but Eastern Europe to U.S. exports. And the Chinese revolution meant that this region, which had been destined for much exploitative activity, was also cut off. Three alternative areas were available and each was pursued with assiduity. First, Western Europe had to be rapidly "reconstructed," and it was the Marshall Plan which thus allowed this area to play a primary role in the expansion of world productivity. Secondly, Latin America became the reserve of U.S. investment from which now Britain and Germany were completely cut off. Thirdly, Southern Asia, the Middle East and Africa had to be decolonized. On the one hand, this was necessary in order to reduce the share of the surplus taken by the Western European intermediaries, as Canning covertly supported the Latin American revolutionaries against Spain in the 1820s.[45] But also, these countries had to be decolonized in order to mobilize productive potential in a way that had never been achieved in the colonial era. Colonial rule after all had been an *inferior* mode of relationship of core and periphery, one occasioned by the strenuous late-nineteenth-century conflict among industrial states but one no longer desirable from the point of view of the new hegemonic power.[46]

But a world capitalist economy does not permit true imperium.

Charles V could not succeed in his dream of world-empire. The Pax Britannica stimulated its own demise. So too did the Pax Americana. In each case, the cost of *political* imperium was too high economically, and in a capitalist system, over the middle run when profits decline, new *political* formulae are sought. In this case the costs mounted along several fronts. The efforts of the U.S.S.R. to further its own industrialization, protect a privileged market area (eastern Europe), and force entry into other market areas led to an immense spiralling of military expenditure, which on the Soviet side promised long-run returns whereas for the U.S. it was merely a question of running very fast to stand still. The economic resurgence of western Europe, made necessary both to provide markets for U.S. sales and investments and to counter the U.S.S.R. military thrust, meant over time that the west European state structures collectively became as strong as that of the U.S., which led in the late 1960s to the "dollar and gold crisis" and the retreat of Nixon from the free-trade stance which is the definitive mark of the self-confident leader in a capitalist market system. When the cumulated Third World pressures, most notably Vietnam, were added on, a restructuring of the world division of labor was inevitable, involving probably in the 1970s a quadripartite division of the larger part of the world surplus by the U.S., the European Common Market, Japan, and the U.S.S.R.

Such a decline in U.S. state hegemony has actually *increased* the freedom of action of capitalist enterprises, the larger of which have now taken the form of multinational corporations which are able to maneuver against state bureaucracies whenever the national politicians become too responsive to internal worker pressures. Whether some effective links can be established between multinational corporations, presently limited to operating in certain areas, and the U.S.S.R. remains to be seen, but it is by no means impossible.

This brings us back to one of the questions with which we opened this paper, the seemingly esoteric debate between Liu Shao-Chi and Mao Tse-Tung as to whether China was, as Liu argued, a socialist state, or whether, as Mao argued, socialism was a *process* involving continued and continual class struggle. No doubt to those to whom the terminology is foreign the discussion seems abstrusely theological. The issue, however, as we said, is real. If the Russian Revolution emerged as a reaction to the threatened further decline of Russia's structural position in the world-economy, and if fifty years later one can talk of the U.S.S.R. as entering the status of a core power in a *capitalist* world-economy, what then is the meaning of the various so-called socialist revolutions that have occurred on a third of the world's surface? First let us notice that it has been neither Thailand nor Liberia nor Paraguay that has had a "socialist revolution" but Russia, China, and Cuba. That is to say, these revolutions have occurred in countries that, in terms of their internal economic structures in the pre-revolutionary period, had a certain minimum strength in terms of skilled personnel, some manufacturing, and other factors which made it plausible that, within the framework of a capitalist world-economy, such a country could alter its role in the world division of labor within a reasonable period (say 30–50 years) by the use of the technique of mercantilist semi-withdrawal. (This may not be all that plausible for Cuba, but we shall see). Of course, other countries in the geographic regions and military orbit of these revolutionary forces had changes of regime without in any way having these characteristics (for example, Mongolia or Albania). It is also to be noted that many of the countries where similar forces are strong or where considerable counter-force is required to keep them from emerging also share this status of minimum strength. I think of Chile or Brazil or Egypt—or indeed Italy.

Are we not seeing the emergence of a political structure for *semi-peripheral* nations adapted to stage four of the capitalist world-system? The fact that all enterprises are nationalized in these countries does not make the participation of these enterprises in the world-economy one that does not conform to the mode of operation of a capitalist market-system: seeking increased efficiency of production in order to realize a maximum price on sales, thus achieving a more favorable allocation of the surplus of the world-economy. If tomorrow U.S. Steel became a worker's collective in which all employees without exception received an identical share of the profits and all stockholders were expropriated without compensation, would U.S. Steel thereby cease to be a capitalist enterprise operating in a capitalist world-economy?

What then have been the consequences for the world-system of the emergence of many states in which there is no private ownership of the basic means of production? To some extent, this has meant an internal reallocation of consumption. It has certainly undermined the ideological justifications in world capitalism, both by showing the political vulnerability of capitalist entrepreneurs and by demonstrating that private ownership is irrelevant to the rapid expansion of industrial productivity. But to the extent that it has raised the ability of the new semi-peripheral areas to enjoy a larger share of the world surplus, it has once again depolarized the world, recreating the triad of strata that has been a fundamental element in the survival of the world-system.

Finally, in the peripheral areas of the world-economy, both the continued economic expansion of the core (even though the core is seeing some reallocation of surplus internal to it) and the new strength of the semi-periphery has led to a further weakening of the political and hence economic position of the peripheral areas. The pundits note that "the gap is getting wider," but thus far no one has succeeded in doing much about it, and it is not clear that there are very many in whose interests it would be to do so. Far from a strengthening of state authority, in many parts of the world we are witnessing the same kind of deterioration Poland knew in the sixteenth century, a deterioration of which the frequency of military coups is only one of many signposts. And all of this leads us to conclude that stage four has been the stage of the *consolidation* of the capitalist world-economy.

Consolidation, however, does not mean the absence of contradictions and does not mean the likelihood of long-term survival. We thus come to projections about the future, which has always been man's great game, his true hybris, the most convincing argument for the dogma of original sin. Having read Dante, I will therefore be brief.

There are two fundamental contradictions, it seems to me, involved in the workings of the capitalist world-system. In the first place, there is the contradiction to which the nineteenth-century Marxian corpus pointed, which I would phrase as follows: whereas in the short-run the maximization of profit requires maximizing the withdrawal of surplus from immediate consumption of the majority, in the long-run the continued production of surplus requires a mass demand which can only be created by redistributing the surplus withdrawn. Since these two considerations move in opposite directions (a "contradiction"), the system has constant crises which in the long-run both weaken it and make the game for those with privilege less worth playing.

The second fundamental contradiction, to which Mao's concept of socialism as process points, is the following: whether the tenants of privilege seek to co-opt an oppositional movement by including them in a minor share of the privilege, they may no doubt eliminate opponents in the short-run; but they also up the ante for the next oppositional movement created in the next crisis of the world-economy. Thus the cost of "co-option" rises ever higher and the advantages of co-option seem ever less worthwhile.

There are today no socialist systems in the world-economy any more than there are feudal systems because there is only *one* world-system. It is a world-economy and it is by definition capitalist in form. Socialism involves the creation of a new kind of world-system, neither a redistributive world-empire nor a capitalist world-economy but a socialist world-government. I don't see this projection as being in the least utopian but I also don't feel its institution is imminent. It will be the outcome of a long struggle in forms that may be familiar and perhaps in very new forms, that will take place in *all* the areas of the world-economy (Mao's continual "class struggle"). Governments may be in the hands of persons, groups or movements sympathetic to this transformation but *states* as such are neither progressive nor reactionary. It is movements and forces that deserve such evaluative judgments.

Having gone as far as I care to in projecting the future, let me return to the present and to the scholarly enterprise which is never neutral but does have its own logic and to some extent its own priorities. We have adumbrated as our basic unit of observation a concept of world-systems that have structural parts and evolving stages. It is within such a framework, I am arguing, that we can fruitfully make comparative analyses — of the wholes and of parts of the whole. Conceptions precede and govern measurements. I am all for minute and sophisticated quantitative indicators. I am all for minute and diligent archival work that will trace a concrete historical series of events in terms of all its immediate complexities. But the point of either is to enable us to see better what has happened and what is happening. For that we need glasses with which to discern the dimensions of difference, we need models with which to weigh significance, we need summarizing concepts with which to create the knowledge which we then seek to communicate to each other. And all this because we are men with hybris and original sin and therefore seek the good, the true, and the beautiful.

NOTES

1. George Lukacs, 'The Marxism of Rosa Luxemburg,' in *History and Class Consciousness* (London: Merlin Press, 1968), p. 27.
2. Robert A. Nisbet, *Social Change and History* (New York: Oxford University Press, 1969), pp. 302-3. I myself would exempt from this criticism the economic history literature.
3. Fernand Braudel, 'History and the Social Sciences,' in Peter Burke (ed.) *Economy and Society in Early Modern Europe* (London: Routledge and Kegan Paul, 1972), pp. 38-9.
4. See Andre Gunder Frank, Ch. IV (A), 'The Myth of Feudalism' in *Capitalism and Underdevelopment in Latin America* (New York: Monthly Review Press, 1967), pp. 221-42.
5. See Frederic Lane's discussion of 'protection costs' which is reprinted as Part Three of *Venice and History* (Baltimore: Johns Hopkins Press, 1966). For the specific discussion of tribute, see pp. 389-90, 416-20.
6. See Karl Polanyi, 'The Economy as Instituted Process,' in Karl Polanyi, Conrad M. Arsenberg and Harry W. Pearson (eds.), *Trade and Market in the Early Empire* (Glencoe: Free Press, 1957), pp. 243-70.
7. See my *The Modern World-System: Capitalist Agriculture and the Origins of the European World-Economy in the Sixteenth Century* (New York: Academic Press, 1974).
8. Philip Abrams concludes a similar plea with this admonition: 'The academic and intellectual dissociation of history and sociology seems, then, to have had the effect of deterring both disciplines from attending seriously to the most important issues involved in the understanding of social transition.' 'The Sense of the Past and the Origins of Sociology,' *Past and Present*, No. 55, May 1972, 32.
9. Frank, *op. cit.*, p. 3.
10. Frank's critique, now classic, of these theories is entitled 'Sociology of Development and Underdevelopment of Sociology,' and is reprinted in *Latin America: Underdevelopment or Revolution* (New York: Monthly Review Press, 1969), pp. 21-94.
11. See Theotonio Dos Santos, *La Nueva Dependencia.* (Buenos Aires: s/ediciones, 1968).
12. Ernesto Laclau (h), 'Feudalism and Capitalism in Latin America,' *New Left Review*, No. 67, May-June 1971, 37-8.
13. *The Accumulation of Capital* (New York: Modern Reader Paperbacks, 364-5). Luxemburg however, as is evident, lends herself further to the confusion by using the terminology of 'capitalistic' and 'non-capitalistic' modes of production. Leaving these terms aside, her vision is impeccable: 'From the aspect both of realising the surplus value and of producing the material elements of constant capital, international trade is a prime necessity for the historical existence of capitalism — an international trade which under actual conditions is essentially an exchange between capitalistic and non-capitalistic modes of production,' *Ibid.*, 359. She shows similar insight into the need of recruiting labor for core areas from the periphery, what she calls 'the increase in the variable capital.' See *ibid.*, p. 361.
14. The debate begins with Maurice Dobb, *Studies in the Development of Capitalism* (London: Routledge and Kegan Paul, 1946). Paul Sweezy criticized Dobb in 'The Transition from Feudalism to Capitalism,' *Science and Society*, XIV, 2, Spring 1950, 134-57, with a 'Reply' by Dobb in the same issue. From that point on many others got into the debate in various parts of the world. I have reviewed and discussed this debate *in extenso* in Chapter 1 of my work cited above.
15. It would take us into a long discursus to defend the proposition that, like all great thinkers, there was the Marx who was the prisoner of his social location and the Marx, the genius, who could on occasion see from a wider vantage point. The former Marx generalized from British history. The latter Marx is the one who has inspired a critical conceptual framework of social reality.

W.W. Rostow incidentally seeks to refute the former Marx by offering an alternative generalization from British history. He ignores the latter and more significant Marx. See *The Stages of Economic Growth: A Non-Communist Manifesto* (Cambridge: at the University Press, 1960).

16. Laclau, *op. cit.*, 25, 30.

17. Cited in F. Burlatsky, *The State and Communism* (Moscow: Progress Publishers, n.d., *circa* 1961), p. 95.

18. *Ibid.*, p. 97.

19. Mao Tse-Tung, *On The Correct Handling of Contradictions Among The People*, 7th ed., revised translation (Peking: Foreign Languages Press, 1966), pp. 37–8.

20. *Long Live The Invincible Thought of Mao Tse-Tung!*, undated pamphlet, issued between 1967 and 1969, translated in *Current Background*, No. 884, July 18, 1969, 14.

21. This is the position taken by Mao Tse-Tung in his speech to the Work Conference of the Central Committee at Peitaiho in August 1962, as reported in the pamphlet, *Long Live . . .* , p. 20. Mao's position was subsequently endorsed at the 10th Plenum of the 8th CCP Central Committee in September 1962, a session this same pamphlet describes as 'a great turning point in the violent struggle between proletarian headquarters and the bourgeois headquarters in China.' *Ibid.*, 21.

22. Remarks made by Mao at 10th Plenum, cited in *ibid.*, 20.

23. Mao Tse-Tung, 'Talk on the Question of Democratic Centralism,' January 30, 1962, in *Current Background*, No. 891, Oct. 8, 1969, 39.

24. 'Communiqué of the 10th Plenary Session of the 8th Central Committee of the Chinese Communist Party,' *Current Background*, No. 691, Oct. 5, 1962, 3.

25. Yuri Sdobnikov (ed.), *Socialism and Capitalism: Score and Prospects* (Moscow: Progress Publ., 1971), p. 20. The book was compiled by staff members of the Institute of World Economy and International Relations, and the senior contributor was Prof. V. Aboltin.

26. *Ibid.*, p. 21.

27. *Ibid.*, p. 26.

28. *Ibid.*, p. 24.

29. *Ibid.*, p. 25.

30. See Raymond Aron, *Dix-huit leçons de la société industrielle* (Paris: Ed. Gallimard, 1962).

31. This is the dilemma, I feel, of E.J. Hobsbawm in explaining his so-called 'crisis of the seventeenth century.' See his *Past and Present* article reprinted (with various critiques) in Trevor Aston (ed.), *The Crisis of the Seventeenth Century* (London: Routledge and Kegan Paul, 1965).

32. Maurice Dobb, *Capitalism Yesterday and Today* (London: Lawrence and Wishart, 1958). p. 21. Italics mine.

33. *Ibid.*, pp. 6–7.

34. *Ibid.*, p. 21.

35. See my *The Modern World-System, op. cit.*, Chap. 2.

36. I give a brief account of this in 'Three Paths of National Development in the Sixteenth Century,' *Studies in Comparative International Development*, VII, 2, Summer 1972, 95–101.

37. See Arghiri Emmanuel, *Unequal Exchange* (New York: Monthly Review Press, 1972).

38. Charles Bettelheim, 'Theoretical Comments' in Emmanuel, *op. cit.*, 295.

39. See J. Siemenski, 'Constitutional Conditions in the Fifteenth and Sixteenth Centuries,' *Cambridge History of Poland, I*, W. F. Reddaway *et al.* (eds.), *From the Origins to Sobieski (to 1696)* (Cambridge: At the University Press, 1950), pp. 416–40; Janusz Tazbir, 'The Commonwealth of the Gentry,' in Aleksander Gieysztor *et al.*, *History of Poland* (Warszawa: PWN—Polish Scientific Publ., 1969), pp. 169–271.

40. See my fuller analysis in 'Social Conflict in Post-Independence Black Africa: The Concepts of

Race and Status-Group Reconsidered' in Ernest W. Campbell (ed.), *Racial Tensions and National Identity* (Nashville: Vanderbilt Univ. Press, 1972). pp. 207–26.

41. Range in this sentence means the number of different occupations in which a significant proportion of the population is engaged. Thus peripheral society typically has its occupations well-distributed over all of Colin Clark's three sectors. If one shifted the connotation of range to talk of style of life, consumption patterns, even income distribution, quite possibly one might reverse the correlation. In a typical peripheral society, the differences between a subsistence farmer and an urban professional are probably far greater than those which could be found in a typical core state.

42. See my 'The Two Modes of Ethnic Consciousness: Soviet Central Asia in Transition?' in Edward Allworth (ed.), *The Nationality Question in Soviet Central Asia* (New York: Praeger, 1973), pp. 168–75.

43. A. Adu Boahen cites the instructions of the British Board of Trade in 1751 to the Governor of Cape Castle (a small British fort and trading-settlement in what is now Ghana) to seek to stop the local people, the Fante, from cultivating cotton. The reason given was the following: 'The introduction of culture and industry among the Negroes is contrary to the known established policy of his country, there is no saying where this might stop, and that it might extend to tobacco, sugar and every other commodity which we now take from our colonies; and thereby the Africans, who now support themselves by wars, would become planters and their slaves be employed in the culture of these articles in Africa, which they are employed in America.' Cited in A. Adu Boahen, *Topics in West Africa History* (London: Longmans, Green and Co., 1966), p. 113.

44. Robert Michels, 'The Origins of the Anti-Capitalist Mass Spirit,' in *Man in Contemporary Society* (New York: Columbia University Press, 1955), Vol. I, pp. 740–65.

45. See William W. Kaufman, *British Policy and the Independence of Latin America, 1804–28* (New Haven: Yale University Press, 1951).

46. Cf. Cathérine Coquery-Vidrovitch, 'De l'impérialisme britannique à l'impérialisme contemporaine — l'avatar colonial,' *L'Homme et la société*, No. 18, oct.–nov.–déc. 1970, 61–90.

6—Modernization: Requiescat in Pace

This short polemic was delivered in a debate with Alex Inkeles at the meetings of the American Sociological Association in 1975. I was trying to bury modernization theory, or at least to indicate why I had rejected it after having been taught it by my predecessors. I fear modernization theory has survived nonetheless, in altered clothing, but I feel what I said about it still holds true.

When a concept has died, some try to revive it by invoking it as ritual incantation, some regret its passing wistfully, some pretend it never existed, and some are impatient with any reference to it. But only the American Sociological Association holds a funeral service.

De mortuis nil nisi bonum? A good slogan perhaps for personal matters, but not very helpful in intellectual or political ones. I should like therefore very briefly to review how world social science ever got into this cul-de-sac known as modernization theory and, now that some of us are out of it, what lies on the horizon ahead.

I hesitate to review the history of this idea since it seems to me that this has been done already on a number of occasions. But memorials involve familiar memories. Until 1945 it still seemed reasonable to assume that Europe was the center of the world. Even anti-imperialist movements outside of Europe and against Europe often tended to assume it. But the world moved inexorably on. And everyone's geographical horizons expanded. To cope with this changing world, Western scholars invented development, invented the Third World, invented modernization.

Let us start by citing the merits of these inventions. The new terms replaced older, distasteful ones. Backward nations were only underdeveloped. The Yellow Horde became instead the Third World. And progress no longer involved Westernization. Now one could antiseptically modernize.

Above all, the new concepts offered hope. No doubt Africa had never invented the wheel, no doubt Asian religions were fatalist, no doubt Islam preached submission, no doubt Latins combined racial miscegenation with a lack of entrepreneurial thrift; but it could now be asserted confidently that these failings were not biological, merely cultural. And if, like the Japanese, the underdeveloped were clever enough to invent an indigenous version of Calvinism, or if they could be induced to change the content of their children's readers (the children first being taught to read, of course), or if transistors were placed in remote villages, or if far-sighted elites mobilized benighted masses with the aid of altruistic outsiders, or if . . . then the underdeveloped too would cross the river Jordan and come into a land flowing with milk and honey. This was the hope offered up by the modernization theorists.

It was unquestionably a worthy parable for the times. It would be easy to show how this parable was manipulated by the masters of the world. Let us recognize nonetheless that it served to spur devoted and well-intentioned scholarship and liberal social action. But the time has come to put away childish things, and look reality in its face.

We do not live in a modernizing world but in a capitalist world. What makes this world tick is not the need for achievement but the need for profit. The problem for oppressed strata is not how to communicate within this world but how to overthrow it. Neither Great Britain nor the United States nor the Soviet Union is a model for anyone's future. They are state-structures of the present, partial (not total) institutions operating within a singular world-system, which however is and always has been an evolving one.

The last thing we need to do is to make comparative measurements of noncomparable and nonautonomous entities when the social system in which we all operate is for the first time in human history a single unit in which the entire game is resumed in the internal relationships to be found within the capitalist world-economy: of core to periphery, of bourgeois to proletarian, of hegemonic culture to cultures of resistance, of dominant strata with their demand for universalistic individual measurement to institutionally oppressed racial and ethnic strata, of the party of order to the party of movement. These relationships can be measured too, but we have not been measuring them.

The first step we must make if we wish to understand our world is radically to reject any and all distinction between history and social science, and to recognize that we are part of a single discipline of study: the study of human societies as they have historically evolved. There are no generalizations that are not historically time-bound, because there are no systems and no structures that are unchanging. And there is no set or sequence of social events that is comprehensible without reference to a theoretical construct whose function is to create meaning out of reality.

What was primarily wrong with all the concepts linked to the paradigm of modernization was that they were so ahistorical. After all, the modern world did not come out of nowhere. It involved the *transformation* of a particular variant of the redistributive mode of production, that found in feudal Europe, into a European world-economy based on a capitalist mode of production. It involved the strengthening of state-structures in the core areas of this world-economy and the correlative weakening of them in the periphery.

And once capitalism was consolidated as a system and there was no turnback, the internal logic of its functioning, the search for maximum profit, forced it continuously to expand—extensively to cover the globe, and intensively via the constant (if not steady) accumulation of capital, the pressure to mechanize work in order to make possible still further expansion of production, the tendency to facilitate and optimize rapid response to the permutations of the world market by the proletarianization of labor and the commercialization of land. This is what modernization is about, if one wants to use such a contentless word.

But whatever word we use, let us remember that the suffix "-ization" in the English language contains an antinomy. It refers both to the state of something and to the process of becoming that something. The capitalist world-economy has not yet, after four to five hundred years of existence, realized a free market, free labor, unentailed land, unbounded flows of capital. Nor do I believe it ever will do so. For I believe that the essence of the capitalist mode of production is the *partial* freedom of the factors of production. It will in fact only be with a socialist world-system that we will realize true freedom (including the free flow of the factors of production). This is indeed what lies behind Marx's phrase about moving from the "realm of necessity into the realm of freedom."

I do not intend here to preach a faith. Those who wish will believe. And those who do not will struggle against it. I wish rather to suggest an agenda of intellectual work for those who are seeking to understand the world-systemic transition from capitalism to socialism in which we are living, and thereby to contribute to it.

I think top priority must go to the original concern of the nineteenth-century fathers of social science, the understanding of the capitalist world-economy in which we live as a gestalt. But how do we do that? I see five major arenas of research, each large in scope.

1. The first arena is the internal functioning of the capitalist world-economy as a system: the institutional ways in which areas get located at the core, the periphery, and the semiperiphery of that system, and how units can and do change their location; the mechanisms of transfers of surplus toward the core; the ways in which classes emerge, consolidate, and disintegrate; the multiple expressions of class struggle; the creation, sustenance, and destruction of all varieties of "status-groups" (ethnonational groups, racial castes, age and sex groups), and the ways these "status" groupings interweave with class structure; the cultural expressions of conflicting interests; the pattern of interplay between cyclical processes of expansion and contraction and the secular evolutionary processes that undermine the basis stability of the system; the modalities of and resistances to the proletarianization of labor and the commercialization of land; the role of the state in affecting the world market and aiding specific groups within it; the rise of antisystemic revolutionary movements.

This is a long list, but it is only one arena. We must also and simultaneously work in other arenas:

2. We must reopen the question of how and when the capitalist world-economy was created in the first place: why the transition took place in feudal Europe and not elsewhere; why it took place when it did and not earlier or later; why earlier attempts of transition failed. This is not merely an exercise in archeological reconstruction; it is rather essential to the full comprehension of the nature of our present system.

3. Allied with this issue is another on which almost no work has been done. For at least three centuries (the sixteenth to the eighteenth), the capitalist world-economy functioned side by side with noncapitalist social systems outside it. How did it relate to them? And in particular, what were the processes that made it possible for the capitalist world-economy to incorporate them?

4. In the light of these interests, it will be clear why we must also turn

to a comparative study of the various historical forms of social system, the alternative modes of production. I myself believe there have only been three such modes up to now: the reciprocal (lineage) mode found in minisystems; the redistributive (tributary) mode found in world-empires (either full blown or largely disintegrated); the capitalist (market) mode found in world-economies. But this is a contentious formulation. In any case enormous work has to be done simply to identify properly which historical constructs reflected which modes and to make appropriate comparisons primarily within the systems or modes and secondarily among them.

5. This then brings me to the fourth system based on a socialist mode of production, our future world-government. We are living in the transition to it, which has begun and will continue for some time to come. But how are we relating to it? As rational militants contributing to it, or as clever obstructors of it (whether of the malicious or cynical variety)? In any case, here too we must look afresh at the various "socialist" experiences, seen as regimes that are seeking both to transform the world-system and partially to prefigure the future one, with greater or lesser success. And we must look to the relationship of revolutionary movements in the various political subdivisions of the world-system to each other.

You may ask whether this agenda is not far wider than the narrow field "modernization" was to cover. Yes, indeed it is. But that is the point. Modernization theory has served to deflect us from the agenda that would be able to speak to the problems with which it was supposedly concerned. This agenda requires redoing our historical narratives, accumulating new world-systemic quantitative data (almost from scratch), and above all reviewing and refining our conceptual baggage.

There are those who will say that such an agenda is a throwback from the scientific advances of modern social science to the imprecise and ideological musings of the nineteenth century. To such a contention, one can only give the answer of Thomas Kuhn when he discussed the problem of the historical use of measurement in physical science:

> [M]uch qualitative research, both empirical and theoretical, is normally pre-requisite to fruitful quantification of a given research field. In the absence of such prior work, the methodological direction, "Go ye forth and measure," may well prove only an invitation to waste time. . . .

The full and intimate quantification of any science is a consummation devoutly to be wished. Nevertheless, it is not a consummation that can effectively be sought by measuring. As in individual development, so in the scientific group, maturity comes most surely to those who know how to wait. [1961:55,60]

We have been impatient for the past thirty years. And the wine has turned sour. Let us go back to where we once were: understanding the reality of our world, which is that of a capitalist world-economy in the early stages of its transition to a socialist world-government. The road is hard, intellectually and politically. But it is the road both of scholarly integrity and of scientific promise.

7—Societal Development, or Development of the World-System?

In 1984, I was invited to give a talk at the German Sociological Congress, which was being held on the theme "Sociology and Social Development." I decided to use this occasion to challenge the historic antinomy of *Gemeinschaft-Gesellschaft*, and to insist that states do not "develop," only the modern world-system as a whole. To illustrate my argument, I used the somewhat shocking comparison of Germany and Puerto Rico as "societies."

The theme of this German Sociological Congress is "Sociology and Societal Development." This title includes two of the most common, most ambiguous, and most deceptive words in the sociological lexicon—society *(Gesellschaft)* and development *(Entwicklung)*. That is why I have entitled my talk in the form of a question, Societal Development or Development of the World-System?

Society of course is an old term. The *Oxford English Dictionary* (OED) gives twelve principal meanings to it, of which two seem most relevant to our present discussion. One is "the aggregate of persons living together in a more or less ordered community." The second, not very different, is "a collection of individuals comprising a community or living under the same organisation of government." The OED has the merit of being an historical dictionary and therefore indicating first usages. The first usages listed for these two senses are 1639 and 1577 respectively—hence, at the beginning of the modern world.

Looking in German dictionaries, I find the *Grosse Duden* (1977) offers the following relevant definition: *"Gesamtheit der Menschen, die unter bestimmten politischen, wirtschaftlichen und sozialen Verhältnissen zusammen leben,"* followed immediately by these examples: *"die bürgerliche, sozialistische Klassenlose Gesellschaft."* The *Wörterbuch der deutschen Gegenwartssprache* (1967), published in the GDR, gives a rather similar definition: *"Gesamtheit der unter gleichartigen sozialen und ökonomis-*

chen sowie auch politischen Verhältnissen lebenden Menschen," and it follows this by various examples including: *"die Entwicklung der (menschlichen) Gesellschaft. . . ; die neue sozialistische, kommunistische Gesellschaft; die Klassenlose Gesellschaft. . . ; die bürgerliche, kapitalistische Gesellschaft."* It precedes this definition with a notation that reads: *"ohne Plural."*[2]

Now, if one regards these definitions closely, which are probably typical of what one would find in most dictionaries in most languages, one notes a curious anomaly. Each of the definitions refers to a political component which seems to imply that each society exists within a specific set of political boundaries, yet the examples also suggest that a society is a type of state defined in terms of less specific, more abstract phenomena, with the last-mentioned dictionary specifically adding "no plural." In these examples, "society" is modified by an adjective, and the combined phrase describes the kind of structure which a "society" in the other usage, that of a politically bounded entity, is said to have. This latter usage of society can then take a plural, whereas the former cannot.

Perhaps you see no anomaly here. Yet I would like to start by endorsing the opening remark of one of the first serious attempts in modern social science to treat this matter. It is a German attempt. Lorenz von Stein's largely forgotten work on *Der Begriff der Gesellschaft und die soziale Geschichte der Französischen Revolution bis zum Jahre 1830.*[3] Stein says in the Introduction that *"Der Begriff der Gesellschaft gehört . . . zu den schwierigsten in der ganzen Staatswissenschaft . . ."* (1959 I : 12).

Why does Stein talk of *Gesellschaft* as a concept in *Staatswissenschaft*? To be sure, one answer is that *Staatswissenschaft* was the term then in use in Germany that included the domain of what today in Germany is called *Sozialwissenschaften*, although the boundaries of the two are not identical. The use of the term *Staatswissenschaften* in nineteenth-century Germany, but not in England or France, is itself a significant phenomenon, reflecting an understanding of the social sciences from the vantage point of what I would call a semi-peripheral state, but one outside the cultural circle of the hegemonic power. Yet this is not the whole answer. *Gesellschaft* is a concept of *Staatwissenschaft*, and the "most difficult one," because, as is clear from Stein's work itself, the concept "society" has its meaning for us primarily (even only) in the classic antinomy, society/state. And this antinomy in turn has its origin in the

attempt of the modern world to come to grips with the ideological implications of the French Revolution.

Monarchs had been ousted before 1792, and/or forced by rebellions
to change the constitutional structures of their regime. But the legitimation of such changes had previously been sought in the existence of some
illegitimate act or acts of the monarch. The French Revolution was not
justified on this basis, or at least came not to be so justified. Instead, the
revolutionaries asserted with some vigour a new moral or structural basis
on which to assign legitimacy, the concept of the popular will. As we
know, this theoretical construct swept the world in the two centuries that
have followed the French Revolution, and there are few today who contest it, despite all the attempts of conservative theorists from Burke and
de Maistre on to disparage the doctrine, and despite the numerous instances in which popular sovereignty has been de facto ignored.

There are two problems with a theory that sovereignty resides in the
people. First of all, we must know who and where are the people, that is
who are and ought to be the "citizens" of a "state." I remind you that the
central term of honorific address in the heyday of the French Revolution
was *"citoyen."* But it is the "state" which decides who are the "citizens,"
and in particular decides who are the full-fledged members of the polity.
Even today, nowhere is every resident of a state a citizen of that state, or
a voter in that state. The second problem is how one knows what the
popular will is. This is of course even more difficult than the first problem. I do not believe it is very much of an exaggeration to say that a very
large part of the historical and social scientific enterprise in the nineteenth and twentieth centuries has been one vast attempt to solve these
two problems, and that the key conceptual tool that has been used is the
idea that there exists something called a "society" that is locked into a
complicated, partially symbiotic, partially antagonistic relationship with
something called the "state." If, however, you feel (as I do) that after 150
or so years we have not resolved these problems very well, perhaps the
reason is that we have not given ourselves very adequate conceptual
tools. Of course, if this is so, one would have to analyse why this has
occurred, and I will come to this matter.

Let us now look briefly at the other term of our title, which is "development." Development too has many, many meanings. The one in the
OED most relevant to its usage here is as follows: "the growth or unfold-

ing of what is in the germ: (b) of races of plants and animals." The OED traces this usage only to 1871, to a work of social science in fact: Tylor's *Primitive Culture*, Volume I. Tylor is cited as saying: "Its various grades may be regarded as stages of development or evolution, each the outcome of previous history." Development, the OED adds, is "the same as evolution."

We get something similar in the German dictionaries. The *Grosse Duden* seems to avoid almost all usages in our sense until it comes to the compound *"Entwicklungsgesetz"* which it tells us refers to *"Wirtschaft und Gesellschaft."*[4] The GDR dictionary similarly treats the matter indirectly, through an example, *"die kulturelle, gesellschaftliche, geschichtliche, politische, ökonomische, soziale Entwicklung unseres Volkes."*[5]

The English definitions make it abundantly clear how tied this usage in social science is to the doctrine of biological evolution which emerged in the latter half of the nineteenth century. This is of course true of German as well. Duden's *Das Fremdwörterbuch* defines the *"Entwicklungsgesetz,"* a direct borrowing from English, as follows: *"Theorie der Entwicklung aller Lebewesen aus niedrigen, primitiven Organismen."*[6]

If we now combine the two terms, as you have done in the title of this congress (not at all in an unusual fashion), and talk of "Societal Development," we seem to be dealing with how some entity (an entity that is not the state, but also is not divorced from the state, and usually one sharing more or less the same boundaries as the state) has evolved over time from some lower to some more "complex" state of being.

Where then is the "germ" from which one can trace this evolution, and how far back can one trace it? Let me mention briefly two possible examples of a "society" and ask some naive questions about them. One example I will take is German society. The second example is Puerto Rican society. I do not plan to review the abundant literature of scholarly and public debate on these two instances. This would be a monumental task in the case of the German example, and not such a small one in the case of the Puerto Rican example. I merely want to show that there are some very elementary problems in using the concept "society" in either instance. I know that these two cases have their peculiarities, and that some may say they are somehow not "typical" or "representative." But one of the realities of history is that every example is specific and particular, and I frankly am skeptical that there are any representative "instances" anywhere. So I chose these because you know the German case, and you may be intrigued by the Puerto Rican case, which most of you probably do not know.

Let me ask the simple question: where is German society? Is it within the present boundaries of the Federal Republic The official answer seems to be that today there are *"zwei deutsche Staaten"* (two German States) but only *"ein Volk"* (one nation). So the one "nation" or "people" seems to be defined, at least by some as including both those persons found in the Federal Republic and those in the GDR.

What then about Austria? Are Austrians part of German "society," of the German "people"? Austria was only briefly, from 1938 to 1945, formally incorporated into the German state. Nevertheless, as you know, in the middle of the nineteenth century, Austria's incorporation into a then only potential German state was widely discussed as a distinct possibility. There seems to exist a long nationalist tradition, or at least one long nationalist tradition, that would define Austria as part of German society.

Despite this, the official answer to my question, Is Austria part of German society?, today seems to be a no—but only today. That is, because of the efforts of the present-day Federal Republic to dissociate itself morally from the Third Reich, itself associated with *Anschluss*, any suggestion that Austria is not and will not always be a separate state (and therefore nation? therefore "society"?) is distinctly frowned upon, both in the Federal Republic and in Austria. But if a "society" is something which "develops" out of a "germ," how is it possible that a mere political event, the outcome of the Second World War, or further back the outcome of the Austro-Prussian War of 1866, could affect the definition of the social space of German society? After all, a "society" is supposed to be different from a state, a sort of underlying and developing reality, at least in part against and in spite of the state. If, however, every time we change state boundaries we change the boundaries of "society," how can we argue that the legitimacy of a government provided by a "society" is different from the legitimacy of a government provided by a state? The concept of "society" was supposed to give us something solid on which to build. If it turns out to be mere putty, which we can reshape at will, it will do us precious little good—little analytical good, little political good, little moral good.

If the German case is one in which there are today two, perhaps three, sovereign "German" states, the Puerto Rican case seems virtually the opposite. As against a society with several states, here may be a society without any state. Ever since the sixteenth century there has been an administrative entity called Puerto Rico, but at no point in time has there ever been a sovereign state, a fully recognised member of the interstate system. To be sure, the United Nations does debate from time to time whether there ever will be one in the future, and so of course do the inhabitants of Puerto Rico.

If there is no state at all, how do we define the "society"? Where is it located? Who are its members? How did it come into existence? These, as you may immediately intuit, are political questions that have given rise to much passion. Recently, this intellectual controversy has been reopened in an unusual way by José Luis González who in 1980 published a book entitled *El país de cuatro pisos*. González is a man of letters who considers himself a Puerto Rican nationalist. The book, however, is a polemic against certain Puerto Rican *independistas*, and in particular against Pedro Albizu Campos, not because they stood for independence, but because they based their claims on a totally wrong analysis of what is Puerto Rican "society."

González starts, in the best tradition of Max Weber, with an observed anomaly. Of all Spain's colonies in the Western Hemisphere, Puerto Rico alone has never obtained an independent status. How come? His answer revolves around his belief that Puerto Rican "society" precisely did *not* evolve out of some "germ." He suggests an alternative analogy: Puerto Rican "society" is a house of four stories, each story being added at specific historical moments. The first story is that created in the sixteenth to eighteenth centuries, mixing the three historical "races": the Taina (or indigenous Carib Indians), the Africans (brought over as slaves), and the Spanish settlers. Since the Taina were largely wiped out and the Spaniards were few in number and often only temporary residents, the Africans came to predominate. "Hence my conviction, expressed on various occasions and disconcerting or irritating to some people, that the first Puerto Ricans were in fact Black Puerto Ricans." (González 1980 : 20)

It was only in 1815 that this ethnic mix changed in Puerto Rico. In 1815, the *Real Cédula de Gracias* opened the island to refugees from the various other Hispano-American colonies that were in the midst of wars of independence—and not only to Spaniards loyal to the Crown, but to English, French, Dutch, and Irish persons as well. Note well the date: 1815. It is the year of Napoleon's definitive exile, the founding of the Holy Alliance, the enthronement of British hegemony in the world-system. In addition, in the course of the late nineteenth century, Puerto Rico was the recipient of a recorded further wave of immigration, coming primarily from Corsica, Majorca, and Catalonia. Hence, by the end of the century, says González, a second story had been erected by these white settlers of the nineteenth century, and they constituted in Puerto Rico a "privileged minority" (p.24). Thus, continues González, it is not true, as Albizu Campos and others had claimed, that when American colonisation began in 1898, Puerto Rico had a homogeneous "national culture." Quite the contrary, it was a "people divided."

González uses this fact to explain the differential response of Puerto Ricans to U.S. colonisation, which created the third story. To simplify his argument, he argues that the *hacendados* at first welcomed the Americans since they thought that the U.S. intended to incorporate them eventually as part of the U.S. bourgeoisie. When it became clear within ten years that this was not to be, the "privileged minority" turned to nationalism. Meanwhile, the Puerto Rican working class had initially also greeted favourably the U.S. invasion, but for opposite reasons. They saw it as opening the door to "squaring their accounts" (p.33) with the land-owning classes, who "were seen by the Puerto Rican masses for what they in fact were: foreigners and exploiters" (p.35).

And then there is the fourth story, that constructed not as a result of the initial cultural "Northamericanisation" but rather as the result of the economic transformations beginning in the 1940s. It led initially to a "modernisation-within-dependency" (p.41) of Puerto Rican society, but then subsequently to the "spectacular and irreparable breakdown" (p.40) of this fourth story in the 1970s. González does not discuss directly the further complication, that since the 1940s there has also been a massive migration of Puerto Ricans to the continental United States, and that today a substantial proportion of all Puerto Ricans were born and live outside Puerto Rico. Are these latter still part of Puerto Rican "society," and if so for how long will this be true?

I cite González not to debate the future of Puerto Rico, nor merely to remind us of the profound social divisions in our so-called societies, which are to be sure class divisions, but ones often (even usually) over-laid with and linked to ethnic divisions. Rather, I cite the Puerto Rican case, as I did the German case, to underline the changing and debatable definitions of the boundaries of a "society" and to the close link such changing definitions have with historical events which are not products primarily of some "development" *intrinsic* to the "society."

What is fundamentally wrong with the concept of society is that it rei-fies and therefore crystallises social phenomena whose real significance lies not in their solidity but precisely in their fluidity and malleability. The concept "society" implies we have before us to analyse something that is a tangible reality, albeit, to be sure, a "developing" one. In fact what we have before us is primarily a rhetorical construct, and therefore, as Lorenz von Stein says, a "difficult concept" of *Staatswissenschaft* (that is, in this case, of political philosophy). We do not, however, have an analytical tool for the summation or dissection of our social processes.

One of the underlying elements of world social science for the last 150 years has been a particular reading of modern European history. This reading of history is not limited to professional historians and social sci-entists. It constitutes a deep layer of our common culture, taught via the secondary school system to all, and simply assumed as a basic structur-ing of our comprehension of the social world. It has not been the subject of major controversy. Rather it has been the *common* property of the two major principal *Weltanschauungen* of the last century, liberalism and Marxism, which otherwise have stood in stark opposition one to the other.

This reading of history takes the form of an historical myth which comprises two main statements. The first statement is that, out of a Eu-ropean medieval feudal world where seigneurs ruled over peasants, there arose (emerged, was created) a new social stratum, the urban bourgeoi-sie, who first economically undermined and then politically overthrew the old system (the *Ancien Régime*). The result was a market-dominated capitalist economy combined with a representative political system based on individual rights. Both the liberals and Marxists described Eu-ropean history in this way; they also both applauded this historical pro-cess as "progressive."

The second statement in this historical myth is most clearly captured in the book by Karl Bücher, *Die Entstehung der Volkswirtschaft*, in which Bücher distinguishes three successive stages of European economic history—*geschlossene Hauswirtschaft*, *Stadtwirtschaft*, and *Volkswirtschaft*.[7] The key element here, the one in which Bücher represents the liberal-Marxist consensus, is the perception of modern history as the story of widening economic circles, in which the major jump was to go from a "local" economy to a "national" economy, a national economy located of course in a national state. Bücher underlines the connection insisting that *"die Volkswirtschraft das Produkt einer jahrtausendelangen historischen Entwicklung ist, das nicht älter ist als der moderne Staat"* (1913 : 90).[8] Note incidentally once again the term "development." Bücher brings out explicitly the spatial implications that are implicit in the generic, descriptive categories found in the works of many other major figures of nineteenth-century social science: Comte and Durkheim, Maine and Spencer, Tönnies and Weber.

I think both of these statements comprising the dominant historical myth of modern European history are great distortions of what really happened. I will not discuss here why I believe the concept of the rise of a bourgeoisie, which somehow overthrew an aristocracy, is more or less the opposite of what really happened, which is that the aristocracy reconverted itself into a bourgeoisie in order to salvage its collective privilege. I have argued this case elsewhere (Wallerstein 1982). I prefer to concentrate my attention on the second myth, that of the widening circles.

If the essential movement of modern European history was from town economy to national economy, from the local arena to the national state, where does the "world" come into the picture? The answer is essentially as an epiphenomenon. National states are seen as spending a portion of their time and energy (a relatively small portion for the most part) on *inter*-national activities—international trade, international diplomacy. These so-called international relations are somehow "external" to this state, this nation, this "society." At the very most, some might concede that this situation has been evolving in the direction of the "internationalisation" of the economy and of the political and cultural arenas, but only very recently (since 1945, or even since only the 1970s). So, we are told, there may now be, "for the very first time," something we can call world production or a world culture.

This imagery, which frankly seems to me more and more bizarre the more I study the real world, is the heart of the operational meaning of the concept, the "development of society." Allow me to present to you another imagery, another way of summarising social reality, an alternative conceptual framework, which I hope can be said to capture more fully and more usefully the real social world in which we are living.

The transition from feudalism to capitalism involves first of all (first logically and first temporally) the creation of a world-economy. That is to say, a social division of labor was brought into being through the transformation of long-distance trade from a trade in "luxuries" to a trade in "essentials" or "bulk goods," which tied together processes that were widely dispersed into long commodity chains. The commodity chains consisted of particular linked production processes whose linkage made possible the accumulation of significant amounts of surplus-value and its relative concentration in the hands of a few.

Such commodity chains were already there in the sixteenth century and predated anything that could meaningfully be called "national economies." These chains in turn could only be secured by the construction of an interstate system coordinate with the boundaries of the real social division of labor, the capitalist world-economy. As the capitalist world-economy expanded from its original European base to include the entire globe, so did the boundaries of the interstate system. The sovereign states were institutions that were then created within this (expanding) interstate system, were defined by it, and derived their legitimacy from the combination of juridical self-assertion and recognition by others that is the essence of what we mean by "sovereignty." That it is not enough merely to proclaim sovereignty in order to exercise it is illustrated well by the current examples of the "independent" Bantustans in South Africa and the Turkish state in northern Cyprus. These entities are not sovereign states because the other members of the club of sovereign states (in each case with one single exception, which is insufficient) do not recognise them as sovereign states. How many recognitions, and whose, it takes to legitimate a claim to sovereignty is unclear. That there is a threshold somewhere becomes evident when we observe how firmly Morocco stands opposed to the wish of the majority (a bare majority, to be sure) of members of the Organization of African Unity (OAU) to admit the Sahraoui Arab Democratic Republic to full status in this regional interstate structure. Clearly, Morocco feels that a recognition by the OAU would create pressure on the great powers, and the claim might thereby pass the threshold.

It has been the world-system then and not the separate "societies" that has been "developing." That is, once created, the capitalist world-economy first became consolidated and then over time the hold of its basic structures on the social processes located within it was deepened and widened. The whole imagery of going from acorn to oak, from germ to fulfilment, if plausible at all, makes sense only if it is applied to the singular capitalist world-economy as an historical system.

It is within that developing framework that many of the institutions we often describe quite mistakenly as "primordial" came into existence. The sovereignty of jurisdictions became ever more institutionalised, as (and to the degree that) some kind of social allegiance evolved to the entities defined by the jurisdictions. Hence, slowly, and more or less coordinate with the evolving boundaries of each state, a corresponding nationalist sentiment took root. The modern world-system has developed from one in which these "nationalisms" were weak or non-existent to one in which they were salient, well-ensconced, and pervasive.

Nor were the nations the only new social groupings. The social classes, as we have come to know them, were also created in the course of this development, both objectively and subjectively. The pathways of both proletarianisation and bourgeoisification have been long and sinuous, but above all they have been the outcome of world-scale processes. Even our present household structures—yes, even they—are constructed entities, meeting simultaneously the double need of a structure to socialise the labor force and one to give this labor force partial shelter against the harsh effects of the work-system.

In all of this description, the imagery I am employing is not of a small core adding on outer layers but of a thin outer framework gradually filling in a dense inner network. To contrast *Gemeinschaft* und *Gesellschaft* in the way conventionally done not only by German but by all of world sociology is to miss the whole point. It is the modern world-system (that is, the capitalist world-economy whose political framework is the interstate system composed of sovereign states) which is the *Gesellschaft* within which our contractual obligations are located. To legitimate its structures, this *Gesellschaft* has not only destroyed the multiple *Gemein-*

schaften that historically existed (which is the point normally stressed) but has created a network of new *Gemeinschaften* (and most notably, the nations, that is, the so-called societies). Our language thus is topsy-turvy.

I am tempted to say we are really going not from *Gemeinschaft* to *Gesellschaft* but from *Gesellschaft* to *Gemeinschaft*, but that is not quite right either. Rather it is that our only *Gesellschaft*, the capitalist world-economy (and even it is only a partially-contractualised structure) has been creating our multiple, meaningful *Gemeinschaften*. Far from *Gemeinschaften* dying out, they have never been stronger, more complex, more overlapping and competing, more determinative of our lives. And yet never have they been less legitimate. Nor have they ever been more irrational, substantively irrational, and this is precisely because they have emerged out of a *gesellschaftliche* process. Our *Gemeinschaften* are, if you will, our loves that dare not speak their names.

Of course this is an impossible situation and we find ourselves amidst a worldwide cultural rebellion against these pressures all around us, one which is taking the widest of forms—the religious fundamentalisms, the hedonisms of withdrawal and the hedonisms of total self-interestedness, the multiple "countercultures," the Green movements, and not least the seething of really serious and really powerful anti-racist and anti-sexist movements. I do not mean to imply that these diverse groups are at all the same. Far from it. But they are the common consequence of the relentless spread of the ever more formally rational and ever more substantively irrational historical social system in which we all find ourselves collectively trapped. They represent screams of pain against the irrationality that oppresses in the name of a universal, rationalising logic. Had we really been moving from *Gemeinschaft* to *Gesellschaft*, all this would not be occurring. We should instead be bathing in the rational waters of an Enlightenment world.

At one level, there is much hope. Our historical system, as all historical systems, is full of contradictions, of processes which force us to go in one direction to pursue our short-run interests and in another to pursue our middle-run interests. These contradictions are built into the economic and political structures of our system and are playing themselves out. Once again, I do not wish to repeat here analyses I have made elsewhere about what I call "the crisis of transition" (Wallerstein 1982b), a long process taking perhaps 150 years, which has already begun and which will result in the demise of our present system and its replacement by something else, without, however, any guarantee that this something else will be substantively better. No guarantee, but a meaningful possibility. That is to say, we are before an historical, collective choice, the kind that comes rarely and is not the lot of every generation of mankind.

I would prefer to develop here the question of the possible role of the historical social sciences in this collective choice, which is of course a moral choice, hence a political choice. I have argued that the basic concept of "society" and the basic historical myths of what I have called the liberal-Marxist consensus of the nineteenth century, which combined to form the framework of social science as the principal ideological expression of the world-system, are fundamentally offbase. Of course, this was no accident. The concept of society and the historical myths were part of the machinery that made the modern world-system operate so well in its heyday. In a period of relative systemic equilibrium, the consciousness of the intellectuals is perhaps the finest-tuned reflection of the underlying material processes.

However, we are no longer in a time of relative systemic equilibrium. It is not that the machine has been working poorly, but rather that it has been working only too well. The capitalist world-economy has showed itself over 400 years magnificently adept at solving its short-run and middle-run problems. Furthermore, it shows every sign of being able to do more of the same in the present and near future. But the solutions themselves have created changes in the underlying structure, which are eliminating over time this very ability to make the constant necessary adjustments. The system is eliminating its degrees of freedom. I am unable here to argue this case. I simply assert it, and use it to explain the fact that, amid the constant hosannas to the efficiency of capitalist civilisation, we see everywhere the signs of malaise and cultural pessimism. The consensus has therefore begun to break down. And this is what is reflected in the myriad of anti-systemic movements that have begun to develop momentum and get out of hand.

Among the intellectuals, this malaise is reflected in the growing questioning of fundamental premises. Today we have physical scientists who are doubting the whole philosophical description of science as the "disenchantment of the world," one that goes from Bacon to Newton to Einstein, and are asking us to understand that science is rather the "reenchantment of the world" (Prigogine and Stengers 1979). And I am coming before you to express what many have come to feel, that it is futile to analyse the processes of the *societal development* of our multiple (national) "societies" as if they were autonomous, internally evolving structures, when they are and have been in fact primarily structures created by, and taking form in response to, world-scale processes. It is this world-scale structure and the processes of its development that provide the true subject of our collective enquiry.

If I am anywhere near right, it has consequences for us. It means of course that we must collectively rethink our premises, and therefore our theories. But it has an even more painful side. It means we must reinterpret the meaning of our entire stock of slowly-accumulated "empirical data," a stock whose constant growth is making our libraries and our archives bulge, and which serves as the historically created and distorted basis of almost all our current work.

But why will we do this? And in whose name, in whose interest? One answer that has been given for at least 75 years now has been "in the name of the movement, or the party, or the people." I do not reject that answer because of some belief in the separation of science and values. But that answer is no answer, for two reasons. First, the movement is not singular. Perhaps at one time, the family of anti-systemic movements could lay claim to a semblance of unity, but surely no longer. And in terms of world-scale processes, there is not merely a multiplicity of movements, but even of types of movements. Secondly, the collectivity of movements is undergoing a collective crisis concerning the efficacy of the strategy of change which emerged out of the nineteenth-century debates. I refer to the strategy of achieving transformation through the acquisition of state power. The fact is that the anti-systemic movements have themselves been the product of the capitalist world-system. As a consequence, they have by their actions not merely undermined the world-system (their ostensible objective, partially achieved) but they have also sustained this same system, most particularly by taking state power and operating within an interstate system which is the political superstructure of the capitalist world-economy. And this has created inbuilt limits on the ability of these movements to mobilize effectively in the future. Thus it is that, while the world-system is in crisis, so are its anti-systemic movements, and so I may add are the analytic self-reflective structures of this system, that is, the sciences.

The crisis of the movements has its locus in their collective increasing inability to transform their growing political strength into processes that could truly transform the existing world-system. One of their present constraints, though surely not the only one, has been the ways in which their own analyses have incorporated large segments of the ideology of the existing world-system. What the historical social sciences can contribute in this crisis of transition is therefore an involvement that is simultaneously engaged with the movements and disengaged from them. If science cannot offer praxis, it can offer the insights that come from distance, provided it is not neutral. But scientists are never neutral, and hence the science they produce is never neutral. The commitment of which I am speaking is of course the commitment to substantive rationality. It is a commitment in the face of a situation where collective choice is being made possible by the decline of the historical social system in which we are living, but where the choice is made difficult by the absence of a clear-cut alternative social force standing for a wise choice.

In this situation, in purely intellectual terms, it means we have to re-think our conceptual apparatus, to rid it of the nineteenth century's ideological patina. We will have to be radically agnostic in our empirical and theoretical work, while trying to create new heuristic frameworks which will speak to the absence, not the presence, of substantive rationality.

You will forgive me if, before a congress of German sociologists, I invoke Max Weber. We all know his passionate address to the students in 1919, "Politics as a Vocation." There is a deep pessimism in that talk:

> Not summer's bloom lies ahead of us, but rather a polar night of icy darkness and hardness, no matter which group may triumph externally now. Where there is nothing, not only the Kaiser but also the proletarian has lost his rights. When this night shall have slowly receded, who of those for whom spring apparently has bloomed so luxuriously will be alive? (Gerth and Mills 1946 : 128).

We must wonder if the polar night which did indeed come as Weber predicted is yet behind us or whether still worse is to come. Whether the one or the other, the only possible conclusion we should draw is the one that Weber did draw:

Politics is a strong and slow boring of hard boards. It takes both passion and perspective. Certainly all historical experience confirms the truth—that man would not have attained the possible unless time and again he had reached out for the impossible. (Gerth and Mills 1946: 128).

I have said that our concepts can be traced to the intellectual conundra bred by the French Revolution. So can our ideals and our solutions. The famous trinity, "liberté, égalité, fraternité," is not a description of reality; it has not infused the structures of the capitalist world-economy, in France or anywhere else. This phrase was in fact not really the slogan of the so-called bourgeois revolution but rather the ideological expression of the first serious anti-systemic movement in the history of the modern world that was able to shape and inspire its successors. Liberty, equality, and fraternity is a slogan directed not against feudalism but against capitalism. They are the images of a social order different from ours, one that might one day be constructed. For this we need passion and perspective. It scarcely will be easy. It cannot be done without a fundamental reassessment of strategy on the part of the anti-systemic movements, another subject I have not been able to discuss here. (See, however, Wallerstein 1984, Part II.) But it will also not be done unless those who say that they strive to understand social reality, that is, we, the historical social scientists, will be ready to repeat, in science as in politics, Weber's final plea, "in spite of all!"

NOTES

1. The English translation is: 'the aggregate of persons living together under particular political, economic and social conditions' . . . 'the bourgeois, socialist classless society.'

2. The English translation is: 'the aggregate of persons living together under homogeneous social and economic as well as political conditions' . . . 'the development of (human) society. . . ; the new socialist, communist society; the classless society. . . ; the bourgeois capitalist society' . . . 'no plural.'

3. In the published English version we have two problems. One is the title which is rendered as *The History of the Social Movement in France, 1789–1850*. This omits from the title the fact that Stein was concerned with the *concept* of society. The passage is rendered as: 'Society is one of the most difficult concepts in political theory.' (1964, 43) This translates the untranslatable *'Staatwissenschaft'* into an imperfect equivalent, 'political theory.' It so happens that the point I am making, the *a priori* definitional link between 'society' and 'state,' comes out even more clearly in the German version.

4. The English translation is: 'theory of evolution' . . . 'economy and society.'

5. The English translation is: 'the cultural, societal, historical, political, economic, social development of our nation.'

6. The English translation is: 'theory of evolution' . . . 'the theory of the development of all living beings from lower primitive organisms.'
7. The published English-language translation once again changes the title. It becomes *Industrial Evolution*. The three stages are translated as independent economy, town economy and national economy.
8. The English translation reads: 'National economy is the product of a development extending over thousands of years, and is not older than the modern State . . .' (1901 : 88).

BIBLIOGRAPHY

Bücher, Karl. 1901. *Industrial Evolution*. New York: Henry Holt.

Bücher, Karl. 1913. *Die Entstehung der Volkswirtschaft*. Ninth edition. Tübingen: H. Laupp'schen Buchhandlung.

Gerth, H.H. and Mills, C. Wright. 1946. From *Max Weber: Essays in Sociology*. New York: Oxford University Press.

González, José Luis. 1980. *El pais de cuatro pisos*. Rio Piedras, P.R.: Ed. Huracán.

Prigogine, Ilya and Stengers, Isabelle. 1979. *La nouvelle alliance*. Paris: Gallimard. (English translation: *Order Out of Chaos*. New York: Bantam. 1984.)

Stein, Lorenz von. 1959. *Der Begriff der Gesellschaft und der soziale Geschichte der Französischen Revolution bis zum Jahre 1830*. Three volumes. Hildesheim: Georg Olma Verlagsbuchhandlung.

Wallerstein, Immanuel. 1982a. 'Economic Theories and Historical Disparities of Development,' in: *Eighth International Economic History Congress, Budapest 1982*. J. Kocka and G. Ránki, eds. B. 1: *Economic Theory and History*. Budapest: Akadémiai Kiado. 17–26.

Wallerstein, Immanuel. 1982b. 'Crisis as Transition,' in: S. Amin, G. Arrighi, A.G. Frank and I. Wallerstein, *Dynamics of Global Crisis*. New York: Monthly Review Press, 11–54 and London: Macmillan.

Wallerstein, Immanuel. 1984. *The Politics of the World-Economy*. Cambridge: Cambridge University Press.

8—World-Systems Analysis

This article was the result of an invitation to expound in a short space the distinctive theoretical premises of "world-systems analysis." I think this is the clearest piece I have written on this subject. It explains why I think of world-systems analysis as a perspective and not as a theory, and why centrally it is about what I would call in a subsequent book "unthinking" nineteenth-century social science.

W orld-systems analysis is not a theory about the social world, or about part of it. It is a protest against the ways in which social scientific inquiry was structured for all of us at its inception in the middle of the nineteenth century. This mode of inquiry has come to be a set of often unquestioned a priori assumptions. World-systems analysis maintains that this mode of social scientific inquiry, practised worldwide, has had the effect of closing off rather than opening up many of the most important or the most interesting questions. In wearing the blinkers which the nineteenth century constructed, we are unable to perform the social task we wish to perform and that the rest of the world wishes us to perform, which is to present rationally the real historical alternatives that lie before us. World-systems analysis was born as a moral, and in its broadest sense, political, protest. However, it is on the basis of scientific claims, that is, on the basis of claims related to the possibilities of systematic knowledge about social reality, that world-systems analysis challenges the prevailing mode of inquiry.

This is a debate, then, about fundamentals, and such debates are always difficult. First of all, most participants have deep commitments about fundamentals. Second, it is seldom the case that any clear, or at least any simple, empirical test can resolve or even clarify the issues. The empirical debate has to be addressed at a very complex and holistic level. Does the sum of derived theorizing starting from one or another set of premises encompass known descriptions of reality in a more "satisfactory manner?" This involves us in all sorts of secondary dilemmas. Our known "descriptions" of reality are to some extent a function of our premises: future "descriptions" may of course transform our sense of reality. Does the "theorizing" said today to encompass reality really encompass it? And last but not least, what does it mean to encompass reality "in a satisfactory manner"? Is this latter criterion anything more than an aesthetic adjunct?

Not only are debates about fundamentals frustrating for all these reasons, but each side has a built-in handicap. The defenders of existing views must "explain away" the anomalies, hence our present challenge. But the challengers must offer convincing "data" in a situation where, compared to the 150 years or so of traditional social scientific inquiry, they have had far less time to accumulate appropriately relevant "data." In a subject matter inherently recalcitrant to experimental manipulation, "data" cannot be accumulated rapidly. So a dispute about fundamentals may be thought of as analogous to a heavyweight championship bout, but without a referee and between two somewhat dyspeptic boxers, each with his left hand tied behind his back. It may be fun to watch, but is it boxing? Is it science?

And who will decide? In some sense, the spectators will decide—and probably not by watching the boxers, but by fighting it out themselves. So why bother? Because the boxers are part of the spectators, who are of course all boxers.

Lest we get lost in analogies, let me return to the discussion of fundamentals. I propose to take seven common assumptions of social scientific inquiry and indicate what it is that makes me feel uncomfortable about them. I shall then explore whether alternative (or even opposing) assumptions are not as plausible or more plausible and indicate the direction in which these alternative assumptions would lead us.

I

The social sciences are constituted of a number of "disciplines" which are intellectually-coherent groupings of subject matter distinct from each other.

These disciplines are most frequently listed as anthropology, economics, political science and sociology. There are, to be sure, potential additions to this list, such as geography. Whether history is or is not a social science is a matter of some controversy, and we shall return to this later (see section II). There is a similar debate about psychology, or at least about social psychology.

It has been a growing fashion, since at least 1945, to deplore the unnecessary barriers between the "disciplines" and to endorse the merits of "interdisciplinary" research and/or teaching. This has been argued on two counts. One is the assertion that the analysis of some "problem areas" can benefit from an approach combining the perspectives of many disciplines. It is said, for example, that if we wish to study "labour," pooling the knowledge offered by the disciplines of economics, political science and sociology might be of great advantage. The logic of such an approach leads to multidisciplinary teams, or to a single scholar "learning several disciplines," at least in so far as they relate to "labour."

The second presumed basis for "interdisciplinary" research is slightly different. As we pursue our collective inquiry it becomes clear, it is argued, that some of our subject matter is "at the borderline" of two or more disciplines. "Linguistics," for example, may be located at such a "border." The logic of such an approach may lead eventually to the development of a new "autonomous discipline," which in many ways is what has been happening to the study of linguistics during the last thirty years.

We know that there are multiple disciplines, since there are multiple academic departments in universities around the world, graduate degrees in these disciplines, and national and international associations of scholars of these disciplines. That is, we know *politically* that different disciplines exist. They have organizations with boundaries, structures, and personnel to defend their collective interests and ensure their collective reproduction. But this tells us nothing about the validity of the *intellectual* claims to separateness, claims which presumably justify the organizational networks.

The lauding of the merits of interdisciplinary work in the social sciences has so far not significantly undermined the strengths of the organizational apparatuses that shield the separate disciplines. Indeed, the contrary may be true: what has enhanced the claim of each discipline to represent a separately coherent level of analysis linked to appropriate methodologies is the constant assertion by practitioners of the various disciplines that each has something to learn from the other which it could not know by pursuing its own level of analysis with its specific methodologies, and that this "other" knowledge is pertinent and significant to the resolution of the intellectual problems on which each is working. Interdisciplinary work is in no sense an intellectual critique *per se* of the existing compartmentalization of social science, and lacks in any case the political clout to affect the existing institutional structures.

But are the various social scientific disciplines really "disciplines"? For a word so widely used, what constitutes a "discipline" is seldom discussed. There is no entry for this term in the *International Encyclopaedia of the Social Sciences* nor in the *Encyclopaedia of Philosophy* nor in the *Encyclopaedia Britannica*. We do better by going to the *Oxford English Dictionary*, which tell us that:

> Etymologically, *discipline*, as pertaining to the disciple or scholar, is antithetical to *doctrine*, the property of the doctor or teacher; hence, in the history of the words, *doctrine* is more concerned with abstract theory, and *discipline* with practice or exercise.

But having reminded us of the term's origins, the *OED* does no better for us in the actual definition than describing it as "a branch of instruction or education; a department of learning or knowledge; a science or art in its educational aspect." The emphasis here seems to be on the reproduction of knowledge (or at least its dissemination) and not on its production. But surely the concept, "discipline," cannot be unrelated to the process of producing knowledge?

The history of the social sciences is quite clear, at least in broad brush strokes. Once, there were no social sciences, or only "predecessors." Then slowly but steadily there emerged over the course of the nineteenth century a set of names, and then of departments, degrees and associations, that by 1945 (although sometimes earlier) had crystallized into the categories we use today. There were other "names" which were discarded and which presumably involved different "groupings" of "subject-matter." What is, or was, encompassed by such terms as "moral economy" or *Staatswissenschaft* is not entirely clear. This is not because their advocates were insufficiently clear-thinking but because a "discipline" in some real sense defines itself over a long run in its practice. An interrupted practice means an unfulfilled discipline. For example, the famous quadripartite subdivision of anthropology (physical anthropology, social or cultural anthropology, archaeology, and linguistics) was (and to some extent still is) a "practice" rather than a "doctrine." It then became a doctrine, taught and justified by doctors or teachers. But did the whole add up to a coherent, defensible level of analysis or mode of analysis, or just to segregated subject matter?

We know where all these divisions of subject matter came from. They derive intellectually from the dominant liberal ideology of the nineteenth century which argued that state and market, politics and economics, were analytically separate (and largely self-contained) domains, each with their particular rules ("logics"). Society was adjured to keep them separate, and scholars studied them separately. Since there seemed to be many realities that apparently were neither in the domain of the market nor in that of the state, these realities were placed in a residual grab-bag which took on as compensation the grand name of sociology. There was a sense in which sociology was thought to explain the seemingly "irrational" phenomena that economics and political science were unable to account for. Finally, since there were people beyond the realm of the civilized world—remote, and with whom it was difficult to communicate—the study of such peoples encompassed special rules and special training, which took on the somewhat polemical name of anthropology.

We know the historical origins of the fields. We know their intellectual itineraries, which have been complex and variegated, especially since 1945. And we know why they have run into "boundary" difficulties. As the real world evolved, the contact line between "primitive" and "civilized," "political" and "economic," blurred. Scholarly poaching became commonplace. The poachers kept moving the fences, without however breaking them down.

The question before us today is whether there are any criteria which can be used to assert in a relatively clear and defensible way boundaries between the four presumed disciplines of anthropology, economics, political science, and sociology. World-systems analysis responds with an unequivocal "no" to this question. All the presumed criteria—level of analysis, subject-matter, methods, theoretical assumptions—either are no longer true in practice or, if sustained, are barriers to further knowledge rather than stimuli to its creation.

Or, put another way, the differences between permissible topics, methods, theories or theorizing *within* any of the so-called "disciplines" are far greater than the differences *among* them. This means in practice that the overlap is substantial and, in terms of the historical evolution of all these fields, is increasing all the time. The time has come to cut through this intellectual morass by saying that these four disciplines are but a single one. This is not to say that all social scientists should be doing identical work. There is every need for, and likelihood of, specialization in "field of inquiry." But let us remember the one significant organizational example we have. Somewhere in the period 1945–55, two hitherto organizationally separate "disciplines," botany and zoology, merged into a single discipline and has generated many sub-fields, but none of them, as far as I know, bears the name or has the contours of botany or zoology.

The argument of world-systems analysis is straightforward. The three presumed arenas of collective human action—the economic, the political, and the social or sociocultural—are not autonomous arenas of social action. They do not have separate "logics." More importantly, the intermeshing of constraints, options, decisions, norms, and "rationalities" is such that no useful research model can isolate "factors" according to the categories of economic, political, and social, and treat only one kind of variable, implicitly holding the others constant. We are arguing that there is a single "set of rules" or a single "set of constraints" within which these various structures operate.

The case of the virtually total overlap of the presumed domains of sociology and anthropology is even stronger. By what stretch of the imagination can one assert that Elliot Liebow's *Tally Corner* and William F. Whyte's *Street-Corner Society*—both "classic" works, one written by an "anthropologist" and the other by a "sociologist"—are works in two different "disciplines"? It would not be hard, as every reader knows, to assemble a long list of such examples.

II

History is the study of, the explanation of, the particular as it really happened in the past. Social science is the statement of the universal set of rules by which human/social behavior is explained.

This is the famous distinction between idiographic and nomothetic modes of analysis, which are considered to be antithetical. The "hard" version of this antithesis is to argue that only one of the modes (which one varies according to one's views) is legitimate or interesting or even "possible." This "hard" version is what the *Methodenstreit* was about. The "soft" version sees these two modes as two ways of cutting into social reality. Though undertaken separately, differently and for dissimilar (even opposing) purposes, it would be fruitful for the world of scholarship to combine the two modes. This "soft" view is comparable to arguing the merits of "interdisciplinary" work in the social sciences. By asserting the merits of combining two approaches, the intellectual legitimacy of viewing them as two separate modes is reinforced.

The strongest arguments of the idiographic and nomothetic schools both seem plausible. The argument of the idiographic school is the ancient doctrine that "all is flux." If everything is always changing, then any generalization purporting to apply to two or more presumably comparable phenomena is never true. All that one can do is to understand emphatically a sequence of events. Conversely, the argument of the nomothetic school is that it is manifest that the real world (including the social world) is not a set of random happenings. If so, there must be rules that describe "regularities," in which case there is a domain for scientific activity.

The strongest critiques of each side about the other are also plausible. The nomothetic critique of the idiographic view is that any recounting of "past happenings" is by definition a selection from reality (as it really happened) and therefore implies criteria of selection and categories of description. These criteria and categories are based on unavowed but nonetheless real generalizations that are akin to scientific laws. The critique of the nomothetic view is that it neglects those transformational phenomena (due in part to the reflexiveness of social reality) which makes it impossible to "repeat" structural arrangements.

There are various ways of dealing with these mutual criticisms. One way is the path of "combining" history and the social sciences. The historian is said to serve the social scientist by providing the latter with wider, deeper sets of data from which to induce his law-like generalizations. The social scientist is said to serve the historian by offering him the results of research, reasonably-demonstrated generalizations that offer insight into the explication of a particular sequence of events.

The problem with this neat division of intellectual labour is that it presumes the possibility of isolating "sequences" subject to "historical" analysis and small "universes" subject to "social scientific" analysis. In practice, however, one person's sequence is another's universe, and the neutral observer is in some quandary as to how to distinguish between the two on purely logical as opposed to, say, stylistic or presentational grounds.

The problem however is deeper than that. Is there a meaningful difference between sequence and universe, between history and social science? Are they two activities or one? Synchrony is akin to a geometric dimension. One can describe it logically, but it can be drawn only falsely on paper. In geometry, a point, a line or a plane can be drawn only in three (or four) dimensions. So is it in "social science." Synchrony is a conceptual limit, not a socially usable category. All description has time, and the only question is how wide a band is immediately relevant. Similarly, unique sequence is only describable in non-unique categories. All conceptual language presumes comparisons among universes. Just as we cannot literally "draw" a point, so we cannot literally "describe" a unique "event." The drawing, the description, has thickness or complex generalization.

Since this is an inextricable logical dilemma, the solution must be sought on heuristic grounds. World-systems analysis offers the heuristic value of the *via media* between trans-historical generalizations and particularistic narrations. It argues that, as our format tends toward either extreme, it tends toward an exposition of minimal interest and minimal utility. It argues that the optimal method is to pursue analysis within systemic frameworks, long enough in time and large enough in space to contain governing "logics" which "determine" the largest part of sequential reality, while simultaneously recognizing and taking into account that these systemic frameworks have beginnings and ends and are therefore not to be conceived of as "eternal" phenomena. This implies, then, that at every instant we look both for the framework (the "cyclical rhythms" of the system), which we describe conceptually, and for the patterns of internal transformation (the "secular trends" of the system) that will eventually bring about the demise of the system, which we describe sequentially. This implies that the task is singular. There is neither historian nor social scientist, but only a historical social scientist who analyses the general laws of particular systems and the particular sequences through which these systems have gone (the grammatical tense here deliberately not being the so-called ethnographic present). We are then faced with the issue of determining the "unit of analysis" within which we must work, which brings us to our third premise.

III

Human beings are organized in entities we may call societies, which constitute the fundamental social frameworks within which human life is lived.

No concept is more pervasive in modern social science than society, and no concept is used more automatically and unreflectively than society, despite the countless pages devoted to its definition. The textbook definitions revolve around the question: "What is a society?" whereas the arguments we have just made about the unity of historical social science lead us to ask a different question: "When and where is a society?"

"Societies" are concrete. Furthermore, society is a term which we might do well to discard because of its conceptual history and hence its virtually ineradicable and profoundly misleading connotations. Society is a term whose current usage in history and the social sciences is coeval with the institutional emergence of modern social science in the nineteenth century. Society is one half of an antithetic tandem in which the other is the state. The French Revolution was a cultural watershed in the ideological history of the modern world-system in that it led to the widespread acceptance of the idea that social change rather than social stasis is normal, both in the normative and in the statistical sense of the word. It thereby posed the intellectual problem of how to regulate, speed up, slow down, or otherwise affect this normal process of change and evolution.

The emergence of social science as an institutionalized social activity was one of the major systemic responses to this intellectual problem. Social science has come to represent the rationalist ideology that if one understands the process (whether idiographically or, more commonly, nomothetically) one can affect it in some morally positive manner. (Even "conservatives," dedicated to containing change, could broadly assent to this approach.)

The political implications of such an enterprise escaped (and escapes) no one. But it is also why in the nineteenth century the concept "society" was opposed to that of "state." The multiple sovereign states that had been and were being constituted were the obvious focuses of political activity. They seemed the locus of effective social control, and therefore the arena in which social change could be affected and effected. The standard nineteenth-century approach to the intellectual-political issue was concerned with the question of how to "reconcile" society and state. In this formulation, the state could be observed and analysed directly. It operated through formal institutions by way of known (constitutional) rules. The "society" was taken to mean that tissue of manners and customs that held a group of people together without, despite or against formal rules. In some sense "society" represented something more enduring and "deeper" than the state, less manipulable and certainly more elusive.

There has ever since been enormous debate about how society and state related to each other, which one was or should be subordinate to the other, and which incarnated the higher moral values. In the process we have become accustomed to thinking that the boundaries of a society and of a state are synonymous, or if not should (and eventually would) be made so. Thus, without explicitly asserting this theoretically, historians and social scientists have come to see current sovereign states (projected hypothetically backward in time) as the basic social entities within which social life is conducted. There was some sporadic resistance to this view on the part of anthropologists, but they resisted in the name of a putative earlier political-cultural entity whose importance remained primary, many of them asserted, for large segments of the world's population.

Thus, by the back door, and unanalysed, a whole historiography and a whole theory of the modern world crept in as the substratum of both history and social science. We live in states. There is a society underlying each state. States have histories and therefore traditions. Above all, since change is normal, it is states that normally change or develop. They change their mode of production; they urbanize; they have social problems; they prosper or decline. They have the boundaries, inside of which factors are "internal" and outside of which they are "external." They are "logically" independent entities such that, for statistical purposes, they can be "compared."

This image of social reality was not a fantasy, and so it was possible for both idiographic and nomothetic theorists to proceed with reasonable aplomb using these assumptions about society and state, and to come up with some plausible findings. The only problem was that, as time went on, more and more "anomalies" seemed to be unexplained within this framework, and more and more lacunae (of uninvestigated zones of human activity) seemed to emerge.

World-systems analysis makes the unit of analysis a subject of debate. Where and when do the entities within which social life occurs exist? It substitutes for the term "society" the term "historical system." Of course, this is a mere semantic substitution. But it rids us of the central connotation that "society" has acquired—its link to "state"—and therefore of the presupposition about the "where" and "when." Furthermore, "historical system" as a term underlines the unity of historical social science. The entity is simultaneously systemic and historical.

Having opened up the question of the unit of analysis, there is no simple answer. I myself have put forth the tentative hypothesis that there have been three known forms or varieties of historical systems, which I have called mini-systems, world-empires and world-economies. I have also suggested that it is not unthinkable that we could identify other forms or varieties.

I have argued two things about the varieties of historical systems: one concerns the link of "logic" and form; the other concerns the history of coexistence of forms. In terms of forms, I have taken as the defining boundaries of a historical system those within which the system and the people within it are regularly reproduced by means of some kind of on-going division of labour. I argue that empirically there have been three such modes. The "mini-systems," so-called because they are small in space and probably relatively brief in time (a life-span of about six generations), are highly homogeneous in terms of cultural and governing structures. The basic logic is one of "reciprocity" in exchanges. The "world empires" are vast political structures (at least at the apex of the process of expansion and contraction which seems to be their fate) and encompass a wide variety of "cultural" patterns. The basic logic of the system is the extraction of tribute from otherwise locally self-administered direct producers (mostly rural) that is passed upward to the centre and redistributed to a thin but crucial network of officials. The "world economies" are vast uneven chains of integrated production structures dissected by multiple political structures. The basic logic is that the accumulated surplus is distributed unequally in favour of those able to achieve various kinds of temporary monopolies in the market networks. This is a "capitalist" logic.

The history of coexistence of forms can be construed as follows. In the pre-agricultural era, there were a multiplicity of mini-systems whose constant death may have been largely a function of ecological mishaps plus the splitting of groups grown too large. Our knowledge is very limited. There was no writing and we are confined to archaeological reconstructions. In the period between, say, 8000 BC and 1500 AD, there coexisted on the earth at any one time multiple historical systems of all three varieties. The world empire was the "strong" form of that era, since whenever one expanded it destroyed and/or absorbed both mini-systems and world-economies and whenever one contracted it opened up space for the re-creation of mini-systems and world economies. Most of what we call the "history" of this period is the history of such world-empires, which is understandable, since they bred the cultural scribes to record what was going on. World economies were a "weak" form, individual ones never surviving long. This is because they either disintegrated or were absorbed by or transformed into a world empire (by the internal expansion of a single political unit).

Around 1500, one such world economy managed to escape this fate. For reasons that need to be explained, the "modern world-system" was born out of the consolidation of a world economy. Hence it had time to achieve its full development as a capitalist system. By *its* inner logic, this capitalist world economy then expanded to cover the entire globe, absorbing in the process all existing mini-systems and world empires. Hence by the late nineteenth century, for the first time ever, there existed only one historical system on the globe. We are still in that situation today.

I have sketched my hypotheses about the forms and the history of co-existence of historical systems. They do not constitute world-systems analysis. They are a set of hypotheses within world-systems analysis, open to debate, refinement, rejection. The crucial issue is that defining and explicating the units of analysis — the historical systems — becomes a central object of the scientific enterprise.

Within the discussion I have just related there lies hidden a further debate about the modern world and its defining characteristics. This is a

debate in which the two main versions of nineteenth-century thought—
classical liberalism and classical Marxism—share certain crucial premises about the nature of capitalism.

I V

Capitalism is a system based on competition between free producers using free
labour with free commodities, "free" meaning its availability for sale and purchase on a market.

Constraints on such freedoms, wherever they exist, are leftovers from an
incomplete evolutionary process and mean, to the extent that they exist,
that a zone or an enterprise is "less capitalist" than if there were no such
constraints. This is essentially the view of Adam Smith. Smith thought of
the capitalist system as the only system consonant with "human nature,"
and saw alternative systems as the imposition of unnatural and undesirable constraints on social existence. But this too was essentially the view
of Karl Marx. In characterizing the system, Marx placed particular emphasis on the importance of free labor. He did not regard the capitalist
system as eternally natural, and he did not consider it desirable. But he
did regard it as a normal stage of humanity's historical development.

Most liberals and Marxists of the last 150 years have regarded this
picture of "competitive capitalism" as an accurate description of the
capitalist norm, and have therefore discussed all historical situations that
involved non-free labour/producers/commodities as deviations from this
norm and thus as phenomena to be explained. The norm has largely reflected an idealized portrait of what was thought to be the quintessential
exemplar of the normal—England after the "Industrial Revolution,"
where proletarian workers (essentially landless, toolless urban workers)
laboured in factories owned by bourgeois entrepreneurs (essentially private owners of the capital stock of these factories). The owner purchased
the labour-power of (paid wages to) the workers—primarily adult
males—who had no real alternative, in terms of survival, than to seek
wage-work. No one has ever pretended that all work situations were of
this model. But both liberals and Marxists have tended to regard any
situation that varied from this model as less capitalist to the extent that it
varied.

If each work situation could be classified on a degree-of-capitalism scale, as it were, then each state, as the locus of such work situations, can be designated as falling somewhere on that scale. The economic structure of a state, then, can be seen as "more" or "less" capitalist, and the state structure itself can be viewed as reasonably congruent with the degree of capitalism in the economy, or as inconsistent with it—in which case we might expect it somehow to change over time in the direction of greater congruence.

What is to be made of work situations that are less than fully capitalist under this definition? They can be seen as reflecting a not-yet-capitalist situation in a state that will eventually see capitalist structures become dominant. Or they can be seen as anomalous continuances from the past in a state where capitalist structures are dominant.

How the "dominance" of a particular way of structuring the work units within a spatial entity (the state) can be determined has never been entirely clear. In a famous U.S. Supreme Court decision, Justice William Brennan wrote of the definition of pornography: "I know it when I see it." In a sense, both liberals and Marxists have defined dominance of capitalism in a similar fashion: they knew it when they saw it. Obviously, there is implicitly a quantitative criterion in this approach. But insofar as there is such a counting of heads, it is crucial to know what heads are being counted. And thereby hangs a tale.

A distinction was made between productive and unproductive labour. Although the exact definitions of the physiocrats, Saint-Simon and Marx were quite different, they all wished to define certain kinds of "economic activity" as non-work, that is, as non-productive. This has created an enormous and very useful loophole in the definition of capitalism. If among the various kinds of activity eliminated as non-productive fall a significant number which do not meet the model of a capitalist work-situation—the most obvious, but certainly not the only example, is housework—then it becomes far easier to argue that the "majority" of work situations in some countries are of the kinds described in the model, and thus we really do have some "capitalist" countries in terms of the definition. All this manipulation is scarcely necessary were the deduced "norm" in fact the statistical norm. But it was not, and is not. The situation of free labourers working for wages in the enterprises of free producers is a minority situation in the modern world. This is certainly true if our unit of analysis is the world economy. It is probably true, or largely true, even if we undertake the analysis within the framework of single high-industrialized states in the twentieth century.

When a deduced "norm" turns out not to be the statistical norm, that is, when the situation abounds with exceptions (anomalies, residues), then we ought to wonder whether the definition of the norm serves any useful function. World-systems analysis argues that the capitalist world-economy is a particular historical system. Therefore if we want to ascertain the norms, that is, the mode of functioning of this concrete system, the optimal way is to look at the historical evolution of this system. If we find, as we do, that the system seems to contain wide areas of wage and non-wage labour, wide areas of commodified and non-commodified goods, and wide areas of alienable and non-alienable forms of property and capital, then we should at the very least wonder whether this "combination" or mixture of the so-called free and the non-free is not itself the defining feature of capitalism as a historical system.

Once the question is opened up, there are no simple answers. We discover that the proportions of the mixes are uneven, spatially and temporally. We may then search for structures that maintain the stability of any particular mix of mixes (the cyclical trends again) as well as for underlying pressures that may be transforming, over time, the mix of mixes (the secular trends). The anomalies now become not exceptions to be explained away but patterns to be analysed, so inverting the psychology of the scientific effort. We must conclude that the definition of capitalism that dominated the nineteenth-century thought of both liberals and Marxists accounts for the central historiographical insight that has been bequeathed to us.

V

The end of the eighteenth and the beginning of the nineteenth century represent a crucial turning-point in the history of the world, in that the capitalists finally achieved state-societal power in the key states.

The two great "events" that occurred in this period, the Industrial Revolution in England and the French Revolution, were, it is argued, crucial in the development of social scientific theory. A simple bibliographical check will verify that a remarkably large proportion of world history has been devoted to these two "events." Furthermore, an even larger proportion has been devoted to analysing other "situations" in terms of how they measure up to these two "events."

The link between the historical centrality accorded these two "events" and the prevailing definition of capitalism is not difficult to elucidate. We have already pointed out that the concept of degrees of capitalism leads necessarily to an implicit exercise in quantification so that we can ascertain when capitalism becomes "dominant." This theory assumed that a mismatch between "economic" dominance and state-societal power is possible, and that it can be overcome.

The Industrial Revolution and the French Revolution are of interest because they presumably represent the overcoming of a mismatch. The French Revolution highlights the political arena. According to the now strongly-challenged but long predominant "social interpretation," the French Revolution was the moment when the bourgeoisie ousted the feudal aristocracy from state power and thereby transformed the pre-capitalist *ancien régime* into a capitalist state. The Industrial Revolution highlights the fruits of such a transformation. Once the capitalists achieve state power (or in Smithian terms reduce the interference of the state) then it is possible to expand significantly the triumphal possibilities of a capitalist system.

Given these assumptions, it is possible to treat both these phenomena as "events" and to concentrate on the details of what happened and why they happened in that particular way. Books on the Industrial Revolution typically debate which factor (or factors) was more important to its occurrence, what its precise dating was and which of the various features encompassed by the term was the most consequential for future transformations. Books on the French Revolution typically debate when it started and ended, what factor or factors triggered it, which groups were involved in key processes and how and when there were alterations in the cast of characters, and what legacy the revolution left.

Of course such a close and ultimately idiographic scrutiny of these "events" inevitably breeds scepticism. Increasingly there are voices doubting how revolutionary the revolutions were. Nonetheless, virtually all these analyses (of both believers and sceptics) presume the analytical frame of reference that led to these two "events" being singled out in the first place: the assumption that capitalism (or its surrogate, individual freedom) had in some sense to "triumph" at some point within particular states.

Furthermore, lest one think that history is central only to historians, we should notice how it immediately became central to the analytical exercises of social scientists. The idea of *the* "Industrial Revolution" has been transformed into the process of *an* "industrial revolution" or of "industrialization" and bred a whole family of sub-categories and therefore of sub-issues: the idea of a "take-off," the notions of both "pre-industrial" and "post-industrial" societies, and so on. The idea of the "bourgeois revolution" has become the analysis of when and how a "bourgeois revolution" (or the middle classes in power) could or would occur. I do not suggest that these debates are not about the real world. Clearly, twentieth-century Brazil can be discussed in terms of industrialization, or of the role of the national bourgeoisie, or of the relation of the middle classes to the military. But once again, key assumptions are being made which should be examined.

What world-systems analysis calls for is an evaluation of the centrality of these purportedly key "events" in terms of the long *durée* of the historical system within which they occurred. If the unit of analysis of the modern world-system is the capitalist world-economy (and this remains an "if"), then we will need to ask whether the received categorical distinctions—agriculture and industry, landowner and industrialist—do or do not represent a *leitmotiv* around which the historical development centered. We can only be in a post-industrial phase if there was an industrial phase. There can only be disjunctures of the tenants of state power and economic power if we are dealing with analytically-separable groups. All these categories are now so deep in our subconscious that we can scarcely talk about the world without using them. World-systems analysis argues that the categories that inform our history were historically formed (and for the most part only a century or so ago). It is time that they were re-opened for examination.

Of course, this prevailing history is itself informed by the dominant metaphysics of the modern world. The triumph of this modern metaphysics required a long struggle. But triumph it did, in the Enlightenment, which brings us to the sixth premise.

V I

Human history is progressive, and inevitably so.

To be sure, the idea of progress has had its detractors, but they have for two centuries been in a distinct minority. I do *not* count in this minority all those who have criticized the *naive* view of progress and have concentrated their efforts on explaining the so-called irrational. These people have been making rational the irrational. Nor do I include the growing number of disabused believers who embrace a sort of hopelessness or despair about progress. They are rather like lapsed Catholics in a Graham Greene novel, always searching for the faith they once had.

The true conservatives, the ones who do not believe that systematic change or improvement in the world is a desirable or fruitful collective activity, are actually quite rare in the modern world. But notice once again how the dominant assumptions have circumscribed the sceptics and the opponents. To the notion that progress is inevitable, the only response seems to have been despair: despair because the thesis is incorrect, or despair because it is correct.

World-systems analysis wants to remove the idea of progress from the status of a trajectory and open it up as an analytical variable. There may be better and there may be worse historical systems (and we can debate the criteria by which to judge). It is not at all certain that there has been a linear trend — upward, downward or straightforward. Perhaps the trend line is uneven, or perhaps indeterminate. Were this conceded to be possible, a whole new arena of intellectual analysis is immediately opened up. If the world has had multiple instances of, and types of, historical systems, and if all historical systems have beginnings and ends, then we will want to know something about the process by which there occurs a succession (in time-space) of historical systems.

This has typically been discussed as the problem of "transitions," but transitions have been analysed within the framework of linear transformations. We detail the process of the transformation toward some inevitable end-point which we presume to be, to have been, the only real historical alternative. But suppose the construction of new historical systems is a stochastic process. Then we have a totally new arena of intellectual activity before us.

The debate of "free will" versus "determinism" is a hoary one. But it has been traditionally pursued as an either-or proposition. What the re-opening of the issue of transition does—transitions as really occurring, transitions as moving toward uncertain outcomes— is to suggest a differ-ent formulation of this debate. Perhaps it is the case that what we call "determinism" is largely the process internal to historical systems in which the "logic" of the system is translated into a set of self-moving, self-reinforcing institutional structures that "determine" the long-term trajectory. But perhaps it is also the case that what we call "free will" oc-curs largely in the process of "transition" when, precisely because of the breakdown of these very structures, the real historical choices are wide and difficult to predict.

This would then turn our collective attention to the study of precisely how these stochastic process work. Perhaps they will turn out not to be stochastic at all but have an inner hidden key, or perhaps the inner key is some process that keeps these processes stochastic (that is, not really subject to human manipulation). Or perhaps, least acceptable to the present inhabitants of the globe no doubt, God plays dice. We shall not know unless we look. We may of course not know even then. But how do we look? This brings us to the last and deepest of the assumptions, the assumptions concerning the nature of science.

VII

Science is the search for the rules which summarize most succinctly why every-thing is the way it is and how things happen.

Modern science is not a child of the nineteenth century. It goes back at least to the sixteenth, perhaps to the thirteenth, century. It has come down strongly on the determinist side of the equation, on the side of lin-earity and concision. Scientists have brought more and more domains of the universe under their aegis, the world of man being no doubt the last such domain. It was in the name of this tradition that nomothetic social science asserted itself.

The methodology that nomothetic social science adopted emulated the basic principles of its socially successful predecessor, the natural sci-ences: systematic and precise empirical inquiry, then induction leading to theories. The more elegant the theory, the more advanced the science.

Practical applications would of course follow. Nomothetic social science has been haunted by its inadequacies—in a comparison with physics—but sustained by its certainty that science was cumulative and unilinear.

In our doubts concerning the previous assumptions there has been implicit—it should now be clear—another view of science. If we reject the utility of the nomothetic–idiographic distinction, then we are casting doubt on the usefulness of the Newtonian view of science. We do not do this, as the idiographers did, on the basis of the peculiarity of social inquiry (humans as reflexive actors). We doubt its utility for the natural sciences as well (and indeed there has emerged in the last two decades a thrust toward a non-linear natural science, wherein stochastic processes are central).

Specifically, in terms of what we have been calling historical social science, we raise the question of whether the method of going from the concrete to the abstract, from the particular to the universal, should not be inverted. Perhaps historical social science must *start* with the abstract and move in the direction of the concrete, ending with a coherent interpretation of the processes of particular historical systems that accounts plausibly for how they followed a particular concrete historical path. The determinate is not the simple but the complex, indeed the hyper-complex. And of course no concrete situation is more complex than the long moments of transition when the simpler constraints collapse.

History and social science took their current dominant forms at the moment of fullest unchallenged triumph of the logic of our present historical system. They are children of that logic. We are now however living in the long moment of transition wherein the contradictions of that system have made it impossible to continue to adjust its machinery. We are living in a period of real historical choice. And this period is incomprehensible on the basis of the assumptions of that system.

World-systems analysis is a call for the construction of a historical social science that feels comfortable with the uncertainties of transition, that contributes to the transformation of the world by illuminating the choices without appealing to the crutch of a belief in the inevitable triumph of good. World-systems analysis is a call to open the shutters that prevent us from exploring many arenas of the real world. World-systems analysis is not a paradigm of historical social science. It is a call for a debate about the paradigm.

9—Hold the Tiller Firm: On Method and the Unit of Analysis

I had long taken the position that world-systems analysis had carved out for itself a narrow epistemological space between the idiographic and the nomothetic pretensions. This article was the result of the virtually inevitable fact that even those who try to go down this path slip readily into one or the other temptation. This article is a call for intellectual carefulness in negotiating difficult terrain.

Historical/social analysis is like sailing a boat in rough waters. The dangers come from all sides. It requires not merely good judgment, but the ability and the will to hold the tiller firm. When I first started writing *The Modern World-System* in 1970, I thought the issue was primarily substantive, that is, that I was entering into a debate about what is the most useful interpretation of what happened historically. World-systems analysis was for me a set of protests against prevailing modes of interpretation, at first primarily against modernization theory (see Wallerstein, 1979). But I soon came to see that, in order to arrive at a useful interpretation of what happened historically, one had to dispose of a useful method. And that has turned out to be not merely an even more controversial matter than the question of the substantive interpretation of historical reality, but a more slippery one as well.

In my venture into worrying about method, I decided that one key issue was the "unit of analysis," which is why one speaks of "world-systems analysis." The assumption is that the appropriate unit of analysis is a world-system, by which I at least originally meant something other than the modern nation-state, something larger than this nation-state, and something that was defined by the boundaries of an effective, ongoing division of labor. Hence I started with spatial or geographic concerns. The basic metaphor of core/periphery is in origin and etymology a spatial metaphor.

But as I proceeded, it seemed to me that space could never be sepa-

149

rated analytically from time, and that the unit of which we were talking was therefore one kind of TimeSpace (see Wallerstein, 1991), specifically that which I denoted as structural TimeSpace. To give it a language of easy reference, I thought of structural TimeSpace as divided into "historical systems." I liked the term because it caught what I thought of as the essential tension of structural TimeSpace, that it is a system (meaning it has continuing rules of relation/process, and therefore contains cyclical rhythms) but that it is also historical (meaning that it is different at every moment, and therefore contains secular trends). By combining in one concept both cyclical rhythms and secular trends, I was clearly using an organic analogy. An historical system has a life: it is born or generated, it lives or proceeds, it dies or disintegrates. Each of these three moments of the organism can be analyzed and located in TimeSpace.

From its institutional outset, what came to be called in the nineteenth century the "social sciences" was beset by a *Methodenstreit*. The classical formation of this methodological debate was posed in terms of two alternative epistemologies. On the one hand, there were those who believed that the object of research was the discerning of general laws of human behavior, true of all time and space. Their avowed model was to imitate the methods of classical physics to the degree possible and thereby replicate its scientific (and social) success. Windelband called this the nomothetic method, and its proponents became dominant in the emerging university "disciplines" of economics, sociology, and political science. On the other hand, there were those who believed that the search for general laws was not merely futile but dangerous, in that it pushed scholars away from what this group saw as their primary task: ascertaining empirical reality, which was always particular, indeed idiosyncratic. What really happened, in the famous phrase of Ranke, could indeed be discerned and, once discerned, empathetically reconstructed. This was called the idiographic method, and its proponents became dominant in history and for the most part in anthropology.

This difference between nomothetic and idiographic, between synchronic and diachronic, between objective and subjective, between structure and agency, has been renewed and rediscussed under many labels and in many avatars. While the organizational linkages of epistemology and specific disciplines largely reflected university realities between, say, 1880 and 1945, it has tended to break down since then, particularly since the 1970s. That is to say, the debate is still there, but the persons on each side are not so easily recognizable by the name of the university department in which they teach.

Of course, this debate was seldom crude. From its subtleties emerged not two but a thousand positions. Nonetheless, the cleavage was profound. Furthermore, there were always schools of thought which specifically refused the terms of the debate, and suggested either that the dilemma was false, or that the correct position was an intermediate one or one proceeding from an *Aufhebung*. This group was always a numerical minority, if a vocal one. I count myself among them, and I have called this conducting a "war on two fronts" (Wallerstein, 1980).

In the period since 1945, there have been a growing number of scholars who became unhappy with Establishment social science (including of course history) on the grounds that its methodological imperatives (whether they were nomothetists or idiographers) had pushed them de facto into the study of the infinitely small in time and space, and that thereby the problems, the realities of large-scale, long-term social change had become eliminated from the purview of scholarship. There was a call for intellectual renewal, and for new (actually revived) foci of analysis. This call had many names: dependency theory, civilizational analysis, world history, world-systems analysis, historical sociology, long-run economics, international political economy, and still others. The list is long. Let me call this the family of dissidents, in the sense that they all were dissenting from the views that had dominated, still largely dominate, the universities.

The seas are rough in two senses. Historical/social reality is enormously complex. Indeed, it represents the most complex of all realities. And we know so little still. But the seas are rough in another sense. The study of historical/social reality is a highly sensitive subject, which has immense consequences for the existing structures of power in our existing world-system. Hence, the analyses are closely surveyed, pressured, and kept in check. The Establishment views are not only wrong; they are powerfully protected by extra-intellectual means. If we are to proceed in such rough seas, we must hold the tiller firm, and in particular we must not fall prey to the temptations of the world, which are primarily three: to become nomothetic, to become idiographic, to reify. I see very many persons in the family of dissidents paying, in my view, insufficient attention to these dangers. I shall discuss each in turn.

THE NOMOTHETIC TEMPTATION

Since all explanation is ultimately in terms of a covering law, however implicit and even if specifically denied, it is tempting to wish to make the covering laws we use as general and as simple as possible. But, of course, there is a price to be paid for generalizing our laws. The more general, the more different things they explain, but the fewer aspects they explain about each thing. It depends on what we want to have explained. For most things, if we use too general a law, the explanation is vacuous, and if we use too narrow a generalization, the explanation is specious. So there is a pragmatic judgment to be made, in terms of payoff. We need to do constant, if not always explicit, cost-benefit analyses.

In world-systems analysis, Christopher Chase-Dunn and others have put to themselves a very simple, obvious proposition. If our unit of analysis is a world-system, and if there are several kinds of world-systems (not an enormous number, but more than one), would it not be useful to compare the three or four or five kinds of world-systems with each other, to discern their similarities and differences, and therefore to arrive at more general explanations of the functioning of world-systems? This is a nomothetic temptation. Chase-Dunn has put his case this way:

> The world-systems perspective has expanded the temporal and spatial scope of theorizing about social change. Our understanding of modernity has been radically transformed by the study of the Europe-centered world-system over the past 500 years. But the analysis of a single system encounters methodological and theoretical limitations. If we would fathom fundamental change we need to comprehend the causes of those structural constants which are usually taken for granted in the modern world-system. These structural "constants" exhibit variation when we broaden the scope of comparison to include very different kinds of world-systems. Are interstate systems of core/periphery hierarchies inevitable features of all organizational wholes? Do all world-systems share a similar underlying developmental logic, or do systemic logics undergo fundamental transformations? These questions can only be scientifically addressed by a comparative perspective which employs the corpus of evidence produced by historians, ethnographers, and archaeologists regarding human activities over very long periods of time much longer than the five hundred year span of the modern world-system (Chase-Dunn, 1992:313).

Hence, Chase-Dunn is ready to compare the "world-system" of Cahokia within the middle Mississippian tradition with Mesopotamia and with the modern capitalist world-system. To do this, he adds that "concepts developed for the analysis of the modern system be applied with care; some of them need to be redefined in order to avoid projecting contemporary reality on the past."

This may work, but I remain skeptical. One of the major reasons I remain skeptical is that I wonder if one can take a set of concepts developed for the analysis of one historical system, consider the concepts one by one, redefine each in some more general form (of which consequently the form in the modern world-system becomes but one variant), and then recombine them for the analysis of Cahokia or Mesopotamia. This presumes a certain independence of the concepts from each other which, it seems to me, is doubtful. To be specific, the concept "core/periphery" is not analytically dissociable from the concept "class conflict" or the concept "interstate system" or the concept "endless accumulation of capital." That is to say, the set of concepts developed for a fruitful analysis of the modern world-system is a set. Dissociated, redefined (in the sense of giving different values to each), and reassembled, they may have the coherence of an awkwardly patched pottery bowl.

There are no doubt similarities one can find between Cahokia, as an example of a stateless, classless (?) structure; Mesopotamia, as an example of a world-empire (if that is what it was); and the modern world-system, as an example of a capitalist world-economy. But are these similarities and therefore the differences analytically interesting for problems we wish to solve? There might be some, but looking at these problems does not seem to be the line the "comparative study of world-systems" has been following. The work up to now has emphasized the comparison of the rules governing the system, which I would call looking at the ongoing lives of the systems. Here I think we are comparing apples and oranges, and I don't think we'll get much further than saying they're both fruit and not vegetables.

What might possibly be a fruitful line of enquiry is to compare both the geneses and the terminal crises of systems, to see if there are any patterns, which could then (a) give us some insight into "world history," if by that we mean the synchronic unfolding of human social existence, and (b) illuminate how system bifurcations (vide Prigogine) work in historical systems, which in turn might help us with (c) the practical question of how best to navigate the current bifurcation (or systemic demise, or transformation from one historical system to one or more other such systems).

I have said that where we draw the line in our work in this nomothetic/idiographic divide (or intrinsic tension) is a pragmatic matter, and I have suggested reasons to believe that the "comparative study of world-systems" is not where I would place my bets in terms of useful interpretations. But of course I may be wrong. I would feel more comfortable about this line of work if its practitioners were more cautious about the nomothetic temptation.

THE IDIOGRAPHIC TEMPTATION

In the same article sited above, Chase-Dunn criticizes two extremes on a continuum, what he calls the "lumpers" and the "splitters." "The extreme lumpers are those who see only one global system far back in time. . . . Extreme splitters are those who focus only on local processes to the exclusion of more distant connections" (1992:317). He comes out sensibly for an in-between position. But the way he puts it, the story is not quite clear. One of his extremes is temporal (too much time), and the other is spatial (too local). Of course, both are in reality spatio-temporal. Most important of all, the two "extremes" are in fact only one: they are both forms of the idiographic temptation. To say that everything is one single thing, or to say that every "unit" is local, that is, different from all the other units, are both ways to avoid structural explanation. In one case, there can be no variation and therefore no alternative structures; in the other, there is nothing but variation, and no two things can be lumped together as structures.

We readily recognize in localism a familiar particularizing face, the standard undergirding of idiographic analysis. Presumably, the dissidents of whom I spoke above have all been allergic to such self-defeating localism. But one big single story is just another form of the idiographic temptation, and this is the route Andre Gunder Frank has chosen to take in his recent writings about "world system history":

I now also stress and examine "systemic connections in a single historical process" extending back much earlier than 1500. I now examine these systemic connections in a single historical process over a much wider social and geographical range, including at least the entire Afro-Eurasian ecumene, of which Europe and its world is only a part. Thus the historical and socio-graphical scope of this process is no longer seen as beginning and centered in Europe, which, on the contrary, joined it rather late. I will also question the supposed historical uniqueness and perhaps the social-theoretical relevance of the modern capitalist mode of production (Frank, 1990:164).

This is not the place to review Frank's version of the evolution of world history. Here we are only raising methodological doubts. Everything that can be denoted as a system can be shown to be "open" at some points of its perimeter. One can always take this opening and insist that the presumed system is really part of some larger system. It will not take long to arrive at the largest of all possible systems, the universe from the beginning of its existence to now. Whether even this supersystem is open is itself a matter of philosophical and scientific debate. And in this sense everything is determined by the big bang, if there was a big bang. But while it is salutary to remember this, it is not very useful to build our analysis on this quicksand, which will very rapidly engulf us. Once again, the question is pragmatic.

Frank says the story does not start in A.D. 1500, but rather in 3000 B.C. (or so). Perhaps, but by what logic do we stop at 3000 B.C.? Why not 10,000 B.C.? Why not go back to Australopithecus, or to prehominids? Once again, it depends on what question we want to answer. And that depends on your chronosophy (Pomian, 1979). If you think the history of the world has been a linear upward curve, then it is very important to pursue Frank's line of argument. It is explicitly aimed at undermining a Eurocentric reading of world progress. Basically, it says that the Europeans, whether circa 1800 or circa 1500, did nothing special. They were a part, a "rather late" part, of the story of humanity's achievements. This is the salutary message Frank bears. And I sympathize with it, except that I do not think that the history of the world has been a linear upward curve. I think, to put it crudely, that the curve essentially went up with the so-called agricultural revolution (despite its social negatives), then essentially went down with the arrival of a capitalist world-system (despite some pluses which have been much exaggerated), and may go up again (but then again may not) with the future demise of the world capitalist system. If this chronosophy is adopted, then it positively impedes clarity of vision to efface the 1500 line. Rather we must exert much more energy than we have up to now on the question of genesis—what it was about the situation of the Europeans that accounts for their taking this major, backward step (see Wallerstein, 1992). And we need to spend much time as well on the question of bifurcation, demise and/or transition, which may require a comparative look (along the lines I suggested in my discussion of Chase-Dunn).

It is always easy, as I said, to find generalizations that are plausible (if often not very interesting). It is always possible to insist that every particular situation is different from every other in some way, and that therefore all the generalizations are false. And it is always easy to prove continuity of a single reality, in that there are always some things which do not seem to have changed. In any case, there are no caesuras in history that are vacuums, or unbridgeable chasms. The world goes on, microsecond by microsecond. The hard thing is to find the appropriate balance, and to be certain that it is the most relevant balance for the question you wish to answer.

THE TEMPTATION TO REIFY

Analysts do not manipulate data, though many of them like to think that is what they are doing. Rather, analysts manipulate concepts. Concepts become our friends, even our children. They take on a certain life of their own, and it is tempting to stretch their usage beyond the purpose for which they were created. This is what reification is about. In the context of the study of long-term, large-scale social change, one of the concepts most frequently and lovingly employed is that of civilization. Indeed, most of us have a fairly standard list in mind when we use the word: the West (or Christianity), perhaps Russia (or maybe the whole Orthodox world), Islam (or the Arab-Islamic world), Persia, India, China, perhaps Japan and Korea separate from the Sinic world, and then the ones no longer surviving: Byzantium, Mesopotamia, the Incas, Pharaonic Egypt, classical Antiquity (or are Rome and Greece separate?), and so forth. Are there African civilizations, or one African civilization? The list is of course open to amendment, but that is beside the point. It is a some-what limited list, usually 20 or 30 examples at most.

What is a "civilization"? It is hard to say because different analysts use different criteria. For most analysts, it usually involves a linguistic element, a religious (or cosmological) element, a distinctive pattern of "everyday life," a spatial locus (however blurred or shifting) and there-fore perhaps an ecological element, and perhaps, least convincingly, continuous ethnicity and some genetic coherence. This list too could go on. If one looks at the names listed above, the one that appears to have the longest continuous history is, by common accord, China. We talk of a Chinese civilization that presumably goes back to the earliest dynasty and continues to today. What continuity does this imply? We can of course find continuities—not perhaps the same exact language, but mostly (*sic*!) related ones; not the same religion(s), but some links be-tween older forms and later ones; not the same patterns of everyday life, but some long-lasting peculiarities; more or less the same geography, provided one is not too fussy about the breadth of the boundaries; a lim-ited case for ethnic and genetic descendence.

As with the case for a single world history, one can make a case for a single Chinese history at about the same level of plausibility, or perhaps at a stronger level. And certainly we can make the case that many/most Chinese today (Chinese thinkers, Chinese politicians) believe in this continuity and act in function of this belief. Suppose, however, that someone were to postulate that China since 1945 or since 1850 is closer overall on a multitude of measures of social relations to Brazil since 1945/1859 than it is to the "China" of the Han dynasty. We could not reject the case out of hand.

Of course, one can avoid the decision by a common sense dismissal of the issue—in some ways the one, in some ways the other. The question doesn't thereby disappear. For many purposes, we have to decide whether it is more profitable to consider contemporary China and Brazil as two instances of the same phenomenon (say, very large underdevel-oped nations within the modern world-system or the capitalist world-economy) or to consider the China of today and Han China as two instances of Chinese civilization, comparing it then (I suppose) with the Brazil of today descended from an uncertain something else of 1500 years ago as two instances of I'm not sure what (perhaps Christian civilization).

Would it not be more useful if we didn't reify civilizations? One way to think about China is to think of it as a name linked to a geographical location in which there existed successive historical systems, which had a few features in common, and each of which sustained (for a good deal of the time) myths concerning civilizational continuity. In that case, instead of China the civilization, we are perhaps talking empirically of five, six, or seven different historical systems (each of which could be grist for the eventual fourfold tables that will derive from the nomothetic temptation). At least, I wouldn't like to close off this way of viewing "Chinese history" by a too rapid embrace of "civilizational analysis." (Of course, one can see why there would be social pressure against adopting such a perspective on "China" or "the West" or most of the names we use for "civilizations.") China is no doubt the strongest case for a civilizationist thesis. It becomes harder to demonstrate inherent cultural continuities everywhere else. To be sure, if we narrow our analysis to the scale and scope of a single historical system, then a "geoculture" is part of its "systemness."

I have discussed the civilizational hypothesis under the heading of the temptation to reify. It is of course most frequently a variant of the idiographic temptation but occasionally a variant of the nomothetic temptation. But reification as such is a recurring problem because we deal in concepts, and concepts are inherently ambiguous tools. Civilization is by no means the only concept we reify, but for the purposes of the analysis of long-term, large-scale social change, it is the exemplary one.

CONCLUSION

What is there to conclude? I suppose that the scholar should be intellectually monastic, and resist temptations. But product that I am of "American civilization," I urge that the resistance be modulated by pragmatism. I see no other way. The issues are too important that they not be faced, and they are too urgent to be closed off to analysis by failing to fight the war on two—indeed on all—fronts at the same time. Above all, I urge prudence in any haste to shout Eureka!

REFERENCES

Chase-Dunn, Christopher. 1992. "The Comparative Study of World-systems." *Review* 15,3(Summer):313–33.

Frank, Andre Gunder. 1990. "A Theoretical Introduction to 5000 Years of World System History." *Review* 12,2(Spring):155–248.

Pomian, Krzysztof. 1979. "The Secular Evolution of the Concept of Cycles." *Review* 2,4(Spring):563–646.

Wallerstein, Immanuel. 1979. "Modernization: Requiescat in Pace." Pp. 132–37 in *The Capitalist World-Economy*, by Immanuel Wallerstein. Cambridge: Cambridge University Press. [Ch. 6 this volume]

———. 1980. "The Annales School: The War on Two Fronts." *Annals of Scholarship* 1,3(Summer):85–91.

———. 1991. "The Invention of TimeSpace Realities: Towards an Understanding of our Historical Systems." Pp. 135–48 in *Unthinking Social Science*, by Immanuel Wallerstein. Cambridge: Polity Press.

———. 1992. "The West, Capitalism, and the Modern World-System." *Review* 15,4(Fall):561–619.

10—Time and Duration: The Unexcluded Middle, or Reflections on Braudel and Prigogine

Both Braudel and Prigogine had influenced my treatment of epistemo-logical issues, and especially the question of time and duration. I had been struck by the extent to which each of them had sought to trace a narrow *via media* amid the standard epistemological divides of modern knowledge systems. In the end, I decided the issue was how to con-struct an "unexcluded middle."

While epistemological debates are no doubt eternal, there are moments when they seem to reach higher intensity than usual. We are experiencing such a moment in the last decade of the 20th century. Science appears to be, it is said, under fierce attack, and with it rationality, modernity, and technology. Some see this as a crisis of civilization, of Western civilization—even the end of the very concept of a civilized world. Whenever the defenders of prevailing intel-lectual concepts seem to be screeching in pain rather than ignoring their critics or answering them calmly and (dare I suggest) rationally, it may be time to take a step backwards in order to make a cooler appraisal of the underlying debate.

For at least two centuries now, science has been enthroned as the most legitimate path, even the only legitimate path, to truth. Within the structures of knowledge this has been sanctified by the belief that there exist "two cultures"—that of science and that of philosophy (or letters)—which have not only been thought to be incompatible with each other but have also been de facto ranked in a hierarchy. As a result, the universities of the world have almost everywhere separated these two cultures into distinct faculties. If the universities have asserted formally the view that the two faculties were equally important, governments and economic enterprises have not hesitated to manifest a clear preference.

They have invested heavily in science and for the most part barely tolerated the humanities.

The belief that science is something different from and even antagonistic to philosophy, the so-called divorce between the two, is in fact relatively new. It evolved as the endpoint of the process of the secularization of knowledge that we associate with the modern world-system. Just as philosophy came to displace theology as the basis of statements of truth by the end of the Middle Ages, so science came to displace philosophy by the end of the 18th century. I say "science" did this, but it was a very particular version of science: that associated with Newton, with Francis Bacon, and with Descartes. Newtonian mechanics posited a series of premises and propositions which achieved canonic status in our modern world: systems are linear; they are determined; they tend to return to equilibria. Knowledge is universal and can ultimately be expressed in simple covering laws. And physical processes are reversible. This last statement is the one that seems most counterintuitive, because it suggests that fundamental relations never change, and that time is therefore irrelevant. Yet this last proposition is essential if one is to maintain the validity of the other parts of the Newtonian model.

Thus, in terms of this model, "time and duration" cannot be a meaningful or significant topic, or at least not one about which scientists can make statements. Yet here is Ilya Prigogine, a physical scientist, talking on this topic, and here am I, a social scientist, talking on it. How can this be? To understand this, we have to take into account the history of the epistemological debates in the 19th and 20th centuries.

Let me start with social science. Social science is a concept that was invented quite recently, only in the 19th century. It refers to a body of systematic knowledge about human social relations that was put forward and institutionalized in these two centuries. In the divisionalization of knowledge into two cultures, social science inserted itself as somewhere and somehow in-between. It is crucial to note that most social scientists did not do this boldly, asserting the legitimacy (not to speak of the superiority) of some third culture. Social scientists intruded in-between uneasily, uncomfortably, and with divided ranks. Social scientists continually debated whether social science was closer to the natural sciences or closer to the humanities.

Those who considered that social science was nomothetic, that is, in search of universal laws, generally argued that there was no intrinsic methodological difference between the scientific study of human phenomena and the scientific study of physical phenomena. All seeming differences were extrinsic, and were therefore transitory, if difficult to overcome. In this view, sociologists were simply backward Newtonian physicists, destined in principle one day to catch up. The road to catching up involved the replication of the theoretical premises and the practical techniques of the elder brother disciplines. From this point of view, time (that is, history) was as little relevant to nomothetic social scientists as it was to solid state physicists or microbiologists. What was far more relevant was the replicability of the data and the axiomatic quality of the theorizing.

At the other end of the spectrum of the social sciences stood idiographic historians, who insisted that human social action was non-repetitive, and therefore not susceptible to large-scale generalizations that held true across time and space. They emphasized the centrality of diachronic sequences—history as stories, as narratives—as well as the aesthetics of literary style. I suppose it could not be said that they rejected time altogether since they emphasized, indeed embraced, diachrony, but their time was exclusively chronological time. What they ignored was duration, because duration could only be defined by abstraction, by generalization, and indeed by a chronosophy. Usually, these scholars preferred to call themselves humanists, and insisted on being located in the Faculty of Letters, to indicate their disdain for nomothetic social science.

But even these humanistic, idiographic historians were caught up in the idolatry of Newtonian science. What they feared far more than generalizations (and therefore science) was speculation (and therefore philosophy). They were Newtonians *malgré soi*. They conceived of social phenomena as atomic in nature. Their atoms were historical "facts." These facts had been recorded in written documents, largely located in archives. They were empiricists with a vengeance. They held to a very close-up vision of the data, and the faithful reproduction of the data in historical writing. Close-up tended to mean very small-scale in both time and space. So these humanist historians were also positivist historians, and most of them saw little contradiction between the two emphases.

This definition of the tasks of the historian became ascendant throughout the academic world between 1850 and 1950. It was not, to be sure, without its harsh critics. One major such current was in France, and the journal *Annales*, founded by Lucien Febvre and Marc Bloch. In a letter written in 1933 to Henri Pirenne, who shared their discomfort with positivist history, and whose influence on the *Annales* school was profound (see Lyon and Lyon, 1991), Lucien Febvre said of a book by Henri Seignobos:

> A dusty, old-fashioned atomism, a naive respect for "facts," for the tiny fact, for the collection of tiny facts which are though to exist "in themselves" (Lyon and Lyon, 1991:154).

But the clearest, and fullest, statement of the critique of the dominant mode of historical writing was that made in 1958 by Fernand Braudel, who continued the *Annales* tradition after 1945 (Braudel, 1969). I shall examine the text.

Let us start with the title, "Histoire et science social. La longue durée." If there is one term that is thought to summarize Braudel's emphasis and contribution, it is *la longue durée*. This is of course the duration of which we are speaking, although in fact Braudel's term tends not to be translated when used in English-language social science. The term is polemical. Braudel wishes to attack the predominant practice of historians concentrating their energy on recording short-term happenings or events, which he calls (following Paul Lacombe and François Simiand) *l'histoire événementielle*. (This latter is a term difficult to translate into English; I believe the closest equivalent is "episodic history.")

For Braudel, the mass of "small details" (some dazzling, some obscure) that comprise the bulk of traditional history, which is almost always political history, is only a part of reality, indeed only a small part. Braudel notes that nomothetic social science "is almost horrified by the event. Not without reason: the short term is the most capricious and most deceptive of all durations" (1969: 46). This assessment is the clue to Braudel's famous *boutade* in *La Méditerranée*: "Events are dust" (1949).

Thus, against the chronological time of events, Braudel counterposes duration, *la longue durée*, with which he associates the term of "structure," giving the latter a very precise definition:

By *structure*, social analysts understand something organized, something coherent, relatively fixed relations between social realities and groups. For us historians, a structure is no doubt something put together, an architecture, but
even more a reality that time affects only slightly and maintains over a long
period. . . . All structures are simultaneously underpinnings and obstacles.
(1969: 50)

Against a time that is just there, a mere external physical parameter,
Braudel insists on the plurality of *social* times, times that are created and
which, once created, both aid us in organizing social reality and exist as
constraints to social action. But having asserted the limits and misdeeds
of *l'histoire événementielle*, he is quick to add that it is not only the historians who are at fault:

Let us be fair. If there are those who sin by leaning to centering analysis around
events, history, albeit the main culprit, is not the only guilty party. All the social
scientists participate in this error. (1969: 57)

It seems, says Braudel, that nomothetic social science is no more virtuous than idiographic history in this regard. He focuses his discussion
on Lévi-Strauss's search for underlying social relations that exist in all
social interaction, a set of elementary cells that are both simple and mysterious (once more, our atoms), which the scientist is supposed to seek
to "grasp as a substratum of all languages, in order to translate it into a
Morse code" (Braudel, 1969:71). To this, he says no, this is not what I
mean by *longue durée*. Quite the contrary:

Let us reintroduce duration into what we do. I've said that models were of
varying duration. The time of which they speak is valid insofar as it represents
a particular reality. . . . I have compared models to ships. Shipwrecks are
perhaps the most significant moment. . . .

Am I wrong to think that the models of qualitative mathematics . . . do not
lend themselves well to such voyages, above all because they circulate on only
one of the numerous routes of time, that of the long, the very *long*, duration,
sheltered from all accidents, cyclical movements, ruptures? (1969:71–2)

Thus, says Braudel, the search for the infinitely small (by the idiographic historian) and the search for not long but *very* long duration (by
the nomothetic social scientist) — he says of the very long, "if it exists, it
can only be the time of the sages" (1969: 76) — share the same defect.
Braudel ends by making two claims in effect. First, there are multiple

social times which interweave and owe their importance to a sort of dialectic of durations. Hence, second, neither the ephemeral and microscopic event nor the dubious concept of infinite eternal reality can be a useful focus for intelligent analysis. We must rather stand on the ground of what I shall call the unexcluded middle—both time and duration, a particular and a universal that are simultaneously both and neither—if we are to arrive at a meaningful understanding of reality.

Braudel saw traditional history as privileging time (a certain time) over duration, and he sought to reinstate *la longue durée* as a key epistemological tool for social science. Prigogine sees traditional physics as privileging duration (a certain duration) over time, and he seeks to reinstate "the arrow of time" as a key epistemological tool for the natural sciences.

Here too a history of the controversy seems necessary to understand the debate. The history of the natural sciences in the last two centuries is somewhat different from that of the social sciences. Newtonian science has followed a steady trajectory since at least the 17th century, both as an intellectual construct and as an ideology for the organization of scientific activity. By the early 19th century, it was given canonic (and if you will, textbook) status by Laplace. Many of its practitioners felt that major scientific theorizing was at an end, and that all that was left for working scientists was to clean up some of the minor loose ends, as well as to continue to utilize the theoretical knowledge for practical purposes.

But as we know, or as we should know, theorizing (just like history) is never at an end because all our knowledge, however valid it seems in the present, is in a cosmic sense transitory because it is tied to the social conditions out of which it was learned and constructed. In any case, Newtonian science came up against physical realities that it found difficult to explain, and by the end of the 19th century, when Poincaré demonstrated the impossibility of solving the three-body problem, it was in trouble, even though most scientists were not yet ready to acknowledge this.

It is only in the 1970s that the discomfort with Newtonian mechanics as the paradigm for all scientific activity was sufficiently widespread that we can speak of a significant intellectual movement within the natural sciences challenging the predominant and formerly substantially unchallenged views. This movement goes by many names. For shorthand purposes, it may be called "complexity studies." One of the central figures of this challenge has been Ilya Prigogine, who received the Nobel Prize for his work on dissipative structures. I shall use as my text his recent summation of his views, *La Fin des Certitudes*, which has as its subtitle *Temps, Chaos, et les Lois de la Nature* (Prigogine, 1996). Just as we may take *la longue durée* to signal Braudel's central emphasis, so we may take "the arrow of time" (a term Prigogine took from Arthur Eddington but which is now associated with him) to signal Prigogine's central emphasis.

As his point of departure in this book, he reproduces the conclusions he (and Isabelle Stengers) drew in their earlier *La Nouvelle Alliance*.

1. Irreversible processes (associated with the arrow of time) are as *real* as the reversible processes described by the traditional laws of physics; they cannot only be interpreted as approximations to fundamental laws.
2. Irreversible processes play a *constructive* role in nature.
3. Irreversibility calls for an extension of dynamics. (1996: 32)

Newtonian mechanics, says Prigogine, describes stable dynamic systems. But just as, for Braudel, *l'histoire événementielle* described a part, but only a small part, of historical reality, so for Prigogine, stable dynamic systems are a part, but only a small part, of physical reality. In unstable systems, slightly varying initial conditions, which are always and necessarily particular, produce vastly different results. The impact of initial conditions are essentially unexamined within Newtonian mechanics.

And just as, for Braudel, the effects of *la longue durée* are most clear in macroscopic as opposed to microscopic structures, so for Prigogine, "it is in macroscopic physics that the importance of irreversibility and probabilities becomes most evident" (1996:51). Finally, just as for Braudel, "events are dust," so for Prigogine, "where we are dealing with *transient* interactions, the diffusion effects are negligible" (1996:51). The situation, however, becomes quite the opposite for Prigogine in Braudel's *longue durée*: "In short, it is in *persistent* interaction that diffusion effects become dominant" (1996: 62).

For Braudel, there are multiple social times. It is only of the *very* long duration (a duration of which, I remind you, he said: "if it exists, it can only be the time of the sages") that truly universal laws may be asserted. Such nomothetic social science presumes the ubiquity of equilibria, as does Newtonian mechanics. Here too, Prigogine takes aim:

While the laws of nature are *universal* when we are dealing with equilibrium or something close to it, they become specific as we move away from the equilibrium, and they depend on the type of irreversible processes. . . . Far from the equilibrium . . . matter becomes more active. (1996: 75)

Nor is Prigogine embarrassed by the concept of an active nature. Again, quite the contrary: "It is because . . . we are both 'actors' and 'spectators' that we can learn something from nature" (1996: 173–4).

There is, however, one important difference between Braudel and Prigogine: their starting points. Braudel had to fight against a dominant view in history that ignored structure, that is, duration. Prigogine had to fight against a dominant view in physics that ignored non-equilibria situations, and the consequences of the uniqueness of initial conditions, that is, time. Hence Braudel talked of the importance of *la longue durée* and Prigogine of the importance of the arrow of time. But just as Braudel did not want to leap out of the frying pan of *l'histoire événementielle* into the fire of the *très longue durée*, but insisted on staying in the unexcluded middle, so Prigogine does not seek to renounce reversible time to jump into the fire of the impossibility of order and explanation.

Prigogine's unexcluded middle is called determinist chaos:

In fact, equations are as deterministic as Newton's Laws. But in spite of that, they give rise to behaviour that has an air (*allure*) of uncertainty. (1996: 35)

Well, perhaps more than just *allure*, because he also says that probabilities are "intrinsically uncertain" (1996: 40). This is why I speak of this position as being situated in the unexcluded middle. It is clearly middle:

Pure chance is as incompatible with reality as determinism and with our demand to understand the world. What we have tried to construct is a narrow path between the two conceptions both of which lead to alienation: that of a world governed by laws which leave no place for novelty, and that of an absurd, a-causal world, where nothing can be predicted or described in general terms. (Braudel, 1969: 222).

Prigogine himself calls this "a median description" (1996: 224), but I wish to insist that it is not merely the assertion of merits of a golden mean, but those of the unexcluded middle—a determinist chaos and a chaotic determinism: one in which both time and duration are central, and constantly constructed and reconstructed. This may not be a simpler universe than the one classical science thought it was describing, but the claim is that it is closer to being a real universe, harder to know than the one we used to perceive, but more worth knowing, more relevant to our social and physical realities, ultimately more morally hopeful.

Let me conclude, on this American Day, celebrated in Belgium, with two quotations. The first is from that great Belgian scholar, Henri Pirenne:

> Every historical construction . . . is based on a postulate: that of the identity of human nature throughout the ages . . .

> But a brief reflection is enough to make it clear that two historians with the same information at their disposal will not treat it in the same fashion. . . . Historical syntheses are thus to a very high degree dependent not only on the personality of their authors, but also on their social, religious or national environment. (1931: 16, 19–20)

The second is from the American philosopher Alfred North Whitehead:

> Modern science has imposed on humanity the necessity for wandering. Its progressive thought and its progressive technology make the transition through time, from generation to generation, a true migration into uncharted seas of adventure. The very benefit of wandering is that it is dangerous and needs skill to avert evils. We must expect, therefore, that the future will disclose dangers. It is the business of the future to be dangerous, and it is among the merits of science that it equips the future for its duties. (1948: 125)

I opened by saying that science is said to be under severe attack today. It is not true. What is under severe attack is Newtonian science and the concept of the two cultures, of the incompatibility of science and the humanities. What is being constructed is a renewed vision of scientia, which is a renewed vision of philosophia, whose centerpiece, epistemologically, is not merely the possibility but the requirement of standing in the unexcluded middle.

NOTE

This paper was first presented at a Conférence de prestige sur le thème, 'Temps et Durée,' Université Libre de Bruxelles, 25 September 1996.

REFERENCES

Braudel, F. (1949) *La Méditerranée et le monde méditerranéen à l'époque de Philippe II*. Paris: Lib. Armand Colin.

Braudel, F. (1969) 'Histoire et sciences sociales: La longue durée', in *Ecrits sur l'histoire*. Paris: Flammarion. 41–83 [original in *Annales E.S.C.* 1958; XII (4):725–53].

Lyon, Bryce and Mary Lyon. (1991) *The Birth of Annales History: The Letters of Lucien Febvre and Marc Bloch to Henri Pirenne (1921–1935)*. Bruxelles: Académie Royale de Belgique, Commission Royale.

Pirenne, H. (1931) 'La tâche de l'historien', *Le Flambeau* XIV: 5–22.

Prigogine, I. (1996) *La Fin des Certitudes: Temps, Chaos et les Lois de la Nature*. Paris: Odile Jacob.

Whitehead, A. N. (1948) *Science and the Modern World*. New York: Mentor [ninth printing, 1959] [original publication 1925].

11—What Are We Bounding, and Whom, When We Bound Social Research

> I had taken the position since at least 1974 that what I called historical social science was a single discipline, which had been erroneously carved up into multiple containers in the nineteenth century. I needed to explain why. The international commission I chaired between 1993–95 issued a report in 1996, *Open the Social Sciences*, which did this. This article is my own personal and reduced response to this issue. It illustrates why world-systems analysis is not a specialization within social science, and *a fortiori* not one within sociology but a call to restructure the social sciences as a whole.

O nce upon a time, there was knowledge and/or wisdom. Whatever its source or its intellectual framework, it was more or less a seamless whole. As knowledge accumulated, it became more and more clear that no individual could retain it all or even be competent about every kind of problem. It seemed plausible and natural to divide knowledge into sectors and expect people to specialize, that is, to work primarily in one sector. This simple differentiation model fits well within the differentiation models for social structures in general. As with all differentiation models, however, it presumes the "naturalness" of the process, and, in this case of two things in particular, that these sectors have "boundaries," and the boundaries that have come into existence are self-evident or at least inherent in the nature of things.

But it ain't so, Charlie! "Creating boundaries" around "sectors" is a social decision, fraught with both short-run and long-run consequences for the allocation of power and resources and the maintenance of the legitimacy of social institutions. The boundaries that have been erected are far from self-evident. They have been enduring to be sure, but they have also been plastic and impermanent. And what has been socially created can be socially uncreated.

The social creation of boundaries for social enquiry is not very ancient. As of 1750, they scarcely could be said to exist. To be sure, we can today, looking back, make distinctions among the work then done, say in western Europe. We can use such descriptive terms as political arithmetic or *Kameralwissenschaft* to designate types of work. And some of these terms were actually used by some persons at the time. But there were no real boundaries that individuals felt obliged to respect in any meaningful way.

Between circa 1750 and 1850, in western Europe, various efforts were made to argue the case for some kinds of boundaries. But looking back we can see that most of these efforts were unsuccessful. As of 1850, a clear set of categories denoting domains within social enquiry still did not exist in any firm way. It was only in the period 1850–1914 that our present boundaries emerged, blossomed, and crystallized, becoming firmer still in the period 1914–1945. The categories that triumphed reflected the times and harbored three great cleavages: past/present; West/non-West; state/market/civil society.

PAST/PRESENT

Those who studied the past were called historians. Those who studied the present were called, generically, social scientists—a category that included (minimally and largely) economists, political scientists, and sociologists. The cleavage was given a methodological patina in the *Methodenstreit*, in which the historians were largely the champions of the idiographic stance and the social scientists of the nomothetic.

The temporal specialization is hard to understand or defend on purely intellectual grounds. It can be thought of as two alternate modes of the search for objective truth. The historians argued that if one wanted to know what really happens in the social world, one must look at what people actually do and the arguments they give for doing it. But since people may embellish the truth if faced with an investigator, it is best to observe people in circumstances in which they are unaware of being observed, or in which what they say is in fact the action being observed. If the actors are dead, they are in no position to embellish the truth for public presentation.

Furthermore, since in practice we cannot observe everything, it is best to observe important things. It is thus that we arrive at the view that the best source of data about important things (events) are archives in which documents about past events are stored. The documents that are stored there tend to be momenta of important events — for example, the letter of an ambassador to his minister concerning strategies to pursue in negotiations.

As soon as one builds one's search for reliable evidence on archival sources, the distinction past/present makes methodological sense. In the present, important people/agencies are likely to try to keep their internal files secret and, therefore, refuse access to the scholar. Or if they accord access, they might doctor the archives deliberately in order to emit disinformation. Furthermore, we need to worry not merely about the *a posteriori* public presentation of the actor but, the argument goes, of the potential biases of the researcher. It is thought that the scholar is less likely to maintain a neutral stance about current events about which he may have strong feelings and, therefore, about which he may wish to influence the future outcome by altering the account of current events. But since the scholar cannot affect past outcomes (though, of course, he may fail to record them), he may feel more detached from them. Therefore, in investigating the past as opposed to the present, the scholar was considered to be more likely to be neutral and, hence, "objective."

A close look at past events in their archival detail leads quite naturally to a realization of and therefore an emphasis on their complexity, and quite often their murkiness. Archival data impress the scholar with their singularity, even their idiosyncrasy. They tend to suggest the limited applicability of simple generalizations. Consequently, an idiographic stance seemed by far the most plausible and the most natural to these readers of the archives.

The social scientists pursued an absolutely inverse logic in their search for objectivity. In essence, they topped the requirement of observing human action via the reading of archives by calling in addition for more direct observation in situations in which the scholar could verify independently the data. This meant that the scholar could not restrict data collection to past events but necessarily had to observe current events as well. The logic of this search carried them still further. As they engaged in data collection, the better and more reliable the data — certainly the more replicable. Indeed, as their exigencies about the quality of data grew, they began to feel that *only* current data were worth utilizing, that earlier data were for the most part mere speculative reconstructions of low reliability.

The historians sought to ensure the researcher's neutrality by insisting that the subject be one of low affectivity for the researcher. Remoteness in time was taken as a minimal guarantee of objectivity. The social scientists thought they could eliminate the intrusion of subjective judgments by moving from qualitative statements (necessarily based on an internal, non-reproducible, and non-verifiable assessment by the researcher) with quantitative statements derived from the researcher's external world and available to all other researchers. The identification of objectivity with quantification reinforced the orientation to the present of the social scientist.

But how could social scientists justify ignoring virtually all of past history? Here is where the nomothetic stance became essential. The social scientists saw themselves as scientists, by which they were asserting, as the natural scientists in the Newtonian-Cartesian tradition were asserting, that they wished to go beyond "common sense." Common sense could be wrong, and indeed often was wrong.[1] The function of the scientist was to verify, to discover the secrets that lay beneath the surface of the observations or beliefs of ordinary people. But if one searches for secrets beneath the surface, one is necessarily theorizing. And if one is generalizing, it is safest and simplest to believe in the existence of universal truths. But if universal truths exist, it does not matter where and when one accumulates the data, provided that they are rigorous, that is, that they are collected appropriately and analyzed in logically tight ways. At this point, we have a methodological justification for an orientation to the present at least as powerful as the historian's methodological justification for an orientation to the past.

Still, this cleavage was not inevitable, since it really had not been there, or at least had not been encrusted, until the late nineteenth century. What was there about the epoch that encouraged such a cleavage to crystallize? If we look at the social location of the researchers, we discover that a good 95 percent (if not more) of the world's historians and social scientists in this period were located in five countries: Great Britain, France, the Germanies, the Italies, and the United States. And what do we know about the political-cultural ambiance of these five countries at that time? They were all struggling with a basic political issue: how to deal with the increasingly assertive demands of the growing number of urban proletarians in the wake of considerable industrial development and a marked development of consciousness about popular sovereignty.

The basic political response developed in these five countries over the nineteenth century was the establishment of the "liberal national state." This state was to be "national" insofar as it accorded rights to and demanded loyalties of its "citizens," a category that was juridically defined. The state was to be "liberal" in that it recognized as its central function the promotion of rational gradual reforms that would alleviate injustices, suffering, and inefficiencies. By establishing a liberal national state, those who had power hoped to tame the "dangerous classes" and keep them at bay. This political program was enormously successful.[2]

Where then does the past-present cleavage enter? The orientation to the past, history based on idiographic prejudices, was admirably suited to the creation of national identity. It is no accident that in Germany and Italy, the two countries out of the five that had the most recent national integration, history should virtually blank out social science in this period. On the other hand, social science, with its present orientation and its nomothetic prejudice, was admirably adaptable to policy planning, the necessary tool of rational reformism. Of course, the detailed history of the disciples is more complicated than this division. But, in broad brush strokes, the cleavage past/present had a strong social base. It was supported and rewarded by public authorities. It was useful.

WEST/NON-WEST

As the four disciplines of which we have been speaking—history, economics, political science, and sociology—emerged with distinctive structures and fairly clear boundaries in the period 1850–1914/45, their loci of research were in practice virtually exclusively "the West." They constituted studies of the "civilized" world by the civilized world.

There were several reasons for this focus. First of all, there was the social prejudice that only the West was worth studying since only the West had historically "progressed." Furthermore, it was thought that only the West possessed the necessary data for the researcher—archives for the historian, quantifiable data for the social scientist. In addition, it was thought that only by studying the West could one speak usefully to the issues of national identity and rational reform. These issues were seen as Western issues, which could only be posed about so-called historic nations that were technologically advanced. It seemed so self-evident that one should spend one's time studying the West that the question was never seriously debated. In 1900, a British historian who would have devoted himself to the study of Argentine history, an American sociologist who would have done research on urbanization in Japan, a French economist who would have used Turkish data to generalize about price equilibria would have been considered bizarre, to say the least.

Still, there was a social need to study the world beyond the West. For one thing, the period 1850–1914/45 was the heyday of imperial expansion, and all five "core countries of social enquiry" were heavily involved in such expansion. And even where direct colonial rule was not imposed by the West, the West had come to be in immediate and constant political contact with all zones of the non-Western world. If history and the three nomothetic social sciences were not appropriate mechanisms of studying the non-West, other separate modes of social enquiry needed to be invented and institutionalized. Two were: anthropology and Oriental studies. New boundaries were being created.

Anthropology was invented as the study of peoples different from those who studied them, peoples who were primitive (a term that was fully acceptable in the second half of the nineteenth century). Which "peoples" were primitive? The answer seemed empirically obvious. Primitive peoples were most (but not quite all) of the non-white human populations who lived under the political aegis of Western peoples. These peoples shared, in the eyes of Western analysts, certain defining characteristics. Their populations were small, as was their land area, and their geopolitical weight was slight at most. Their "pre-conquest" technologies were no match for Western technology in terms of military or productive efficacy. They had no system of writing and, hence, no texts. Their gods were specific to their group. They had a language more or less specific to their group. They were for the most part either hunters and gatherers or small-scale agricultural producers.

Of what did the study of such peoples consist? At first, it was merely an attempt to describe that which was strange to a Westerner. This was not mere curiosity but a useful aid to the two kinds of Westerners in most continual contact with such peoples: colonial officials seeking to maintain public order, and Christian missionaries seeking to convert pagans. It comes then as no surprise that a large number of early ethnographic accounts were written by colonial officers or missionaries.

As the academic component of anthropology became institutionalized, a methodological justification of the descriptive mode obtained widespread assent. It was argued that the only way in which a researcher could learn the mores of another culture, especially one radically strange to him/her, was by "participant observation." The essence of the method was a stay by the researcher for several years among the people being studied, during which time the researcher was to observe and to question members of the group—directly and via "interpreters" about all facets of social organization and behavior, seeking to compile a complete picture of the normative structure.

The past/present cleavage was irrelevant here since all such peoples were presumed to be living in unchanging and undynamic social systems, at least unchanging prior to "culture contact" with the Western world. And their "primitivism" made it impossible to separate the study into economic, political, and social spheres as in the West, since their system had not yet been "differentiated" in this way.

Even if anthropology as a discipline was useful to colonial authorities and churches, many (even most) anthropologists did not think of themselves as agents of these groups. Rather, they thought of themselves as interlocutors of their peoples with the Western world as a whole. In the face of universalistic norms, they offered relativist evaluations. What was exotic, they argued, was not thereby irrational, perhaps not even primitive. Primarily, it was different. However, precisely because it was different, it needed a specialized (and sympathetic/empathetic) group of researchers to engage in the scholarly work, the anthropologists.

The traits that were used to characterize primitive groups—smallness in size, low level of technology, absence of writing—were not applicable to all non-Western areas. To take only the most obvious example, China was very big, had a very high level of technology, and had a very ancient system of writing. The same could be said of other areas where there were, in the terminology of the late nineteenth century, "high civilizations"—for example, India, Persia, the Arab-Islamic world. All such high civilizations became the domain of Oriental studies, an ancient discipline refurbished in the late nineteenth century.

Oriental studies in the West go back to the Middle Ages. It was the purview of monk-scholars who were concerned with religious issues and the possibilities of proselytization. They concentrated on learning languages and understanding the classical religious texts of the Orient. Their nineteenth-century successors were not monk-scholars and, by and large, little interested in proselytization. But the methods they used were not significantly different. In a sense, the basic intellectual question they posed was why these other high civilizations were not like the West, that is, why that had not known the "progress" of the West. In post-1945 terminology, the question was: how is it that they did not "modernize"? The answer seems to have been they could not, or they could not without the active intrusion of the Western world into their locales. The reason they could not was that they had features which made them resistant to basic change. Their social structures were somehow "frozen" in molds without an internal dynamic for evolution. They were, in one form or another, "despotisms."[3]

Unchanging despotisms do not need to be studied by historians, precisely because they are unchanging. The tools of the nomothetic social scientists seemed most dubious, since they could not describe adequately the peculiarities of each such high civilization. And participant observation seemed a very crude tool with which to appreciate their complexities. Hence, Oriental studies focused on studying the texts, for which then philology became a principal form of training.

It seems hardly necessary to demonstrate the social function of the West/non-West antinomy. The era of the institutionalization of the social sciences was the era of high imperialism and Western arrogance. There was a social science for the civilized world that had invented modernity, and there was a social science for the rest of the world, a zone that had no history and whose virtues, whatever they might be, held no candle to those of Western civilization.

STATE/MARKET/CIVIL SOCIETY

The third fault line (or rather set of fault lines) was among the nomothetic social sciences. In the process of their institutionalization, the latter "differentiated" into three principal separate disciplines: economics, political science, and sociology. A quick look at the history of these disciplines will show that in most of the major countries there was an early stage when scholars (and public figures) were grouped together in a single social science structure, one, furthermore, that combined an interest in empirical research and social reform. Then, there was a move to "professionalize" their activity, which meant separating the research and the reform components, placing the former exclusively in a university setting, after which they were carved out into differentiated domains.

Why could the professionalization not have occurred without the differentiation? Logically, it was certainly possible, and there were many who resisted the differentiation. But it occurred nonetheless in one university after another, in one country after another, steadily. By 1900, the pattern seemed in place, and by 1945 there were only rare pockets of resistance remaining. As social science transformed itself into three separate disciplines, it became necessary intellectually and organizationally to justify the distinctions, and many scholars turned to the task of staking out the "boundaries." What kinds of arguments were offered to limit the scope of each discipline and to assert its *chasse gardée*? The economists basically argued that economic transactions followed certain eternal rules (such as, prices vary according to supply and demand), and that their task was to elaborate this set of rules (for example, governments) could alter the functioning of these rules, more or less *manu militari*, but they excluded the study of these elements, precisely because they were seen to be "exogenous" to the economic transactions themselves. Economists used the so-called *ceteris paribus* clause to justify and enforce this exclusion. The economists of this era were quite the opposite of university imperialists. They preferred to *exclude* various matters from their purview, rather than intrude on turf they defined as belonging to others.[4]

The political scientists took a parallel route. On the one hand, those who wished to study political processes had been excluded from the discipline of economics by the fact that those who now called themselves economists had repudiated the label of political economy, a label that had been in use since at least the eighteenth century. On the other hand, the students of political processes felt the need to carve out a domain that distinguished them not only from the rest of social science but additionally from the faculty of law, which had its claims and which was very powerful in the university systems of the Western world. It was this latter constraint that in fact slowed down the emergence of an autonomous discipline of political science, making it the last of the three nomothetic social sciences to obtain clear recognition as a separate university department. The case that political scientists made to justify their distinctness vis-à-vis the faculty of law was that they were not primarily studying jurisprudence but the exercise of political power. At first, this referred primarily to the construction, patterns, and functioning of governments, but later, by extension, power was also studied as exercised through and in para-governmental political structures, such as political parties.

If the economists studied economic transactions *ceteris paribus*, and the political scientists studied the exercise of power in and around governments, what was there that the sociologists might claim to be studying? This was not an easy question to answer, and there are many long methodological tomes to testify to the general anxiety. Basically, the sociologists argued two quite different points. On the one hand, they argued the case for residue. There were many social phenomena not being treated either by the economists or by the political scientists yet were worthy of study: for example, the family, social deviance, demography. Sociology became a catch-all label for this residue.

There was, however, a more sophisticated (and perhaps less demeaning) argument. Sociologists argued that there were social structures/conventions/processes that underlay and preceded what other social scientists studied, more hidden but more fundamental. Sociologists studied what held "societies" together. Their domain was the civil society. Just as political scientists had to resist the territorial claims of jurisprudence, sociology had to resist the territorial claims of psychology, which also asserted it was studying how people interacted with each other. Sociologists did this by appealing to the reality of trans-individual emergent structures, what Durkheim called "social facts." There were always some sociologists, to be sure, who sought to bridge this gap by engaging in what they called social psychology. If this group never really succeeded, it was primarily because most psychologists preferred to reinforce rather than break down the boundaries with sociology.

Whence came the pressure to have this threefold differentiation? It is hard to miss the degree to which these divisions reflected the dominant liberal ideology of the times, which argued that the state, the market, and civil society were the three separated pillars upon which modern social structures were built. It was argued—indeed, it is still being argued today—that this differentiation constitutes the distinctive feature that distinguishes the modern world from all the pre-modern societies (where, it was argued, the three domains were inextricably interwoven). But if the reality of the modern world was its differentiation into three spheres, it seemed obvious that the scholarly enterprise should respect this reality. Or perhaps to state it more strongly, social science would not be able to comprehend adequately the social world if it did not take into account the different kinds of rules and structures that governed each of the modern domains.

What has happened to these boundaries today? That is another long story, and I will not tell it here.[5] Let me just summarize it in a paragraph. The enormous postwar expansion of the world university system led to the search for niches and to extensive academic poaching outside the recognized boundaries of each discipline. The cold war concerns of the United States led to the funding and encouragement of "area studies," which led the four "Western disciplines" to do research for the first time in the Third World. This in turn both ended the territorial monopolies of and undermined the traditional justifications for both anthropology and Oriental studies. The world revolution of 1968 dealt a further blow to the traditional divisions of the disciplines by fostering a general questioning of the liberal verities and thereby created the social space for the flourishing of studies of and by the "forgotten" groups—women, people of color, gays and lesbians, and so on—as well as permitting the rise of "cultural studies." All of this together led to an immense blurring of the boundaries, to the irrelevance of most of the historic justifications for the boundaries as they were constructed between 1850 and 1945, and to widespread intellectual confusion. This state of professional anomie has been compounded by the worldwide fiscal crises of the states, which has led to a squeeze on university resources, acute competition, and urgent concern by administrators on how to reduce costs.

The question is, what to do?

There are really only three possible answers. One is to scrap everything that has occurred intellectually and organizationally since 1945 and return to the "golden age" of the traditional disciplines. Aside from the fact that this is sociologically and politically improbable, the fact is that the golden age was not one. Still, this is essentially the program of the neo-conservative intellectuals.

The second is to encourage further multidisciplinarity. The argument here takes the form of the classical reformist stance. Yes, the old boundaries were unduly rigid and constricting. Yes, most important problems cross the disciplinary boundaries. But one cannot erase historical structures at the stroke of a pen, and, furthermore, one should not. There are still significant differences in the ways people trained in different disciplines approach the same problem. And there is richness in this variety. So, encourage cooperation, interrelations, flexibility. And slowly, slowly, things will improve. As to intellectual confusion, there is always intellectual confusion, which is merely another name for intellectual vitality.

There are a few problems with this attractive and moderate stance. First of all, multidisciplinarity has been around in force since 1945 (and has indeed an older history that dates from circa 1920), and, if anything, it has made the situation worse. Multidisciplinarity, by definition, assumes the meaningfulness of the existing boundaries and builds on them. But the changing real world and the changing intellectual world have both undermined seriously the legitimacy of these boundaries. Multidisciplinarity is, therefore, building on sand.

Furthermore, the issues of the boundaries have become sharply politicized, both because of the intense social conflicts throughout the world and because of the global financial squeeze. This means that university structures have moved into the public limelight. If the scholars do not get their house in order, the administrators will do it for them, if not the politicians. I do not have much faith in the scholars, but at the moment I think the politicians will do an even worse job.

Third, recruiting for scholarship, like recruiting for any other activity, depends on social ambience. If young potential recruits do not believe that social science is going somewhere, they will try other things. I believe we have reached a point where much skepticism exists, and we risk losing the social role for social science that we have painfully constructed over two centuries. I believe this will be a social loss.

Hence, reformism (that is, more multidisciplinarity) will not do.

What then will? There is no easy solution. In my view, what is necessary is a complete overhaul of the boundaries. None of the three present cleavages is plausible or desirable. The distinction past/present is totally without merit. The distinction West/non-West must be fundamentally rethought. The distinction state/market/civil society must be abolished. Are there other cleavages that make more sense? Perhaps macro-micro; global-local. I am not sure this distinction is totally defensible epistemologically. I note, however, two things. It has come to be used de facto as a very real cleavage in social science work of the last twenty years. Scholars seem to be more comfortable with other scholars working on the same side of this cleavage than on the other. In addition, both the physical scientists and the biological scientists utilize this kind of cleavage in organizing their work. We ought at least to look at it as the basis of organizational structures and training programs.

I do not think world social science is ready yet to make any far-reaching decisions about restructuring. I do, however, think it is ready to discuss possibilities and to explore them. And I think it is urgent to do so. I think we ought to set in place mechanisms that will encourage and foster such discussion and debate. One such mechanism is overlap. As opposed to multidisciplinarity, in which, say, an historian collaborates with a sociologist, overlap means that the historian *also* teaches in a sociology department, *also* becomes an active participant in the associations of sociologists, and so forth. Overlap should minimally be optional and perhaps maximally be mandatory. Of course, the overlaps would be incredibly diverse. Hence, at any university one could have n! combinations. As a result, interesting things might begin to happen. Clarity might even emerge from the muddle. At the very least, intellectual excitement might be ignited.

Another mechanism might be life-limited floating groups. Now, whenever a group exists with a new thrust, they seek to have their concepts institutionalized as a "program" and eventually as a department. Administrations sometimes yield to fads and oftentimes resist other ideas because of the fear of proliferation. If, however, such structures were created with a built-in sunset clause—say, five years—this would still be long enough for some common research and maybe one real cohort of graduate students. These would constitute try-outs of every semi-serious bright idea about realignments. Confusing? Yes, to be sure, but the present situation is one of massive confusion masquerading as continuity. At least floating groups would be a more straightforward and honest mode of dealing with the confusion.

There is another matter on which I can touch only in the most fleeting way. In the period 1850–1945, we saw not merely the institutionalization of the boundaries *within* the social sciences but also the boundaries *between* the social sciences and the natural sciences on the one hand and between the social sciences and the humanities on the other. This trinitarian construction of the world of knowledge was also unknown in the eighteenth century. It has been undermined as well in the period since 1945. It may also need restructuring. One question, therefore, is whether we will be able to justify something called social science in the twenty-first century as a separate sphere of knowledge.

And there is one final question. In the period 1850–1945, we constructed not only the multiple social sciences and the trinitarian division of the world of knowledge, but also the modern university itself as the primary, virtually exclusive locus of knowledge production and reproduction. This, too, is threatened. The enormous expansion of the world university system has led to pressures for the "high-school-ization" of the universities. Amidst the fiscal crises of the states, we hear calls all about by politicians to force the pace of this process under the guise of making university instruction more "productive." My guess is that these pressures will be hard to resist, and that scholarship may begin to turn elsewhere for secure bases. Indeed, this has already begun. But it is not a simple matter to create secure and somewhat autonomous bases for knowledge production. It will not be easy but we may have to find a substitute for universities. We should at the very least be discussing this question.

NOTES

1. See the famous article by Paul F. Lazarsfeld (1949). Lazarsfeld begins the article by reciting six obvious truths, all of which turned out to be wrong according to the data collected in the book.
2. This view of the historical role of liberalism as an ideology elaborated in Wallerstein, 1995.
3. The concept of despotism is, of course, a modern invention. In a fascinating study of Venetian diplomats' reports on the Ottoman Empire from the sixteenth to the eighteenth centuries, Lucette Valensi demonstrates how these reports shifted from initial admiration to denigration. The term "despotic" was first used in 1579, but "the invention of the abstract concept of despotism [did] not occur until the end of the seventeenth century" (Valensi, 1993, p. 77).

4. Alfred Marshall, the father of neo-classical economics, devoted himself, quite effectively, to this process of academic exclusion. See Mahoney, 1985.
5. It is told in some detail in Part II of Wallerstein, et. al., *Open the Social Sciences* (1996). The story of area studies is explicated also in Wallerstein (1997).

REFERENCES

Lazarsfeld, Paul F., "The American Soldier—An Expository Review," *Public Opinion Quarterly*, XIII (Fall 1949): 377–404.

Mahoney, John, *Marshall, Orthodoxy and the Professionalism of Economics* (Cambridge: Cambridge University Press, 1985).

Valensi, Lucette, *The Birth of the Despot: Venice and the Sublime Porte* (Ithaca, NY: Cornell University Press, 1993).

Wallerstein, Immanuel, *After Liberalism* (New York: New Press, 1997), 195–231.

Wallerstein, Immanuel, "The Unintended Consequences of Cold War Area Studies," in *The Cold War and the University, Volume I* (New York: New Press, 1997), 195–231.

Wallerstein, Immanuel, et. al., *Open the Social Sciences*, Report of the Gulbenkian Commission on the Restructuring of the Social Sciences (Stanford, CA: Stanford University Press, 1996).

12—Social Science and the
Quest for a Just Society

The intellectual history of the nineteenth and twentieth centuries was dominated by the profound disjuncture between the quest for the true and the quest for the good and the beautiful. This disjuncture was a modern invention, and I try to argue here why it has not been a fruitful one, and why we have to reunite today the two quests.

Macro and micro constitute an antinomy that has long been widely used throughout the social sciences and indeed in the natural sciences as well. In the last twenty years, the antinomy global/local has also come into wide use in the social sciences. A third pair of terms, structure/agency, has also come to be widely adopted and is central to the recent literature of cultural studies. The three antinomies are not exactly the same, but in the minds of many scholars they overlap very heavily, and as shorthand phrases they are often used interchangeably.

Macro/micro is a pair that has the tone merely of preference. Some persons prefer to study macrophenomena, others microphenomena. But global/local, and even more structure/agency, are pairs that have passions attached to them. Many persons feel that only the global or only the local make sense as frameworks of analysis. The tensions surrounding structure/agency are if anything stronger. The terms are often used as moral clarion calls; they are felt by many to indicate the sole legitimate rationale for scholarly work.

Why should there be such intensity in this debate? It is not difficult to discern. We are collectively confronted with a dilemma that has been discussed by thinkers for several thousand years. Beneath these antinomies lies the debate of determinism versus free will, which has found countless avatars within theology, within philosophy, and within science. It is therefore not a minor issue, nor is it one about which, over the thousands of years, a real consensus has been reached. I believe that our inability to find a way beyond this opposition constitutes a major obstacle to our collective ability to create a form of knowledge that is adequate for what I expect will be a quite transformed world in the coming century and millennium. I therefore propose to look at how this long-standing debate has been conducted within our community, that is, within the framework of that very recent construct "social science." I intend to argue that the way the problem has been posed heretofore has made it insoluble. I intend also to argue that we are today at a point where we may be able to overcome the social constructions of the nineteenth century in ways that will allow us to move forward constructively, and collectively, on this question.

Let me start with determinism and free will in theological discourse. The concept that everything is determined seems to derive quite directly from the concept of the omnipotence of God, central to all the monotheistic religions at least. On the one hand, if there is an omnipotent God, then everything is determined by the will of God, and to suggest otherwise would seem to be blasphemous. On the other hand, the churches of the world are in the business of regulating moral behavior. And determinism provides an easy excuse for the sinner. Has God indeed determined that we shall sin? And if so, should we try to counter the will of God? This is a conundrum that has plagued theologians from the beginning. One way out is to argue that God has bestowed upon us free will, that is, the option to sin or not to sin. It is however too easy a solution. Why would it have been necessary or desirable for God to have done this? It makes us seem like God's playthings. Furthermore, it does not provide a logically tight argument. If God has given us free will, can we exercise it in unpredictable ways? If so, is God omnipotent? And if not, can we really be said to have free will?

Let me say once again how impressed I have always been with the astuteness of Calvin's attempt to resolve this dilemma. The Calvinist argument is very simple. Our destinies are indeed not predetermined, not because God could not predetermine everything, but because if humans assert that everything is predetermined, they are thereby limiting God's ability to determine. In effect, Calvin is saying, perhaps *we* cannot change our minds, but God can, or else God is not omnipotent. Still, as you well know, Calvinists were not persons to countenance immoral behavior. How then could humans be induced to make the necessary effort to behave according to the norms that Calvinists believed they ought to observe? Remember, Calvin was part of the Reformation attempt to refute the doctrine of the Catholic Church that good deeds are rewarded by God (a view that, by derivation, justified the sale of indulgences). To get out of the box, Calvinists resorted to the concept of negative grace, which is in reality a familiar and very modern device of science, the concept of disproof. While we could not have foreknowledge of who was saved, since that would limit God's decisions, we could have foreknowledge of who was *not* saved. It was argued that God displays the prospect of damnation in the sinful behavior of humans, as sinful behavior is defined by the Church. Those who sin are surely *not* saved, because God would not permit the saved so to act.

The Calvinist solution is so astute that it was subsequently adopted by its successor expression, the revolutionary movements of the nineteenth and twentieth centuries. The analogous argument went like this. We cannot know for sure who is advancing the revolution, but we can know for sure who is *not* advancing it, those who act in ways that are sinful, that is, in ways that run counter to the decisions of the revolutionary organization. Every member is a potential sinner, even if the militant has behaved appropriately in the past. Members are thus continuously subject to the judgment of the revolutionary authorities as to whether or not they have gone against the will of God, that is, against the will of the revolutionary organization.

Nor was it only the revolutionary organizations that adopted the Calvinist solution. Essentially, modern science adopted it as well. We can never know with certainty whether a scientist has reached truth, but we can know when the scientist has sinned. It is when he has failed to follow the norms of appropriate scientific methods, as defined by the community of scientists, and therefore has ceased to be "rational," that is, when the scientist has stooped to politics, or to journalism, or to poetry, or to other such nefarious activities.

The Calvinist solution is astute, but it has one enormous drawback. It confers inordinate power on those humans—church authorities, revolutionary authorities, scientific authorities—who are the interpreters of whether or not other human actors are showing signs of negative grace. And who will guard the guardians? Is there then a remedy to this drawback? The consecrated remedy is to proclaim the virtue of human freedom. That good Calvinist, John Milton, wrote a marvelous poem extolling this remedy. It was called *Paradise Lost*. There are many read-ers who have said that behind Milton's ostensible vindication of God, his real hero was Lucifer, and that Lucifer's rebellion represented hu-manity's attempt to rise up against the constraint of the will of an unsee-able and unknowable God. But the remedy seems almost as bad as the malady. Shall we praise Lucifer? After all, in whose interests does he act?

I have come to bury Caesar, not to praise him.

Consider the Enlightenment. What was the sermon? It seems to me the essential message was anticlerical: humans were capable of rational judg-ment and hence had the ability to arrive at both truth and goodness di-rectly, through their own best efforts. The Enlightenment represented the definitive rejection of religious authorities as judges of either truth or goodness. But who were substituted for them? I suppose one has to say the philosophers. Kant was anxious to take away from the theologians the right to judge either truth or goodness. He found it easy enough to do this for truth, but more difficult to do for goodness. Having decided that one cannot prove laws of morality as though they were laws of physics, he might have conceded goodness to the theologians. But no, he insisted that here too the philosophers could offer the answer, which for Kant was located in the concept of the categorical imperative.

However, in the process of secularizing knowledge, the philosophers enshrined doubt, and this proved to be their own subsequent undoing. For along came the scientists to proclaim that the philosophers were merely disguised theologians. The scientists began to challenge the right of philosophers as well as of theologians to proclaim truth, asserting very stridently that scientists were *not* philosophers. Is there anything, the scientists asked, that legitimates the speculations, the ratiocinations, of the philosophers, anything that allows us to say that they are true? The scientists asserted that they, on the contrary, possessed a firm basis for truth, that of empirical investigation leading to testable and tested hy-potheses, to those provisional universals called scientific theorems. The scientists, however, unlike Kant, wiser or perhaps less courageous than Kant, wanted nothing to do with moral laws. They laid claim therefore to only one-half of the task the philosophers had inherited from the theolo-gians. Scientists would search only for truth. As for goodness, they suggested that it was uninteresting to search for it, asserting that goodness was incapable of being an object of knowledge as science was defining knowledge.

The claims of the scientists that science represented the unique path to locate truth gained wide cultural support, and they came to be the pre-eminent constructors of knowledge in the course of the late eighteenth and early nineteenth centuries. However, at that very moment, there was a small happening called the French Revolution, a happening whose protagonists claimed they were acting in the furtherance of goodness. Ever since, the French Revolution has served as the source of a belief system at least as powerful as that provided by the rise to cultural pre-dominance of science. As a result, we have spent the last two hundred years trying to reunite the search for truth and the search for goodness. Social science, as it came to be established during the nineteenth cen-tury, was precisely the heir to both searches, and in some ways offered itself as the ground on which they could be reconciled. I must however admit that social science has not been very successful in its quest since, rather than reunifying them, it has itself been torn apart by the disso-nance between the two searches.

The centrifugal pressure of the "two cultures" (as we now call them) has been impressively strong. It has provided the cultural themes of the rhetoric of public discourse about knowledge. It has determined the structures of the universities in the course of their being rebuilt and rein-vigorated in the nineteenth century. Its continuing strength explains the persistingly high degree of passion about the antinomies to which I re-ferred. It explains the fact that social science has never achieved true au-tonomy as an arena of knowledge nor ever acquired the degree of public esteem and public support to which it aspires and that it believes it mer-its.

The gulf between the "two cultures" was the deliberate construction of Newtonian-Cartesian science. Science was very sure of itself in this struggle. This is well illustrated by two famous declarations of the Mar-quis de Laplace. One was his *bon mot* in replying to Napoleon's query about the absence of God in his physics—"Sire, I have not found any need for that hypothesis."[1] The other was his unyielding statement about how much science could know:

The present state of the system of nature is evidently a resultant of what it was in the preceding instant, and if we conceive of an Intelligence who, for a given moment, embraces all the relations of beings in the Universe, It will be able to determine for any instant of the past or future their respective positions, motions, and generally their affections.[2]

Triumphant science was not prepared to admit any doubts or to share the state with anyone else.

Philosophy and, more generally, what came to be called in the nineteenth century the humanities fell in public esteem and retreated to a defensive stance. Unable to deny science's capacity to explain the physical world, they abandoned that domain entirely. Instead, they insisted that there existed another quite separate domain—the human, the spiritual, the moral—that was as important as, if not more important than, the domain of science. That is why, in English at least, they assumed the label of the humanities. From this human domain they sought to exclude science, or at the very least relegate it to a very secondary role. As long as the humanities engaged in metaphysics or literature, science was quite willing to allow itself to be excluded, on the deprecatory grounds that these were nonscientific matters. But when the subject matter was the description and analysis of social reality, there was no accord, even a tacit one, between the two camps. Both cultures laid claim to this arena.

A cadre of professional specialists on the study of social reality emerged slowly and, be it said, unsurely. In many ways, the most interesting story is that of history. Of all the fields that we today call social science, history has the longest lineage. It was a concept and a term long before the nineteenth century. But the basis of the modern discipline of history was the historiographical revolution we associate with Leopold von Ranke. And the modern version of history, which Ranke and his colleagues called *Geschichte* and not *Historie*, was extraordinarily scientistic in its fundamental premises. Its practitioners asserted that social reality was knowable. They asserted that such knowledge could be objective—that is, that there were correct and incorrect statements about the past—and that historians were obliged to write history "as it really happened," which is why they gave it the name of *Geschichte*. They asserted that scholars must not intrude their biases into the analysis of the data or its interpretation. Hence they asserted that scholars must offer evidence for their statements, evidence based on empirical research, evidence subject to control and verification by the community of scholars. Indeed, they even defined what kind of data would be acceptable evidence (primary documents in archives). In all these ways they sought to circumscribe the practices of the "discipline" and eliminate from history anything that was "philosophical," that is, speculative, deductive, mythical. I have called this attitude "history in search of science."[3] But historians proved in practice to be timid scientists. They wished to stick extremely close to their data and to restrict causal statements to statements of immediate sequences—immediate particular sequences. They balked at "generalizations," which is what they called either inductions of patterns of behavior from specific instances or assertions of causal sequences in which two variables were less immediately linked in time and space. We may be generous and say they did this because they were sensitive to the thin basis the collected empirical data in the nineteenth century afforded them for sound inductions. In any case, they were haunted by the fear that to generalize was to philosophize, that is, to be antiscientific. And so they came to idolize the particular, the idiographic, even the unique, and thereupon to shun, for the most part, the label of social science, despite the fact that they were "in search of science."

Other practitioners were more audacious. The emerging disciplines of economics, sociology, and political science by and large wrapped themselves in the mantle and the mantra of "social science," appropriating the methods and the honors of triumphant science (often be it noted to the scorn and/or despair of the natural scientists). These social science disciplines considered themselves nomothetic, in search of universal laws, consciously modeling themselves on the good example of physics (as nearly as they could). They had, of course, to admit that the quality of their data and the plausibility/validity of their theorems were far beneath the level achieved by their confreres in the physical sciences, but they defiantly asserted optimism about future progress in their scientific capacities.

I should like to underline that this great *Methodenstreit*, as it was called, between idiographic history and the nomothetic trio of "real" social sciences was in many ways huff and puff, since *both* sides of this disciplinary and methodological debate fully acknowledged the superiority of science over philosophy. Indeed, science might have won the battle for the soul of the social sciences hands down were the natural scientists not rather snobbish in refusing to accept the importuning social scientists into full membership in the fraternity.

History and the nomothetic trio remained up to 1945 very much social sciences of the civilized world, by the civilized world, and about the civilized world. To deal with the colonized world of what were called primitive peoples, a separate social science discipline was constructed, anthropology, with its separate set of methods and traditions. And the remaining half of the world, that of non-Western, so-called high civilizations—that is, China, India, the Arab-Islamic world, among others—was left to a special group of persons engaged in something that was given the name of "Oriental studies," a discipline that insisted on its humanistic character and refused to be considered part of the social sciences. It is obvious today why a cleavage between a social science of and for the civilized world and a second social science of and for the rest of the world seemed so natural to nineteenth-century European scholars, and why it seems so absurd today. I shall not dwell on this issue.[4] I wish merely to note that both the anthropologists and the Orientalist scholars, by virtue of the logic of engaging in a social science about the others/the nonmodern world/the barbarians, felt very much more comfortable on the idiographic side of the *Methodenstreit*, since the universalist implications of nomothetic social science seemed to leave no place for what they wanted to say.

In the nineteenth century, the idiographers and the nomothetists were in great competition as to who could be more objective in their work, which had a strange consequence for the macro/micro distinction. If one looks at the earliest works and major figures in each of these emerging disciplines, one notices that they wrote about very large themes, such as universal history or stages of civilization. And the titles of their books tended to be all-encompassing. This fit in very well with the turn that modern thought was taking in that century, the turn to evolution as the fundamental metaphor. These books were very "macro" in the sweep of their subject matter, and they described the evolution of mankind. They were seldom monographic. But this macro quality of the research did not seem to last very long.

In the interests of creating corporate structures, the various social science disciplines sought to control the training and career patterns of those who would enter the fraternity. They insisted on both originality and objectivity, and this turned them against macroscholarship. As originality required that each successive scholar say something new, and the easiest way to do that was to divide up the subject matter into subjects of ever smaller scope, the disciplines believed they were making it more possible for scholars to be careful in their collection and analysis of data. It was the mentality of the microscope, and it pushed scholars to using ever more powerful microscopes. It fit in well with a reductionist ethos.

This microscopization of social science reinforced the gulf between idiographic and nomothetic social science. The two camps were equally in search of objectivity but pursued diametrically opposite paths to achieving it, because they singled out opposite risks of subjectivity. The idiographic camp had two principal fears. They saw the danger of subjectivity deriving on the one hand from inadequate contextual understanding and on the other hand from the intrusion of self-interest. Insofar as one was dependent upon primary documents, one was obliged to read them correctly, and not anachronistically or from the prism of another culture. This required considerable knowledge of the context: the empirical detail, the definition of boundaries, the use of the language (even in many cases the handwriting), and the cultural allusions in the documents. The scholars hence sought to be hermeneutic, that is, to enter into the mentality of persons and groups who were remote from them, and to try to see the world as the persons under study saw it. This required long immersion in the language and culture under observation. For the historians, it seemed easiest therefore to study their own nation/culture, in which they were already immersed. For the anthropologists, who by definition could not follow this path, it required so great an investment to know enough to study a particular group of "others" that it seemed sensible to devote one's life work to the study of one such people. And for the Orientalist scholars, doing well their philological exercises required a lifelong improvement of difficult linguistic skills. There were thus, for each field, objective pressures that led scholars to narrow the scope of their research and to attain a level of specialization at which there were at most a few other persons in the world who had a matching profile of skills.

The problem of noninvolvement was also a serious one for idiographic scholars. The historians solved it first of all by insisting that history could not be written about the present and then by ending the "past" at a point relatively distant from the present. The argument was that we are all inevitably committed politically in the present, but that as we move backward in time we may feel less involved. This was reinforced by the fact that historians made themselves dependent upon archives, and the states that provided the materials for the archives were (and are) unwilling to make the documents available about current happenings, for obvious reasons. The Orientalist scholars ensured their neutrality by avoiding real intercourse with the civilizations they studied. Theirs being primarily a philological discipline, they were immersed in reading texts, a task they could and largely did conduct in their study. As for the anthropologists, the great fear of the discipline was that some colleagues would "go native," and thereby be unable to continue to play the role of the scientific observer. The main control employed was ensuring that the anthropologist did not stay out in the "field" too long. All of these solutions emphasized remoteness as the mechanism of controlling bias. In turn validity was guaranteed by the interpretative skills of carefully trained scholars.

The nomothetic trio of economics, political science, and sociology turned these techniques on their head. They emphasized not remoteness but closeness as the road to avoiding bias; but it was a very particular kind of closeness. Objective data were defined as replicable data, that is, precisely data that were *not* the result of an "interpretation." The more quantitative the data, the easier it was to replicate them. But data from the past or from remote parts of the world lacked the infrastructural basis for the necessary guarantees of quality, of "hardness." Quite the opposite: the best data were the most recent, and collected in the countries with the best infrastructure for the recording of data. Older or remoter data were necessarily incomplete, approximate, perhaps even mythical. They might be sufficient for the purposes of journalism or travel reports but not for science. Furthermore, even newly collected data rapidly became obsolete, since the passing of time brought ever-increased quality of data collection, especially in terms of the comparability of data collected in two or more sites. So the nomothetic trio retreated into the present, even into the immediate and instantaneous present.

Furthermore, insofar as one wanted to perform sophisticated operations on quantitative data, it was optimal to reduce the number of variables and to use indicators about which one could collect good data, hard data. Thus, reliability pushed these social scientists into constantly narrowing the time and space scope of the analyses and into testing only carefully limited propositions. One might wonder then about the validity of the results. But the epistemological premises solved this problem. Insofar as one believed that there existed universal laws of human behavior, the locus of the research became irrelevant. One chose sites of data collection according to the quality of the data it was possible to obtain, not because of their superior relevance.

I draw from this the conclusion that the great methodological debates that illustrated the historical construction of the social sciences were sham debates, which distracted us from realizing the degree to which the "divorce" between philosophy and science effectively eliminated the search for the good from the realm of knowledge and circumscribed the search for truth into the form of a microscopic positivism that took on many guises. The early hopes of social scientists that they could be modern philosopher-kings proved totally vain, and social scientists settled into being the handmaidens of governmental reformism. When they did this openly, they called it applied social science. But for the most part they did this abashedly, asserting that their role was merely to do the research, and that it was up to others, the political persons, to draw from this research the conclusions that seemed to derive from this research. In short, the neutrality of the scholar became the fig leaf for their shame, in having eaten the apple of knowledge.

As long as the modern world seemed to be one long success story of technological triumph, the necessary political base to maintain a certain equilibrium in the system continued to exist. Amid the success, the world of science was carried from honor to honor within this system, as though it were responsible for the triumph. The social sciences were swept along in the tide. No one was seriously questioning the fundamental premises of knowledge. The many maladies of the system—from racism to sexism to colonialism as expressions of the manifestly growing polarization of the world, from fascist movements to socialist gulags to liberal formalisms as alternative modes of suppressing democratization—were all defined as transitory problems because they were all thought to be capable of being brought under control eventually, as so many turbulent deviations from the norm, in a world in which the trajectory always returned to the curve of linear upward-moving equilibrium. The political persons on all sides promised that goodness was coming at the end of the horizon, a prospect presumably guaranteed by the continual progress in the search for truth.

This was an illusion, the illusion bred by the separation and reification of the two cultures. Indeed the separation of the two cultures was one of the main factors pushing the trajectories far from equilibrium. Knowledge is in fact a singular enterprise, and there are no fundamental contradictions between how we may pursue it in the natural and in the human world, for they are both integral parts of a singular universe. Nor is knowledge separate from creativity or adventure or the search for the good society. To be sure, knowledge will always remain a pursuit, never a point of arrival. It is this very fact, however, that permits us to see that macro and micro, global and local, and above all, structure and agency are not unsurpassable antinomies but rather yin and yang.

There have been two remarkable intellectual developments of the last two decades that constitute an entirely new trend, signs that the world may be now in the process of overcoming the two cultures. These trends are only marginally the doing of social scientists, but they are wonderfully encouraging about the future of social science. I refer to what has been called complexity studies in the natural sciences and what has been called cultural studies in the humanities. I am not going to review the now immense literature in each of these two fields. Rather I shall try to situate each of these fields in terms of their epistemological implications for knowledge and their implications for the social sciences.

Why are complexity studies given that name? It is because they reject one of the most basic premises of the modern scientific enterprise. Newtonian science assumed that there were simple underlying formulas that explained everything. Einstein was unhappy that $e=mc^2$ explained only half the universe. He was searching for the unified field theory that would in an equally simple equation explain everything. Complexity studies argue that all such formulas can at best be partial, and at most explain the past, never the future. (We must of course be careful to distinguish between the dubious belief that truth is simple and the sound methodological injunction of Occam's razor, that we ought always to try to eliminate logical curlicues from our reasoning and include in our equations only the terms necessary to stating them clearly.)

Why is truth complex? Because reality is complex. And reality is complex for one essential reason: the arrow of time. Everything affects everything, and as time goes on, what is everything expands inexorably. In a sense, nothing is eliminated, although much fades or becomes blurred. The universe proceeds — it has a life — in its orderly disorder or its disorderly order. There are of course endless provisional orderly patterns, self-established, holding things together, creating seeming coherence. But none is perfect, because of course perfect order is death, and in any case enduring order has never existed. Perfect order is what we may mean by God, which is by definition beyond the known universe. So the atoms, the galaxies, and the biota pursue their paths, their evolution if you will, until the internal contradictions of their structures move them further and further away from whatever temporary equilibria they enjoy. These evolving structures repeatedly reach points at which their equilibria can no longer be restored, at points of bifurcation, and then new paths are found, new orders established, but we can never know in advance what these new orders will be.

The picture of the universe that derives from this model is an intrinsically nondeterministic one, since the aleatory combinations are too many, the number of small decisions too many, for us to predict where the universe will move. But it does not follow that the universe can therefore move in any direction whatsoever. It is the child of its own past, which has created the parameters within which these new paths are chosen. Statements about our present trajectories can of course be made, and can be made carefully, that is, can be stated quantitatively. But if we try to overdo the accuracy of the data, the mathematicians tell us we get unstable results.[5]

If physical scientists and mathematicians are now telling us that truth in their arena is complex, indeterminate, and dependent on an arrow of time, what does that mean for social scientists? For, it is clear that, of all systems in the universe, human social systems are the most complex structures that exist, the ones with the briefest stable equilibria, the ones with the most outside variables to take into account, the ones that are most difficult to study.

We can only do what the natural scientists can only do. We can search for interpretative patterns, of two sorts. We can search for what might be called *formal* interpretative patterns, of the kind that state, for example, that all human social systems are historical social systems, not only in the sense that they follow a historical trajectory, but in the sense that they are born or emerge at certain times and places for specific reasons, operate according to specific sets of rules for specific reasons, and come to a close or die or disintegrate at certain times and places because they are unable any longer to handle their contradictions for specific sets of reasons. Such formal interpretative patterns are of course themselves subject to a finite relevance. One day, a given particular formal pattern may no longer operate, though for the moment this day may seem remote.

We can also search, however, for what might be called *substantive* interpretative patterns, such as the description of the rules of a particular historical social system. For example, when I term the modern world-system a capitalist world-economy, I am laying claim to the existence of a particular substantive pattern. It is of course a debatable one, and it has been much debated. Furthermore, like a series of boxes within boxes, there are substantive patterns within substantive patterns, such that, even if we all agree that the world in which we live is a capitalist world-economy, we may nonetheless differ about whether it has had discernible stages, or about whether unequal exchange has been its norm, or about endless other aspects of its functioning.

What is crucial to note about complexity studies is that they have in no sense rejected scientific analysis, merely Newtonian determinism. But in turning some premises on their head, and in particular by rejecting the concept of reversibility in favor of the concept of the arrow of time, the natural sciences are taking a giant's step in the direction of the traditional terrain of social science, the explanation of reality as a constructed reality.

If we now turn to cultural studies, let us start with the same question. Why are they called cultural studies? For a group of scholars so taken with linguistic analysis, to my knowledge this question has never been posed. The first thing I note is that cultural studies are not really studies of culture but studies of cultural products. This is the consequence of their deep root in the humanities and explains in turn their deep attraction to the humanities. For the humanities, in the division of the two cultures, were attributed above all the domain of cultural products.

They were also attributed the domain of goodness, but they were very reluctant to seize hold of it. It seemed so political, so uncultural, so fleeting and unsolid, so lacking in eternal continuities. The personal path of Wordsworth from poet of the French Revolution to poet of poetry illustrates the repeated flight of the artists and the scholars of cultural products to the surer ground of "art for art's sake," an aesthetic turning inward. They comforted themselves with Keats's lines in "Ode on a Grecian Urn": "Beauty is truth, truth beauty—that is all / Ye know on earth, and all ye need to know."

To be sure, there were always those who asserted that cultural products were a product of the culture and that this could be explained in terms of the structures of the system. Indeed, cultural studies as we know it today originated in England in the 1950s with persons who were arguing this long-standing theme. They were, let us remember, in search of a workers' culture. But then cultural studies took what has been called a linguistic turn or a hermeneutic turn, but which I think of as a 1968 turn. The revolutions of 1968 were against the liberal center and put forward the argument not only that the Old Left was part of this liberal center, but also that this liberal center was as dangerous as (if not more dangerous than) the true conservatives.

In terms of the study of cultural products, it meant that the enemy became not merely those who would study cultural products according to conservative, traditional aesthetic norms (the so-called canons), but also those (the Old Left) who would analyze cultural products in terms of their presumed explanations in the political economy. An explosion followed, in which everything was deconstructed. But what is this exercise? It seems to me the core of it is to assert the absence of absolute aesthetics, to insist that we have to explain how particular cultural products were produced when they were produced and why in that form, and then to proceed to ask how they were *and are* being received by others, and for what reasons.

We are clearly involved here in a very complex activity, one in which equilibria (canons) are at best transient and one in which there can be no determinate future, since the aleatory elements are too vast. In the process, the study of cultural products has moved away from the traditional terrain of the humanities and onto the terrain of the social sciences, the explanation of reality as a constructed reality. This is of course one of the reasons why so many social scientists have been receptive to it.

The move of natural scientists toward the social sciences (complexity studies) and the move of scholars in the humanities toward the social sciences (cultural studies) have not been without opposition within the natural sciences and within the humanities. The opposition has in fact been ferocious, but it seems to me that it has been largely a rearguard operation. Nor have the proponents of complexity studies or the proponents of cultural studies defined themselves as moving into the camp of the social sciences. Nor have all (or even most) social scientists analyzed the situation in this way.

But it is time that we all call a spade a spade. We are in the process of overcoming the two cultures via the social scientization of all knowledge, by the recognition that reality is a constructed reality and that the purpose of scientific/philosophical activity is to arrive at usable, plausible interpretations of that reality, interpretations that will inevitably be transitory but nonetheless correct, or more correct, for their time, than alternative interpretations. But if reality is a constructed reality, the constructors are the actors in the real world, and not the scholars. The role of the scholars is not to construct reality but to figure out how it has been constructed, and to test the multiple social constructions of reality against each other. In a sense, this is a game of never-ending mirrors. We seek to discover the reality on the basis of which we have constructed reality. And when we find this, we seek to understand how this underlying reality has in turn been socially constructed. In this navigation amid the mirrors, there are however more correct and less correct scholarly analyses. Those scholarly analyses that are more correct are more socially useful in that they aid the world to construct a substantively more rational reality. Hence the search for truth and the search for goodness are inextricably linked the one to the other. We are all involved, and involved simultaneously, in both.

In his latest book, Ilya Prigogine says two things very simply. "The possible is richer than the real. Nature presents us in effect with the image of creation, of the unforeseeable, of novelty"; and, "Science is a dialogue with nature."[6] I should like to take these two themes as the basis of my concluding remarks.

The possible is richer than the real. Who should know this better than social scientists? Why are we so afraid of discussing the possible, of analyzing the possible, of exploring the possible? We must move not utopias, but utopistics, to the center of social science. Utopistics is the analysis of possible utopias, their limitations, and the constraints on achieving them. It is the analytic study of real historical alternatives in the present. It is the reconciliation of the search for truth and the search for goodness.

Utopistics represents a continuing responsibility of social scientists. But it represents a particularly urgent task when the range of choice is greatest. When is this? Precisely when the historical social system of which we are a part is furthest from equilibrium, when the fluctuations are greatest, when the bifurcations are nearest, when small input has great output. This is the moment in which we are now living and shall be living for the next twenty-five to fifty years.[7]

If we are to be serious about utopistics, we must stop fighting about nonissues, and foremost of these nonissues is determinism versus free will, or structure versus agency, or global versus local, or macro versus micro. It seems to me that what we can now see clearly is that these antinomies are not a matter of correctness, or even of preference, but of timing and depth of perspective. For very long and very short timespans, and from very deep and very shallow perspectives, things seem to be determined, but for the vast intermediate zone things seem to be a matter of free will. We can always shift our viewing angle to obtain the evidence of determinism or free will that we want.

But what does it mean to say that something is determined? In the realm of theology, I can understand it. It means we believe that there is an omnipotent God and that he has determined everything. Even there, we get quickly into trouble, as I have suggested. But at least, as Aristotle would have put it, we are dealing with an efficient cause. But if I say that the possibility of reducing unemployment in Europe in the next ten years is determined, who or what is doing this determining, and how far back shall I trace it? Even if you were to convince me that this had some analytical meaning (and that would be difficult), does it have any practical relevance? But does it follow then that it is merely a matter of free will, and that, were Dutch or German or French politicians, or entrepreneurs, or trade union leaders, or someone else to do specific things, then I could assure you that the unemployment would in fact be reduced? Even if they, or I, knew what these things were, or believed we knew, what would motivate us to do them now when we did not do them previously? And if there were an answer to this, does that mean that our free will is determined by something prior? And if so, what? This is an endless, pointless, sequential chain. Starting with free will, we end up with determinism, and starting with determinism, we end up with free will.

Can we not approach this another way? Let us agree that we are trying to make sense of the complexity, to "interpret" it usefully and plausibly. We could start with the simple task of locating seeming regularities. We could also try provisionally to assess the relative strength of various constraints on individual and collective action. This task we might call locating structures of the *longue durée*. I call this a simple task, but of course it is not at all an easy task. It is simple rather in the sense that it explains little, and also in the sense that it is a prior task, prior, that is, to other more complex tasks. If we don't have the structures clearly in mind, we cannot go on to analyze anything more complex, like for example so-called microhistories or texts or voting patterns.

Analyzing structures does not limit whatever agency exists. Indeed, it is only when we have mastered the structures, yes have invented "master narratives" that are plausible, relevant, and provisionally valid, that we can begin to exercise the kind of judgment that is implied by the concept of agency. Otherwise, our so-called agency is blind, and if blind it is manipulated, if not directly then indirectly. We are watching the figures in Plato's cave, and are thinking that we can affect them.

This brings me to Prigogine's second apothegm: "Science is a dialogue with nature." A dialogue has two partners. Who are they in this case? Is science a scientist or the community of scientists or some particular scientific organization(s), or is it everyman insofar as he or she is a thinking being? Is nature a living entity, some sort of pantheistic god, or God omnipotent? I do not think we know for sure who is engaged in this dialogue. The search for the partners in the dialogue is part of the dialogue itself. What we must hold constant is the possibility of knowing more and of doing better. This remains only a possibility, but not an unattainable one. And the beginning of realizing that possibility is ceasing to debate the false issues of the past erected to distract us from more fruitful paths. Science is at its very earliest moments. All knowledge is social knowledge. And social science lays claim to being the locus of self-reflection of knowledge, a claim it makes neither against philosophy nor against the natural sciences, but at one with them.

Much as I think that the next twenty-five to fifty years will be terrible ones in terms of human social relations—the period of disintegration of our existing historical social system and of transition toward an uncertain alternative—I also think that the next twenty-five to fifty years will be exceptionally exciting ones in the world of knowledge. The systemic crisis will force social reflection. I see the possibility of definitively ending the divorce between science and philosophy, and, as I have said, I see social science as the inevitable ground of a reunited world of knowledge. We cannot know what that will produce. But I can only think, as did Wordsworth about the French Revolution in *The Preludes:* "Bliss was it in that dawn to be alive. / But to be young was very Heaven!"

NOTES

1. Cited in Alexandre Koyré, *From the Closed World to the Infinite Universe.* Baltimore: Johns Hopkins University Press, 1957, p. 276.

2. Cited in Roger Hahn, "Laplace as a Newtonian Scientist." Paper presented to the Seminar on the Newtonian Influence, University of California, Los Angeles, William Andrews Clark Memorial Library, April 8, 1967, p. 15.

3. Immanuel Wallerstein, "History in Search of Science," *Review*, XIX, 1, Winter 1996, 11–22.

4. See I. Wallerstein et al., *Open the Social Sciences: Report of the Gulbenkian Commission on the Restructuring of the Social Sciences.* Stanford: Stanford University Press, 1996.

5. The crystal has been shattered, Ivar Ekeland tells us: "The qualitative approach is not a mere stand-in for quantitative methods. It may lead to great theoretical advances, as in fluid dynamics. It also has a significant advantage over quantitative methods, namely, stability." (*Mathematics and the Unexpected*, Chicago: University of Chicago Press, 1988, p. 73).

6. Ilya Prigogine, *La fin des certitudes*. Paris: Ed. Odile Jacob, 1996, pp. 83, 177.

7. I have no place to argue this here but I have articulated this elsewhere. See Immanuel Wallerstein, "Peace, Stability, and Legitimacy, 1990–2025" (ch. 27 this volume).

Part Three

INSTITUTIONS

OF THE CAPITALIST

WORLD-ECONOMY

13—Long Waves
as Capitalist Process

One of my basic arguments is that the capitalist world-economy, like any other system, has both cyclical rhythms and secular trends, and that one of the most important cyclical rhythms is the so-called Kondratieff cycles, more or less 60 years in length. A description of what happens when the cycle goes up and down is not too difficult. Attempting to account for why it is going up and down is more difficult and more controversial. This is my version of this central issue.

> *Qui dit alors hausse courte, hausse convulsive, dit en gros recul économique: recul de la production dans sa masse, recul des revenus, non pas universelle, mais générale, tension sociale, et . . . politique. Qui dit baisse des prix évoque des phénomènes contraires . . . (réserve faite d'un secteur industriel secondaire et effacé). . . . A la différence de la hausse courte et convulsive, la hausse longue et progressive a dans une large mesure sa signification d'aujourd'hui. Qui dit hausse dit ici expansion, prospérité. Qui dit baisse dit régression économique* (C.-E. Labrousse, 1943: xv–xvi).

Absolutely no one claims that quantitative indicators of social life in the modern world are monotone. We all agree that they fluctuate; that is, they go up and down. To talk of "cycles" is to suggest more, however; it is to suggest some element of regularity, that is, some pattern in these fluctuations. And to suggest a pattern is thereby to suggest structures that explain the pattern.

As we know, a whole panoply of presumed cycles, of varying presumed lengths, has been elaborated: the Kitchin (2–3 years), the Juglar (6–10 years), the Kuznets (15–20 years), the Kondratieff (45–60 years, and the "logistic" or *"trend séculaire"* (150–300 years). Some insist that none of these cycles exist, or at least that their existence has never been demonstrated adequately (in terms of statistical reasoning). Some even argue their inherent implausibility.[1] Some on the contrary believe that all of these cycles exist, and even that they "fit" within each other. Still others take an intermediate position, arguing the greater plausibility of some cyclical lengths than of others, preferring, say, the Kuznets to the Kondratieffs (see Aldcroft & Fearon, 1972: 59; Spree, 1980; Morineau, 1984).

The curious result of this range of views is that, on a scale of skepticism or controversiality, the Kondratieff clearly ranks highest. Although the Kondratieff is often called the "long wave," it is in fact only medium-length in this range of presumed cycles. The first puzzle therefore is why, relatively speaking, scholars should find it easier to give credibility to shorter and longer cycles than to the medium-length Kondratieff.

Even among those who give some *prima facie* acceptance to the Kondratieff, there are sharp divisions as to the historical period to which the concept of Kondratieff cycles is applicable. Kondratieff himself, writing in the 1920's, started his calculations and descriptions as of the 1780's. In his classic text he gave as the reason for his starting date a purely technical (as opposed to a theoretical) explanation. He said he started at that point in order "to remain within the realm of reliable data" (1979: 520). Schumpeter was even clearer about the fact that historically Kondratieffs could be traced "certainly as far back as the sixteenth century"[2] and that the long wave of 1787–1842 "was not the first of its kind" but merely "the first to admit of reasonably clear statistical description" (1939: I, 250, 252).

Nonetheless, many who consider themselves in the tradition of Kondratieff and Schumpeter argue that the issue is not merely one of the availability of data but rather that 1780 (or 1800) was a theoretical turning-point, marked by the beginning of the industrial revolution. The argument of Delbeke is typical of this perspective:

> The long wave is a phenomenon inherent to the development of industrial society. Also in agrarian societies we can find long term fluctuations, but these are determined by other mechanisms (1982:I).

Many of those who have been collecting data on the Kondratieff-length waves of the sixteenth to eighteenth centuries would agree that the phenomena they are describing are somehow different from those found after 1780 (or after 1850).

There are two further problems of inclusiveness, one at each end of our time span. Guy Bois, describing what is a clearly medieval, clearly feudal period in Normandie, nonetheless describes Kondratieff-length movements, what he calls "movements of medium length (of the 30-years type)" (1976: 246). And, in the post-1945 period, two problems are posed. One is that Rostow (1978) gives a dating for the cycle radically at odds with most other Kondratieff describers (see Wallerstein, 1979). The second is that many insist that these cyclical processes, even if they exist, do not apply to the socialist world. Yet other disagree.

Behind these two debates — do Kondratieffs exist at all in any reasonable view? If they do exist, during what time span can one talk of them? — lie some basic differences about the nature of capitalism as an historical system.

Why after all are we interested in cycles? Cycles are of course a construct of the analyst. Apparently, some statisticians believe that to say this is to condemn cycles as somehow unreal. But all our concepts are constructs, ways of viewing and interpreting the real world. We cannot speak about reality or even think about it without such constructs. Obviously, a construct must have an empirical base; it is to be distinguished from a fantasy. But a construct is not a "fact," somehow there, irremediably objective, unmediated by collective representations and social decisions. A construct is an interpretative argument, to which may be counterposed alternative, even opposite, interpretative arguments. Its justification is in its defensibility and its heuristic value. Its utility lies in its implications. We should therefore play the game with some cards on the table.

I believe we are interested in cycles because they are both a mechanism that represents the life of an historical system and one through which such a system operates. Our interest is akin to the interest of a physiologist in the breathing of animal life. Physiologists do not argue about whether or not breathing occurs. Nor do they assume that this regular, repetitive phenomenon is always absolutely identical in form or in length. Neither do they assume that it is easy to account for the causes and consequences of a particular instance. Such accounting is perforce extraordinarily complex. But it would be hard to describe the physiology of animal life without taking into account that all animals breathe, repetitively and reasonably regularly, or they do not survive.

Of course, that still leaves open the question of whether the study of such a construct per se will be a rewarding way of learning very much more about the operation of the system being studied. The investment of scholarly energy is a decision and a risk, and will be pursued only if it seems to be rewarded by additional interpretative insight. Most scholars have not been willing to invest at all in the construction of Kondratieffs. A few, however, have. It is reasonable to assess whether or not we should continue to do so, and in what form.

I should say myself, as one who believes the investment will pay off, that the rewards to date have been meager. At the level of empirical data, a half-century of spasmodic empirical work since Kondratieff has not added all that much to the basic findings he presented. The skeptics remain unconvinced, while the adepts debate among themselves about which of the cyclical processes it is preferable to measure and what causes what—a debate that is itself dilatory and one that manifests, if I may say so, insufficient passion but all too much narrow-mindedness. I think in this respect Gordon is absolutely right when he says that the Achilles heel of Kondratieff analysts is their failure "to elaborate a coherent (much less a unified) theoretical foundation for their interpretation of long cycles" (1980: 10).

I believe the starting point must be a vision (hopefully coherent, perhaps one day unified) of the processes of capitalism as an historical system. I think, furthermore, we must start with the premise that Schumpeter enunciated in his book on cycles: "Capitalism itself is, both in the economic and sociological sense, essentially one process, with the whole world as its stage" (1939: II, 666).

If one starts with this premise, it follows logically that, to the degree that Kondratieff or any other cyclical processes exist, they must first of all be phenomena of the world-economy as a whole.[3] A quick look at the quantitative data thus far collected about Kondratieff cycles suffices to indicate, however, that they are overwhelmingly data about individual states, and for the most part, data about western Europe and the United States.

It follows therefore that, to the extent that such data seem to confirm our hypotheses, they may be misleading, since the correlations may not hold for the world-economy as a whole. And, to the extent such data seem not to confirm our hypotheses, they may also be misleading, since they may still hold true about the world-economy as a whole, even if they are disconfirmed for intrastate measurements.

Worst of all, as Forrester correctly complains, "The literature of the Kondratieff wave is particularly confused by the failure of authors to recognize that different modes are to be expected in different places in the economy" (1977: 536)—*a fortiori*, I would add, in different zones of the world-economy.

Even, however, if we were to agree that what needs to be measured is the world-economy as a whole (in its complexity, as a vector of multiple forces located in different sectors and zones), the question would remain what it is we ought to measure. What is it that goes up and down? It seems to me that we have collectively spent most of our energy measuring the *consequences* of the cycles rather than the cycles themselves— prices of various kinds (including price ratios), innovations, production, money supply. All of these, I have little doubt myself, go up and down in complex interlinkage with the Kondratieffs, but they are Plato's shadow in the cave.

If Kondratieffs are a phenomenon of capitalism, then the key issue surely is profit rates. Authors of very different persuasion indeed tell us this. Mandel says that "any Marxist theory of the long waves of capitalist development can only be an accumulation-of-capital theory, [that is,] a rate-of-profit theory" (1980:9). But Simiand says the same thing, defining an A-phase as one in which "the central factor [is] a level of profit that is increasing and high for the entirety of economic activities" (1932:45). And Dupriez explains the downturn by a glutting of markets, which is another way of talking about declining profits (1978: 204). Finally, Schumpeter, warning against undue emphasis on prices, points to the crucial issues behind prices: "[A] fall in prices is not the same as a fall in money earnings, which in turn is not the same as a fall in real earnings" (1939: II, 450).

Why then have we not been measuring profit-rate? I think the answer is very simple and given by Labrousse in an article he devoted to methodological problems. Comparing the measurements of prices, production, rent, wages, and profits, he says that "the movement of profit remains the most obscure of all of them" (1975: 592). Facing this difficulty, Mandel proposes to use interest rates as a barometer of profit because, he says, over the long run they "fluctuate parallel to the average rate of profit" (1980: 19). I doubt that this is true, however, since, insofar as money too is a commodity, the overall rate of profit is a vector of the profit rate of multiple sectors of investment, including investments in money.

I do not wish to minimize the conceptual and technical difficulties of measuring the rates of profit, especially if I simultaneously suggest that we want to know these rates for the world-economy as a whole. But we may never discover our patterns if we do not invent some ways of approximating a measure of profit-rates. Furthermore, let me suggest one reason not to despair about such a measure. It seems obvious that capitalists in the real world are constantly making decisions about investments based on their assessment of comparative rates of profit. No doubt their knowledge is limited and faulty. No doubt they make mistakes. But if the capitalist system is to work at all, and it has been working for a very long time now, capitalists as a whole must make more correct decisions than wrong ones, or we should find ourselves in a situation of far wilder oscillations than we do now. Cannot scholars collectively retrace the path of investors in order to arrive at some reasonable approximation of their measurements?

I do not suggest a new single measurement. Obviously, as Schumpeter reminds us, "the cycle is a process within which all elements of the economic system interact in certain characteristic ways and . . . no one element can be singled out for the role of prime mover" (1939: II, 449). It is because of this complexity that Morineau urges us to substitute the study of "sequences" for that of "cycles," the distinction being that sequences are defined as being of irregular length, with a characteristic form for each, and the advantage being that we would then look at all the movements at the same time, "in depth, in the middle of the waters and on the surface, distinguishing among them and unifying them."

I am all for looking at the cycles, and indeed each cycle, in their complexity, but in their political and social complexity as well. But there needs to be some *fil conducteur* if we are to make sense of it all, and it seems to me we are more likely to find this *fil conducteur* in the global profit-rate than anywhere else. Once found, we will discover that the historical working-out of the patterns is extraordinarily intricate, thus presenting us with a different concrete picture in each successive phase—or sequence (why not?).

Even, however, if we agree that we should concentrate on the cycle of the global profit-rate as our *fil conducteur*, we are still faced with what Morineau calls "the apple of the discord of the pre- and post–1780 or 1800."[4] Can we really talk of a single pattern that applies from the sixteenth to the twentieth centuries? I think so, provided that we are explicit as to what one would mean by a single pattern.

The heart of the traditional distinction between the 1500–1800 period and the post-1800 period lies in the presumed difference between an economic system still overwhelmingly agricultural and one that has a significant industrial component. In both, "crises" occurred, but in the former they were *"crises de l'Ancien Régime."* That is to say, they were crises of the harvest. In the classical explanations, a poor harvest led naturally to high prices for cereals and for bread. This was a catastrophe not only for the ordinary buyer but for the ordinary producer. The small rural producers, when the harvest was poor, had nothing or little left to sell, after deducting their subsistence and seed. The high prices benefited them not at all, whilst the consumer—whether townsman or rural producer buying a part of his food on the market (which part increased because of the poor harvest)—was faced not only with higher prices but lowered employment and/or wages as well. Thus price rise was negatively correlated with good times. Presumably, in the post-1800 period, this was no longer true. First, because the caprices of the harvest were no longer dominant (due to improvement of agronomy, transport, and the like). Secondly, because "industrial" crises showed an opposite correlation: Good times and price rise went together.

Stated in this bald way, it is clear that the distinction, pre-1800/post-1800, is far from self-evident, on many grounds. In the first place, "good times" is a very ambiguous concept, since we must ask, Good times for whom? Note that, in the very description of the *crises de l'Ancien Régime*, the difficulties for the producer are specified as being those of the *small* producer. This question of the "positive" or "negative" character of phases of a cycle is one to which we shall return, but it is by no means clear that the phases can be appreciated in opposite manners on the two sides of the time frontier.

Second, the double negativity of the *crises de l'Ancien Régime* (high prices for the consumer, whose wage income was declining simultaneously) which Labrousse, among others, presumed (1945: v) to have disappeared with the industrial revolution, has been rediscovered recently in the allegedly new phenomenon of "stagflation."

But third, and most important, there is a confusion of temporalities. *Crises de l'Ancien Régime* refer primarily to short-run crises (i.e.,

Kitchins) on the local market.[5] But Slicher van Bath (1977: 50) reminds us that in the pre-1800 period there were three kinds of agricultural markets: local, regional, and international, and it was only in the first that the *crises de l'Ancien Régime* occurred. In the others we find the familiar post-1800 phenomenon; in the medium run, high prices lead to an increase in production, and low prices the inverse. Prices and "good times" are thus correlated, *grosso modo*.

Let us review, therefore, the various current major explanations for the post-1800 Kondratieffs to see how relevant they might be to the 1500–1800 situation. I find three different emphases in the recent literature: (a) exhaustion of technology, (b) capital overexpansion, and (c) overexpansion of primary production. To illustrate each of these views, which come in many variants and often in great elaboration, I reproduce three summary statements:

(a) Stagnations have their roots in the exhaustion of the possibilities for improvements in old technologies, which then facilitates the concentration of supply and a satiation of demand (Mensch, 1979: 111).

(b) The theory suggests that the early phases of a long wave create employment opportunities as the capital and goods-producing industries expand. As the capital-producing sector begins to overexpand, it begins to push capital into the rest of the economy, thereby displacing further employment (Senge, 1982: 13).

(c) Kondratieff cycles are "caused primarily by periodic undershooting and overshooting of the dynamic optimum levels of capacity and output for food and raw materials in the world economy (Rostow & Kennedy, 1979: 1–2).

It seems to me evident when one places these three statements side by side that they share one common characteristic. They all assert that there is some process whereby over time there grows to be a significant discrepancy between some supply and some demand, and that this process is structural, not conjunctural. I do not contest this. Far from it, I embrace this common argument. We must then of course ask how come such a structural divergence between supply and demand occurs, and how come it occurs repeatedly, that is, cyclically. Logically, it seems to me this can only be because the factors that determine supply and demand, albeit linked, are different and therefore move at different rates.

What could such factors be? Given that we are speaking of a capitalist system, in which producers seek to accumulate, it seems plausible that producers will adjust their production to their expectations about profitability. Hence, as long as there is presumed to be an unsatisfied demand at what is considered a high price level, producers will tend to expand their production (or new producers will enter the market). As production is expanded, unless the global demand changes, further production automatically reduces its own *raison d'être*.

But does not production create its demand? Obviously not; else we should be living in an economically tranquil world. The reason it does not is that demand is a function of the distribution of surplus. (We have but to remember Engel's law on food consumption to underline this.) The distribution of surplus, however, unlike the variation of supply, is not the consequence of largely individual decisions made with a view to accumulation. The distribution of surplus is primarily determined in the sociopolitical arena, the outcome of the *rapport de forces* globally and locally of various contending classes and strata. The conflicts of interest are permanent, but the acute struggles are more discontinuous, giving rise to compromises that last for medium periods.

The *continuous* variation in supply combined with the *discontinuous* variation in demand is what gives us the medium-length cycle, the Kondratieff. The innovations cycle is of course part of the pattern. At the point where a discrepancy between supply and demand becomes acute, and the situation is defined as overproduction/satiation of demand, it becomes quite desirable to seek means of reducing costs of production or taking the risks of new production lines. This in no sense contradicts the other two explanations, "overinvestment" in production goods or "overshooting" in basic commodities. Nor does it seem to me we have to decide definitely a sequence for the latter two, because the interplay can be very complex. In all cases, the basic process is that what is, from a short-term perspective, rational and efficient behavior by the producer adds up to medium-term "wastages" or "over-production."

Was the "overshooting" of oil prices as of 1973 cause or consequence of the increased investment in industrial capacity in the world-economy in the 1950's and 1960's, leading to "overinvestment"? In terms of a concrete analysis of the immediate situation, it may make a difference to decide this. But, in terms of seeing a pattern whereby a long Kondratieff A-phase came to an end and was supplanted by a B-phase, the two factors (as well as "exhaustion" of the old technology) were all blended together.

Once it is recognized that the discrepancy between supply and demand that matters is the *global* discrepancy, and that the "sequences" that can lead to such a result are immensely varied, not only can we expect the concrete variations in the observed Kondratieffs of the post-1800 period, but we also see that it is perfectly plausible to utilize such a schema for the pre-1800 period. To be sure, the world-economy was less structured and less commodified in 1700 than in 1800, but this is equally true if one compares 1800 with 1900, or 1900 with the present, since the process of commodification is one of the secular trends of the capitalist world-economy.

It remains to be asked why such a pattern of global discrepancy should take the average length of 45–60 years. Gordon argues that it has to do with the scale of infrastructural investment and the length of time it takes to accumulate a "supply of potentially investible funds available to finance that investment" (1980: 29). He seems to suggest that such infrastructural investment is a phenomenon only of the post-1800 era. I do not see why this should necessarily be so. Surely, on a smaller absolute scale (but not inevitably on a smaller relative scale), there had to be prior accumulation in order to finance the investments in the shipbuilding or metallurgical or textile production of the 1500–1800 period, in new mining, even in opening up new agricultural zones.

The presumed length of the Kondratieff seems to me also linked, however, to political processes. If one key element in the process is the distribution of surplus, and if this is the consequence of major political struggles, it takes time to ignite, mobilize, and summarize the political struggles in the *various parts* of the world-economy such that the total effect would be to expand global effective demand, which in turn would be a major element in the launching of an A-phase after a long downturn. There is nothing magic in the period, 45–60 years, but there is nothing implausible either in such a periodicity.

If then we turn to the still longer run, to the "logistics" or *"trends séculaires,"* what could account for such cycles of 150–300 years? Even if the process resembled that of the Kondratieffs—the assemblage of discrepancies—we would need some additional factor to account for them.

The logistics are identified, even more strongly than the Kondratieffs, as price movements—the "longest of the long price movements" (Braudel & Spooner, 1967: 391). The pattern of secular inflation and deflation, which we can trace back to 1100 and which continues today, has been regularly described but almost never explained. "The serious scientific study of historical logistics has scarcely begun" (Cameron, 1973: 146). Let me suggest one possible approach. In his analysis of long cycles, Gordon distinguishes "infrastructural investment" from what he calls "world-market control investments," which "require long periods for installation and repayment" (1980: 31). But what are world-market control investments? They are both *global* infrastructure (transport, communications, financial networks) and politico-military infrastructure (armed forces, diplomatic networks *lato sensu*, networks of subversion). They are what goes with and sustains the existence of a hegemonic power in the capitalist world-economy. Elsewhere (1982), I have developed the ways in which the "cycle" of hegemony seems to correlate quite well with the "logistics"—the slow rise of the hegemonic power correlating with the long-term acquisition of economic relative efficiencies, culminating in a "world war/thirty years' war" that establishes the hegemony definitely and restructures the interstate system, followed by an equally slow decline of relative efficiencies, but the early end of the short-lived true hegemonic phase, with a return to the normal state of rivalry among the powers.[6]

One further word should be said about these patterns. To argue in favor of cyclical rhythms is never to deny secular trends. The rhythms are rhythms of an historical system. Since they are rhythmic but never symmetrical, they compose the secular trends. It is these trends themselves, in their contradictory development, that lead to a point of bifurcation, the eventual decline of the historical system, the transition to some other historical system. This process of transition itself is long, and during the transition the cyclical rhythms of the existing system do not cease operating. Quite the contrary, it is their continued operation that is forcing the transition.[7] Forrester addresses this same problem by discussing what he calls the "life cycle of economic development . . . [of] any one civilization." He suggests we are in a "transition . . . between the past of exponential growth and a future of equilibrium" (1977: 540). Equilibrium, however, precisely is not possible for capitalism, for which existence is expansion.

In the end we must return to the question of the implicit assessments of cyclical hypotheses. Simiand called the A-phases "positive" and the B-phases "negative" (1932: 17). This is because A-phases are phases of expansion, B-phases ones of relative stagnation, and, as I have just said, for capitalism existence is expansion. But the terminology is deceptive for two reasons.

From the point of view of the capitalist world-economy as an historical system, the B-phases are an essential element of its existence. To return to the analogy of breathing, in the A-phases, one inhales the oxygen of new innovations, investments, expansions; in the B-phases, one exhales the poisons (elimination of inefficient producers and lines of production and so on), which permits revitalization. In this sense the cyclical behavior of the Kondratieffs and the "logistics" are the lifeline of the capitalist system. It is all "positive" from the standpoint of the system.

From the point of view of particular groups within the system (various clusters of capitalists and various groups of workers; different states; core zones versus peripheral zones), there is no simple correlation of "positiveness" with A- or B-phases. They are always better for some than for others. In a B-phase, for example, there may be a decline in salaried employment, but it may also be true that, for those who continue to be employed, real wages may rise. The decline in employment in one zone may mean its increase in another. The launching of new kinds of enterprises may offer high profits for those who obtain a temporary quasi-monopoly. But this may entail catastrophe for other entrepreneurs. The "development" of a particular semiperipheral country may mean a real increase in the living standards of many within its borders, but entail a significant decline somewhere else in the world.

We should therefore strip of its connotations of "well-being" the concept of A-phase or of expansion. Indeed, Schumpeter already gave the same advice. "[Our model] does not give to prosperity and recession . . . the welfare connotations which public opinion attached to them" (1939: I, 142). Having done that, we can perhaps be less emotional, more clinical in our research on the long waves which are so central a feature of capitalism. Indeed, it is well to close with Schumpeter's sober reminder.

> Analyzing business cycles means neither more nor less than analyzing the economic processes of the capitalist era. Most of us discover this truth which at once reveals the nature of the task and also its formidable dimensions (1939: I, v).

NOTES

1. Wassily Leontieff was quoted as saying, "It is most implausible that over 200 years a periodicity exists" (*Business Week*, Oct. 11, 1982; 130).
2. Braudel and Spooner go further. Kondratieffs exist, they say, "no doubt earlier than [the sixteenth century]" (1967: 437).
3. Thomas Kuczynski, who remains skeptical about the utility of Kondratieffs, nonetheless says the same in his set of hypotheses about them: "The Kondratieff cycles are a phenomenon typical not of national economies but of the capitalist world economy" (1978: 80).
4. This "apple of discord" has been a central concern of the Research Working Group on Cyclical Rhythms and Secular Trends of the World-Economy of the Fernand Braudel Center since 1976. See its early statements (1977, 1979).
5. Morineau notes, however, that Labrousse *also* uses the expression to refer to the downturn of the intercycle, which manifests a discordance between prices and rent (1978: 390, Fn. 36).
6. This analysis resolves, be it said in passing, Mandel's criticism of Gordon's denial of "exogenous" factors in the explanation of the Kondratieffs (Gordon, 1980: 22; Mandel, 1980: 55). What is exogenous in the Kondratieff for Mandel is clearly endogenous to the longer "logistic."
7. For a debate on whether or not Kondratieff cycles will continue to be part of the functioning of the capitalist world-economy during the current transition, see the discussion between Samir Amin, Giovanni Arrighi, Andre Gunder Frank, and Immanuel Wallerstein in the "Conclusion" of their joint book (1982: 233–34).

REFERENCES

Aldcroft, Derek H. & Fearon, Peter (1972). *British Economic Fluctuations, 1790–1939.* London: Macmillan; & New York: St. Martin's Press.

Amin, Samir; Arrighi, Giovanni; Frank, Andre Gunder & Wallerstein, Immanuel (1982). *Dynamics of Global Crisis.* New York & London: Monthly Review Press (French ed., *La crise, quelle crise?* Paris: Maspéro, 1982).

Bois, Guy (1976). *Crise du féodalisme.* Paris: Presses de la Fondation Nationale des Sciences Politiques.

Braudel, Fernand & Spooner, Frank (1967). "Prices in Europe from 1450 to 1750," in *Cambridge Economic History of Europe*, IV: E.E. Rich & C.H. Wilson, eds., *The Economy of Expanding Europe in the Sixteenth and Seventeenth Centuries.* Cambridge: Cambridge Univ. Press, 374–486.

Cameron, Rondo (1973). "The Logistics of European Economic Growth: A Note on Historical Periodization," *Journal of European Economic History*, II, I, Spr., 145–48.

Delbeke, Jos (1982). "Towards an Endogenous Interpretation of the Long Wave. The Case of Belgium, 1830–1930," Discussion Paper 82.02, Workshop on Quantitative Economic History, Kath. Univ. te Leuven, Centrum voor Economische Studien.

Dupriez, Léon H. (1978). "1974, A Downturn of the Long Wave?" *Banca Nazionale del Lavoro Quarterly Review*, No. 126, Sept., 199–210.

Forrester, Jay W. (1977). "Growth Cycles," *De Economist*, CXXV. 4, 525–43.

Gordon, David M. (1980). "Stages of Accumulation and Long Economic Cycles" in T.K. Hopkins & I. Wallerstein, eds., *Processes of the World-System.* Beverly Hills: Sage, 9–45.

Kondratieff, N. D. (1979). "The Long Waves in Economic Life," *Review.* 11,4, Spr., 519–62. (Originally published in part in English in 1935, in German in 1926, in Russian in 1925.)

Kuczynski, Thomas (1978). "Spectral Analysis and Cluster Analysis as Mathematical Methods for the Periodization of Historical Processes—A Comparison of Results Based on Data about the Development of Production and Innovation in the History of Capitalism. Kondratieff Cycles—Appearance or Reality?" *Proceedings of the International Congress of Economic History*, Edinburgh. II, 79–86.

Labrousse, C.-E. (1943). *La crise de l'économie française à la fin de l'Ancien Régime et au début de la Révolution*, t. I. Paris: Presses Univ. de France.

Labrousse, C.-E. (1945). "Préface," to A. Chabert, *Essai sur les mouvements des prix et des revenus en France, 1798 à 1820*. Paris: Lib. des Médicis, i–x.

Labrousse, C.-E. (1975). "Aspects d'un bilan méthodologique de l'histoire conjoncturelle (XVIe–XVIIIe siècles)," in *Metodología de la historia moderna: Economía y demografía*. Univ. de Santiago de Compostela. Actas de las I Jornadas de Metodología Aplicada de los Ciencias Históricas, 587–93.

Mandel, Ernest (1980). *Long Waves of Capitalist Development: The Marxist Interpretation*. Cambridge: Cambridge Univ. Press; and Paris: Ed. de la Maison des Sciences de l'Homme.

Mensch, Gerd (1979). *Stalemate in Technology: Innovations Overcome the Depression*. Cambridge, MA: Ballinger. (Originally published, Frankfurt, 1975).

Morineau, Michel (1978). "Trois contributions au colloque de Göttingen" in E. Hinrichs et al., eds., *Von Ancien Regime zur Französische Revolution*. Göttingen: Vandenhoeck & Ruprecht, 374–419.

Research Working Group on Cyclical Rhythms and Secular Trends (1977). "Research Proposal: Patterns of Development of the Modern World-System," *Review*, 1,2, Fall, 111–45.

Research Working Group on Cyclical Rhythms and Secular Trends (1979). "Cyclical Rhythms and Secular Trends of the Capitalist World-Economy: Some Premises, Hypotheses, and Questions," *Review*, 11, 4. Spr., 483–500.

Rostow, W.W. (1978). *The World Economy: History and Prospect*. Austin: Univ. of Texas Press.

Rostow, W.W. & Kennedy, Michael (1979). "A Simple Model of the Kondratieff Cycle," *Research in Economic History*, IV. 1–36.

Schumpeter, Joseph (1939). *Business Cycles*, 2 vols. New York & London: McGraw-Hill.

Senge, Peter W. (1982). "The Economic Long Wave: A Survey of Evidence," unpubl. mimeo D-3262-1, Systems Dynamics Group, M.I.T., April.

Simiand, François (1932). *Les fluctuations économiques à longue période et la crise mondiale*. Paris: Lib. Félix Alcan.

Slicher van Bath, B. H. (1977). "Agriculture in the Vital Revolution," in *Cambridge Economic History of Europe*, V: E. E. Rich & C. H. Wilson, eds., *The Economic Organization of Early Modern Europe*. Cambridge: Cambridge Univ. Press, 42–137.

Spree, Reinhard (1980). "'Lange Wellen' des Wirtschaftswachstums," in W. H. Schröder & R. Spree, Hrsg., *Historische Konjunkturforschung* (Bd. II of *Historisch-Sozialwissenschaftliche Forschungen*). Stuttgart: Klett-Cotta, 304–15.

Wallerstein, Immanuel (1979). "Kondratieff Up or Kondratieff Down?" *Review*, II, 4, Spr., 663–73.

Wallerstein, Immanuel (1983). "The Three Instances of Hegemony in the History of the Capitalist World-Economy." *International Journal of Comparative Sociology*, XXIV, 1–2, Jan.–Apr., 100–08.

14—(With Terence K. Hopkins) Commodity Chains in the World-Economy Prior to 1800

> Hopkins and I invented the term "commodity chains" to underline a basic process of capitalism: that it involved linked production processes that had always crossed multiple frontiers and that had always contained within them multiple modes of controlling labor. Furthermore, we believed that a close study of such chains would indicate how and why surplus-value was distributed among its appropriators, and hence explain how the system of "unequal exchange" worked in practice.

I. STATEMENT OF THE PROBLEM

During the course of the last ten years the political economy of the world-system has emerged as a major field of inquiry within social science in general and within sociology in particular. At the heart of the development of this new field has been the documentation of the patterns of the capitalist world-economy, a historical system marked by a world-scale division of labor and phases of expansion and contraction.

Although there are an increasing number of scholars of social change who have come to accept the premises of an organizing capitalist world-economy for their accounts of trends and events occurring in the nineteenth and twentieth centuries, there remains considerable dispute about the very existence of a world-economy in the sixteenth, seventeenth, and eighteenth centuries, let alone about its scope and sway as an organizing force in the explanation of events and trends of that period.

Our proposed research is addressed directly to this debate, the question of whether or not there are substantial historical/empirical grounds for the claim that by the seventeenth and eighteenth centuries world-economic forces were organizing production over a growing portion of the "world" delimited by the scope of their operations.

The principal counter-claim is the incrementalist thesis of scalar enlargement (most sharply etched classically by Bucher) that development in Europe starts, as it were, with large-scale estate-centered economies, proceeds to town-centered economies, and culminates (at the beginning of the seventeenth century) in national or state-centered economies. This view is maintained today by those who argue that, as of perhaps 1945, for the first time we are seeing the "internationalization of capital."

This research is designed to validate a directly opposite claim, namely, that the development of productive forces in Europe (what Adam Smith called the "wealth of nations") was initiated primarily through the transformation of the trade of surpluses between distant points into a true division of labor with integrated production processes crosscutting political jurisdictions, and that the state-level and local processes ensued therefrom. The boundaries of this division of labor are therefore appropriately defined by the effective geographical reach of the production and labor processes thereby integrated, and not by town or national boundaries.

This counter-claim is to be tested through the empirical investigation of the operations involved in the production of two of the major consumable commodities of the earlier period (sixteenth to eighteenth century), namely, ships and wheat flour. A project of the scale proposed can hardly lay to rest the many detailed issues informing the dispute. But it can, and we believe it will, establish the plausibility of the kind of claim we are asserting. To the extent that this is achieved, subsequent inquiries, proposing differing accounts of changes in that period, will be required at least to address the line of argument substantiated by the results of the proposed research.

We could, of course, be wrong. It is not a conclusion we regard with equanimity. Still, it is possible. And accordingly we have so framed the proposed inquiry that if, with respect to at least two major products of the time—the capital good, ships, and the staple good, wheat flour—we are wrong, it will be all too evident from our results. If the results of this limited study are positive, that of course won't validate our whole perspective. It will only mean, as we said, that the line of argument advanced isn't implausible, and therefore others ought to take account of it.

II. BASIC RESEARCH ISSUES
AND PROCEDURES

Our basic query is whether and to what extent a capitalist world-economy was an organizing force and structural reality during the sixteenth, seventeenth, and eighteenth centuries. This requires examining two issues.

First, to what degree were production processes in different political jurisdictions and geographical areas integrated parts of a complex "world-scale" division of labor marked by phases of expansion and contraction? From our knowledge of changes in the locations and types of commodity production between (and indeed even within) the seventeenth and eighteenth centuries as opposed to the nineteenth and twentieth centuries, comes a second question: Exactly what major changes in commodity production occurred as part of the hypothetical periodic restructuring of the world-scale division of labor?

Pursuing these two inquiries requires constructing and tracking relations among production operations across time and space. Toward this end, we shall utilize the concept of "commodity chains." The concept "commodity chain" refers to a network of labor and production processes whose end result is a finished commodity. In building this chain we start with the final production operation and move sequentially backward (rather than the other way around — see below) until one reaches primarily raw material inputs.

Use of this concept has considerable advantages over other methods of tracking and depicting a trans-state division of labor. The predominant current procedure is to trace primarily the economic flows between states (that is, across frontiers) such as trade, migration, or capital investment. (Because of the bureaucratic processes governing such frontier crossings, we have probably more systematic data on these particular economic operations than on any other.) Research organized along these lines effectively shows movements from one state jurisdiction to another, helping to delineate direct or indirect exchange between states. Such efforts do not, however, and for the most part cannot, show the totality of the flows or movements that reveal the real division, and thus the integration, of labor in complex production processes. Analyses of the component production processes that result in a finished commodity are able, by way of contrast, to address directly the issue of the existence of a complex division of labor, and of the real economic alternatives at each point of the chain. It should be noted, moreover, that the concept of a commodity chain does not *presume* either a geographically dispersed division of labor or the interrelation or separation of states via commodity movements. By being agnostic on these issues in its designation of linked labor processes, research organized by the concept is able, in ways currently not possible, to examine claims regarding the transnational interdependence of productive activities.

The construction of a commodity chain proceeds through two steps. Delineation of the anatomy of the chain begins from the point of final production of a consumable. We take, however, one step "forward." The points to which the end product was sent for consumption are noted first. The other steps move in the reverse direction. We move backward rather than forward because we are interested in seeing the loci of the sources of value in a finished product and not the multiple uses to which raw materials are put.

Delineation of production proper begins by designating each major operation, working backward from the end product. Each of these operations constitutes one "node" of the chain. The most elemental form of a chain would look like Figure 1.

A fully sketched chain would reveal a much more complex division of labor: Multiple subcomponents would each have their own chains reaching back to their respective materials, processed raw materials used in final production operations would have their own chain segments, and so forth. The source of the labor (and, in turn, major food staples for this labor) required for each of these operations would also have to be established. Parallel different subchains, or even whole chains, may in addition need to be constructed whenever different major production loci are linked to quite distinct and separate sets of operations as offered by competing technologies. The particular configuration that one would establish would thus depend upon the product and time period under examination.

The second step in constructing a chain is to record four properties for each operation or node (except for labor):

(1) the usual nature of flows between the node and those operations that occur immediately prior to and after it;

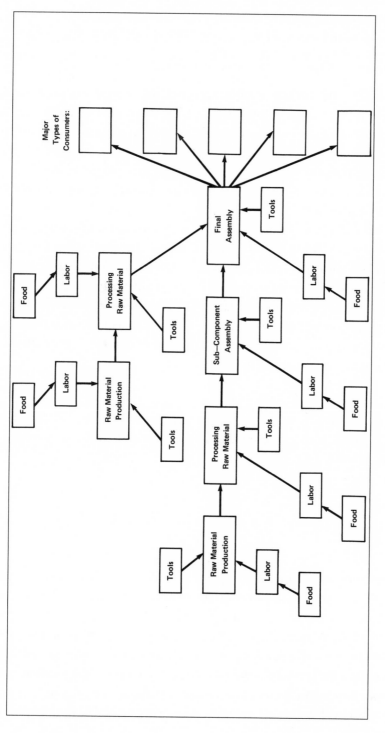

Figure 1

(2) the dominant kinds of relations of production within the node;

(3) the dominant organization of production, including technology and the scale of the unit of production; and

(4) the geographical loci of the operation in question.

A commodity chain constructed in such detail adequately depicts the division of labor in the production of the commodity in question. Cohesion/segmentation between operations, and inequalities in the organizational properties of different sets of operations, may be directly read off the anatomy of the chain. The geographic dispersion of any of these operations or combinations thereof across state jurisdictions may be readily calculated.

Equally, if not more important, the examination of a commodity chain over time allows the observer to assess the nature and degree of structural transformations of the organization of the chain. Such changes may range from transformations of a segment within a chain to the wholesale replacement of one chain by another. Significant variations in any of the following four facets would, we believe, constitute indications of a significant transformation of the division of labor as represented by the commodity chain under observation:

(1) the geographical distribution of operations;

(2) the forms of the labor force encompassed by the chain;

(3) the technology and relations of production; and

(4) the degree of dispersion/concentration of operations within each site of production.

III. RESEARCH DESIGN AND DATA COLLECTION

A. The Subject Matter

In order to test the claim of a world-scale division of labor over the period 1590 to 1790 (the justification for which period we give below), we propose to construct commodity chains resulting in two of the leading products of the period: ships and wheat flour as consumed in urban areas. The choice of ships rests upon the recognition that ships constituted in this epoch the principal infrastructure for commodity exchanges as well as an important locus of production (fish, whale oil, etc.). Wheat flour represents by contrast a staple commodity crucial to the sustenance and reproduction of the urban labor force in the most economically advanced areas of Europe. In the mid-seventeenth century, for example, over half the inhabitants of the Dutch provinces of Holland, Utrecht, Friesland, and Groningen were fed with imported grain. The choice of wheat flour production and shipbuilding also controls for variability between urban-industrial and agrarian-centered commodity production. Together these two commodities thus give us a sound empirical basis for evaluating the character of economic activity in the period under examination. Both goods, moreover, meet a final criterion: Each has formed the subject matter of a large body of secondary research, providing us with ample materials for the construction of commodity chains. This material is of course of varied quality, depending on the author and the archives used. We shall generally try to cross-check alternative secondary sources, and also rely on tertiary evolution of the quality of secondary sources.

B. Chain Construction

The major research task is to construct the commodity chains for wheat flour production and shipbuilding. This primarily involves establishing (1) the major productive operations through which the commodity was produced, (2) the central properties of each operation, and (3) the geographical and political dispersion of these operations.

Both shipbuilding and wheat flour production involved a large number of sequenced and distinguishable productive operations. This may be illustrated by way of reference to our previous work on shipbuilding between 1650 and 1733. Operations of the shipbuilding chain for this period may be depicted in a simplified fashion as in Figure 2. Delineation of our two chains will begin from the locus of final production (i.e., the shipyard and the flour mill). After noting points of distribution and consumption, the operations are traced *backward*, ending when raw material production is reached.

In practice, a much more complex chain emerges than that depicted in Figure 2. For each operation, data regarding the tools, labor force, and food supply for the labor force will be collected, at which point our tracing of the nodes of the chain is stopped. (We could, of course, trace each of these items further back, but this would involve us in an infinite regress and a total description of all conceivable economic activity, which

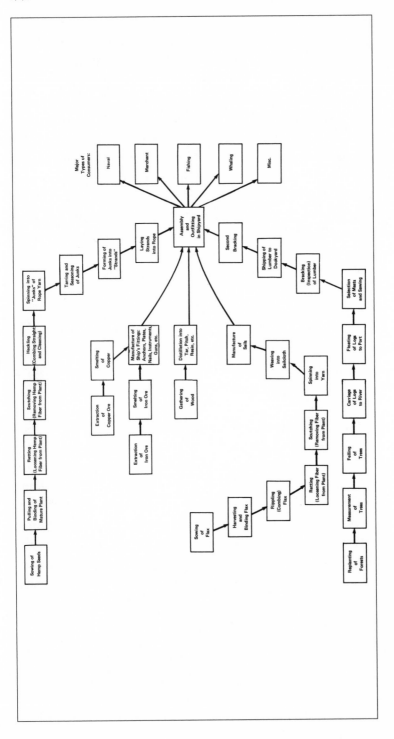

Figure 2

would be pointless and counterproductive.) We recognize that at any one moment, and even more so for a long period of time, several such commodity chains may need to be constructed insofar as multiple producers, employing multiple and alternative sets of operations, may exist.

The second research task involves the coding of data in relation to the four key properties of each production operation. These four categories and an initial working list of possible variations by which data will be coded are as follows:

(1) flows to and from node:
    (a) item being transferred
    (b) mode of transfer (market transfer; within workshop; nonmarket, non-workshop transfer)
(2) relations of production and labor force characteristics:
    (a) waged labor: wage rates
    (b) nonwaged labor: household labor
        "share" labor
        slave labor
        serf labor
        other coerced labor
(3) organization of production:
    (a) technology: energy source
        degree and type of mechanization
    (b) unit of production: factory or large workshop (over 10 persons)
        small workshop
        household
        estate
        peasant plot
(4) location of operation: geographical location
        political unit.

Data compiled from the fourth category provide the material to construct the chain across geographical and political space, pinpointing the degree to which operations are evenly or unevenly dispersed. In this regard, the number of operations within each political unit is noted.

C. Data Sources

Data for the research procedures described immediately above are to be derived first of all from the readily available accounts of economic and social historians. Research on shipbuilding and wheat production has been extensive. Given the various regions, languages, and topics our research encompasses, it may be expected that data gaps will occur as our work proceeds. When these remain after we have exhausted the secondary literature, we will seek assistance from acknowledged specialists in European economic history of the sixteenth to the eighteenth centuries, who have knowledge either of agrarian processes or of commercial and industrial processes relevant to the topics under examination here. After exhausting such sources, we do not propose to estimate any remaining data gaps, as the whole development of economic history has indicated that this is a very dangerous procedure.

D. Time Span of the Research

A crucial research problem arises once it is admitted that the chains, or parts of them, may alter over time; it is clearly necessary to observe the chains at successive moments over our two-century time span. Yet what temporal points should mark one's observations?

In this matter we have been guided by the economic histories of the period. It is widely argued in many separate accounts, for widely disparate areas and countries, that economic activity in Europe in this period underwent alternating phases of expansion and contraction. No one, to our knowledge, has documented these phases for the whole of the European economic arena. Insofar as phases of contraction and expansion have been recorded, the following dates represent a plausible tentative Europe-wide consensus (albeit one that we know is controversial):

Contraction	Expansion
1590–1620	1620–50
1650–72	1672–1700
1700–33	1733–70
1770–90	

We have accordingly chosen as our moments of observation the eight probable turning points suggested in the above: 1590, 1620, 1650, 1672, 1700, 1733, 1770, and 1790. This choice of intervals, as opposed to arbitrary ones (say of 25 years), remains, however, provisional and subject to revision. Nonetheless, it provides us with a starting point. Needless to say, we will want to see if the empirical material justifies this chronology. At each of our eight points we will thus recheck the details of our chains, and reconstruct them as and when it appears necessary.

E. Evaluation of the Constructed Chains

The construction of commodity chains for our two products, at our eight points in time, provides the materials for evaluating the debate over the existence of a world-economy in the seventeenth and eighteenth centuries. Five issues are to be assessed.

(1) A *WORLD-ECONOMY-WIDE* DIVISION OF LABOR?

Under question here are the scale and degree of the division of labor for shipbuilding and wheat flour production. From the completed commodity chains we shall assess the interdependence of production operations. Of overriding importance here is the extent to which the completed chains reveal operations that are geographically dispersed, in particular crossing multiple political units. As noted above, differing claims about the existence of a world-economy in this period present us with two very opposed accounts: a social division of labor predominantly within national boundaries versus a division of labor integrating labor processes dispersed across territorial boundaries. To the extent that the latter is found to be the case, we shall also seek to establish the degree to which points of political differentiation correspond to differences in production and labor processes (e.g., wage labor versus coerced labor versus household labor; levels of technology, remuneration of labor, and scale of units of production). There always remains the possibility, of course, that the chains will demonstrate the opposed claim, showing primarily state-centered production operations.

(2) AN *EXPANDING* WORLD-ECONOMY?

One of the defining characteristics of the modern world-economy in the nineteenth and twentieth centuries has been the secular, if fitful, expansion of its boundaries. In order to determine if this trend existed in our earlier period we shall examine our chains at our eight points in time in order to assess whether the geographical and political boundaries of these chains expanded, contracted, or stayed the same over the two centuries in question. To the extent that our chains expanded—by encompassing new sources of labor, raw materials, and so forth—we shall have obtained significant support for asserting the existence of a division of labor that grew through world-economic processes.

(3) A *RHYTHMIC* PRODUCTION SYSTEM?

As noted above, it is acknowledged by many that the economic activity organized through the world-economy exhibits alternating phases of expansion and contraction in the nineteenth and twentieth centuries. A number of authors have noted such cycles in addition for individual areas of seventeenth- and eighteenth-century Europe. Examination of the data collected on the activity of our chains over two centuries enables us to assess, for the first time, if such cyclical rhythms were *broadly* evident between 1590 and 1790. To the degree that the production activities joined in these chains followed the putative rhythms of the capitalist world-economy, we would have strong evidence of world-economy-wide processes as *organizing* these chains, while their absence would weaken the case for the existence of a world-economy in this period.

(4) PERIODIC *RESTRUCTURING* OF THE DIVISION OF LABOR?

Research on the capitalist world-economy indicates that its division of labor has gone through periodic transformations over long periods of time, and that these transformations in the characteristics and allocations of tasks within the modern division of labor occur predominantly in the periods of economic crisis or stagnation. Taking the materials assembled on the shipbuilding and wheat flour chains, we shall attempt to locate such redivisions of labor and the moments of their occurrence. The degree to which these can be established we will accordingly assist to dis/confirm the existence of (1) strong similarities between the two centuries prior to 1790 and the almost two-century-long period after 1790, and (2) the processes by which such world-economy-wide commodity production was reorganized. One of the primary features obscuring the continuity of world-economy-wide activity—and we would argue the debate over a world-economy prior to the nineteenth century—is precisely the successively and radically different faces assumed by commodity production on a world scale.

(5) THE *SOURCES* OF STRUCTURAL TRANSFORMATIONS?

If phases of expansion and contraction or periodic structural transformations of the commodity chains are found to occur, it follows that the sources of such changes should be investigated. Such a task can only be minimally approached in a project of this design and size. We shall nevertheless seek to record and evaluate in the course of our work the processes facilitating or inhibiting such transformations. Many may be expected to be revealed in the course of describing the chains and their alterations over time: Innovative technologies may be introduced at a specific moment, triggering wholesale reorganization of the chain(s); new areas of the supply of raw material or cheaper labor may be opened up; pressures of economic stagnation may eliminate selected producers in sharply etched periods; and so on. Other important factors in this period are found in the arena of interstate relations, a sphere of activity not directly under observation. It is often argued, for example, that the rise of shipbuilding in Great Britain owes as much to the Anglo-Dutch struggle for hegemony as it did to strictly formal economic considerations. Wherever and whenever such elements are recorded in the annals of the histories pertinent to the construction of our chains they shall be noted and assessed. Although we cannot on this basis offer a systematic assessment of the weight of such factors, we shall in this manner be able to pose an avenue of approach for the future consideration of the sources of such transformations.

15—(With Joan Smith)
Households as an Institution
of the World-Economy

Households are probably the most neglected institutional pillar of the capitalist world-economy. Joan Smith and I wrote this article as the theoretical introduction to our research project, published as *Creating and Transforming Households* in 1992. It constitutes an argument that households as they function today are a modern invention; that we all participate in the world-economy via our households; and that the revenue of households comes from five distinct sources, only one of which is wage-labor.

For the past 100 to 150 years, we have had a generally accepted image of the family and its historical evolution that has permeated our consciousness and served as part of the general conceptual apparatus with which we have viewed the world. This image had three main elements. One, the family was previously large and extended, but today (or in modern times) it has been getting smaller and more nuclear. Two, the family was previously engaged primarily in subsistence production but today it draws its income primarily from the wage-employment of adult (but nonaged) members. Three, the family was previously a structure virtually indistinguishable from economic activities but today it is a quite segregated or autonomous institutional sphere.

CHALLENGES TO THE
CONVENTIONAL IMAGE

Though still quite pervasive as a basic assumption in the world view of the majority, in the last 20 years or so this image of the family has come under severe scholarly attack. There are at least four themes in that attack.

First, this conventional image of the family involves an evolutionary premise that all families everywhere are moving in a given direction, and

234

that the degree to which they have thus moved is a measure of the degree to which the society in which they are located may be thought of as advanced or modern. That is to say, this image of the family is an integral part of a developmentalist notion, which assumed that there exist multiple societies in the world, evolving in parallel directions, if at different paces, and that all are evolving furthermore in the direction of "progress" (Goode, 1963).

But developmentalism itself has come under severe challenge in recent years as a framework within which to interpret modern historical change. The logical and historical autonomy of the various societies presumably evolving in parallel fashions has been questioned. Rather, some have argued, all these so-called societies have in fact been or become part of an integrated historical system—that of the capitalist world-economy—which is arranged hierarchically in a self-reproducing system, and in which so-called core and peripheral zones perform very different roles and, hence, are structured quite differently. It would presumably follow from this that the patterns of the family (its composition, its modalities) might look systematically different in the different zones.

Second, the idea of the nuclear family as something historically progressive has been very much associated with the idea that the adult male was thereby liberated from the tutelage of his father and assumed independently his own responsibilities. This same adult male came to be identified as the breadwinner because it was he who presumably sought wage work outside the household with which to support his family. This notion in turn became a basic element in our concepts of the world of work and the world of politics, peopled presumably ever more by these adult proletarian male individuals who faced employers and (sometimes) banded together politically. Along with this conceptualization of the male breadwinner has gone the concept of the (adult) female housewife (Parsons, 1955).

These concepts of "normal" family roles have of course also been under severe challenge—first of all by feminist scholarship and women's studies in general, which have contested the degree to which this kind of nuclear family (which of course has in fact existed, at least in some places at some times) can be considered to be "progressive" or "liberatory," in that the "liberation" of the adult male from his father was bought, if you will, at the expense of the increased subordination of the adult female to this same adult male, not to speak of the increased subordination of the aged father to his adult male son (Eisenstein, 1979).

In addition, quite apart from the political and moral conclusions to draw about this kind of family structure, women's studies has raised basic questions about the assumptions the concepts have made about economic value and its creation. Specifically, we find ourselves in the midst of a long, still ongoing, debate about how best to conceptualize the economic significance of housework and where it fits in the macroeconomy as well as in the budgetary realities of the household itself.

Third, since the 1970s there has been a growing literature on the so-called "second economy," variously referred to as "informal" or "underground" or "submerged." The image of the nuclear family implied a parallel image of a "nuclear economy," with equally clear boundaries and a specified, specialized role. This nuclear economy was in theory composed of legal, autonomous enterprises, each with its employer and employees, producing goods and services for the market within the framework established by state laws. This new literature has called attention to the multitudinous economic activities that occur outside this framework—evading legal restrictions or obligations, such as taxation, minimum wage laws, and forbidden production (Redclift & Mingione, 1985).

Once again, the implications were double. It was not only that the model of economic production that underlay analysis was shown to be wrong, or at least inadequate to cover empirical reality, but also that the model of family income sources was correspondingly wrong. The adult male often had two employments, not one, and the second employment was frequently one in which the income was not wage-income. Similarly, both the unemployed adult male and the adult female housewife were frequently quite actively involved in this informal economy, and, therefore, the basic description of their occupation—unemployed, housewife—was wrong, or at least incomplete (Smith, 1984).

A fourth challenge to the traditional image has resulted from the enormous expansion of the so-called welfare state, particularly since World War II, and particularly in Western (or core) countries. These states have come to accept a wide series of obligations vis-à-vis citizens and/or national residents in general and additionally vis-à-vis specific categories of persons in particular, obligations which involve the periodical alloca-tion of revenues to individuals on some specified criteria.

As the amounts have grown and the political encrustation has become deeper (despite continuing shrill opposition), it has become impossible to ignore the impact of such so-called "transfer payments" on income, and that in two respects. On the one hand, transfer payments have come to represent an even larger percentage of total income, indeed for some families the majority. And on the other hand, transfer payments are fre-quently conditional, and thus it becomes apparent that the "state" has thereby a very potent and quite obvious mechanism of affecting, even di-recting, the structure of the family (Donzelot, 1979).

And if all these were not enough, the careful reconstruction of family history that has become a major subfield of social history in the last 20 years has shown that factually the widespread image of the rise of the nuclear family does not bear the weight of careful archival inspection. The picture in empirical reality turns out to be extremely complex with no very simple trend-line, and one that varies considerably from region to region.

RECONCEPTUALIZING THE HOUSEHOLD AS AN INCOME-POOLING ENTITY

It seems, therefore, that there is much demand for a reconceptualization of the ways in which these presumably basic institutional spheres—the family, the workplace, the state—relate to each other in our modern world. We shall start with three rather simple empirical observations and argue that no conceptualization which does not encompass these three observations will be adequate as an explanatory model.

Observation Number 1

Observation number 1 is that most individuals live on a daily basis within a *household*, which is what we call the entity responsible for our basic and continuing reproduction needs (food, shelter, clothing), and this house-hold puts together a number of different kinds of income in order to pro-vide for these reproduction needs. We make a distinction between households and families. The former refers to that grouping that assures some level of pooling income and sharing resources over time so as to reproduce the unit. Often the members of a household are biologically related and share a common residence, but sometimes they do not.

We can classify the multiple forms of income into five major varieties and observe that most households get some of their income in *each* of the five forms, at least if you measure their income not on a daily basis but on an annual or multiannual basis. These five forms are wages, market sales (or profit), rent, transfer, and subsistence (or direct labor input). None of these five categories is as straightforward and uncomplicated as we sometimes pretend.

Wages means the receipt of income (usually cash, but often partially in kind) from someone or some entity outside the household for work performed. The work is usually performed outside the household and hours of work are normally circumscribed (and legally constrained). We speak of someone being employed full-time when this person works a prescribed number of hours per week (these days, circa 35–45), 52 weeks a year (including vacation time, often legally prescribed). Someone is unemployed if, having been employed full-time, this person is no longer so employed but is seeking to resume being so employed. But, of course, we know that many persons receive wages for work that is part-time — in hours per week, in weeks per year (such as "seasonal" employment), in years per lifetime (such as "target" employment). And we know that sometimes this employment can involve work in the home, especially as the wages are based on piecework rather than on hourly compensation.

Market (or profit) income seems straightforward in the case of commodity sales. If someone in the household makes something and sells it in the local market, then the net income is clearly "profit" and the profit can be used (and normally is, in large part) for expenditure on immediate consumption, although some part of the net income may be used for "investment." Petty commerce is only a minor variant on petty manufacture in terms of its significance for providing household income. It is more difficult, however, to decide what is happening when services are being offered. If one babysits, or takes in washing, the income is often thought of as market income, similar to petty commodity production or marketing. If, however, one is a free-lance editor or computer programmer, the income is more often thought of as akin to wages. It may not be terribly important to resolve such a classificational problem.

Rental income seems to cover any income deriving from the remunerated use by someone outside the household of some entity to which we
have (legal) property rights. We rent space in our own home to lodgers.
We rent tools or facilities to neighbors. We deposit money in banks and
draw interest therefrom. These days we also invest money in stocks and
bonds and receive dividends. In theory, this last is a process of joining
others to produce market income (and, therefore, a form of profit), but in
practice it is a form of income much closer to that obtained by renting
our property. It requires no work, only the forgoing of use. We can also
rent our own persons. If one stands in a line for someone else, that is
called selling a service. But suppose we substitute our presence for someone else's legal obligation (say, military service), as was once legal in
many parts of the world, is this not more akin to rental (forgoing "normal" civilian life in return for an income)? And how is one to classify the
newest of all commodifications, the income of the "substitute" uterine
progenitor?

Transfers are receipts of income for which there is no immediate
work-input counterpart. But of course the "immediacy" of the counterpart is difficult to circumscribe. If one receives state transfer income (old
age insurance, unemployment benefits, work-injury compensation, welfare), it is certainly possible to argue that there have been significant
counterparts at some prior point in time. To the extent that such transfers are based on "insurance" there have been cash inputs at previous
times that required work-inputs to earn them. And even when the transfer payments require no prior insurance payments, it may be argued in
many cases that they represent deferred compensation, collectively distributed, for previous work-inputs.

Private transfers are even more obscure in form. Most households receive irregular but predictable (and anticipated) private transfers of income (frequently denominated *gifts*). They receive these transfers from
their "extended" families (annually on anniversaries, but often more importantly on the occasion of births, marriages, and deaths). They also
receive such transfers from those superextended families we sometimes
call *communities*, a category that overlaps but is not identical with another superextended group, our circle of friends. But are such transfers
transfers? Are there not obligations of reciprocity, more or less faithfully

observed? Perhaps these transfers should be thought of as ways of adjusting lifetime income to uneven curves of expenditure (for example, on the occasions of births, marriages, deaths).

Finally, subsistence income is the most confusing category of all. Our use of the term derives from a model of a virtually nonexistent entity, the self-sufficient household that reproduces itself fully from what it produces and is thus truly autarkic. This autarkic model is largely a fantasy. However, it should not therefore be forgotten that virtually every household produces *some* of what it requires to reproduce itself, that is, produces some subsistence income.

The household may do this by hunting, gathering, or agriculture to obtain food for consumption. Obviously, this kind of household subsistence production is of diminishing significance, as the percentage of world labor-time (however remunerated) in such activities is on the decline. Household self-manufacture seems on the other hand as important a source of income as it ever was, even if the items thus produced are less likely to be the presumed basics (preserved foods, clothing, the house itself) and more likely to be the increasing number of do-it-yourself manufactures (in whole, or more often in part). And household subsistence services on the other hand seem to be actually increasing overall, rather than decreasing in labor-input. Households not only still for the most part prepare their own food, but they continue to maintain their shelter and clothing. Indeed, they probably spend far more time maintaining their shelter and clothing as the number of appliances available to be tools in this process increases. The tools do not seem to reduce the labor-input in terms of time—probably, the reverse—even if they usually make the labor-input require less muscle-power (Smith, 1987).

The mere listing of the multiple forms of income makes it very obvious that real income for real households is normally made up of all these components. The percentages vary (and are, as we shall see, difficult to compute), but two things at least seem clear. First, few households in the modern world, anywhere, can afford over a lifetime to ignore any of these sources of income. Second, wage-income, even for households that are thought of as fully dependent on it, remains only *one of five* components, and as a percentage probably rarely approaches, even today, a massive proportion of the total.

Observation Number 2

Observation number 2 is that there seem to exist rather dramatic differences in the real wage-levels of persons doing more or less identical work at more or less identical skill levels across world space and world time. That is to say, to put it in its most concise form, a skilled mason employed in construction activities receives considerably higher wages (however measured) in London than in New Delhi, and in London in the late twentieth century as compared to London in the early nineteenth century. This is such common knowledge that it is often not regarded as something that requires explanation.

Yet, on the face of it, this empirical reality flies in the face of almost all standard economic explanations for wage-levels. It should not be thus, and if it is thus momentarily, normal economic flows should end such anomalies over a relatively short space of time.[1] It is irrational in a capitalist world-economy that similar/identical activities should not be similarly compensated. In general, when explanations for such an anomaly are offered, they tend to be self-consciously noneconomic in character. The wage-differentials are said to be attributable to historic factors, or to cultural differences or to variations in political systems. Of course there are no explanations at all, but simply the listing of possible intermediate processes. One would want to know how these other constraints came into existence and when. This is all the more true when we observe both that particular wage differentials can and do change and that the pattern of wage differentials nonetheless persists.

Observation Number 3

Observation number 3 is that all the members of a household (or virtually all) produce *some* income for the household (on an annual basis probably, on a lifetime basis surely), and that the various sources of income are not to be *exclusively* identified with any particular members of the household. That is not to say, however, that there are not systematic patterns or correlations that vary with gender, age, class, or ethnic group.

Wages are identified with adult males. They are identified to the point that female wage work, child labor, employment of the aged or of retired workers constitute a phenomenon that is noticed and therefore that is studied. Yet we know that wage work has never been exclusively the pre-

serve of adult males. To be sure, the amount of wage-work by adult females, children, and the aged has varied considerably (although without
as yet long trend lines) in what may be cyclical patterns. Still it is probably true to say that at most times and in most places the majority of
wage-workers have been adult males and the majority (or at least a large
plurality) of adult males have engaged in at least some wage-work during
their lifetimes.

The earning of market income on the other hand is so flexible a procedure that it is hard to identify it consistently with gender or age roles.
Worldwide and over time, men and women have engaged in it, even if
some parts of the world seem to show cultural biases toward the higher
participation (and the nonparticipation) of certain groups in market activities. One of the flexible features of market activities is that they are less
tied to collective schedule-making than wage activities. It is therefore
usually quite easy to do them for small amounts of time, facilitating their
combination with other income-producing activities, and allowing them
to be, so to speak, schedule fillers.

Many rental activities are collective household acts (at least in theory)
and in addition require very little time. After all, what we mean by *rent* is
income derived from a legal claim rather than from current activity. Of
course the renter may be simultaneously purchasing services or commodities in addition to paying a rent, as when a lodger is served food or
has clothes laundered. The rental of persons (which is not the most common of phenomena) may however be gender- and age-specific.

Transfers are also made in a sense to the collective household, but,
not unlike other forms of income, they are usually made via an individual
who is the legal recipient or the excuse for a transfer. The forms of transfers are many and the recipients, therefore, are in fact widely distributed
across gender and age.

Finally there is subsistence income. Subsistence income shares with
market income a considerable flexibility in the allocation (when and for
how long a particular activity occurs) and shares with wage income an
imperfect correlation with a particular age-gender role. We do identify
subsistence income with the adult female, but that is for the same reasons
we identify wage labor with the adult male. On the other hand,
everyone—men and women, adults, children, and the aged—does some
subsistence work, with variations according to time and place, with per-

haps cyclical patterns, and with no long-term trend-line. But on the other hand, at most times and places the majority of the subsistence income has been produced by adult females, as this is what is implied by the concept "housewife," which has been a constant of the organizational pattern of the capitalist world-economy.

What then may we conclude from these observations? One thing surely: All members of the household (except infants and total invalids) are capable of obtaining income for the household by their labor inputs, and in most cases participate in income-securing activities. One other thing, which must however be stated more hesitantly: there are some patterns of gender-age correlation with income-procuring activities but it is far from perfect, and most persons engage in several different income-producing activities—in a week, in a year, in a lifetime.

One last point should be made about income-pooling. What we are describing is how income comes *into* the household. This says nothing necessarily about how it is spent. Households may be structured in more or less authoritarian fashions. The income may be allocated unequally. Furthermore, the inflow of the income may be hypothetical. A particular member of the household, somehow earning cash income, may short-stop the process, by keeping part or all of the cash to spend. This is a "political" act. From the point of view of this analysis, this cash is still household income, because it in fact forms part of the pool that is redistributed. A member who shortstops income and spends it may not be allocated other income for the expenditures in question. In any case, the internal structure of households, and how power and goods are distributed internally, is not treated in this discussion.

THE HOUSEHOLD, THE WORKPLACE, AND THE STATE

How should we reconceptualize the interrelations between the household, the workplace, and the state? We suggest that we can make most sense of what is going on if we utilize a set of five orienting propositions, alerting us to what seem to be the processes at work.

1. The appropriate operational unit for analyzing the ways in which people fit into the labor force is not the individual but the household, defined for these purposes as the social unit that effectively over long

periods of time enables individuals, or varying ages and of both sexes, to pool income coming from multiple sources in order to ensure their individual and collective reproduction and well-being. We shall call the multiple processes by which they pool income, allocate tasks, and make collective decisions *householding*.

The composition of the effective household becomes a central object for empirical research. We do not presume that all members of the household are necessarily kin, much less a nuclear family, although no doubt in most cases most members of a household are kin and probably close kin. Nor do we presume that household is necessarily a group resident in the same house, or even in the same locality, although once again this is often the case. Households are defined as those who have de facto entered into long-term income-pooling arrangements. To be sure, this entails some set of mutual obligations, although no particular set is included in the definition.

This mode of defining the household is beset by all sorts of boundary problems. How long is long-term? How much pooling constitutes pooling? How many obligations constitute an ongoing set of mutual obligations? As persons enter and leave households periodically (certainly by birth and death, and quite often for other reasons), over what sequence of time ought one to measure the pooling activities? We deliberately leave these issues without answers at the level of definition, making defining households both an object of study and not presuming that there is only one set of possible boundaries for a household.

2. There is a further reason for our vagueness about boundaries. The household as an income-pooling unit is not a primordial essence. It is an historically created institution, both as an institution in general and in its particular varieties. Of course it is not the only such historically created institution. Our holistic conception of the capitalist world-economy as an historical system leads us to consider all the institutions of this system as a collective mutual creation. The states and the interstate system, the enterprises, the classes, the nations and ethnic groups, the social movements, the sciences, the educational and health structures are all equally historically created in a single, interrelated process, which is a continuing one.

It follows that we must ask why any of these institutions has taken the form that it has, generically as a form and specifically in all its variations.

None of this history is to be considered theoretically accidental, having no explanation other than it just happened to be that way for historical or cultural reasons.

In this case, the bounding of households is itself an historical process, which not only can but must be analyzed, as it is probably the key process in the functioning of householding and is what integrates this particular structure into the larger network of structures that constitute the capitalist world-economy. If bounding is key, then it behooves us to see what are the kinds of pressures to which the households are subject that lead them (or even force them) to modify their boundaries. We see three major kinds of pressures, which constitute our third, fourth, and fifth orienting propositions.

3. The capitalist world-economy operates through an axial division of labor that is hierarchical and involves commodity chains of production processes, some of which are more corelike and some of which are more peripheral. Any particular unit of production participates in one or multiple commodity chains. Furthermore, any particular unit of production competes with other units of production for its percentage of the total production for a specific point in the one or multiple commodity chains.

The number of competing units of production at particular nexuses of the commodity chain(s) is continually varying and can vary hypothetically from one to a very, very large number. This is the continuum of monopoly competition. It is quite clear that as the number of competing units in the world-economy as a whole goes down at any nexus toward one, the ability of the units of production located at this nexus to increase their net profit goes up, and as the number goes up toward some very large number, the ability to obtain net profit goes down. This is essentially the difference between being corelike and being peripheral.

It is further clear that the total net profit extracted at any nexus of a chain is related to the total net profit (or extracted surplus value) in the sum of all the nexuses. Thus, as one nexus becomes more or less profitable, it affects the level of profitability of other nexuses in the commodity chain or chains of which it is a part. That is to say, coreness or peripherality is a relation of one nexus to other nexuses. The nature of the actual economic activity is irrelevant, only the degree to which at any given point in time, participants (owners) at this nexus are in a more or less favorable position to obtain a larger or less large proportion of the total surplus value created in the commodity chain.

Commodity chains typically are very long with very many nexuses. Typically, too, the production units of a given nexus are located in a large number of political units, although the more corelike the nexus, the fewer the number of countries containing production units belonging to that nexus. And typically, it is difficult to go from one end of a commodity chain to the other without crossing frontiers (often many frontiers).

The modes of remunerating labor at different nexuses of the commodity chain are multiple. Two things are true: Most commodity chains will have various modes at different nexuses. Many nexuses will have more than one mode; that is, different production units on the same nexus may use different modes of remuneration.

Finally, it is clear that as the world-economy goes through its cyclical patterns of global expansion and global contraction, which reflect global ability to extract surplus value and, therefore, to accumulate capital, there will be pressures of varying intensities on the units of production to reduce costs. Global contraction will lead to squeezes that force units of production to find ways of reducing costs. One such way of course is to reduce the cost of labor. This may in turn lead to changes in the mode of remunerating labor.

Now what has all this to do with the structure of households? A very great deal. A household is a unit that pools income for purposes of reproduction. If the income it receives is reduced, it must either live on less income or find substitute income. Of course, there comes a point where it cannot survive on less income (or survive very long) and, therefore, the only alternative is to find substitute income.

The household with the least flexibility, as total income goes down, is the household most dependent on wage-income, since the ability to obtain wage-income (or a certain level of wage-income) is a function of the offer by someone outside the household of that wage-employment. A household can most readily affect its total income by investing its labor power in activities it can autonomously launch. It can do this most obviously in terms of subsistence income, and it can also try to do this in the securing of market and rent income. It can even try to invest its time in the securing of additional transfer-income, though this may be more difficult.

But the ability to secure nonwage forms of income is itself a function of the boundaries of the household. One that is too small (say, a truly nuclear family) may simply not have the hours available to generate the necessary income. On the other hand, a very extended household may have too much of a gap in income realistically to hope to overcome it. Such very extended households have however become relatively rare in the poorer strata of the world's households, which tend to vary from very small to medium in size. Ergo, typically, stagnations in the world-economy create pressures on small household structures to enlarge boundaries and to self-exploit more.

Seen from the perspective of the employer of wage-labor, it is preferable, other things being equal, to employ persons who are less rather than more dependent on wage-income (let us call such households *semi-proletarian* households). A wage-worker in a semiproletarian household is more able to accept a low real wage since this worker may be able to assume that, via self-exploitation, other compensating forms of income will be available to him or her. The more proletarian (that is, wage-dependent) the *household*, the more the individual wage-worker is compelled to demand higher real wages (a so-called living wage). This is for example why we see, in times of stagnation in the world-economy, relocation of industries from one zone to another. They are moving primarily to reduce wage costs, and they can do this because of the household structures prevalent in the zone into which they are moving.

If this is so, then both the cyclical rhythms and the secular trends of the capitalist world-economy should affect the modal boundaries of household structures. The cyclical rhythms and the secular trends of the capitalist world-economy should affect the modal boundaries of household structures. The cyclical rhythms—the expansions and contractions of the world-economy—should lead to a shifting rhythm of modal household composition. Periods of expansion should see a shift in the direction of relatively greater wage-dependence and relatively narrower boundaries of inclusion, while periods of stagnation should see a shift in the reverse direction. Obviously, we are talking only of shifts and not sudden and complete transformation. And obviously too this will vary according to the degree to which particular subareas benefit from or are hurt by the global rhythms.

In addition, however, the world-economy has secular trends. The stagnation phases of the world-economy's rhythms are not symmetrical to its expansion phases. There results a certain "ratchet" effect, which leads to some long-term *slow* upward curves. The one that is most relevant here is the slow upward curve of worldwide proletarianization, which should find some reflection in a *slow* upward curve of the type of household structures most consonant with wage-dependence.

4. Thus far, the pressures on household boundaries of which we have been speaking seem to be nontangible, proceeding from obscure market forces to whose abstract consequences households feel it necessary to respond by altering their composition and perhaps their mode of functioning and internal decision-making. No doubt these obscure market forces are real and no doubt, too, households can perceive their effects and respond to them. There is a growing literature that suggests that households respond relatively rapidly to economic conditions altering their composition and boundaries.

There are other forces which are more direct, more immediate, and more imperious. We tend to call such forces *political* and to locate them primarily in the state-machinery—or rather in the multiple levels and forms of state machinery—laws and policies that direct households about a large number of possibilities, and issues that determine their composition: possibilities and requirements of co-residence; financial and legal responsibilities; fiscal obligations; right to physical movement; constraints on the physical location of economic activities; rules concerning house and remuneration of work; rules about market behavior; and eligibility for transfer income.

Indeed the list of matters about which the state legislates is extremely long, even in the more laissez-faire-oriented political regimes. Not only does the state legislate on a vast gamut of matters affecting the structure and composition of households, but it legislates constantly. That is, the rules are never set once and for all. They are regularly being revised.

The bases on which particular states decide to revise their rules are, to be sure, multiple. One major factor is the attempt of the state to maintain its own budgetary balance and the collectivity's economic survival (as reflected say in a "balance of payments") as this faces the changing realities of the world economy within which it operates. A state may decide it wishes to be the locale to which a large industry in another state may consider relocating because of world economic stagnation. It may then take concrete steps to ensure that the household structures of at least a portion of its citizenry are such, or become such, that the owners of the large industry will find a local market for wage-labor at wage-levels they find attractive.

Or a state may need to restore its budgetary balance which has been upset by some changes in the realities of the world-economy. It may then decide on major fiscal or social welfare reforms, which will affect the inflows and outflows of the state's treasure. Such changes may have a significant impact on budgetary calculations for particular groups of household structures, forcing them, in order to survive, to recompose the household.

Of course, the state may even be more direct. It may actually ordain household structures, by controlling the right to migrate (across frontiers, from rural to urban areas), or by decreeing certain legal obligations of kin to each other, or by making its own obligations to provide household income contingent on households being structured in specific ways, or by forbidding urban land to be used for agricultural purposes.

Thus, our fourth orienting proposition is that states always have policies about household composition and boundaries and, furthermore, that such policies are not simply givens, but change. States therefore constrain households. But conversely the state itself is the vector of political forces and households participate in these political forces that put pressure upon the state to move in specific directions.

5. Both the obscure market forces and the more visible state machineries appear to the household as something external to it, to which it has to respond in some way. But the realities of the world-system of which we are a part enter into the internal mental frameworks that we utilize to respond to these other apparently external forces.

Households think of themselves as belonging to communities, multiple communities. If the boundaries of the community are derived from the obscure market forces, we call it a *class*. If the boundaries are derived from or related to existing or potential state structures, we call it a *nation*. In some sense, both class-consciousness and nationalism are conceived of as simultaneously subjective and objective realities. That is, we feel ourselves to be of a given class, of a given nation, but we also know that because they are defined in terms of external phenomena, membership is alterable. We can theoretically change our class affiliation, our national allegiance. Some people do (even if most do not). The possibility is nonetheless felt to be there, and by and large it is considered "legitimate" for a household to make a change should it wish to and/or should it be possible to do so. The "legitimacy" of such change is subject to certain constraints relating to the moment of change—it is frowned upon to shift membership at moments when the community is in crisis.

There is a third type of community affiliation which, in common conception, is thought simply to be there and which people claim is not somehow determined by external structures. We call this *ethnicity*, and by this we mean a collection of cultural norms, perhaps a common language, sometimes a religious affiliation, which mark us off from others *of the same class and nation*. It is furthermore believed that this community membership is not subject to change. That this is not in fact true does not diminish the importance of the widespread belief that it is true.

Our *ethnicity*, our *culture* (or *subculture*) is a crucial defining category for household structures—in two ways. Households are the prime socializing agency into the norms of ethnicity. We learn these norms as children within a household, and we are most immediately constrained to observe them—as adults or children—by others in the same household.

But what norms are they that we learn in a household and consider to be our culture or a good part of it? The norms relate to all areas of activity, but first of all and most importantly to the operation of the household itself. We are taught rules of legitimacy concerning sexual behavior. We are taught obligations (and their limits) of observing *non*market criteria in internal household transactions. We are taught norms about our sharing obligations, that is, with whom we ought to pool income that is juridically defined as owned by an individual.

We are also taught norms about how to relate to the work world and to the state. We are taught to be more (or less) industrious. We are taught to be oriented to upward mobility or to accepting our place. We are taught to be more submissive to the state (law-abiding) or more intransigent (individual independence or collective rebelliousness). We are taught to be more or less self-denying or self-indulgent. We are taught to define intercommunity obligations narrowly or broadly.

As one draws up the list of all the things that are involved in one's ethnicity, two things become obvious. It is a very broad list, impinging not merely upon the household structure but quite explicitly on how these structures should relate to economic and political institutions. Second, the list itself is constantly evolving. That is, the norms of a given ethnic group are themselves changing; indeed the very boundaries (and names) of the groups evolve. We see then that, far from being somehow just there, somehow more internal, ethnicity is simply a third modality by which the forces in the total historical system mold each other.

It consequently should come as no surprise to find a triple correlation which, while not total, is strong: ethnicity, type of household structure, ways in which household members relate to the overall economy. We are very aware of this phenomenon in its most unpalatable form: discrimination in the work (or political) arena. But it operates as well, and more frequently, in subtler guises: by orienting households to greater or lesser wage-dependence, by legitimating (or not) certain kinds of market or subsistence involvement, by pressing toward or away from certain kinds of transfer payments.

A household normally has a single ethnicity. If, by marriage, there is a mixture, the intrusive element tends to convert, if not formally, at least de facto. If this does not happen, the household has survival problems. The household's ethnicity constitute a set of rules that very largely ensure that it will operate in specific ways. If, because of changes in the world-economy, such modalities of action are no longer useful, ethnic groups find themselves under external pressure to evolve, that is, to change their norms, even to change their ethnic boundaries.

There is at this point one bugaboo to set aside. It may be said that our concept seems to diminish, underplay, or even eliminate the autonomous role of the household—the household as actor, and not as dependent variable. Not at all! The household is as autonomous as the state, the firm, the class, or indeed as any other actor. As autonomous or as little autonomous. All these so-called actors are part of one historical system; they compose it. They are determined by it, but they also determine it, in a process of constant interaction that is so imbricated that there is no prime mover. Had we set out to reconceptualize and analyze the state or the firm or the class it might have equally seemed, once the matter was laid out, that its autonomy as an actor had been denied. What is inherent in a holistic view of an historical system is that the actors are simultaneously produced by the system and produce (that is, constitute) the system. The whole issue of who is autonomous is a nonissue.

These then are our five orienting processes: the household as an income-pooling unit as our basic unit of analysis; the household as an entity whose boundaries and composition are subject to continuing change; the impact of the cycles and trends of the world-economy upon household structures; the role of the state-machinery in molding and re-molding household structures; the role of ethnicity as a modality of so-cializing household members into particular economic roles, and the changeability of these norms. They add up to a concept of *household* and therefore of *householding* that serves as a basis of our analysis of empirical reality.

NOTE

1. According to most conventional accounts discrimination is impossible to maintain since "if all firms are profit-maximizers, then all will demand the services of the low-wage individuals, bid-ding their wages up until the wage differential is eliminated" (Stiglitz, 1973, p. 287).

REFERENCES

Eisenstein, Z.R. (1979). *Capitalist Patriarchy and the Case of Socialist Feminism*. New York: Monthly Review Press.

Donzelot, J. (1979). *The Policing of Families*. New York: Pantheon.

Goode, W.J. (1963). *World Revolution and Family Patterns*. New York: John Wiley.

Parsons, T. (1955). *Family Socialization and Interaction Processes*. Glencoe, Il.: Free Press.

Redclift, N., & Mingione, E. (Eds.). (1985). *Beyond Employment: Household, Gender, and Sub-sistence*. London: Basil Blackwell.

Smith, J. (1984). "The Paradox of Women's Employment: The Importance of Being Marginal." *Signs, X*, 291–310.

Smith, J. (1987). "Transforming Households: Working Class Women and Economic Crisis." *Social Problems, XXXIV*, 416–436.

Stiglitz, J.F. (1973). "Approaches to the Economics of Discrimination." *American Economic Review*, Papers and Proceedings of the 85th Annual Meeting, *LXIII*, 280–298.

16—The Three Instances of Hegemony in the History of the Capitalist World-Economy

A crucial element in the institutionalization of the modern world-system has been the creation of the modern sovereign state and of the modern interstate system, the combination of which provide the political framework within which the capitalist division of labor occurs. One crucial element of its functioning is that there is a cyclical rhythm marked by the rise and fall of hegemonic powers within the system. It is argued here that this has occurred only three times.

When one is dealing with a complex, continuously evolving, large-scale historical system, concepts that are used as shorthand descriptions for structural patterns are only useful to the degree one clearly lays out their purpose, circumscribes their applicability, and specifies the theoretical framework they presuppose and advance.

Let me therefore state some premises which I shall not argue at this point. If you are not willing to regard these premises as plausible, you will not find the way I elaborate and use the concept of hegemony very useful. I assume that there exists a concrete singular historical system which I shall call the "capitalist world-economy," whose temporal boundaries go from the long sixteenth century to the present. Its spatial boundaries originally included Europe (or most of it) plus Iberian America but they subsequently expanded to cover the entire globe. I assume this totality is a *system*, that is, that it has been relatively autonomous of external forces; or to put it another way, that its patterns are explicable largely in terms of its internal dynamics. I assume that it is an *historical* system, that is, that it was born, has developed, and will one day cease to exist (through disintegration or fundamental transformation). I assume lastly that it is the dynamics of the system itself that explain its historically changing characteristics. Hence, insofar as it is a system, it has structures and these structures manifest themselves in cyclical rhythms, that is, mechanisms which reflect and ensure repetitious patterns. But insofar as this system is historical, no rhythmic movement ever returns the system to an equilibrium point but instead moves the system along various continua which may be called the secular trends of this system. These trends eventually must culminate in the impossibility of containing further reparations of the structured dislocations by restorative mechanisms. Hence the system undergoes what some call "bifurcating turbulence" and others the "transformation of quantity into quality."

To these methodological or metaphysical premises, I must add a few substantive ones about the operations of the capitalist world-economy. Its mode of production is capitalist; that is, it is predicated on the endless accumulation of capital. Its structure is that of an axial social division of labor exhibiting a core/periphery tension based on unequal exchange. The political superstructure of this system is that of a set of so-called sovereign states defined by and constrained by their membership in an interstate network or system. The operational guidelines of this interstate system include the so-called balance of power, a mechanism designed to ensure that no single state ever has the capacity to transform this interstate system into a single world-empire whose boundaries would match that of the axial division of labor. There have of course been repeated attempts throughout the history of the capitalist world-economy to transform it in the direction of a world-empire, but these attempts have all been frustrated. However, there have also been repeated and quite different attempts by given states to achieve hegemony in the interstate system, and these attempts have in fact succeeded on three occasions, if only for relatively brief periods.

The thrust of hegemony is quite different from the thrust to world-empire; indeed it is many ways almost its opposite. I will therefore (1) spell out what I mean by hegemony, (2) describe the analogies in the three purported instances, (3) seek to decipher the roots of the thrust to hegemony and suggest why the thrust to hegemony has succeeded three times but never lasted too long, and (4) draw inferences about what we may expect in the proximate future. The point of doing all this is not to erect a Procrustean category into which to fit complex historical reality but to illuminate what I believe to be one of the central processes of the modern world-system.

(1) Hegemony in the interstate system refers to that situation in which the ongoing rivalry between the so-called "great powers" is so unbalanced that one power can largely impose its rules and its wishes (at the very least by effective veto power) in the economic, political, military, diplomatic, and even cultural arenas. The material base of such power lies in the ability of enterprises domiciled in that power to operate more efficiently in all three major economic arenas—agro-industrial production, commerce, and finance. The edge in efficiency of which we are speaking is one so great that these enterprises can not only outbid enterprises domiciled in other great powers in the world market in general, but quite specifically in very many instances within the home markets of the rival powers themselves.

I mean this to be a relatively restrictive definition. It is not enough for one power's enterprises simply to have a larger share of the world market than any other or simply to have the most powerful military forces or the largest political role. I mean hegemony only to refer to situations in which the edge is so significant that allied major powers are *de facto* client states and opposed major powers feel relatively frustrated and highly defensive vis-à-vis the hegemonic power. And yet while I want to restrict my definition to instances where the margin or power differential is really great, I do not mean to suggest that there is ever any moment when a hegemonic power is omnipotent and capable of doing anything it wants. Omnipotence does not exist within the interstate system.

Hegemony therefore is not a state of being but rather one end of a fluid continuum which describes the rivalry relations of great powers to each other. At one end of this continuum is an almost even balance, a situation in which many powers exist, all somewhat equal in strength, and with no clear or continuous groupings. This is rare and unstable. In the great middle of this continuum, many powers exist, grouped more or less into two camps, but with several neutral or swing elements, and with neither side (nor *a fortiori* any single state) being able to impose its will on others. This is the statistically normal situation of rivalry within the interstate system. And at the other end lies the situation of hegemony, also rare and unstable.

At this point, you may see what it is I am describing but may wonder why I am bothering to give it a name and thereby focus attention upon it. It is because I suspect hegemony is not the result of a random reshuffling of the cards but is a phenomenon that emerges in specifiable circumstances and plays a significant role in the historical development of the capitalist world-economy.

(2) Using this restrictive definition, the only three instances of hegemony would be the United Provinces in the mid-seventeenth century, the United Kingdom in the mid-nineteenth, and the United States in the mid-twentieth. If one insists on dates, I would tentatively suggest as maximal bounding points: 1625–72, 1815–73, 1945–67. But of course, it would be a mistake to try to be too precise when our measuring instruments are both so complex and so crude.

I will suggest four areas in which it seems to me what happened in the three instances was analogous. To be sure, analogies are limited. And to be sure, since the capitalist world-economy is in my usage a single continuously evolving entity, it follows by definition that the overall

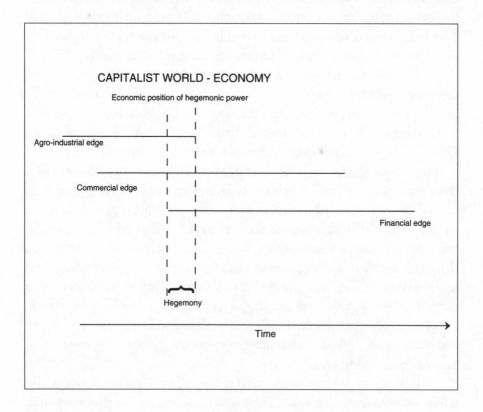

Chart 1

structure was different at each of the three points in time. The differences were real, the outcome of the secular trends of the world-system. But the structural analogies were real as well, the reflection of the cyclical rhythms of this same system.

The first analogy has to do with the sequencing of achievement and loss of relative efficiencies in each of the three economic domains. What I believe occurred was that in each instance enterprises domiciled in the given power in question achieved their edge first in agro-industrial production, then in commerce, and then in finance.[1] I believe they lost their edge in this sequence as well (this process having begun but not yet having been completed in the third instance). Hegemony thus refers to that short interval in which there is *simultaneous* advantage in all three economic domains.

The second analogy has to do with the ideology and policy of the hegemonic power. Hegemonic powers during the period of their hegemony tended to be advocates of global "liberalism." They came forward as defenders of the principle of the free flow of the factors of production (goods, capital, and labor) throughout the world-economy. They were hostile in general to mercantilist restrictions on trade, including the existence of overseas colonies for the stronger countries. They extended this liberalism to a generalized endorsement of liberal parliamentary institutions (and a concurrent distaste for political change by violent means), political restraints on the arbitrariness of bureaucratic power, and civil liberties (and a concurrent open door to political exiles). They tended to provide a high standard of living for their national working classes, high by world standards of the time.

None of this should be exaggerated. Hegemonic powers regularly made exceptions to their anti-mercantilism, when it was in their interest to do so. Hegemonic powers regularly were willing to interfere with political processes in other states to ensure their own advantage. Hegemonic powers could be very repressive at home, if need be, to guarantee the national "consensus." The high working-class standard was steeply graded by internal ethnicity. Nevertheless, it is quite striking that liberalism as an ideology did flourish in these countries at precisely the moments of their hegemony, and to a significant extent only then and there.

The third analogy is in the pattern of global military power. Hegemonic powers were primarily sea (now sea/air) powers. In the long as-cent to hegemony, they seemed very reluctant to develop their armies, discussing openly the potentially weakening drain on state revenues and manpower of becoming tied down in land wars. Yet each found finally that it had to develop a strong land army as well to face up to a major land-based rival which seemed to be trying to transform the world-economy into a world-empire.

In each case, the hegemony was secured by a thirty-year-long world war. By a world war, I shall mean (again somewhat restrictively) a land-based war that involves (not necessarily continuously) almost all the major military powers of the epoch in warfare that is very destructive of land and population. To each hegemony is attached one of these wars. World War Alpha was the Thirty Years' War from 1618–48, when Dutch interests triumphed over Hapsburg in the world-economy. World War Beta was the Napoleonic Wars from 1792–1815, when British interests triumphed over French. World War Gamma was the long Euroasian wars from 1914–45 when U.S. interests triumphed over German.

While limited wars have been a constant of the operations of the interstate system of the capitalist world-economy (there having been scarcely any year when there was not some war some place within the system), world wars have been, by contrast, a rarity. In fact their rarity and the fact that the number and timing seem to have correlated with the achievement of hegemonic status by one power brings us to the fourth analogy.

If we look to those very long cycles that Rondo Cameron has dubbed "logistics," we can see that world wars and hegemony have been in fact related to them. There has been very little scholarly work done on these logistics. They have been most frequently discussed in the comparisons between the A–B sequences of 1100–1450 and 1450–1750. There are only a few discussions of the logistics that may exist after the latter point in time. But if we take the prime observation which has been used to define these logistics—secular inflation and deflation—the pattern seems in fact to have continued.

It therefore might be plausible to argue the existence of such (price) logistics up to today using the following dates: 1450–1730, with 1600–1650 as a flat peak; 1730–1897, with 1810–17 as a peak; and 1897 to ?, with an as yet uncertain peak. If there are such logistics, it turns out that the world war and the (subsequent) hegemonic era are located somewhere around (just before and after) the peak of the logistic. That is to say, these processes seem to be the product of the long competitive expansion which seemed to have resulted in a particular concentration of economic and political power.

The outcome of each world war included a major restructuring of the interstate system (Westphalia; the Concert of Europe; the U.N. and Bretton Woods) in a form consonant with the need for relative stability of the now hegemonic power. Furthermore, once the hegemonic position was eroded economically (the loss of the efficiency edge in agro-industrial production), and therefore hegemonic decline set in, one consequence seemed to be the erosion of the alliance network which the hegemonic power had created patiently, and ultimately a serious reshuffling of alliances.

In the long period following the era of hegemony, two powers seemed eventually to emerge as the "contenders for the succession"—England and France after Dutch hegemony; the U.S. and Germany after British; and now Japan and western Europe after U.S. Furthermore, the eventual winner of the contending pair seemed to use as a conscious part of its strategy the gentle turning of the old hegemonic power into its "junior partner"—the English vis-à-vis the Dutch, the U.S. vis-à-vis Great Britain . . . and now?

(3) Thus far I have been primarily descriptive. I realize that this description is vulnerable to technical criticism. My coding of the data may not agree with everyone else's. I think nonetheless that as an initial effort this coding is defensible and that I have therefore outlined a broad repetitive pattern in the functioning of the interstate question. The question now is how to interpret it. What is there in the functioning of a capitalist world-economy that gives rise to such a cyclical pattern in the interstate system?

I believe this pattern of the rise, temporary ascendancy, and fall of hegemonic powers in the interstate system is merely one aspect of the central role of the political machinery in the functioning of capitalism as a mode of production.

There are two myths about capitalism put forward by its central ideologues (and, strangely, largely accepted by its nineteenth-century critics). One is that it is defined by the free flow of the factors of production.

The second is that it is defined by the non-interference of the political machinery in the "market." In fact, capitalism is defined by the *partially* free flow of the factors of production and by the *selective* interference of the political machinery in the "market." Hegemony is an instance of the latter.

What defines capitalism most fundamentally is the drive for the endless accumulation of capital. The interferences that are "selected" are those which advance this process of accumulation. There are however two problems about "interference." It has a cost, and therefore the benefit of any interference is only a benefit to the extent it exceeds this cost. Where the benefits are available without any "interference," this is obviously desirable, as it minimizes the "deduction." And secondly, interference is always in favor of one set of accumulators as against another set, and the latter will always seek to counter the former. These two considerations circumscribe the politics of hegemony in the interstate system.

The costs to a given entrepreneur of state "interference" are felt in two main ways. First, in financial terms, the state may levy direct taxes which affect the rate of profit by requiring the firm to make payments to the state, or indirect taxes, which may alter the rate of profit by affecting the competitiveness of a product. Secondly, the state may enact rules which govern flows of capital, labor, or goods, or may set minimum and/or maximum prices. While direct taxes always represent a cost to the entrepreneur, calculations concerning indirect taxes and state regulations are more complex, since they represent costs both to the entrepreneur and to (some of) his competitors. The chief concern in terms of individual accumulation is not the absolute cost of these measures, but the comparative cost. Costs, even if high, may be positively desirable from the standpoint of a given entrepreneur, if the state's actions involve still higher costs to some competitor. Absolute costs are only of concern if the loss to the entrepreneur is greater than the medium-run gain which is possible through greater competitiveness brought about by such state actions. It follows that absolute cost is of greatest concern to those entrepreneurs who would do best in open market competition in the absence of state interference.

In general, therefore, entrepreneurs are regularly seeking state interference in the market in multiple forms—subsidies, restraints of trade, tariffs (which are penalties for competitors of different nationality), guarantees, maxima for input prices and minima for output prices, etc. The intimidating effect of internal and external repression is also of direct economic benefit to entrepreneurs. To the extent that the ongoing process of competition and state interference leads to oligopolistic conditions within state boundaries, more and more attention is naturally paid to securing the same kind of oligopolistic conditions in the most important market, the world market.

The combination of the competitive thrust and constant state interference results in a continuing pressure towards the concentration of capital. The benefits of state interference inside and outside the state boundaries is cumulative. In political terms, this is reflected as expanding world power. The edge a rising power's economic enterprises have vis-à-vis those of a competitive rising power may be thin and therefore insecure. This is where the world wars come in. The thirty-year struggle may be very dramatic militarily and politically. But the profoundest effect may be economic. The winner's economic edge is expanded by the very process of the war itself, and the post-war interstate settlement is designed to encrust that greater edge and protect it against erosion.

A given state thus assumes its world "responsibilities" which are reflected in its diplomatic, military, political, ideological, and cultural stances. All conspire to reinforce the cooperative relationship of the entrepreneurial strata, the bureaucratic strata, and with some lag the working-class strata of the hegemonic power. This power may then be exercised in a "liberal" form—given the real diminution of political conflict within the state itself compared to earlier and later periods, and to the importance in the interstate arena of delegitimizing the efforts of other state machineries to act against the economic superiorities of the hegemonic power.

The problem is that global liberalism, which is rational and cost effective, breeds its own demise. It makes it more difficult to retard the spread of technological expertise. Hence over time it is virtually inevitable that entrepreneurs coming along later will be able to enter the most profitable markets with the most advanced technologies and younger "plant," thus eating into the material base of the productivity edge of the hegemonic power.

Secondly, the internal political price of liberalism, needed to maintain uninterrupted production at a time of maximal global accumulation, is the creeping rise of real income of both the working strata and the cad-res located in the hegemonic power. Over time, this must reduce the competitive advantage of the enterprises located in this state.

Once the clear productivity edge is lost, the structure cracks. As long as there is a hegemonic power, it can coordinate more or less the political responses of all states with core-like economic activities to all peripheral states, maximizing thereby the differentials of unequal exchange. But when hegemony is eroded, and especially when the world-economy is in a Kondratieff downturn, a scramble arises among the leading powers to maintain their shares of the smaller pie, which undermines their collec-tive ability to extract surplus via unequal exchange. The rate of unequal exchange thereby diminishes (but never to zero) and creates further in-centive to a reshuffling of alliance systems.

In the period leading to the peak of a logistic, which leads towards the creation of the momentary era of hegemony, the governing parable is that of the tortoise and the hare. It is not the state that leaps ahead politi-cally and especially militarily that wins the race, but the one that plods along improving inch by inch its long-term competitiveness. This re-quires a firm but discreet and intelligent organization of the entrepre-neurial effort by the state-machinery. Wars may be left to others, until the climactic world war when the hegemonic power must at least invest its resources to clinch its victory. Thereupon comes "world responsibility" with its benefits but also its (growing) costs. Thus the hegemony is sweet but brief.

(4) The inferences for today are obvious. We are in the immediate post-hegemonic phase of this third logistic of the capitalist world-economy. The U.S. has lost its productive edge but not yet its commer-cial and financial superiorities; its military and political power edge is no longer so overwhelming. Its abilities to dictate to its allies (western Eu-rope and Japan), intimidate its foes, and overwhelm the weak (compare the Dominican Republic in 1965 with El Salvador today) are vastly im-paired. We are in the beginnings of a major reshuffling of alliances.[2] Yet, of course, we are only at the beginning of all this. Great Britain began to decline in 1873, but it was only in 1982 that it was openly challenged by Argentina, a middle-ranking military power.

The major question is whether this third logistic will act itself out along the lines of the previous ones. The great difference of this third logistic from the first two is that the capitalist world-economy has now entered into a structural crisis as an historical system. The question is whether this fact will obliterate these cyclical processes. I do not believe it will obliterate them but rather that it will work itself out in part through them.[3]

We should not invest more in the concept of hegemony than is there. It is a way of organizing our perception of process, not an "essence" whose traits are to be described and whose eternal recurrences are to be demonstrated and then anticipated. A processual concept alerts us to the forces at play in the system and the likely nodes of conflict. It does not do more. But it also does not do less. The capitalist world-economy is not comprehensible unless we analyze clearly what are the political forms which it has engendered and how these forms relate to other realities. The interstate system is not some exogenous, God-given, variable which mysteriously restrains and interacts with the capitalist drive for the end-less accumulation of capital. It is its expression at the level of the political arena.

NOTES

1. I have described this in empirical detail for the first instance in *The Modern World-System*, II: *Mercantilism and the Consolidation of the European World-Economy, 1600–1750* (New York: Academic, 1980), ch. 2.
2. See my "North Atlanticism in Decline," *SAIS Review*, No. 4, Summer, 1982, 21–26.
3. For a debate about this, see the Conclusion of S. Amin, G. Arrighi, A. G. Frank, & I. Wallerstein, *Dynamics of Global Crisis* (New York: Monthly Review Press, 1982).

17—Culture as the Ideological Battleground of the Modern World-System

The concept of culture has come to the forefront of everyone's attention in the last two decades. But the concept of culture is an extremely confused and confusing one. This article is my attempt to sort out the multiple meanings of the term, and to explain why, in the logic of the modern world-system, it has multiple meanings.

"It is not our human nature that is universal, but our capacity to create cultural realities, and then to act in terms of them." Sidney W. Mintz[1]

I

Culture is probably the broadest concept of all those used in the historical social sciences. It embraces a very large range of connotations, and thereby it is the cause perhaps of the most difficulty. There is, however, one fundamental confusion in our usage which I shall address.

One the one hand, one of the basic building stones of social science's view of the world, most explicitly emphasized by the anthropologists, is the conviction that, while all persons share some traits with all others, all persons also share other traits with only some others, and all persons have still other traits which they share with no one else. That is to say, the basic model is that each person may be described in three ways: the universal characteristics of the specie, the sets of characteristics that define that person as a member of a series of groups, that person's idiosyncratic characteristics. When we talk of traits which are neither universal nor idiosyncratic we often use the term "culture" to describe the collection of such traits, or of such behaviors, or of such values, or of such beliefs. In short, in this usage, each "group" has its specific "culture." To be sure, each individual is a member of many groups, and indeed of groups of very different kinds—groups, classified by gender, by race, by language, by class, by nationality, etc. Therefore, each person participates in many "cultures."

In this usage, culture is a way of summarizing the ways in which groups distinguish themselves from other groups. It represents what is shared within the group, and presumably simultaneously not shared (or not entirely shared) outside it. This is a quite clear and quite useful concept.

On the other hand, culture is also used to signify not the totality of the specificity of one group against another but instead certain characteristics *within* the group, as opposed to other characteristics within the same group. We use culture to refer to the "higher" arts as opposed to popular or everyday practice. We use culture to signify that which is "super-structural" as opposed to that which is the "base." We use culture to signify that which is "symbolic" as opposed to that which is "material." These various binary distinctions are not identical, although they all seem to go in the direction of the ancient philosophical distinctions between the "ideal" and the "real," or between the "mind" and the "body."

Whatever the merits of these binary distinctions, they all go in a quite different structural direction from the other use of culture. They point to a division within the group rather than to the unity of the group (which of course is the basis of division between groups). Now, this "confusion" of the two tonalities of the concept, "culture," is so long-standing that it cannot be a mere oversight, especially given the fact that the discussion of culture in general and of its definition in particular has been so voluminous throughout the nineteenth and twentieth centuries.

It is safest to presume that long-standing intellectual confusions are deliberate and the fact of the confusion should itself be the starting-point of the analysis. Since this voluminous discussion has in fact taken place largely within the confines of a single historical system, the capitalist world-economy, it may be that not only the discussion but the conceptual confusion are both the consequence of the historical development of this system and reflect its guiding logic.

The philosophical distinctions between the "ideal" and the "real" and between the "mind" and the "body" are very ancient, and have given rise, broadly speaking, to two perspectives, at least within the context of so-called Western philosophy. Those who have promoted the primacy of the "ideal" or of the "mind" have tended to argue that the distinction points to an ontological reality, and that the "ideal" or the "mind" is more important or nobler or in some way superior to the "real" or the "body." Those who have promoted the primacy of the "real" or the "body" did not however take the inverse position. Instead, they tended to argue that the "ideal" or the "mind" are not distinct essences but rather social inventions, and that only the "real" or the "body" truly exist. In short they have tended to argue that the very concept of the "ideal" or the "mind" are ideological weapons of control, intended to mask the true existential situation.

Let us thus designate as culture (usage I) the set of characteristics which distinguish one group from another, and as culture (usage II) some set of phenomena which are different from (and "higher" than) some other set of phenomena within any one group. There is one great problem about culture (usage I). Who or what has such a culture? It seems that "groups" have. But if "culture" is the term in our scientific vocabulary that has the broadest and most confusing usage, "group" is the term that has the vaguest usage. A "group" as a taxonomic term is anything anyone wishes to define as a group. There exists no doubt, to follow the *ultima ratio* of such a term, that a "group" consists of all those who are of a given height, or who have a certain color hair. But can such "groups" be said to have "cultures"? There would be few who would claim so. Obviously, it is only certain "groups" then that have "cultures."

We could try this exercise starting from the other direction. To what kinds of groups are "cultures" (usage I) normally attributed? Nations are often said to have a national culture. "Tribes" and/or "ethnic groups" are often said to have a culture. It is not unusual to read about the "culture" of "urban intellectuals," or of the "urban poor." More rarely, but frequently, we might read of the "culture" of "Communists" or of "religious fundamentalists." Now what those "groups" presumed to have "cultures" (always usage I) share in common is that they seem to have some kind of self-awareness (and therefore a sense of boundaries), some shared pattern of socialization combined with a system of "reinforcement" of their values or of prescribed behavior, and some kind of organization. The organization may be quite formalized, as in the case of a nation-state, or it can be quite indirect, as for example the shared newspapers, magazines, and possibly the voluntary associations which act as communication networks between "urban intellectuals."

However, as soon as I raise the question of who or what has a culture, it becomes immediately obvious how slippery is the terrain. What is the evidence that any given group has a "culture"? The answer is surely not that all presumed "members" of any of these groups act similarly to each other and differently from all others. At most, we could argue for a statistically significant relationship between group "membership" and certain behavior, or value-preferences, or whatever.

Furthermore, if we press the matter a little further, it is quite clear that our statistical findings would vary constantly (and probably significantly) over time. That is to say, behavior or value-preferences or however one defines culture is of course an evolving phenomenon, even if it is a slowly-evolving one, at least for certain characteristics (say, food habits).

Yet, on the other hand, it is surely true that people in different parts of the world, or in different epochs, or in different religious or linguistic communities do indeed behave differently from each other, and in certain ways that can be specified and fairly easily observed. For example, anyone who travels from Norway to Spain will note that the hour at which restaurants are most crowded for the "evening meal" is quite different in the two countries. And anyone who travels from France to the U.S. will observe that the frequency with which foreign strangers are invited to homes is quite different. The length of women's skirts in Brazil and Iran is surely strikingly different. And so on. And I have only cited here elements of so-called everyday behavior. Were I to raise more metaphysical issues, it would be easy, as everyone knows, to elucidate group differences.

So, on the one hand, differences are obvious—which is what the concept of culture (usage I) is about. And yet the degree to which groups are in fact uniform in their behavior is distressingly difficult to maintain. When Mintz says that we have a "capacity to create cultural realities and then to act in terms of them," I cannot but agree. But I then wonder how we can know who the "we" are who have this capacity. At that point, I become skeptical that we can operationalize the concept of culture (usage I) in any way that enables us to use it for statements that are more than trivial. The anthropologists, or at least some of them, have argued convincingly that the concept of "human nature" cannot be used to draw meaningful implications about real social situations. But is this not equally true of their proposed substitute, culture?

This then is where I begin. Culture (usage I) seems not to get us very far in our historical analyses. Culture (usage II) is suspect as an ideological cover to justify the interest of some persons (obviously the upper strata) within any given "group" or "social system" against the interests of other persons within this same group. And if, indeed, the very distinction of "ideal" and "real," "mind" and "body" were acknowledged to be an ideological weapon of control, then the confusion of the two usages of culture would be a very logical consequence, since it would no doubt add to the process of making the true existential situation. I would like therefore to trace the actual development of the "culture" (in either or both usages) over time within the historical system which has given birth to this extensive and confusing use of the concept of culture, the modern world-system which is a capitalist world-economy.

II

Let us begin by reviewing some of the realities of the evolution of this historical system, as they have affected the way its participants "theorized" it. That is, I am concerned with the degree to which this historical system became conscious of itself and began to develop intellectual and/or ideological frameworks which both justified it, and impelled its forward movement, and thereby sustained its reproduction. I shall mention six such realities which have implications for the theoretical formulations that have come to permeate the system.

1) The capitalist world-economy is constructed by integrating a geographically vast set of production processes. We call this the establishment of a single "division of labor." Of course, all historical systems are based on a division of labor, but none before was as complex, as extensive, as detailed, and as cohesive as that of the capitalist world-economy. The political framework within which this division of labor has grown up has not however been that of a world-empire, but instead that of an interstate system, itself a product of the historical development of this system. This interstate system has been composed of, and given birth and legitimacy to, a series of so-called sovereign states, whose defining

characteristic is their territorial distinctiveness and congruence combined with their membership in and constraint by this interstate system. It is not the interstate system, however, but the separate states that control the means of violence. Furthermore, their control is in theory exclusive within their respective jurisdictions. Although such total control is a myth, state preemption of violence is at least massive, if never exclusive.

This organization of social life where the predominant "economic" pressures are "international" (a bad term, but the one in common use), and the predominant "political" pressures are "national" points to a first contradiction in the way participants can explicate and justify their actions. How can one explain and justify them nationally and internationally simultaneously?

2) The capitalist world-economy functions, as do most (perhaps all) historical systems by means of a pattern of cyclical rhythms. The most obvious, and probably the most important, of these rhythms is a seemingly regular process of expansion and contraction of the world-economy as a whole. On present evidence, this cycle tends to be 50–60 years in length, covering its two phases.

The functioning of this cycle (sometimes called "long waves," sometimes Kondratieff cycles) is complex and I will not review it here.[2] One part, however, of the process is that, periodically, the capitalist world-economy has seen the need to expand the geographic boundaries of the system as a whole, creating thereby new loci of production to participate in its axial division of labor. Over 400 years, these successive expansions have transformed the capitalist world-economy from a system located primarily in Europe to one that covers the entire globe.

The successive expansions that have occurred have been a conscious process, utilizing military, political, and economic pressures of multiple kinds, and of course involving the overcoming of political resistances in the zones into which the geographic expansion was taking place. We call this process "incorporation," and it too is a complex one.[3] This process points to a second contradiction which the populations of each successively incorporated zone faced. Should the transformations that were occurring in their zone be conceived of as changes from a local and traditional "culture" to a worldwide modern "culture," or were these populations rather simply under pressure to give up their "culture" and adopt that of the Western imperialist power or powers? Was it, that is, a case of modernization or of Westernization?

3) Capitalism is a system based on the endless accumulation of capital. It is therefore a system which requires the maximum appropriation of surplus-value. There are two ways to increase the appropriation of surplus-value. One is that workers work harder and more efficiently, thereby creating greater output with the same amount of inputs (other than human labor-time). The second way is to return less of the value that is produced to the direct producers. In short, capitalism by definition involves a pressure on all direct producers to work more and to be paid less.

This requirement however runs afoul of the logic of the individual's pursuit of his/her own interest. The most obvious incentive for hard work is higher recompense. One can substitute coercion for higher recompense, but of course coercion also has a cost and thereby its use also reduces surplus-value. It follows that, unless one can substitute (at least partially) some motivation for work other than recompense or fear, it is very difficult to obtain simultaneously the twin goals of harder work and lower pay. How can one think about this system in such a way as to achieve the objective?

4) Capitalism as a system requires movement and change, at least formal change. The maximal accumulation of capital requires not only goods and capital to circulate but manpower as well. It requires in addition a constant evolution in the organization of production in terms both of the nature of the leading sectors and of the sites of production. We usually analyze these phenomena under two labels—that of economic innovation and that of the rise and fall of nations.

One principal consequence of this reality is the enormous emphasis placed within the modern world-system on the virtues of "newness." No previous historical system has ever been based on a theory of progress, indeed a theory of inevitable progress. But the emphasis on newness, and its constant implementation (at least at the level of form) raises precisely the question of legitimacy—legitimacy of the historical system in general; legitimacy of its key political institution, the various sovereign states, in particular. From Bodin to Weber to Mao Zedong the question of legitimacy has been constantly debated and seen as an extremely knotty issue to resolve. It is particularly difficult because the very advocacy of the virtues of newness undermines the legitimacy of any authority, however laboriously the legitimacy was achieved.

5) The capitalist system is a polarizing system, both in its reward pattern and in the degree to which persons are increasingly forced to play socially polarized roles. It is however also an expanding system and therefore one in which all the absolute parameters have taken the form of a linear upward projection over time. Since its outset, the capitalist world-economy has had ever more productive activity, ever more "value" produced, ever more population, ever more inventions. Thus, it has had ever more outward signs of wealth.

And yet, if it has been a polarizing system, it must at the least be true that this increase of wealth has been going to only a small proportion of the world's population. It might even be the case that real consumption per world capita has not been keeping pace. For example, it is surely the case that there is less physical space per capita and fewer trees per capita now than 400 years ago. What does this mean in terms of that elusive but very real phenomenon, the "quality of life"?

The contradiction therefore that needs to be handled is that between "progress" and deterioration, between visibly increasing wealth and very real impoverishment. The only way to defuse the resulting angers may well be denial, but how is it possible to deny phenomena that are so public, and whose public character is indeed one of the exigencies of the system? That is, the endless accumulation of capital requires as one of its mechanisms a collective orientation towards consumption.

6) Finally, the capitalist world-economy is an historical system. And being historical, it has a life cycle and, as any other such system, must at some point cease to function as the consequence of the aggregated results of its eventually paralyzing contradictions. But it is also a system which is based on a particular logic, that of the ceaseless accumulation of capital. Such a system therefore must preach the possibility of limitless expansion.

Limitless expansion can seem euphoric, as in the image of wafting upward into heaven, or disastrous, as in the image of hurtling downward into space. In a sense, both images constrain action since there seems to be little an individual can do to affect the pattern. The mundane reality however is more complex, more unsettling, but also more subject to human will.

As systems move towards their natural demise they find themselves in "transition" to uncertain futures. And the very uncertainty, which at one level is liberating, is also disconcerting. Thus we are faced with the dilemma of how to think about such transformation, whether to deny the process of systemic "death" or instead to welcome the process of systemic "birth."

I I I

The "culture," that is the idea-system, of this capitalist world-economy is the outcome of our collective historical attempts to come to terms with the contradictions, the ambiguities, the complexities of the sociopolitical realities of this particular system. We have done it in part by creating the concept of "culture" (usage I) as the assertion of unchanging realities amidst a world that is in fact ceaselessly changing. And we have done it in part by creating the concept of "culture" (usage II) as the justification of the inequities of the system, as the attempt to keep them unchanging in a world that is ceaselessly threatened by change.

The question is, how is this done? Since it is obvious that interests fundamentally diverge, it follows that such constructions of "culture" are scarcely neutral. Therefore, the very construction of cultures becomes a battleground, the key ideological battleground in fact of the opposing interests within this historical system.

The heart of the debate, it seems to me, revolves around the ways in which the presumed antinomies of unity and diversity, universalism and particularism, humanity and race, world and nation, person and man/woman have been manipulated. I have previously argued that the two principal ideological doctrines that have emerged in the history of the capitalist world-economy—that is, universalism on the one hand and racism and sexism on the other—are not opposites but a symbiotic pair. I have argued that their "right dosage" has made possible the functioning of the system, one which takes the form of a continuing ideological zigzag.[4]

It is this zigzag which is at the base of the deliberate confusions inherent in the two usages of the concept of "culture." I should like to illustrate the issues by analyzing some comments made by a political intellectual in Jamaica, Rex Nettleford, in a speech he gave in 1983 to a political party meeting, a party that calls itself the People's National Party. The speech itself, when reprinted, bore the title "Building a Nation, Shaping a Society." Nettleford wished to emphasize the importance of a "sense of history" in building a nation against those who "teach our young that they have no history worth studying, only a future which . . . they are expected to conquer." Here is what Nettleford said:

"Black" does not merely mean skin in the history of the Americas. It means culture—a culture woven out of the encounters between the millions of West Africans brought as slaves and the millions of Europeans who came as masters, settlers, or indentured labourers. In Jamaica and the Caribbean the substance of a truly indigenous life, for all its texture, has been forged in the crucible of the black majority's early efforts to come to terms with the new environment and to survive. That was a struggle of a fundamental and elemental kind, and it is that struggle which is being denied its proper place in the economic, social, and cultural ethos of this society. I sense a *deblackening* of the ethos, a persistent contempt in official and cocktail circles for the fruits of our people's labours, and a hypocritical refuge is being taken in our national motto by those who prefer to emphasize the word "many" since to them the "one" may mean the majority. "Out of many one people" becomes "out of many one." So we keep the country pluralist and divided with the marginalized majority remaining marginal, and a privileged few (with many "roast breadfruits" among them) holding on to the economic, social and cultural power in the land.

The real truth is that our people are better than we like to think: we are not that unsophisticated to be racist, but we are not that foolish not to be race conscious. And on that delicate balancing of sensibilities rests the unusual sophistication of the mass of this population. It is that sophistication which misleads not only our own leaders, but those from outside who say they want to help us. Our people who have gone through centuries of struggle know that "what is pertinent today is not simply freedom from foreign oppression (which in our own primitive way we can deal with), but the creation within this country of socio-economic and political frameworks which accord high values to the human personality." We are very uptight about our personae, about our personal recognition and status, and we hold suspect any class of people inside or outside our nation, who would agree with a once influential Jamaican private sector leader, who in criticising the policies of a certain regime in the recent past said that during the seventies "our rich national culture had been reduced, shrunken to fit into the narrow concept of a vigorous black culture." She was saying this in a country where the vast majority are hopelessly of that "culture." Anything that expresses the image of the majority is a "reduction" and a "shrinking"! We are not likely to shape a society or build a nation with such beliefs in place, and especially if they are to be found among those in the power structure; and so I implore this forum to think seriously on these things.[5]

Notice in this analysis that the definition of a culture is central. Nettleford wants to build and shape an entity he calls a nation or a society. This is of course standard language and seems to refer to culture (usage I), a usage which presumably emphasizes the ways in which Jamaicans are alike. But he proceeds to observe that others, "found among those in the power structure" of this same Jamaica, also claim they wish to do the same.

The two groups seem to be using the national motto "out of many one people" to mean opposite things. Those who Nettleford calls the "privileged few" emphasize "pluralism" within and unity without ("freedom from foreign oppression"). Nettleford says this neglects entirely the "black majority" who are "marginalized" and who are seeking "the creation within [Jamaica] of socio-economic and political frameworks which accord high values to the human personality" (which presumably means an increase in economic and social equality).

How are the privileged few doing this? By "a *deblackening* of the ethos," by hypocritically emphasizing the "many" in the national motto, by failing to teach a fact (one that is a fact however not of the history of Jamaica, but of the history of the Americas, and therefore of the world-system). This fact is that "millions of West Africans [were] brought as slaves" while "millions of Europeans . . . came as masters, settlers or indentured laborers." The historic encounters of these two groups "in Jamaica and the Caribbean" forged the "texture" of a "truly indigenous life." "Black" is the term of the resultant "culture," which is "vigorous" and not a "reduction" or a "shrinking."

So, in the end, what is being said is that the assertion of "blackness" as constitutive of the national "culture" of Jamaica (culture here in usage I) is the mode by which the "marginalized majority" can hope to protect themselves against the claims of the "privileged few" to represent a higher "culture" (usage II). Thus what seems particularist at the level of the world-system ("blackness") serves as an assertion of a universalist theme ("high values to the human personality"). This, says Nettleford, is being "race conscious" but not "racist," which he admits requires a "delicate balancing of sensibilities." In this complicated reasoning, which seems to be more correct, the more "blackness" that Jamaica would exhibit, the more color-blindness (or humanist values) it would exhibit.

Yes, you may respond, perhaps so, but where does this argument end? At what point do we cross the line from "race conscious" to "racism"? For there are clearly many, many cases across the world where the assertion of the particularist "culture" of the (national) "majority" to the exclusion of the minority or minorities could be seen as oppressive. Have Bretons no "cultural" claims in France, Swedes in Finland, Ainu in Japan, Tamils in Sri Lanka, Kurds in Turkey, Hungarians in Romania?

Nettleford might agree—I do not know—that all these latter groups have legitimate claims to their "cultural" assertion, and still argue that the situation is historically different in Jamaica. Why? Essentially because in Jamaica it is the majority that has been historically "marginalized," and not the various "minorities." And, as long as that remains true, then negritude or any similar particularism may serve as the negation of the negation, as Sartre argued in "Black Orpheus."[6]

What the Nettleford quote does is to demonstrate how tangled is the skein of cultural debate in the capitalist world-economy, but also how covered with nettles, and therefore how careful we need to be if we wish to understand and evaluate this ideological battleground.

IV

I would like to take each of the six contradictions of the capitalist world-economy and show how the ideologies of universalism and of racism-sexism help contain each of the contradictions, and why therefore the two ideologies are a symbiotic pair.

1) Since the capitalist world-economy is a world-system, and for some time now one that has expanded to cover the entire globe, it is easy to see how universalism reflects this phenomenon, and indeed this has been one of the most explicit explanations of the ideologists. Today we have a network of United Nations structures, based in theory on the Universal Declaration of Human Rights, asserting the existence of both international law and values of all humanity. We have universal time and space measurements. We have a scientific community who assert universal laws. Nor is this a phenomenon merely of the twentieth century. Uni-

versal science was already being proclaimed in the sixteenth century, and indeed far earlier. Grotius was writing about a universal "law of the seas" in the first half of the seventeenth century. And so on.

At the same time, of course, we have been erecting a network of "sovereign states" with clear territorial boundaries and with national laws, assemblies, languages, passports, flags, money, and above all citizens. The entire land area of the globe is today exhaustively divided into such units, which now number over 150.

There are two ways we can consider these 150 or so sovereign states. We can see them as very strong institutions whose raison d'être is to limit the validity of universal rules. Sovereignty means in theory the right to do within the frontiers of the country whatever the internal (and constitutionally appropriate) authorities decide to do. But of course, at the same time, these 150 or so units are an immense reduction from the number of political authorities (to use a vague term) which existed in the world as of say 1450. Almost every one of the 150 or so units comprises an area that in 1450 included more than one political authority. Thus most of these sovereign states face the issue of how they are to treat this "coming together" historically of what were previously separate entities. All of them, without any exception, do it on the principle of citizenship, a principle which today usually asserts that all persons born in that state are citizens (plus certain others) and that all such citizens enjoy equal rights. (The most notorious exception, South Africa, which as a state refuses to acknowledge the legitimacy of this theory of citizenship, is considered for that very reason a world scandal.) Thus, each state is proclaiming the universality of the equality of citizens, and virtually all states are accepting this principle as a sort of universal moral law.

We can assert, if we wish, that the principle of universalism both on a worldwide scale and within each of the sovereign states that constitute the interstate system is hypocritical. But it is precisely because there is in reality a hierarchy of states within the interstate system and a hierarchy of citizens within each sovereign state that the ideology of universalism matters. It serves on the one hand as a palliative and a deception and on the other as a political counterweight which the weak can use and do use against the strong.

But racism-sexism as an ideology equally serves to contain the contradiction involved in creating sovereign states within an interstate system that contains a single division of labor. For racism-sexism is precisely what legitimates the real inequalities, the always existing (if continually shifting) hierarchies both within the world-system as a whole and within each sovereign state. We know that the peoples of color were subjected to formal colonization as well as to slave labor during the history of this world-system. We know that there exist many formal discriminations concerning the movements of peoples. And we know that these phenomena have been justified by racist theories, sometimes based on pseudo-science (thereby deferring to the ideology of universalism) and sometimes based on unmitigated prejudice, as in the talk of a Yellow Peril which was so widespread in the White areas of the world in the beginning of the twentieth century.

At the state level, the phenomenon of justification by racism of an internal political, economic, and social hierarchy is so familiar that it is scarcely worth recounting. I would only point out two things. Where internal hierarchies cannot be based on skin color, they can always be based on other particularist criteria, as say in Northern Ireland. Secondly, everywhere—in all the states individually, and in the interstate system as a whole—the racist ideology takes the same form. It is argued that one group is genetically or "culturally" (note here, culture in usage II) inferior to another group in such a way that the group said to be inferior cannot be expected to perform tasks as well as the presumably superior group. This is said to hold true either eternally or for a very long period into the future (pending, in another deference to universalist doctrine, some very long-term educational process).

So racism is used, as we all know, to justify these hierarchies. But sexism? Yes, sexism too, and in two ways. First, if one examines racist terminology, one will find that it is regularly clothed in sexist language. The superior "race" is considered to be more masculine, the inferior one to be more feminine. It is as though sexism was even more deeply rooted than racism. Whereas a purely racist ideology might occasionally fail to persuade, the ideologues can find their clinching argument by adding the sexist overtones. So we hear arguments that the dominant group is more rational, more disciplined, more hard-working, more self-controlled, more independent, while the dominated group is more emotional, more self-indulgent, more lazy, more artistic, more dependent.

And this is of course the same set of characteristics that sexist ideology claims distinguish men from women.

There is a second way in which sexism doubles with racism. The dominated racial group, because it is said to be more self-indulgent, is thereby thought more aggressive sexually (and more pan-sexual as well). The males of the dominated group therefore represent a threat to the females of the dominant group who, although women and not men, are somehow more "self-controlled" than the males of the dominated group. But since they are nonetheless physically weaker, because they are women, they therefore require the active physical protection of the males of the dominant group.

Furthermore, we can turn this sexist argument around and still justify world hierarchies. Now that, as a result of recent political developments, women have gained more rights of various kinds in Western countries, the fact that they have not yet done as well politically in some Third World countries, say those countries in which Islam is strong, becomes itself a further justification of racist ideology. The Moslems, it is argued, are not culturally capable of recognizing the same universal principles of man-woman relations that are said to be accepted in the Western (or Judeo-Christian world) and from this it is said to follow that they are also incapable of many other things.

2) We have noted that the historic expansion of a capitalist world-economy originally located primarily in Europe to incorporate other zones of the globe created the contradiction of modernization versus Westernization. The simple way to resolve this dilemma has been to assert that they are identical. Insofar as Asia or Africa "Westernizes," it "modernizes." That is to say, the simplest solution was to argue that Western culture is in fact universal culture. For a long time the ideology remained at this simple level, whether it took the form of Christian proselytization or of the famous "mission civilisatrice" of France's colonial empire.

Of course, this sometimes took the slightly more sophisticated form of arguing that only Western civilization, of all world civilizations, was somehow capable of evolving from a pre-modern form to modernity. In a sense, this is what Orientalism as a discipline clearly implied. Clothed in the legitimation of particularism—Islam or India or China represented complex, high cultures which a Westerner could only appreciate after long, difficult, and sympathetic study—the Orientalists also suggested that these high Oriental cultures were historically frozen and could not evolve, but could only be "destroyed" from without. Various versions of anthropological theory—the search for the pristine pre-contact culture, but also the universalist distinction of structuralist anthropology between cold and hot cultures—led to the same conclusions. The West had emerged into modernity; the others had not. Inevitably, therefore, if one wanted to be "modern" one had in some way to be "Western" culturally. If not Western religions, one had to adopt Western languages. And if not Western languages, one had at the very minimum to accept Western technology, which was said to be based on the universal principles of science.

But at the very same time that the universalist ideologues were preaching the merits of Westernization or "assimilation," they were also (or others were also) preaching the eternal existence and virtue of difference. Thus a universalist message of cultural multiplicity could serve as a justification of educating various groups in their separate "cultures" and hence preparing them for different tasks in the single economy. The extreme version of this, and an explicitly theorized one, is *apartheid*. But lesser versions, perhaps less coherently articulated, have been widespread within the system.

Furthermore, racism and sexism can be justified by a rejection of Westernization which can take the form of legitimating indigenous ideological positions (a so-called revival of tradition) that include blatantly racist and sexist themes. At which point, we have a renewed justification of the worldwide hierarchy. It becomes legitimate to treat Iran as a pariah nation, not only because Iran uses "terrorist" tactics in the international arena, but because Iranian women are required to wear the *chador*.

3) The problem of getting workers to work harder at lower pay is inherently a difficult one. It runs against the grain of self-interest. The question therefore is whether there can exist an ideological motivation that might help achieve this contradictory objective of world capital. Let us see in what ways universalism and racism-sexism can serve this end.

Universalism can become a motivation for harder work insofar as the work ethic is preached as a defining centerpiece of modernity. Those who are efficient, who devote themselves to their work exemplify a value that is of universal merit and is said to be socially beneficial to all. This is true not only at the individual level but at the collective level. Thus states that are low in the hierarchy of the world-system, groups that are low in the hierarchy of states are adjured to overcome the handicap of lower status by joining in the universal ethos. By becoming "competitive" in the market, individuals and groups may obtain what others already have, and thus one day shall achieve equality. Until then, inequality remains inevitable.

Thus, the universal work ethic justifies all existing inequalities, since the explanation of their origin is in the historically unequal adoption by different groups of this motivation. States that are better off than other states, groups that are better off than other groups have achieved this advantage by an earlier, stronger, and more enduring commitment to the universal work ethic. Conversely, those who are worse off, therefore those who are paid less, are in this position because they merit it. The existence of unequal incomes thus becomes not an instance of racism-sexism but rather of the universal standard of rewarding efficiency. Those who have less have less became they have earned less.

But racism and sexism complement this universalizing theorem very well. Racism and sexism, when institutionalized, create a high correlation between low group status and low income. Thus, those at the lower end of the scale are easily identifiable by what may then be termed cultural criteria (culture, that is, in usage II). Culture (usage II) now becomes the explanation of the cause. Blacks and women are paid less because they work less hard, merit less. And they work less hard because there is something, if not in their biology, at least in their "culture" which teaches them values that conflict with the universal work ethos.

Furthermore, we can enlist the dominated groups in their own oppression. Insofar as they cultivate their separateness as "cultural" groups, which is a mode of political mobilization against unequal status, they socialize their members into cultural expressions which distinguish them from the dominated groups, and thus into some at least of the values attributed to them by racist and sexist theories. And they do this, in a seeming paradox, on the grounds of the universal principle of the equal validity of all cultural expressions.

4) Modernity as a central universalizing theme gives priority to newness, change, progress. Through the ages, the legitimacy of political systems had been derived from precisely the opposite principle, that of

oldness, continuity, tradition. There was a straightforwardness to pre-modern modes of legitimation which does not exist anymore. Political legitimacy is a much more obscure objective within the realities of the capitalist world-economy, yet states of course seek constantly to achieve it. Some degree of legitimacy is a crucial element in the stability of all regimes.

Here is where culture (usage I) can be very helpful. For in the absence of the personalized legitimacy of monarchical-aristocratic systems, where real power normally defines the limits of legitimacy, a fictionalized collectivity with a collective soul, a hypothetical "nation" whose roots are located in days of yore, is a marvelous substitute. Few governments in the history of the capitalist world-economy have failed to discover the power of patriotism to achieve cohesion. And patriotism has quite often been reinforced by or transformed into racism (jingoist chauvinism, opposition of the citizen to the stranger or immigrant) and sexism (the presumed martial nature of males).

But in the real world of the capitalist world-economy with its regular rise and decline of nations, a multifarious set of patriotisms offers little in the way of explanation, especially for the losers in the cyclical shifts. Here then legitimacy can be restored by appealing to the universalizing principles of appropriate political and social change which, by a change in state structure (a "revolution") will make possible (for the first time or once again) national development. Thus, by appealing to culture (usage II), the advanced elements of the nation can place the state in the line of universal progress.

Of course, such "revolutions" work to restore (or create) legitimacy by seeking to transform in some significant way the position of the state in the hierarchy of the world-system. Failing that, the revolution can create its own tradition about itself and link this self-appraisal to a perhaps revised but still fictive history of the state. Thus, if culture (usage II) is inefficacious or becomes so, one can fall back on culture (usage I).

5) The capitalist world-economy does not merely have unequal distribution of reward. It is the locus of an increasing polarization of reward over historical time. Here, however, there is an asymmetry between the situation at the level of the world-economy as a whole and that at the level of the separate sovereign states which compose the interstate system. Whereas at the level of the world-system, it seems clear that gap of in-

come between states at the top and the bottom of the hierarchy has grown, and has grown considerably over time, it does not necessarily follow that this is true within each state structure. Nonetheless, it is also the case that one of the moral justifications of the capitalist world-economy, one that is used to justify hard work at low pay (the issue just discussed in the previous section), is that inequalities of reward have been diminishing over time, that such inequalities as exist are transitory and transitional phenomena on the road to a more prosperous, more egalitarian future.

Here, once again, we have a blatant discord between official ideology and empirical reality. How has this been contained? The first line of defense has always been denial. The rising standard of living has been a central myth of this world-system. It has been sustained both by arithmetic sleight of hand and by invoking the paired ideologies of universalism and racism-sexism.

The arithmetic sleight of hand is very straightforward. At the world level, it consists first of all of talking about the numerator and not the denominator, and ignoring the dispersion of the curve. We talk about the numerator when we recite the expanded world volume of production, or total value produced, while failing to divide it by world population. Or we analyze quality of life by observing some linear trends but failing to count others. Thus we measure age of mortality or speed of travel but not average number of hours of work per year or per lifetime, or environmental conditions.

But the real sleight of hand is to engage in national rather than global measures, which involves a double deception. First of all, in an unequal and polarizing world-system, there is geographical dispersion. Hence, it is perfectly possible for real income, as measured by GNP per capita say, to rise in some countries while going down in others and in the system as a whole. But since the countries in which the rise occurs are also those most extensively studied, observed, and measured, it is easy to understand how facile but false generalizations take root. In addition, despite the better statistical systems of such core countries, it is undoubtedly the case that they do not measure adequately the non-citizen component of the population (often illegally in residence). And since this is the poorest component, the bias is evident.

Still, misperception of reality is only a first line of defense, and one that is increasingly difficult to sustain. Hence, in the last 50 years, a worldwide schema of "developmentalism" has been erected and propagated which legitimates the polarization. By this point you will realize how repetitive is the pattern of ideological justification. First of all, there is the universalist theme. All states can develop; all states shall develop. Then come the racist themes. If some states have developed earlier and faster than others, it is because they have done something, behaved in some way that is different. They have been more individualist, or more entrepreneurial, or more rational, or in some way more "modern." If other states have developed more slowly, it is because there is something in their culture (usage I at the state level, usage II at the world level) which prevents them or has thus far prevented them from becoming as "modern" as other states.

The seesaw of ideological explanation then continues into the hypothetical future. Since all states can develop, how can the underdeveloped develop? In some way, by copying those who already have, that is, by adopting the universal culture of the modern world, with the assistance of those who are more advanced (higher present culture, usage II). If, despite this assistance, they are making no or little progress, it is because they are being "racist" in rejecting universal "modern" values which then justifies that the "advanced" states are scornful of them or condescending to them. Any attempt in an "advanced" state to comprehend "backwardness" in terms other than willful refusal to be "modern" is labeled Third-Worldism, or reverse racism or irrationalism. This is a tight system of justification, since it "blames the victim," and thereby denies the reality.

6) Finally, let us turn to the contradiction of limitless and organic death. Any theory of limitless expansion is a gambler's paradise. In the real world, it is not possible. Furthermore, to the limited extent that the theory has seemed to accord with the existential reality of the capitalist world-economy as a world-system, it has not seemed to accord with the realities of separate states. Even the strongest and the wealthiest of states, *especially* the strongest and wealthiest, have risen and declined. We are currently living the beginnings of the long-term decline of the United States, only recently still the hegemonic power of the world-system.

Thus the world-system as a whole must deal with the problem of its eventual demise and, within the ongoing system, the strong states must deal with the problem of their relative decline. The two problems are quite different, but regularly refused and confused. There are basically two ways to deal with demise or decline: to deny them or to welcome the change.

Once again, both universalism and racism-sexism are useful conservative ideologies. First of all, racism-sexism serves to sustain denial. Demise or decline is at most a temporary illusion, caused by momentarily weak leadership, because by definition it is said it cannot occur, given the strength or the superiority of the dominant culture (usage II). Or, if it is really occurring, it is because culture (usage II) has ceded place to a deceptive world humanism in the vain hope of creating a world culture (usage I). Thus, it is argued the demise or decline, which it is now admitted may really be occurring, is due to insufficient emphasis on culture (usage II) and hence to admitting "lower" racial groups or "women" to political rights. In this version of ideology, demise or decline is reversible, but only by a reversion to a more overt racism-sexism. Generally speaking, this has been a theme throughout the twentieth century of what we today call the extreme, or neo-fascist, right.

But there is a universalizing version to this exercise in denial. The demise or decline has perhaps not been caused, or not primarily caused, by an increased political egalitarianism, but much more by an increased intellectual egalitarianism. The denial of the superiority of the scientific elite, and their consequent right to dictate public policy, is the result of an anti-rationalist, antinomian denial of universal culture (usage I) and its worldwide culture-bearers (usage II). Demands for popular control of technocratic elites is a call for "the night of the long knives," a return to pre-modern "primitivism." This is the heart of what is today called neo-conservatism.

But if the overtly "conservative" versions of the ideologies are inadequate to the task, one can put forward "progressive" versions. It is not too difficult to "welcome" the "transition" in ways that in fact sustain the system. There is the universalizing mode, in which progressive transition is seen as inevitable. This can lead on the one hand to postponing the transition until the equally inevitable "preconditions" of transition are realized. It can lead on the other hand to interim measures whose reality is the worsening of conditions on the grounds that this "speeds up" the realization of the preconditions. We have known many such movements.

Finally, the "welcoming" of the transition can have the same conservative effect in a racist form. One can insist that it is only the presently "advanced" groups that can be the leaders of the next presumed "advance." Hence, it is only on the basis of presently-realized culture (usage II) that the transition to a new world will be realized. The more "backward" regions must in some way wait on the more "advanced" ones in the process of "transition."

V

The paired ideologies of universalism and racism-sexism then have been very powerful means by which the contradictory tensions of the world-system have been contained. But of course, they have also served as ideologies of change and transformation in their slightly different clothing of the theory of progress and the conscientization of opposed groups. This has resulted in extraordinarily ambivalent uses of these ideologies by the presumed opponents of the existing system, the antisystemic movements. It is to this last aspect of culture as an ideological battleground that I should like now to turn.

An antisystemic movement is a movement to transform the system. An antisystemic movement is at the same time a product of the system. What culture does such a movement incarnate? In terms of culture (usage I), it is hard to see how the antisystemic movements could conceivably have incarnated any culture other than that of the capitalist world-economy. It is hard to see how they could not have been impregnated by and expressed the paired ideologies of universalism and racism-sexism.

However in terms of culture (usage II) they have claimed to have created a new culture, a culture destined to be a culture (usage I) of the future world. They have tried to elaborate this new culture theoretically. They have created institutions presumably designed to socialize members and sympathizers into this new culture. But of course it is not so easy to know what shall be the culture, a culture, of the future. We design our utopias in terms of what we know now. We exaggerate the novelty of what we advocate. We act in the end, and at best, as prisoners of our present reality who permit ourselves to daydream.

This is not at all pointless. But it is surely less than a sure guide to appropriate behavior. What the antisystemic movements have done, if one considers their global activities over 150-odd years, has been essentially to turn themselves into the fulfillers of the liberal dream while claiming to be its most fulsome critics. This has not been a comfortable position. The liberal dream — the product of the principal self-conscious ideological *Weltanschauung* within the capitalist world-economy — has been that universalism will triumph over racism and sexism. This has been translated into two strategic operational imperatives — the spread of "science" in the economy, and the spread of "assimilation" in the political arena.

The fetishism of science by the antisystemic movements — for example, Marx's designation of his ideas as "scientific socialism" — was a natural expression of the post-1789 triumph of Enlightenment ideas in the world-system. Science was future-oriented; it sought total truth via the perfectibility of human capacities; it was deeply optimistic. The limitlessness of its ambitions might have served as a warning-signal of the deep affinity of this kind of science to its world-system. But the antisystemic thinkers interpreted this affinity to be a transitory misstep, a surviving irrationality, doomed to extinction.

The problem, as the antisystemic movements saw it, was not that there was too much science, but too little. Sufficient social investment in science was still lacking. Science had not yet penetrated into enough corners of economic life. There were still zones of the world from which it was kept. Its results were insufficiently applied. The revolution — be it social or national or both — would at last release the scientists to find and to apply their universal truths.

In the political arena, the fundamental problem was interpreted to be exclusion. The states were the handmaidens of minorities; they must be made the instrument of the whole of society, the whole of humanity. The unpropertied were excluded. Include them! The minorities were excluded. Include them! The women were excluded. Include them! Equals all. The dominant strata had more than others. Even things out! But if we are evening out dominant and dominated, then why not minorities and majorities, women and men? Evening out meant in practice assimilating the weaker to the model of the strong. This model looked suspiciously like Everyman — the man with simple but sufficient means, hard-working, morally upright and devoted to family (friends, large community).

This search for science and assimilation, what I have called the fulfillment of the liberal dream, was located deep in the consciousness and in the practical action of the world's antisystemic movements, from their emergence in the mid-nineteenth century until at least the Second World War. Since then, and particularly since the world cultural revolution of 1968, these movements, or at least some of them, have begun to evince doubts as to the utility, the reasonableness of "science" and "assimilation" as social objectives. These doubts have been expressed in multiple forms. The green movements, the countercultural movements have raised questions about the productivism inherent in the nineteenth-century adulation of science. The many new social movements (of women, of minorities) have poured scorn upon the demand for assimilation. I do not need to spell out here the diverse ways in which this has been manifested.

But, and this is the crucial point, perhaps the real triumph of culture (usage I), the antisystemic movements have hesitated to go all the way. For one thing, the priorities of one kind of antisystemic movement have often been at odds with that of another kind (e.g., ecologists vs. Third World liberation movements). For another thing, each kind of movement itself has been internally divided. The debates within the women's movements or Black movements over such questions as political alliances or the desirability of "protective" legislation for the "weaker" groups are instances of the tactical ambivalences of these movements.

As long as the antisystemic movements remain at the level of tactical ambivalence about the guiding ideological values of our world-system, as long as they are unsure how to respond to the liberal dream of more science and more assimilation, we can say that they are in no position to fight a war of position with the forces that defend the inequalities of the world. For they cede, by this ambivalence, the cultural high-ground to their opponents. The advocates of the system can continue to claim that scientism and assimilation represent the true values of the world culture (usage I) and that their practitioners are the men of culture (usage II), the high priests of this culture (usage I). And, as long as this remains true, we are all enveloped in the paired ideologies (and the false antinomy) of universalism and racism-sexism.

The cultural trap in which we are caught is a strong one, overlain by much protective shrubbery which hides its outline and its ferocity from us. Can we somehow disentangle ourselves? I believe it is possible, though at most I can only indicate some of the directions in which, if we moved along them, I believe we might find ways to disentangle.

Beyond scientism, I suspect there lies a more broadly-defined science, one which will be able to reconcile itself dramatically with the humanities, such that we can overcome what C. P. Snow called the division of the two cultures.[7] (Note the term again, here in usage II.) I suspect we may have to reverse the history of science and return from efficient causes to final causes. I think, if we do, that we may be able to scrape away all that is contingent (that is, all that is Western) to uncover new possibilities.

This will make possible a new rendezvous of world civilizations. Will some "universals" emerge out of this rendezvous? Who knows? Who even knows what a "universal" is? At a moment of world history when the physical scientists are at last (or is it once again?) beginning to talk of the "arrow of time," who is able to say that there are any immutable laws of nature?

If we go back to metaphysical beginnings, and reopen the question of the nature of science, I believe that it is probable, or at least possible, that we can reconcile our understanding of the origins and legitimacies of group particularisms with our sense of the social, psychological, and biological meanings of humanity and humaneness. I think that perhaps we can come up with a concept of culture that sublates the two usages.

I wish that I saw more clearly how this could be done, or where it is leading. But I have the sense that in cultural terms our world-system is in need of some "surgery." Unless we "open up" some of our most cherished cultural premises, we shall never be able to diagnose clearly the extent of the cancerous growths and shall therefore be unable to come up with appropriate remedies. It is perhaps unwise to end on such a medical analogy. Medicine, as a mode of knowledge, has only too clearly demonstrated its limitations. On the other hand, the art of medicine represents the eternal human response to suffering, death, and transition, and therefore incarnates hope, however much it must be tempered by an awareness of human limitations.

NOTES

1. Sidney W. Mintz, *The Power of Sweetness and the Sweetness of Power*, 8th Duijker Lecture (Deventer, NL: Van Loghum Slaterus, 1988), p. 14.

2. I have spelled out the mechanism of these cyclical rhythms in various places. One such explanation is to be found in my "Crisis as Transition," in S. Amin et al., *Dynamics of Global Crisis* (New York: Monthly Review Press, 1982), esp. pp. 12–22.

3. For a discussion of the complexities, see Terence K. Hopkins & Immanuel Wallerstein, "Capitalism and the Incorporation of New Zones into the World-Economy," *Review*, X, 5/6 (Supplement), Summer/Fall 1987, 763–779.

4. See "The Ideological Tensions of Capitalism: Universalism versus Racism and Sexism," in J. Smith et al., eds., *Racism, Sexism, and the World-System* (Westport, CT: Greenwood Press, 1988). [Ch. 22 this volume]

5. Rex Nettleford, "Building a Nation, Shaping a Society," in J. Wedderburn, ed., *A Caribbean Reader on Development* (Kingston, 1986), pp. 9–10.

6. Jean-Paul Sartre, "Orphée noir," *Situations, III* (Paris: Gallimard, 1949), pp. 229–288. He calls negritude "antiracist racism" (p. 237).

7. C. P. Snow, *The Two Cultures and the Scientific Revolution* (New York: Cambridge University Press, 1959).

Part Four

CLEAVAGES IN THE WORLD-SYSTEM: RACE, NATION, CLASS, ETHNICITY, GENDER

18—The Construction
of Peoplehood:
Racism, Nationalism, Ethnicity

> Both scholars and public opinion seem to define "peoples" in the mod-
> ern world in three different ways: as races, as nations, as ethnic groups.
> Why? that is, why three different ways, and how are the three related to
> each other? It seemed to me that clarifying this question was a prereq-
> uisite to any sensible analysis of the cleavages that exist within the mod-
> ern world-system.

Nothing seems more obvious than who or what is a people.
Peoples have names, familiar names. They seem to have long histories. Yet any pollster knows that if one poses the open-ended
question "what are you?" to individuals presumably belonging to the
same "people," the responses will be incredibly varied, especially if the
matter is not at that moment in the political limelight. And any student of
the political scene knows that very passionate political debates hinge
around these names. Are there Palestinians? Who is a Jew? Are Mace-
donians Bulgarians? Are Berbers Arabs? What is the correct label: Negro, African American, Black (capitalized), black (uncapitalized)?
People shoot each other every day over the question of labels. And yet,
the very people who do so tend to deny that the issue is complex or puz-
zling or indeed anything but self-evident.

I would like to start by describing one recent debate about one particular people. It has the rare quality of being a relatively friendly debate,
among people who assert they share common political objectives. It is a
debate that was published in the explicit hope of resolving the issue ami-
cably among comrades.

The setting is South Africa. The South African government has by
law proclaimed the existence of four groups of "peoples," each with a
name: Europeans, Indians, Coloureds, Bantus. Each of these legal categories is complicated and contains multiple possible sub-groups within
it. The sub-groups combined under one legal label are sometimes curi-

ous from the vantage point of an outsider. Nonetheless, these labels have the force of law and have very specific consequences for individuals. Each resident of South Africa is classified administratively into one of these four categories and as a result has different political and social rights. For example, he/she is required to live in a residential area assigned by the state to his category and in some cases to sub-categories.

There are a large number of people in South Africa opposed to this process of legal categorization, which is known as apartheid. The history of their opposition shows, however, at least one significant shift of tactics with regard to the legal labels. Originally, those opposed to apartheid formed organizations within the framework of each separate category. These organizations then formed a political alliance and worked together. For example, in 1955, there occurred a very famous Congress of the People, cosponsored by four groups, each composed of persons belonging to one of the government's four categories of peoples. This Congress of the People issued a Freedom Charter calling for, among other things, the end of apartheid.

The largest of the four opposition organizations was the African National Congress (ANC), which represented what the government called Bantus, some 80 percent of the total population falling under the state's jurisdiction. Somewhere in the 1960s or perhaps 1970s—it is not clear when—the ANC slipped into using the term "African" for all those who were not "Europeans" and thus included under the one label what the government called Bantus, Coloureds, and Indians. Some others—it is not clear who—made a similar decision but designated this group as "non-Whites" as opposed to "Whites." In any case, the consequence was to reduce a fourfold classification into a dichotomy.

The decision, if that is what it was, was not unambiguous, however. For example, the allied organization of the ANC among Indians, the South African Indian Congress (SAIC), continued to exist, though its president and others became simultaneously members of the SAIC and the ANC.

The category "Coloured" has no doubt been the most nettlesome of the four. This "group" was constituted historically out of descendants of various unions between African persons and European persons. It also included persons brought from the East Indies centuries ago, who came to be known as Cape Malays. The "Coloureds" were mostly persons who in other parts of the world have been called "mulattos" and who in the United States were always considered part of the "Negro race," in terms of the now-defunct laws governing racial segregation.

In June 1984, Alex La Guma, member of the ANC and a Coloured from the government's point of view, wrote a letter to the editor of *Sechaba*, the official journal of the ANC. He posed the following issue:

> I have noticed now in speeches, articles, interviews etc. in *Sechaba*, that I am called "so-called Coloured" (sometimes with a small "c"). When did the Congress decide to call me this? In South Africa I was active in the Congress Alliance and was a member of the Coloured People's Congress, not the "so-called Coloured People's Congress." When we worked for Congress of the People and the Freedom Charter we sang, "We the Coloured people, we must struggle to exist. . . ." I remember in those times some people of the so-called unity movement [a rival organization to the ANC] refer to so-called Coloured people, but not our Congress. The old copies of *Sechaba* do not show when it was decided to make this change, or why. Maybe governments, administrations, political and social dealings over centuries called me Coloured. But clever people, the ethnologists and professors of anthropology and so on, did not bother to worry about who I really am.
>
> Comrade Editor, I am confused. I need clarification. It makes me feel like a "so-called" human, like a humanoid, those things who have all the characteristics of human beings but are really artificial. Other minority people are not called "so-called." Why me? It must be the "curse of Ham."

There were three responses to this letter. The first, also in the June issue, was from the editor:

> As far as I can remember there is no decision taken in our movement to change from "Coloured" to "so-called Coloured." All I know is that people at home — like Allan Boesak [Boesak is someone the government labels as Coloured] at the launch of the UDF [United Democratic Front, an anti-apartheid organization] — have been increasingly using the term, "so-called Coloureds." I suspect that what you have noticed is a reflection of this development.
>
> Not long ago, *Sechaba* reviewed Richard Rive's book, *Writing Black*, and in that review we said:
>
> > Our strive for unity should not blind us from seeing the differences which if ignored can cause problems exactly for that unity we are striving to achieve. It is not enough to say the so-called Coloureds or to put the world Coloureds in inverted commas. A positive approach to this problem needs to be worked out because we are dealing with a group of people who are identifiable and distinguishable.

In other words, what we are saying in this review is that a discussion on this issue is necessary, and I think your letter may just as well be a starting point for such a discussion. Any comments on this issue are welcome.

In the August 1984 issue of *Sechaba*, there appeared a letter signed P. G. From the contents, it appears that P. G. is also someone labeled Coloured by the government. Unlike Alex La Guma, he rejects the term unequivocally.

In the Western Cape, I can remember the discussion we used to have about the term Coloured, when we met as groups of the Comrades Movement. These were loosely organised groups of youth brought together in action and study through the uprising of 1976, and who were largely pro-ANC. The term, "so-called Coloured," was commonly used amongst the youth in popular expression of rejection of apartheid terminology.

I am in full agreement with what was said in the *Sechaba* review of Richard Rive's *Writing Black*, but would add that while, as you say, "It is not enough to say the 'so-called Coloureds' or to put the world Coloureds in inverted commas," it would be equally wrong to accept the term, "Coloured." I say this especially in the light of the fact that most people are rejecting the term "Coloured." Congress people, UDF people, those in civic groups, church groups and trade unions, leaders popular with the people speak of "so-called Coloured" without they, or the people they are speaking to feeling like humanoids. In fact the use of the term "Coloured" is cited as making people feel artificial. Coloured is a term which cries of lack of identity.

The term "Coloured" did not evolve out of a distinctive group, but was rather a label pinned on to a person whom the Population Registration Act of 1950 defines as "who in appearance is obviously not White or Indian and who is not a member of an aboriginal race or African tribe." A definition based on exclusion—that is, the isn't people. . . . The term "Coloured" was given to what the racists viewed as the marginal people. The term "Coloured" was fundamental to the racist myth of pure white Afrikaner. To accept the term "Coloured" is to allow the myth to carry on. . . .

Today, people are saying, "We reject the racists' framework, we reject their terminology," and are beginning to build the NEW in defiance of the old, right in the midst of the enemy. The term "Coloured-Kleurling," like "half-caste," "Bruine Afrikaner" and "South Africa's step-children," has been handed down by the racists. Instead of some of us getting offended or taken aback by adopting a very narrow interpretation of this usage, we should see the prefix "so-called" as the first step in coming towards a solution of something which has been a scourge for years.

We have got to move on from the term "so-called Coloured" in a positive way. People are now saying that we have the choice of what we will be called, and most, in the spirit of the nation in the making, opt for "South African." The debate can take many forms, but not a reverting to acceptance of the Baasskap term. If one really needs a sub-identity to that of being a South African, maybe through popular debate the question could be sorted out.

In the September 1984 issue of *Sechaba*, Arnold Selby, someone labeled by the government as a European, entered the debate utilizing a set of categories that distinguished between "nations" and "national minorities":

Let's start the ball rolling viewing some established and accepted facts:

(a) As yet there is no such thing as a South African nation;

(b) The African majority is an oppressed nation, the Coloured people and the Indian people are distinct identifiable oppressed national minorities, the White population comprises the minority oppressor nation;

(c) The Coloured, Indian and White national minorities are not homogeneous but embrace other national or ethnic groups. For example, the Lebanese community is in the main classified and regards itself as White, the Malay and Griqua people regard themselves as part of the Coloured nation, the Chinese minority finds some of its number classified as White, others as Asian and others as Coloured;

(d) The key to South Africa's future and the solution of the national question lies in the national liberation of the African nation. The victory of our national democratic revolution, headed by the African National Congress bringing with it the national liberation of the African nation, will set in motion the process for the birth of a South African nation.

As stated in (b) above, the Coloured people comprise a distinct identifiable oppressed national minority. But the definition, "Coloured," the terminology arising therefrom and its usage in the practice of daily life did not emerge from the natural social causes, nor were they chosen by the Coloured people. They were imposed upon the Coloured people by the successive regimes which came in the wake of successive waves of aggressions, penetration and settlement of South Africa by the European bourgeois nations, in both their trading and imperialist phases, and after the founding of the aggressor South African state in 1910. . . .

Now let me come to the tendency on the part of some of us to talk about the "so-called" Coloured people. This, I believe, arises from two real factors with which we are faced.

First is the question of our work abroad. Other countries and nations have different conceptions about the term "Coloured people," which are far out of keeping with the reality of the nationally oppressed Coloured national minority in our country. When we speak about our country and its struggle and the role and place of the Coloured people in this struggle we have to explain who the Coloured people are, hence we often find ourselves using the words "so-called" (please note inverted commas) to emphasise the aggressors' imposition of the term. Like one could say the "so-called" Indians when referring to the original inhabitants of what is now the USA. This gives a clearer picture to those abroad who want to know more about our liberation struggle.

Secondly, I do not believe that the tendency of some at home to use the words "so-called" means a rejection of our generally accepted term "Coloured people." To my way of thinking the words are used to stress the growing unity of the oppressed Coloured and Indian national minorities with the oppressed majority African nation. The usage of these words, I believe, indicates as identification with Black rather than Coloured separation from Black. At the same time the usage distances the Coloured people from the White oppressor minority nation. Time without number the oppressor White minority nation has sought without success to get acceptance of the idea that the Coloured people are an inferior off-shoot of the White nation, to which it is naturally allied. The usage of "so-called" means a rejection of the aggressor's attempts to get acceptance of such racist ideology clothed in scientific terminology.

Whether we use "so-called" or not, the reality is that there is an oppressed Coloured national minority in our country. In my opinion, under today's conditions, it is not incorrect to use "so-called" provided it is done in the proper context to convey the true meaning and is put in inverted commas. Under no circumstances can there be a rejection of the reality of the existence of the Coloured people as an oppressed minority nation.

Note that Selby's position is really quite different from P. G.'s. While both accept the use of "so-called" before "Coloured," P. G. does it because there are no such thing as Coloureds. Selby thinks Coloureds exist as a people, of a variety of people he calls "national minorities," but defends the use of "so-called" as a tactic in political communication.

Finally, in the November 1984 issue, La Guma responds, unrepentant:

[PG] says that "so-called Coloured" was used in popular expression of rejection of "apartheid terminology." Yet later he says that "most, in the spirit of a nation in the making, opt for 'South African.'" But, Comrade Editor, he does not tell us who gave our country the official name of South Africa? On what or whose authority? There are some who, rejecting this "terminology," call the country "Azania" (again, on whose authority?) and maybe they would call the rest of the population "so-called South Africans." But it would seem that even though the Boer anthem refers to *Suid-Afrika*, the name of South Africa is accepted. Yet for any minority (even so-called) to assume the right to call themselves South African for their own studied convenience seems to me to be somewhat undemocratic, if not downright presumptuous, since the right naturally belongs to the majority.

I regret to say that I did not know (as PG seems to say) that the term "Coloured" emerged as a result of the definition laid down by the Population Registration Act or the Group Areas Act. I was born long before these Acts, so our people must be a little older than that. And we should not believe that all the awful experiences described by PG (divided families, rejection, etc.) are only suffered by us. Mixed race or marginal communities in other parts of the world suffer similar trials and tribulations.

Now PG even says "so-called" is not good enough, but neither is "Coloured," which adds to my confusion, Comrade Editor. But it is not being called Coloured that has been "a scourge for years," but the way our people have been and are being treated, whatever they are called, just as the term "Asiatic" or "Indian" in itself does not mean scourged. . . . While I wait patiently for the outcome of PG's "mass debate," I would still like to know what I am today. So, Comrade Editor, call me what the devil you like, but for God's sake don't call me "so-called."

I have cited this exchange at some length to show first of all that even the most amicable of debates is quite passionate; and secondly, to show how difficult the issue is to resolve on either historical or logical grounds. Is there a Coloured people, or a Coloured national minority, or a Coloured ethnic group? Was there ever? I can say that some people think there is and/or was, others do not, still others are indifferent, and still others are ignorant of the category.

Ergo, what? If there is some essential phenomenon, a Coloured people, we should be able to come to terms about its parameters. But if we find that we cannot come to terms about this name designating a "people" or indeed about virtually any other name designating some people, maybe this is because peoplehood is not merely a construct but one which, in each particular instance, has constantly changing boundaries. Maybe a people is something that is supposed to be inconstant in form. But if so, why the passion? Maybe because no one is supposed to observe upon the inconstancy. If I am right, then we have a very curious phenomenon indeed—one whose central features are the reality of inconstancy and the denial of this reality. Very complicated, indeed bizarre, I should say! What is there in the historical system in which we are located that would give rise to such a curious social process? Perhaps there is a quark to locate.

I propose to address this issue in successive steps. Let us first review briefly the existing views in social science about peoplehood. Let us then see what there is in the structure and processes of this historical system that might have produced such a concept. Finally, let us see if there is some conceptual reformulation that might be useful.

To start with the literature of the historical social sciences, one must note that the term "people" is actually used somewhat infrequently. Rather the three commonest terms are "race," "nation," and "ethnic group," all presumably varieties of "peoples" in the modern world. The last of these three is the most recent and has replaced in effect the previously widely-used term of "minority." Of course, each of these terms has many variants, but nonetheless I think both statistically and logically these are the three modal terms.

A "race" is supposed to be a genetic category, which has a visible physical form. There has been a great deal of scholarly debate over the past 150 years as to the names and characteristics of races. This debate is quite famous and, for much of it, infamous. A "nation" is supposed to be a socio-political category, linked somehow to the actual or potential boundaries of a state. An "ethnic group" is supposed to be a cultural category, of which there are said to be certain continuing behaviors that are passed on from generation to generation and that are *not* normally linked in theory to state boundaries.

The three terms are used with incredible inconsistency, of course, leaving quite aside the multitude of other terms utilized. (We have already seen, in the above debate, one person designate as a "national minority" what others might have called an "ethnic group.") Most users of the terms use them, all three of them, to indicate some persisting phenomenon which, by virtue of its continuity, not only has a strong impact on current behavior but also offers a basis for making present-day political claims. That is, a "people" is said to be or act as it does because of either its genetic characteristics, or its socio-political history, or its "traditional" norms and values.

The whole point of these categories seems to be to enable us to make claims based upon the past against the manipulable "rational" processes of the present. We may use these categories to explain why things are the way they are and shouldn't be changed, or why things are the way they are and can't be changed. Or conversely we may use them to explain why the present structures should indeed be superseded in the name of deeper and more ancient, ergo more legitimate, social realities. The temporal dimension of pastness is central to and inherent in the concept of peoplehood.

Why does one want or need a past, an "identity?" This is a perfectly sensible question to ask and is even on occasion asked. Notice, for example, that P. G. in the cited debate advocates discarding the appelation "Coloured" in favor of a larger category "South African" and then says: "If one really needs a sub-identity to that of being a South African. . . ." If . . . implies why.

Pastness is a mode by which persons are persuaded to act in the present in ways they might not otherwise act. Pastness is a tool persons use against each other. Pastness is a central element in the socialization of individuals, in the maintenance of group solidarity, in the establishment of or challenge to social legitimation. Pastness therefore is preeminently a moral phenomenon, therefore a political phenomenon, always a contemporary phenomenon. That is of course why it is so inconstant. Since the real world is constantly changing, what is relevant to contemporary politics is necessarily constantly changing. Ergo, the content of pastness necessarily constantly changes. Since, however, pastness is by definition an assertion of the constant past, no one can ever admit that any particular past has ever changed or could possibly change. The past is normally considered to be inscribed in stone and irreversible. The real past, to be sure, is indeed inscribed in stone. The social past, how we understand this real past, on the other hand, is inscribed at best in soft clay.

This being the case, it makes little difference whether we define pastness in terms of genetically continuous groups (races), historical sociopolitical groups (nations), or cultural groups (ethnic groups). They are all peoplehood constructs, all inventions of pastness, all contemporary political phenomena. If this is so, however, we then have another analytic puzzle. Why should three different modal terms have developed when one term might have served? There must be some reason for the separation of one logical category into three social categories. We have but to look at the historical structure of the capitalist world-economy to find it.

Each of the three modal terms hinges around one of the basic structural features of the capitalist world-economy. The concept of "race" is related to the axial division of labor in the world-economy, the core-periphery antinomy. The concept of "nation" is related to the political superstructure of this historical system, the sovereign states that form and derive from the interstate system. The concept of the "ethnic group" is related to the creation of household structures that permit the maintenance of large components of non-waged labor in the accumulation of capital. None of the three terms is directly related to class. That is because "class" and "peoplehood" are orthogonally defined, which as we shall see is one of the contradictions of this historical system.

The axial division of labor within the world-economy has engendered a spatial division of labor. We speak of a core-periphery antinomy as constitutive of this division of labor. Core and periphery strictly speaking are relational concepts that have to do with different cost structures of production. The location of these different production processes in spatially-distant zones is not an inevitable and constant feature of the relationship. But it tends to be a normal one. There are several reasons for this. To the extent that peripheral processes are associated with primary production—which has in fact been historically true, although far less today than previously—then there is constraint on the geographical relocatability of these processes, associated with environmental conditions for cultivation or with geological deposits. Secondly, insofar as there are political elements in maintaining a set of core-peripheral relationships, the fact that products in a commodity chain cross political frontiers facilitates the necessary political processes, since the control of frontier transit is among the greatest real powers the states actually exercise. Thirdly, the concentration of core processes in states different from those in which peripheral processes are concentrated tends to create differing internal political structures in each, a difference which in turn becomes a major sustaining bulwark of the inegalitarian interstate system that manages and maintains the axial division of labor.

Hence, to put the matter simply, we tend over time to arrive at a situation in which some zones of the world are largely the loci of core production processes and others are largely the loci of peripheral production processes. Indeed, although there are cyclical fluctuations in the degree of polarization, there is a secular trend towards a widening of this gap. This world-wide spatial differentiation took the political form primarily of the expansion of a Europe-centered capitalist world-economy into one that eventually covered the globe. This came to be known as the phenomenon of the "expansion of Europe."

In the evolution of the human species on the planet Earth, there occurred in a period preceding the development of settled agriculture, a distribution of genetic variants such that at the outset of the development of the capitalist world-economy, different genetic types in any one location were considerably more homogeneous than they are today.

As the capitalist world-economy expanded from its initial location primarily in Europe, as concentrations of core and peripheral production processes became more and more geographically disparate, "racial" categories began to crystallize around certain labels. It may be obvious that there are a large series of genetic traits that vary, and vary considerably, among different persons. It is not at all obvious that these have to be coded as falling into three, five, or fifteen reified groupings we call "races." The number of categories, indeed the fact of any categorization, is a social decision. What we observe is that, as the polarization increased, the number of categories became fewer and fewer. When W. E. B. Du Bois said in 1900 that "the problem of the twentieth century is the problem of the color line," the colors to which he was referring came down in reality to white and non-white.

Race, and therefore racism, is the expression, the promoter, and the consequence of the geographical concentrations associated with the axial division of labor. That this is so has been made stunningly clear by the decision of the South African state in the last twenty years to designate visiting Japanese businessmen not as Asians (which local Chinese are considered to be) but rather as "honorary white." In a country whose laws are supposed to be based on the permanence of genetic categories, apparently genetics follows the election returns of the world-economy. Such absurd decisions are not limited to South Africa. South Africa merely got itself into the box of putting absurdities on paper.

Race is not, however, the only category of social identity we use. It apparently is not enough; we use nation as well. As we said, nation derives from *political* structuring of the world-system. The states that are today members of the United Nations are all creations of the modern world-system. Most of them did not even exist either as names or as administrative units more than a century or two ago. For those very few that can trace a name and a continuous administrative entity in roughly the same geographical location to a period prior to 1450 — there are fewer of these than we think: France, Russia, Portugal, Denmark, Sweden, Switzerland, Morocco, Japan, China, Iran, Ethiopia are perhaps the least ambiguous cases — it can still be argued that even these states came into existence as modern sovereign states only with the emergence of the present world-system. There are some other modern states that can trace a more discontinuous history of the use of a name to describe a zone — for example, Greece, India, Egypt. We get onto still thinner ice with such names as Turkey, Germany, Italy, Syria. The fact is that if we look forward from the vantage-point of 1450 at many entities that then existed — for example, the Burgundian Netherlands, the Holy Roman Empire, the Mughal Empire — we find we have today in each case not one state but at the very least three sovereign states that can argue some kind of political, cultural, spatial descent from these entities.

And does the fact that there are now three states mean that there are three nations? Is there a Belgian, a Dutch, a Luxemburg nation today? Most observers seem to think so. If there is, is this not because there came into existence *first* a Dutch state, a Belgian state, a Luxemburg state? A systematic look at the history of the modern world will show, I believe, that in almost every case statehood preceded nationhood, and not the other way around, despite a widespread myth to the contrary.

To be sure, once the interstate system was functioning, nationalist movements did arise in many zones demanding the creation of new sovereign states, and these movements sometimes achieved their objectives. But two caveats are in order. These movements, with rare exceptions, arose within already constructed administrative boundaries. Hence it could be said that a state, albeit a non-independent one, preceded the movement. And secondly, it is debatable how deep a root "nation" as a communal sentiment took before the actual creation of the state. Take for example the case of the Sahrawi people. Is there a Sahrawi nation? If you ask Polisario, the national liberation movement, they will say yes, and add that there has been one for a thousand years. If you ask the Moroccans, there never has been a Sahrawi nation, and the people who live in what was once the colony of the Spanish Sahara were always part of the Moroccan nation. How can we resolve this difference intellectually? The answer is that we cannot. If by the year 2000 or perhaps 2020, Polisario wins the current war, there will have been a Sahrawi nation. And if Morocco wins, there will not have been. Any historian writing in 2100 will take it as a settled question, or more probably still as a non-question.

Why should the establishment of any particular sovereign state within the interstate system create a corresponding "nation," a "people"? This is not really difficult to understand. The evidence is all around us. States in this system have problems of cohesion. Once recognized as sovereign, the states frequently find themselves subsequently threatened by both internal disintegration and external aggression. To the extent that "national" sentiment develops, these threats are lessened. The governments in power have an interest in promoting this sentiment, as do all sorts of sub-groups within the state. Any group who sees advantage in using the state's legal powers to advance its interests against groups outside the state or in any sub-region of the state has an interest in promoting nationalist sentiment as a legitimation of its claims. States furthermore have an interest in administrative uniformity that increases the efficacy of their policies. Nationalism is the expression, the promoter, and the consequence of such state-level uniformities.

There is another reason for the rise of nationalism, even more important. The interstate system is not a mere assemblage of so-called sovereign states. It is a hierarchical system with a pecking order that is stable but changeable. That is to say, slow shifts in rank order are not merely possible, but historically normal. Inequalities that are significant and firm but not immutable are precisely the kind of processes that lead to ideologies able to justify high rank but also to challenge low rank. Such ideologies we call nationalisms. For a state not to be a nation is for that state to be outside the game of either resisting or promoting the alteration of its rank. But then that state would not be part of the interstate system. Political entities that existed outside of and/or prior to the development of the interstate system as the political superstructure of a capitalist world-economy did not need to be "nations," and were not. Since we misleadingly use the same word, "state," to describe both these other political entities and the states created within the interstate system, we often miss the obvious inevitable link between the statehood of these latter "states" and their nationhood.

If we then ask what is served by having two categories—races and nations—instead of one, we see that while racial categorization arose primarily as a mode of expressing and sustaining the core-periphery anti-nomy, national categorization arose originally as a mode of expressing the competition between states in the slow but regular permutation of the hierarchical order and therefore of the detailed degree of advantage in the system as opposed to the cruder racial classification. In an over-simplified formula, we could say that race and racism unifies intrazonally the core zones and the peripheral zones in their battles with each other, whereas nation and nationalism divides core zones and peripheral zones intrazonally in the more complex intrazonal as well as interzonal compe-tition for detailed rank order. Both categories are claims to the right to possess advantage in the capitalist world-economy.

If all this were not enough, we have created the category of the ethnic group, the erstwhile minority. For there to be minorities, there needs to be a majority. It has long been noticed by analysts that minorityhood is not necessarily an arithmetically-based concept; it refers to the degree of social power. Numerical majorities can be social minorities. The location within which we are measuring this social power is not of course the world-system as a whole, but the separate states. The concept "ethnic group" is therefore as linked in practice to state boundaries as is the con-cept "nation," despite the fact that this is never included in the defini-tion. The difference is only that a state tends to have *one* nation and *many* ethnic groups.

The capitalist system is based not merely on the capital-labor anti-nomy that is permanent and fundamental to it but on a complex hierar-chy within the labor segment in which, although all labor is exploited because it creates surplus-value that is transferred to others, some labor-ers "lose" a larger proportion of their created surplus-value than others. The key institution that permits this is the household of part-lifetime wage laborers. These households are constructed in such a way that these wage workers may receive less in hourly wages than what is, on a proportionate calculation, the cost of the reproduction of labor. This is a very widespread institution, covering the majority of the world's work-force. I shall not repeat here the arguments for this analysis which have been made elsewhere (see Wallerstein, 1983: 19-26, 1984). I merely wish to discuss its consequences in terms of peoplehood. Wherever we find wage workers located in different kinds of household structures, from more highly-paid workers located in more "proletarianized" household structures to less highly-paid ones located in more "semiproletarianized" household structures, we tend to find at the same time that these varieties of household structures are located inside "communities" called "ethnic groups." That is, along with an occupational hierarchy comes the "ethnicization" of the workforce within a given state's boundaries. Even without a comprehensive legal framework to enforce this, as in South Africa today, or in the United States yesterday, there has been a very high correlation everywhere of ethnicity and occupation, provided one groups "occupations" into broad and not narrow categories.

There seem to be various advantages to the ethnicization of occupational categories. Different kinds of relations of production, we may assume, require different kinds of normal behavior by the workforce. Since this behavior is not in fact genetically determined, it must be taught. Work forces need to be socialized into reasonably specific sets of attitudes. The "culture" of an ethnic group is precisely the set of rules into which parents belonging to that ethnic group are pressured to socialize their children. The state or the school system can do this of course. But they usually seek to avoid performing that particuliaristic function alone or too overtly, since it violates the concept of "national" equality for them to do so. Those few states willing to avow such a violation are under constant pressure to renounce the violation. But "ethnic groups" not only *may* socialize their respective members differently from each other; it is the very definition of an ethnic group that they socialize in a particular manner. Thus what is illegitimate for the state to do comes in by the rear window as "voluntary" group behavior defending a social "identity."

This therefore provides a legitimation to the hierarchical reality of capitalism that does not offend the formal equality before the law which is one of its avowed political premises. The quark for which we were looking may be there. Ethnicization, or peoplehood, resolves one of the basic contradictions of historical capitalism—its simultaneous thrust for theoretical equality and practical inequality—and it does so by utilizing the mentalities of the world's working strata.

In this effort, the very inconstancy of peoplehood categories of which we have been speaking turns out to be crucially important. For while capitalism as an historical system requires constant inequality, it also requires constant restructuring of economic processes. Hence what guarantees a particular set of hierarchical social relations today may not work tomorrow. The behavior of the work-force must change without under- mining the legitimacy of the system. The recurrent birth, restructuring and disappearance of ethnic groups is thereby an invaluable instrument of flexibility in the operation of the economic machinery.

Peoplehood is a major institutional construct of historical capitalism. It is an essential pillar, and as such has grown more and more important as the system has developed greater density. In this sense it is like sover- eign statehood, which is also an essential pillar, and has also grown more and more important. We are growing more, not less, attached to these basic *Gemeinschaften* formed within our world-historical *Gesellschaft*, the capitalist world-economy.

Classes are really quite a different construct from peoples, as both Marx and Weber knew well. Classes are "objective" categories, that is, analytic categories, statements about contradictions in an historical sys- tem, and not descriptions of social communities. The issue is whether and under what circumstances a class community can be created. This is the famous *an sich/für sich* distinction. Class *für sich* have been a very elusive entity.

Perhaps, and here is where we will end, the reason is that the con- structed "peoples"—the races, the nations, the ethnic groups—correlate so heavily, albeit imperfectly, with "objective class." The consequence has been that a very high proportion of class-based political activity in the modern world has taken the form of people-based political activity. The percentage will turn out to be even higher than we usually think if we look closely at so-called "pure" workers' organizations that quite fre- quently have had implicit and *de facto* "people" bases, even while utiliz- ing a non-people, purely class terminology.

For more than a hundred years, the world left has bemoaned its di- lemma that the world's workers have all too often organized themselves in "people" forms. But this is not a soluble dilemma. It derives from the contradictions of the system. There cannot be *für sich* class activity that is entirely divorced from people-based political activity. We see this in the so-called national liberation movements, in all the new social move- ments, in the anti-bureaucratic movements in socialist countries.

Would it not make more sense to try to understand peoplehood for what it is—in no sense a primordial stable social reality, but a complex, clay-like historical product of the capitalist world-economy through which the antagonistic forces struggle with each other. We can never do away with peoplehood in this system nor relegate it to a minor role. On the other hand, we must not be bemused by the virtues ascribed to it, or we shall be betrayed by the ways in which it legitimates the existing system. What we need to analyze more closely are the possible directions in which, as peoplehood becomes ever more central to this historical system, it will push us, at the system's bifurcation point, towards various possible alternative outcomes in the uncertain process of the transition from our present historical system to the one or ones that will replace it.

REFERENCES

Wallerstein, Immanuel. 1983. *Historical Capitalism*. London: New Left Books.
Wallerstein, Immanuel. 1984. "Household structures in the capitalist world-economy," in J. Smith, I. Wallerstein, and H. D. Evers (eds.). *Households and the World-Economy*: 17–22. Beverly Hills, CA: Sage.

19—Does India Exist?

I asked the absurd question, does India exist?, to try to illustrate how arbitrary our so-called historical categories of nations/civilizations are. I chose India in part because it illustrated the issue well and in part because I was giving this paper in New Delhi at the World Congress of Sociology in 1986. This paper should not be read as an analysis of modern India but as an analysis of the category "nation."

My query, "does India exist?" is absurd. In the contemporary world, there is a political entity named India; hence India obviously exists. But it is not absurd, if the query is taken to be ontological, analogous to the ancient theological query, "does God exist?" If India exists, how do we know it exists: and who created India, and when?

Let us start by a counterfactual proposition. Supose in the period 1750–1850, what had happened was that the British colonized primarily the old Mughal Empire, calling it Hindustan, and the French had simultaneously colonized the southern (largely Dravidian) zones of the present-day Republic of India, giving it the name of Dravidia. Would we today think that Madras was "historically" part of India: Would we even use the word "India"? I do not think so. Instead, probably, scholars from around the world would have written learned tomes, demonstrating that from time immemorial "Hindustan" and "Dravidia" were two different cultures, peoples, civilizations, nations, or whatever. There might be in this case some "Hindustan" irredentists who occasionally laid claim to "Dravidia" in the name of "India," but most sensible people would have called them "irresponsible extremists."

My question then is, how could what historically happened between A.D. 1750 and 1850 have affected what historically happened between say the sixth century B.C. and 1750, presently conventional dates for "premodern India?" It can do so because what happened in the distant past is always a function of what happened in the near past. The present determines the past, and not vice versa, as our logico-deductive analytical frameworks try to force us to think.

I wish to make three points. Each will be made about India. They would equally be true if I substituted Pakistan, or England, or Brazil, or China for India. What I have to say about India is not specific to its history. It is generic about all currently existing sovereign states, members of the United Nations.

The first proposition is that India is an invention of the modern world-system. The operation of the capitalist world-economy is premised on the existence of a political superstructure of sovereign states linked together in and legitimated by an interstate system. Since such a structure did not always exist, it was one that had to be built. The process of building it has been a continuous one in several ways. The structure was first created in only one segment of the globe, primarily Europe, more or less in the period 1497–1648. It was then sporadically expanded to include a larger and larger geographic zone. This process, which we may call the "incorporation" of new zones into the capitalist world-economy, involved reshaping political boundaries and structures in the zones being incorporated and creating therein "sovereign states, members of the interstate system," or at least what we might think of as "candidate sovereign states"—the colonies.

The process was continuous in a second sense. The framework of the system has been continuously strengthened over the past 500 years. The interstate system has been increasingly clearly defined and its powers specified and enhanced. In addition, the "stateness" of the "sovereign states" has been increasingly clearly defined and their powers specified and enhanced. Hence we have been moving in the direction of ever "stronger" state structures that are constrained by an ever "stronger" interstate system.

Within such an optic, we could say that the "sovereign state" of India was created in part by the British in the period 1750–1850. But it was not created by the British alone. Other "great powers" (such as France) also had something to do with this, insofar as they recognized its juridical reality and insofar as they were not strong enough to alter the boundary lines that emerged. But most of all, the populations resident during this period on the Indian subcontinent had a very great deal to do with the creation of "India." The existing political structures, of varying military and social strengths, of varying political objectives, resisted and collaborated in the process in various ways. The British did not meet a tabula rasa but vital structures which they combated. The actual history is complex. The point is that the outcome was the result of this history in all its complex specificity. The point also is that the outcome in terms of boundaries was not at all foreordained, but that whatever would have been the outcome would have become the entity we know as India. Had Nepal been absorbed into "India" in that period, we would no more talk of a Nepalese people/nation/culture today than we speak of a Hyderabad people/nation/culture.

As is well know, when India became a fully sovereign state in 1948, the erstwhile colony was divided in two, and there came into existence Pakistan. Subsequently Pakistan was divided, and there came into existence Bangladesh. None of this was foreordained in 1759–1850. *A fortiori*, it was not foreordained by the history of the pre-1750 period. The freshness of these divisions leads some still to proclaim their "illegitimacy." But legitimacy is a function, among other things, of duration. As the years go by, the realities of the "past" become more and more unquestionable—until of course the day that they are suddenly, dramatically, and above all successfully challenged, which can always happen.

My second proposition is that India's pre-modern history is an invention of modern India. I am not saying it didn't really happen. I presume, given all the inbuilt control mechanisms of world historiography, there are few (or no) statements found in the textbooks which do not have some evidentiary basis. But the grouping of these statements in an interpretative narrative is not a self-producing phenomenon. "Facts" do not add up to "history." The historian invents history, in the same way that an artist invents his painting. The artist uses the colors on his palette and his vision of the world to present his "message." So does the historian. He has a large leeway, as does the artist. The leeway is not total. It is socially constrained. A narrative that reflects some bizarre psychopathology of the individual author will simply not be read, or more importantly, not taught, not believed, not used.

The historian's narrative of past events "interprets" these events in terms of long-term continuities and medium-term "conjunctural" (or cyclical) shifting patterns. We are therefore told that something called India has a "culture," or is the product of a culture. What does this mean? It means that India is said to have or to reflect a certain world-view (or a specific combination of world-views), to have a distinguishable artistic style, to be part of a specific linguistic tradition, to have been the locus of specific religious movements, etc.

But what in turn do such statements mean? They do not mean (were never intended to mean) that every individual resident in this geographic zone, now and from time immemorial, shared these cultural traits. Rather, they are supposed to represent some statistical parameter over some usually unspecified period of time. But which parameter? the mean, the median, the mode? Just to pose the issue this way is to invite ridicule. But it also points up the arbitrariness of all statements about India's (or anyone else's) "culture." India's culture is what we collectively say it is. And we can disagree. We can also change our mind. If 50 years from now we define India's historical culture differently from the way in which we define it today, India's culture will have in fact changed *in the past*.

So how did we come to invent India's current version of its historical culture? In broad brush strokes, the answer is simple. The British specifically, and the Europeans generally, made statements about what they believed it to be, or wanted it to be. Indians, living their "culture," heard these statements, accepted a few of them, rejected many of them, and verbalized an alternative version, or several versions. The single greatest influence on the version that prevailed in the period 1850–1950 was probably that of the Indian nationalist movement. Today the government of independent India authorizes textbooks for schools, and the Indian government has replaced the Indian nationalist movement as the shaper of India's history. India's poets, historians, and sociologists try to get into the act, and no doubt have some influence. So do the millions of scheduled castes when they decide to convert to Buddhism or to Islam, or not to convert. If enough of them convert, the continuity of Indian Buddhism will suddenly reemerge as an interpretative strand of Indian history.

My third proposition is that India currently exists, but no one knows if 200 years from now it will still exist. Perhaps India will have been divided into five separate states. Perhaps India will have reabsorbed Pakistan and Bangladesh. Perhaps the whole system of sovereign states within an interstate system will have disappeared. Any of these occurrences, if they occur, will transform the past. India may come to seem a transitory and unimportant concept. Or it may be deeply reinforced as an enduring "civilization."

There is no question that, at the present time, nationalism in general, certainly including in India, is a remarkably strong world cultural force. It seems stronger today than any other mode of social expression or collective mentality, although in the last ten years or so, religious consciousness has once again surfaced as a serious competitor to nationalist consciousness as a motivating force in many parts of the world. But nationalism, in historical terms, is a very new concept. It is clearly a product, and indeed a late product, of the modern world-system. It would be hard to argue that it existed before the nineteenth century. Perhaps in the twenty-first century, it will have spent itself. It is hard to predict with any confidence. This should make us hesitate at least in asserting the long-lasting quality of Indianness as a social reality.

Let me ask one final question. As I said at the outset, what I have been saying about India, I could equally well say about Pakistan or England or Brazil or China. Is there then nothing special about India, nothing specific to the Indian case? Of course there is. India as a concrete entity is different in multitudinous and important ways from every other state or nation or people or civilization. The real social world is a complex entity composed of incredibly complex groups and individuals. Everything is specific.

We have, however, two choices about specificity. Either we surrender intellectually to it, in which case the world is a "blooming, buzzing confusion." Or we try to explain it. Specificity is not just there. India (that is, the India we think we observe today) is not just there. It is the result of a long historical process, one which it shares in detail only at certain elementary (albeit crucial) levels with other presumably comparable entities.

I am not here to deny in any way the historical specificity of India. Indeed, the whole objective, as I see it, of sociological analysis is to end up with a historical interpretaiton of the concrete. What I am here to assert is that what is included in the description of the historical specificity of India is an ever-changing, very fluid phenomenon. The historical ground on which we stand is about as stable as that covering a fault in the earth. The possibility of an earthquake hangs over us as an ever-present threat. Hence India exists, at least at this instant at which I write.

20—Class Formation in the Capitalist World-Economy

> I tackle here the long-standing debate about the priority of analysis (and hence political priority) of classes and nations. I take the stance that they can only be appreciated in an ever-evolving historical context and that social classes are a social construction just like other cleavage categories, to be seen as a cleavage within the capitalist world-economy.

S ocial class as a concept was invented within the framework of the capitalist world-economy and it is probably most useful if we use it as historically specific to this kind of world-system. Class analysis loses its power of explanation whenever it moves towards formal models and away from dialectical dynamics.

Thus, we wish to analyze here classes as evolving and changing structures, wearing ever-changing ideological clothing, in order to see to whose advantage it is at specific points of time to define class memberships in particular conceptual terms. What we shall attempt to show is that alternative *perceptions* of social reality have very concrete consequences for the ability of contending classes to further their interests. In particular, there are two arguments about the fundamental paradigm of analysis: is class a polarized concept or a multimodal one? Are affiliations to class groupings more or less fundamental or significant than affiliations to "status groups" or ethno-nations? We shall argue that the debate about the paradigm turns out in the end to be the crucial debate and to play a central role in class organization.

Before, however, we can proceed to analyze the nature and workings of social classes, and the process of class formation, we must specify the mode of functioning of this world-system in which they are located. There are three basic elements to a capitalist world-economy. First, it consists (metaphorically) of a single market within which calculations of maximum profitability are made and which therefore determine over some long run the amount of productive activity, the degree of specialization, the modes of payment for labor, goods, and services, and the utility of technological invention.

The second basic element is the existence of a series of state structures, of varying degrees of strength (both within their boundaries, and *vis-à-vis* other entities in the world-system). The state structures serve primarily to distort the "free" workings of the capitalist market so as to increase the prospects of one or several groups for profit within it. The state acts on the market in the short run by the use of its legal prerogatives to constrain economic activities within or across its borders. But it also acts on the market over the long run by seeking to create institutional proclivities (from the conveniences of established currency and trade channels, to taste preferences, to limitations of knowledge of economic alternatives), such that some persons or groups "spontaneously" misjudge the economic activity that would in fact optimize their profits, a misjudgment which favors some other group or groups that a particular state wishes to favor.

The third essential element of a capitalist world-economy is that the appropriation of surplus labor takes place in such a way that there are not two, but three, tiers to the exploitative process. That is to say, there is a middle tier, which shares in the exploitation of the lower tier, but also shares in being exploited by the upper tier. Such a three-tiered format is essentially stabilizing in effect, whereas a two-tiered format is essentially disintegrating. We are not saying that three tiers exist at all moments. We are saying that those on top always seek to ensure the existence of three tiers in order the better to preserve their privilege, whereas those on the bottom conversely seek to reduce the three to two, the better to destroy this same privilege. This fight over the existence of a middle tier goes on continually, both in political terms and in terms of basic ideological constructs (those that are pluralist versus those that are manicheist). This is the core issue around which the class struggle is centered.[1]

These three tiers can be located repetitively throughout all the institutions of the capitalist world-economy: in the trimodal economic role of regions in the world-economy: core, semiperiphery, and periphery;[2] in the basic organizational structure of the productive process (the existence of a foreman role); in the trimodal patterns of income and status distribution in core capitalist countries; in the trimodal pattern of political alliances (left, center, and right), both at the world and national levels.

Once again, let me underline my position: I am not arguing that three tiers *really* exist, any more than I am arguing that two poles *really* exist. I am indifferent to such Platonic essences. Rather, I am asserting that the class struggle centers politically around the *attempt* of the dominant classes to create and sustain a third tier, against the *attempt* of the oppressed classes to polarize both the reality and the perception of the reality.

That is to say, classes do not have some permanent reality. Rather, they are formed, they consolidate themselves, they disintegrate or disaggregate, and they are re-formed. It is a process of constant movement, and the greatest barrier to understanding their action is reification.[3] To be sure, there are patterns we can describe and which aid us to identify concrete realities and explain historical events. But the patterns themselves evolve over time, even with the historically bound phenomenon of the modern capitalist world-economy.

The division of the populace into tiers of relative privilege often takes the form of ethno-national groupings. Max Weber challenged the Marxian perception of social reality by asserting that what he called "status groups" (*Stände*) were a parallel phenomenon to social classes, and that the two realities cross cut. I do not accept this position. I believe "class" and what I prefer to call "ethno-nation" are two sets of clothing for the same basic reality.[4] However, it is important to realize that there are in fact *two* sets of clothing, so that we may appreciate how, when and why one set is worn rather than the other. Ethno-nations, just like social classes, are formed, consolidate themselves, disintegrate or disaggregate, and are constantly re-formed.

It becomes thus part of any concrete analysis to identify the stage at which specific classes or ethno-nations are found: whether a given stratum is an emerging, established, or a declining social class. I would further like to argue that the classic Marxian terminology about social classes refers in fact to these three aspects of the evolution of classes. Emerging classes are classes *an sich*. Established classes are *für sich*. And false consciousness is the defense of the interests of a declining social class.[5]

If we argue that classes and ethno-nations reflect the same social reality, we must furnish some rationale for the existence of two forms. We shall seek to do this by assessing what are the purposes (or advantages) of a social group taking on one or the other identity.

Let us start with social classes. There is a short-run logic in the formation of a class. It is that the gradual perception of common interests (that is, similar relationships to the ownership and control of the means of production, and similar sources of revenue) and the construction of some organizational structure(s) to advance these interests is an indispensable aspect of bargaining (which is the form that all short-run struggle takes). The traditional distinction between objective class status and subjective class membership (common to the majority of both Marxists and functionalists) seems to me totally artificial. An objective class status is only a reality insofar as it becomes a subjective reality for some group or groups, and if it "objectively" exists, it inevitably will be felt "subjectively." The question is not there, but in the degree to which the "objective" reality takes the "subjective" form of class consciousness rather than the form of ethno-national consciousness.

It would seem logical to deduce that short-run organizing is engaged in primarily when the overall political alignment of forces is such that those who organize can reasonably expect significant short-run bargaining advantages. Needless to say, the very success of the process vitiates its polarizing impact on the political system. This is the phenomenon that Lenin called "economism" and the New Left more recently called "co-optation."

But class consciousness also has long-run significance. It is the clearest route to the acquisition of power within a given state structure by any group numerically larger than one that is politically dominant in that state structure. Whether this acquisition of power is sought theoretically by parliamentary or insurrectionary means, the basic thrust is "democratizing." This is, it seems to me, what we mean when we call the French Revolution a "bourgeois democratic revolution." In the eighteenth century, the bourgeoisie did not have a primary role in the governance of the French state, and in the nineteenth century it did. This basic shift came about as a result of "bourgeois class consciousness."

The self-negating aspects of such "class" assumptions of power are a basic theme of the unhappy critics on the sidelines of modern history, especially in the last half-century. See Claudel's trilogy on the impact of the Napoleonic era (*L'otage, le pain dur, Le père humilié*) or di Lampedusa's novel on the social consequences of the *Risorgimento (The Leopard)* or Djilas's analysis of the Yugoslav revolution in *The New Class*.

While I do not condone the basic pessimism that pervades such works, they point (without truly understanding it) to a phenomenon that is real enough. As long as we have a capitalist world-economy, the state machinery is inevitably "prebendal" in spirit, in that control of the state machinery leads to differential access to resources in a system in which production is for profit rather than for use. Hence such power is, if you will, "corrupting," even of those who assume it in order presumably to transform the social structure. We have all been so bedazzled by the phenomenon of bureaucratization in the modern world that we have missed the more important fact that bureaucratization can *never* occur at the level of political decision making of a state structure within a capitalist world-economy.

And yet both Weber and Marx pointed to this fact. Weber, whose works are the fount of contemporary theorizing about bureaucratization, said nonetheless: "Exactly the pure type of bureaucracy, a hierarchy of *appointed* officials, requires an authority (*Instanz*) which has not been appointed in the same fashion as the other officials."[6] And Marx offered as one of the prospects of socialism precisely the end of this anomaly. What else did Engels mean by the "withering away of the state" except the end of precisely this kind of private use of collective machinery? The Karl Marx who denounced the "idiocy of rural life" surely did not envisage a bucolic, unstructured Utopia. Rather, Engels caught his sense accurately when he wrote: "State interference in social relations becomes, in one domain after another, superfluous; and then dies out of itself; the government of persons is replaced by the administration of things, and by the conduct of processes of production. The state is not 'abolished.' It *dies out*."[7]

How this absence of prebendal opportunities will operate in a socialist world is not to the point here. What is to the point is to notice the limitations of the seizure of state power (limitations, not irrelevance) to the achievement of class objectives within the capitalist world-economy.

Thus, classes are formed—to bargain in the short run, and to seize state power in the long run—and then disintegrate by virtue of their success. But they are then re-formed. This is what Mao Tse-Tung meant when he said of the People's Republic of China, "the class struggle is by no means over."[8]

This continuous re-eruption of the class struggle after each political resolution is in my view not a cyclical process, however, but precisely a dialectical one. For the "establishment" of a class, however transient the phenomenon, transforms—to a greater or lesser extent—the world-system and thus contributes directly to the historical evolution of this world-system.

Let us now turn to the alternative organizational form: that of ethno-nations. Here too, we can distinguish between short-run and long-run uses. In the short run, the formation of an "ethno-nation" serves to alter the distribution of goods according to some arbitrarily defined "status"—kinship, language, race, religion, citizenship. Ethno-nations defend or seek to acquire privilege through partial or total monopolies, distinguishing the group and creating organizational cohesion by the manipulation of cultural symbols.[9]

Ethno-national consciousness is the constant resort of all those for whom class organization offers the risk of a loss of relative advantage through the normal workings of the market and class dominated political bargaining. It is obvious that this is frequently the case of upper strata, who thereby justify differential reward on one or another version of racist ideology. Furthermore, insofar as dominant groups can encourage a gen-eralized acceptance of ethno-nationalism as a base for political action, they precisely achieve the three-tiered structure of exploitation which helps maintain the stability of the system.[10]

But ethno-nations that have to rely on overt legislated monopolies are on weak grounds. They are highly visible in their open challenge to the universalistic ideology of the primacy of the capitalist market, which is reflected in the political ideology of "liberalism." It is possible to main-tain legislative discriminations for long periods of time, as we all know. Nonetheless, the more enduring form in which privilege is maintained is the creation of *de facto* but informal privileged access to non-state insti-tutions (education, occupation, housing, health), optimally through the operation of a totally "individual" attribution of advantage. By refusing to "discriminate" in particular situations which "test" one individual against another, the institution abstracts the totality of social factors which accounts for differential performance, and hence widens rather than narrows existing inequalities.[11]

This subtle mechanism of defending upper class interests has become more important in recent years precisely because of the increased diffi-culties of using cruder mechanisms as a result of the ever more effective organization of oppressed classes. It is precisely thus to counter this newly prominent phenomenon of "institutional racism" that the world has seen in the twentieth century an increasing expression of class consciousness in ethno-national forms.

It is no accident that the great social revolutions of the twentieth century (the Russian, Chinese, Vietnamese, Cuban) have been at one and the same time "social" and "national." To be "social," they had to be "national," whereas those "revolutions" which claimed to be "national" without being "social" (for example, that of the Kuomintang) could not in fact defend "national" interests. It is similarly not at all accidental that oppressed lower strata in core capitalist countries (Blacks in the United States, Québécois in Canada, Occitans in France, etc.) have come to express their class consciousness in ethno-national terms. To be sure, this breeds confusion. But there is *less* confusion in the advantages drawn by the upper class hangers-on of an oppressed ethno-nation than in the failure of the working-class movements in the core capitalist countries to represent the interests of the weakest strata of the proletariat (of "minority" ethnic status) and thereby prevent a growing gap—both objective and subjective—between the interests of workers of upper ethnic status and those of lower ethnic status.

Yet the confusion, if less serious, is nonetheless there. And promotion of ethno-national minorities most frequently results simply in a shift in location of the privileged stratum, and a restructuring of ethno-national dividing lines.

So are we then back where we started? Not at all. We must maintain our eye on the central ball. The capitalist world-economy as a totality— its structure, its historical evolution, its contradictions—is the arena of social action. The fundamental political reality of that world-economy is a class struggle which however takes constantly changing forms: overt class consciousness versus ethno-national consciousness, classes within nations versus classes across nations. If we think of these forms as kaleidoscopic reflections of a fundamental reality which has a structure seldom visible to the naked eye of the observer (like the world of the atom for the physicist), but one that can in fact be perceived as an evolving pattern, then we may come closer to understanding the social reality of the capitalist world-system of which we are a part, the better and the faster to transform it.

NOTES

1. Marx himself underlines the political importance of the third tier, the middle stratum: "What [Ricardo] forgets to mention is the continual increase in numbers of the middle classes, . . . situated midway between the workers on one side and the capitalists and land-owners, on the other. These middle classes rest with all their weight upon the working class and at the same time increase the social security and power of the upper class." *Theorien über den Mehrwert* (Kautsky edition, 1905–10) book II, vol. 2, p. 368, translated in T. B. Bottomore and Maximilien Rubel, *Karl Marx: Selected Writings in Sociology and Social Philosphy* (London: Watts and Co., 1956), pp. 190–1.

2. On the way in which the semiperiphery is to be distinguished from the core and the periphery, see my "Dependence in an Interdependent World: The Limited Possibilities of Transformation Within the Capitalist World Economy," *African Studies Review*, 17: (April 1974), 1–26.

3. Lucien Goldmann defines reification as "the replacement of the qualitative by the quantitative, of the concrete by the abstract," a process he argues is "closely tied to production for the market, notably to capitalist production." "La Réification," in *Recherches dialectiques* (Paris: Ed. Gallimard, 1959), p. 92.

4. I have spelled out in some detail my views on the Marx-Weber controversy, and the ways in which I think Weberians by becoming paradoxically a "vulgar Marxist," in "Social Conflict in Post-Independence Black Africa: The Concepts of Race and Status Group Reconsidered," in Ernest Q. Campbell (ed.), *Racial Tensions and National Identity* (Nashville: Vanderbilt University Press, 1972), pp. 207–26.

5. False consciousness presumably refers to the inability of a group to perceive (and *a fortiori* to admit) that they are members of a given social class. The most obvious explanation of such behavior is that the group sees some advantage in this "misperception." If a group of office assistants fails to acknowledge the growing "Proletarianization" of the work force of large bureaucratic structures, or a "lesser nobility" refuses to admit that they are operating as agricultural capitalists quite like non-noble "gentry," but insist they are of a different "stratum" than others performing basically similar economic tasks, they are exhibiting "false consciousness." The benefit they hope to draw from this is to retain privileges associated with an earlier status which they fear will lose by acknowledging that the class to which they once belonged (or to which their predecessors belonged) has "declined" because of the evolving structure of the capitalist world-economy.

6. Max Weber, *Economy and Society* (3 vols., New York: Bedminster Press, 1968), vol. 3, p. 1123.

7. Frederich Engels, *Socialism: Utopian and Scientific* (New York International Publications, 1935), p. 42. In other versions, the italicized phrase "it dies out" has been translated as "it withers away." Weber, unlike Marx and Engels, was not looking forward to a "withering away" of the state. Quite the contrary. He saw the politician as the guarantor of "responsibility," and the danger to be avoided was the one who acted as though he were a bureaucrat and therefore became a *Kleber*, one who sticks to his post. See Weber, *Economy and Society*, vol. 3, pp. 1403–5.

8. See my "Class Struggle in China?," *Monthly Review*, 25: 4 (September 1974), 55–9.

9. In an unpublished paper, Michael Hechter argues that industrialization, far from diminishing ethnicity, leads to the "the proliferation of the cultural division of labor." He concludes that "so long as substantial regional and international economic inequalities persist, it is reasonable to expect the cultural division of labor to be perpetuated." "Ethnicity and Industrialization: On the Proliferation of the Cultural Division of Labor" (mimeographed), p. 10.

10. While this is readily apparent to many analysts in terms of the function of ethnic groups within nation-states, it is less frequently observed that the creation and reinforcement of state structures as such performs exactly the same stabilizing function for the world-system. One author

who sees this clearly is Francisco Weffort. In a criticism of authors who see a "contradiction" between class struggle in the market and a trans-class perspective of struggle on the basis of oppressed nationhood, Weffort argues:

> For example, did there exist, in the almost complete Argentine integration into the international market of the nineteenth century, a *real* contradiction between State and market? Was not the Argentine State itself, making use of the attributes of sovereignty, one of the factors of this incorporation?
>
> To understand this example a bit, it is clear that the oligarchy controlled the State, but who gave to the Argentina of that era its sense of being a Nation, other than this very oligarchy? My view is that the existence of the Nation-State, or call it autonomy and political sovereignty, is not sufficient reason for us to think that there has come about a contradiction between Nation and market in the country that is integrated into the international economic system. On the contrary, under certain internal social and political conditions (which can only be specified by means of class analysis), the groups who have hegemonic power, or who are those who give content to the idea of the Nation, may use political autonomy to advance economic integration.

"Notas sobre la 'teoría de la dependencia'; ¿Teoría de clase o ideología nacional?" *Revista Lationamericana de Ciencia Política*, 1: 3 (December 1970), 394.

See also Amicar Cabral's useful concept of the "nation-class."

> We are not unaware that in the course of the history of our people, there have emerged class phenomena, varying in definition and state of development . . . [But] when the fight against colonial domination begins, it is not the product of one class even though the idea may have sprung up from the class which has become aware more rapidly or earlier of colonial domination and of the necessity of combatting it. But this revolt is not the product of a class as such. Rather it is the whole society that carries it out. This nation-class, which may be more or less clearly structured, is dominated not by people from the colonized country but rather by the ruling class of the colonizing country. This is our view, and hence our struggle is essentially based not on a class struggle but rather on the struggle led by our nation-class against the Portuguese ruling class.

Interview published in *Anticolonialismo*, 2 (February 1972).

11.　It is precisely this danger to which Marx pointed in the *Critique of the Gotha Programme*. One of the clauses of the Programme called for "equitable distribution of the proceeds of labour." Marx commented:

> What we have to deal with here is a communist society, not as it has *developed* on its own foundations, but on the contrary, as it *emerges* from capitalist society; . . .
>
> This equal right is an unequal right for unequal labour. It recognizes no class differences, because everyone is only a worker like everyone else; but it tacitly recognizes unequal individual endowment and thus productive capacity as natural privileges. It is *therefore a right of inequality in its content, like every right* . . . To avoid all these defects, right instead of being equal would have to be unequal.

V. Adoratsky (ed.), *Karl Marx: Selected Works* (New York: International Publications, n.d.) vol. 2, pp. 563–5.

21—The Bourgeois(ie) as Concept and Reality

We have all been talking of proletarianization for over a century. I wished to show that bourgeoisification was a parallel process, and that once one looked at it, one discovered to one's surprise that the bourgeois in historical practice was almost the opposite of what he/she has been pictured to be. Once one sees bourgeoisification as a process, one can both eliminate false issues that we have been long debating and validate empirically Marx's insight that capitalism involves an ever-greater social polarization into two social categories.

> *Définir le bourgeois? Nous ne serions pas d'accord.*
> Ernest Labrousse (1911)

In the mythology of the modern world, the quintessential protagonist is the bourgeois. Hero for some, villain for others, the inspiration or lure for most, he has been the shaper of the present and the destroyer of the past. In English, we tend to avoid the term "bourgeois," preferring in general the locution "middle class" (or classes). It is a small irony that despite the vaunted individualism of Anglo-Saxon thought, there is no convenient singular form for "middle class(es)." We are told by the linguists that the term appeared for the first time in Latin form, *burgensis*, in 1007 and is recorded in French as *burgeis* as of 1100. It originally designated the inhabitant of a *bourg*, an urban area, but an inhabitant who was "free."[1] Free, however, from what? Free from the obligations that were the social cement and the economic nexus of a feudal system. The bourgeois was *not* a peasant or serf, but he was also *not* a noble.

Thus, from the start there was both an anomaly and an ambiguity. The anomaly was that there was no logical place for the bourgeois in the hierarchical structure and value-system of feudalism with its classical three orders, themselves only becoming crystallized at the very moment that the concept of "bourgeois" was being born.[2] And the ambiguity was that bourgeois was then (as it remains today) both a term of honour and a term of scorn, a compliment and a reproach. Louis XI, it is said, took pride in the honorific "bourgeois of Berne."[3] But Molière wrote his scathing satire on "le bourgeois gentilhomme," and Flaubert said: "J'appelle bourgeois quiconque pense bassement."

Because this medieval bourgeois was neither lord nor peasant, he became eventually to be thought of as a member of an intermediary class, that is, a middle class. And thereby commenced another ambiguity. Were all urban-dwellers bourgeois, or only some? Was the artisan a bourgeois, or only a petty bourgeois, or not a bourgeois at all? As the term came to be used, it was in practice identified with a certain level of income—that of being well off—which implied both the possibilities of consumption (style of life) and the possibilities of investment (capital).

It is along these two axes—consumption and capital—that the usage developed. On the one hand, the style of life of a bourgeois could be contrasted with that of either the noble or the peasant/artisan. Vis-à-vis the peasant/artisan, a bourgeois style of life implied comfort, manners, cleanliness. But vis-à-vis the noble, implied a certain absence of true luxury and a certain awkwardness of social behaviour (viz, the idea of the *nouveau riche*). Much later, when urban life became richer and more complex, the style of life of a bourgeois could also be set against that of an artist or an intellectual, representing order, social convention, sobriety and dullness in contrast to all that was seen as spontaneous, freer, gayer, more intelligent, eventually what we today call "counter-cultural." Finally, capitalist development made possible the adoption of a pseudo-bourgeois style of life by a proletarian, without the latter simultaneously adopting the economic role as capitalist, and it is to this that we have given the label "embourgeoisement."

But if the bourgeois as Babbitt has been the centerpiece of modern cultural discourse, it is the bourgeois as capitalist that has been the centerpiece of modern politico-economic discourse. The bourgeois has meant the one who has capitalized means of production, hiring workers for wages who in turn have made things to be sold on a market. To the extent that the revenue from sales is greater than costs of production including wages, we speak of there being profit, presumably the objective of the bourgeois capitalist. There have been those who have celebrated the virtues of this social role—the bourgeois as creative entrepreneur. And there have been those who have denounced the vices of this social role—the bourgeois as parasitical exploiter. But admirers and critics have generally combined to agree that the bourgeois, this bourgeois the capitalist, has been the central dynamic force of modern economic life, for all since the nineteenth century, for many since the sixteenth century, for a few even longer than that.

NINETEENTH-CENTURY DEFINITIONS

Just as the concept "bourgeois" has meant an intermediate stratum between noble/landowner and peasant/artisan, so the bourgeois era, or bourgeois society, came to be defined in two directions, backwards in time as progress over feudalism, and forwards in time vis-à-vis the promise (or threat) of socialism. This definition was itself a phenomenon of the nineteenth century, which thought of itself and has been thought of ever since by most people as the century of bourgeois triumph, the quintessential historical moment for the bourgeois—as concept, and as reality. What represents bourgeois civilization more in our collective consciousness than Victorian Britain, workshop of the world, heartland of the white man's burden, on which the sun never set—responsible, scientific, civilized?

Bourgeois reality—both its cultural and its politico-economic reality—has thus been something we have all known intimately and which has been described in remarkably similar ways by the three great ideological currents of the nineteenth century—conservatism, liberalism, and Marxism. In their conceptions of the bourgeois, all three have tended to agree upon his occupational function (in earlier times usually a merchant, but later an employer of wage labour and owner of the means of production, primarily one whose workers were producers of goods), his economic motor (the profit motive, the desire to accumulate capital), and his cultural profile (non-reckless, rational, pursuing his own interests). One would have thought that with such unanimity emerging in the nineteenth century around a central concept, we would all have proceeded to use it without hesitation and with little debate. Yet Labrousse tells us that we will not agree on a definition, and he therefore exhorts us to look closely at empirical reality, casting as wide a net as possible. Furthermore, although Labrousse made his exhortation in 1955, I do not have the impression that the world scholarly community took up his challenge. Why should this be? Let us look at five contexts in which, in the work of historians and other social scientists, the concept of bourgeois(ie) has been used in ways that result in discomfort—if not theirs, then that of many of their readers. Perhaps by analysing the discomforts, we will find clues for a better fit between concept and reality.

1. Historians frequently describe a phenomenon designated as the "aristocratization of the bourgeoisie." Some have argued, for example, that this occurred in the United Provinces in the seventeenth century.[4] The system in *Ancien Régime* France of a *"noblesse de robe"* created by the venality of office was virtually an institutionalization of this concept. It is, of course, what Thomas Mann described in *Buddenbrooks*—the typical path of transformation in the social patterns of a wealthy family dynasty, from great entrepreneur to economic consolidator to patron of the arts, and eventually these days to either decadent roué or hedonistic-idealistic dropout.

What is it we are supposed to be noticing? That, for some reason and at a certain biographical moment, a bourgeois seems to renounce both his cultural style and his politico-economic role in favour of an "aristo-cratic" role, which since the nineteenth century has not necessarily been that of titled nobility but simply that of old wealth. The traditional formal symbol of this phenomenon has been the acquisition of the landed es-tate, marking the shift from bourgeois-factory owner-urban resident to noble-landowner-rural resident.

Why should a bourgeois do this? The answer is obvious. In terms of social status, in terms of the cultural discourse of the modern world, it has always been true—from the eleventh century to today—that it is somehow "better" or more desirable to be an aristocrat than a bourgeois. Now, this is remarkable on the face of it, for two reasons. One, we are constantly told by everyone that the dynamic figure in our politico-economic process is and has been—since the nineteenth century, since the sixteenth century, since perhaps even longer—the bourgeois. Why would one want to give up being center-stage in order to occupy an ever more archaic corner of the social scene? Secondly, while what we call feudalism or the feudal order celebrated nobility in its ideological pre-sentations, capitalism gave birth to another ideology which celebrated precisely the bourgeois. This new ideology has been dominant, at least in the centre of the capitalist world-economy, for at least 150–200 years. Yet the *Buddenbrooks* phenomenon goes on apace. And in Britain, even today, a life peerage is taken to be an honour.

2. An important polemical concept in contemporary thought—familiar in, but by no means limited to, Marxist writings—is that of the "betrayal by the bourgeoisie" of its historical role. In fact, this concept refers to the fact that, in certain countries, those that are less "developed," the local (national) bourgeoisie has turned away from its "normal" or expected economic role in order to become landowners or rentiers, that is "aristocrats." But it is more than their aristocratization in terms of personal biography; it is their collective aristocratization in terms of this collective biography. That is to say, it is a question of the timing of this shift in terms of a sort of national calendar. Given an implicit theory of stages of development, at a certain point the bourgeoisie should take over the state apparatus, create a so-called "bourgeois state," industrialize the country, and thereby collectively accumulate significant amounts of capital—in short, follow the presumed historical path of Britain. After that moment, perhaps it would be less important if individual bourgeois "aristocratized" themselves. But before that moment, such individual shifts render more difficult (even make impossible) the national collective transformation. In the twentieth century, this kind of analysis has been the underpinning of a major political strategy. It has been used as the justification, in Third International parties and their successors, of the so-called "two-stage theory of national revolution," wherein socialist parties have the responsibility not only to carry out the proletarian (or second-stage) revolution but also to play a very large role in carrying out the bourgeois (or first-stage) revolution. The argument is that the first stage is historically "necessary" and that, since the national bourgeoisie in question has "betrayed" its historic role, it becomes incumbent on the proletariat to play this role for it.

Now, the whole concept is doubly curious. It is curious that one thinks that one social class, the proletariat, has both the obligation and the social possibility of performing the historical tasks (whatever that means) of another social class, the bourgeoisie. (I note in passing that, although the strategy was in fact launched by Lenin or at least with his benediction, it smacks very much of the moralism for which Marx and Engels denounced the Utopian Socialists.) But the idea of "betrayal" is even more curious when looked at from the angle of the bourgeoisie itself. Why should a national bourgeoisie "betray" its historic role? Presumably, it has everything to gain from performing this role. And since everyone—conservatives, liberals, Marxists—agree that bourgeois capitalists always pursue their own interests, how is it that in this instance they appear not to have seen their own interests? It seems more than a conundrum; it seems to be a self-contradicting assertion. The strangeness of the very idea is accentuated by the fact that quantitatively the number of national bourgeoisies that are said to have "betrayed" their historic roles turns out not to be small but very large—indeed, the vast majority.

OWNERSHIP AND CONTROL

3. The language of "aristocratization of the bourgeoisie" has tended to be applied to situations in European countries primarily in the sixteenth to eighteenth centuries, and the language of "betrayal of the bourgeoisie" has tended to be applied to situations in non-European zones in the twentieth century. There is a third language, however, which has been applied primarily to situations in North America and Western Europe in the late-nineteenth and twentieth centuries. In 1932, Berle and Means wrote a famous book in which they pointed out a trend in the structural history of the modern business enterprise, a trend they called the "separation of ownership and control."[5] By this they meant the shift from a situation in which the legal owner of a business was also its manager to one (i.e., the modern corporation) in which the legal owners were many, dispersed and virtually reduced to being merely investors of money capital, while the managers, with all the real economic decision-making power, were not necessarily even partial owners and were in formal terms salaried employees. As everyone now recognizes, this twentieth-century reality does not match the nineteenth-century description, by either liberals or Marxists, of the economic role of the bourgeois.

The rise of this corporate form of enterprise did more than change the structures at the top of the enterprises. It also begat a whole new social stratum. In the nineteenth century, Marx had forecast that, as capital centralized, there would over time occur a growing polarization of classes, such that eventually only a bourgeoisie (very tiny) and a proletariat (very numerous) would remain. By that he meant in practice that, in the course of capitalist development, two large social groupings, the independent small agricultural producers and the independent small urban artisans, would disappear via a double process: a few would become large-scale entrepreneurs (that is, bourgeois), and most would become wage-workers (that is, proletarians). While liberals were not making for the most part parallel predictions, nothing in Marx's own prediction insofar as it was merely a social description was incompatible with liberal theses. Conservatives, such as Carlyle, thought the Marxist prediction essentially correct, and they shivered at the thought.

In fact, Marx was right, and the membership of these two social categories has indeed diminished dramatically worldwide in the last hundred and fifty years. But in the period since the Second World War, sociologists have been noticing, until it has become a veritable commonplace, that the disappearance of these two strata has gone hand in hand with the emergence of new strata. The language that began to be used was that as the "old middle class" was disappearing, a "new middle class" was coming into existence.[6] By the new middle class was meant the growing stratum of largely salaried professionals who occupied managerial or quasi-managerial positions in corporate structures by virtue of the skills in which they had been trained at universities — originally, primarily the "engineers," then later the legal and health professionals, the specialists in marketing, the computer analysts, and so on.

Two things should be noted here. First of all, a linguistic confusion. These "new middle classes" are presumed to be an "intermediate stratum" (as in the eleventh century), but now one located between the "bourgeoisie" or the "capitalists" or "top management" and the "proletariat" or the "workers." The bourgeoisie of the eleventh century was the *middle* stratum, but in the terminology of the twentieth century, the term is used to describe the top stratum, in a situation in which many still refer to three identifiable strata. This confusion was compounded in the 1960s by attempts to rebaptise the "new middle classes" as the "new working classes," thereby seeking to reduce three strata to two.[7] This change in name was fostered largely for its political implications, but it did point to another changing reality: the differences in style of life and income level between skilled workers and these salaried professionals were narrowing.

Secondly, these "new middle classes" were very difficult to describe in the nineteenth-century categories of analysis. They met some of the criteria of being "bourgeois." They were "well-to-do"; they had some money to invest (but not too much, and that mainly in stocks and bonds); they certainly pursued their own interests, economically and politically. But they tended to be comparable to wage-workers, insofar as they lived primarily on current payments for work (rather than on returns from property); to that extent, they were "proletarian." And their often quite hedonistic style of life de-emphasized the puritanical strain associated with bourgeois culture; to that extent they were "aristocratic."

4. There was a Third World analogue to the "new middle classes." As one country after another became independent after the Second World War, analysts began to take note of the rise of a very significant stratum—educated cadres employed by the government, whose income levels made them quite well-to-do in comparison with most of their compatriots. In Africa, where those cadres stood out most sharply in the virtual absence of other varieties of "well-to-do" people, a new concept was created to designate them, the "administrative bourgeoisie." The administrative bourgeoisie was quite traditionally "bourgeois" in style of life and social values. It represented the social underpinning of most regimes, to the point that Fanon argued that African one-party states were "dictatorships of the bourgeoisie," of precisely this bourgeoisie.[8] And yet of course these civil servants were not bourgeois at all in the sense of playing any of the traditional economic roles of the bourgeois as entrepreneur, employer of wage labour, innovator, risk-taker, profit maximizer. Well, that is not quite correct. Administrative bourgeois often played these classic economic roles, but when they did, they were not celebrated for it, but rather denounced for "corruption."

5. There is a fifth arena in which the concept of the bourgeoisie and/or the middle classes has come to play a confusing but central role— namely, in the analysis of the structure of the state in the modern world. Once again, whether we look at conservative, liberal or Marxist doctrine, the advent of capitalism was presumed to be in some way correlated and closely linked with political control of the state machinery. Marxists said that a capitalist economy implied a bourgeois state, a view most succinctly summarized in the aphorism that "the state is the executive committee of the ruling class."[9] The heart of the Whig interpretation of history was that the drive towards human freedom preceded in parallel fashion in the economic and political arenas. Laissez-faire implied repre-

sentative democracy or at least parliamentary rule. And what were conservatives complaining about, if not the profound link between the cash nexus and the decline of traditional institutions (first of all, at the level of the state structures)? When conservatives talked of Restoration, it was the monarchy and aristocratic privilege they were intent on restoring.

And yet note some persistently dissenting voices. In that heartland of bourgeois triumph, Victorian Britain, at the very moment of the triumph, Walter Bagehot examined the continuing essential role of the monarchy in maintaining the conditions which permit a modern state, a capitalist system, to survive and to thrive.[10] Max Weber insisted that the bureaucratization of the world, his choice of the key process of capitalist civilization, would never be feasible at the very top of the political system.[11] And Joseph Schumpeter asserted that, since in effect the bourgeoisie was incapable of heeding the warnings of Bagehot, the edifice of rule must inevitably crumble. The bourgeoisie, by insisting on ruling, would bring about its own demise.[12] All three were arguing that the equation of bourgeois economy and bourgeois state was not as simple as it looked.

In the corner of the Marxists, the theory of the state, of the class basis of the (bourgeois) state, has been one of the most thorny issues of the last thirty years, most notably in the debates between Nicos Poulantzas and Ralph Miliband.[13] The phrase, the "relative autonomy of the state," has become a cliché enjoying wide nominal support. What does it refer to, if not the fact that there now are acknowledged to be so many versions of "bourgeoisie" or "middle classes" that it is hard to argue that any one of them actually controls the state in the direct mode of the Marxist aphorism? Nor does the combination of them seem to add up to a single class or group.

THE CONCEPT RECONSIDERED

Thus the concept, bourgeois, as it has come down to us from its medieval beginnings through its avatars in the Europe of the *Ancien Régime* and then of nineteenth-century industrialism, seems to be difficult to use with clarity when talking about the twentieth-century world. It seems even harder to use it as an Ariadne's thread to interpret the historical development of the modern world. Yet no one seems ready to discard the concept entirely. I know of no serious historical interpretation of this modern world of ours in which the concept of the bourgeoisie, or alternatively of the middle classes, is absent. And for good reason. It is hard to tell a story without its main protagonist. Still, when a concept shows a persistent ill fit with reality—and in all the major competing ideological interpretations of this reality—it is perhaps time to review the concept and reassess what really are its essential features.

Let me begin by noting another curious piece of intellectual history. We are all very conscious that the proletariat, or if you will, waged workers, have not simply been historically there, that they have in fact been created over time. Once upon a time, most of the world's labour were rural agricultural producers, receiving income in many different forms but rarely in the form of wages. Today, a large (and ever larger) part of the world's workforce is urban and much of it receives income in the form of wages. This shift is called by some "proletarianization," by others the "making of the working class."[14] There are many theories about this process; it is the subject of much study.

We are also aware, but it is less salient to most of us, that the percentage of persons who might be called bourgeois (in one definition or another) is far greater today than previously, and has no doubt augmented steadily since perhaps the eleventh century, and certainly since the sixteenth. And yet, to my knowledge, virtually no one speaks of "bourgeoisification" as a parallel process to "proletarianization." Nor does anyone write a book on the making of the bourgeoisie; rather they write books on "*les bourgeois conquérants*."[15] It is as though the bourgeoisie were a given, and therefore acted upon others: upon the aristocracy, upon the state, upon the workers. It seems not to have origins, but to emerge full-grown out of the head of Zeus.

Our nostrils should flair at such an obvious *deus ex machina*—and a veritable *deus ex machina* it has been. For the single most important use of the concept, the bourgeoisie/the middle classes, has been in explaining the origins of the modern world. Once upon a time, so the myth is recited, there was feudalism, or a non-commercial, non-specialized economy. There were lords and there were peasants. There were also (but was it by chance alone?) a few urban burghers who produced and traded through the market. The middle classes rose, expanded the realm of monetary transaction, and unleashed thereby the wonders of the modern world. Or, with slightly different wording but essentially the same idea, the bourgeoisie did not only rise (in the economic arena) but subsequently rose up (in the political arena) to overthrow the formerly dominant aristocracy. In this myth, the bourgeoisie/middle classes must be a given in order for the myth to make sense. An analysis of the historical formation of this bourgeoisie would inevitably place in doubt the explanatory coherence of the myth. And so it has not been done, or not been done very much.

The reification of an existential actor, the urban burgher of the late Middle Ages, into an unexamined essence, the bourgeois—that bourgeois who conquers the modern world—goes hand in hand with a mystification about his psychology or his ideology. This bourgeois is supposed to be an "individualist." Once again, notice the concordance of conservatives, liberals and Marxists. All three schools of thought have asserted that, unlike in past epochs (and, for Marxists in particular, unlike the future ones), there exists a major social actor, the bourgeois entrepreneur, who looks out for himself and himself alone. He feels no social commitment, knows no (or few) social constraints, is always pursuing a Benthamite calculus of pleasure and pain. The nineteenth-century liberals defined this as the exercise of freedom and argued that, a little mysteriously, if everyone did this with full heart, it would work out to everyone's advantage. No losers, only gainers. The nineteenth-century conservatives and the Marxists joined together in being morally appalled at and sociologically skeptical of this liberal insouciance. What for liberals was the exercise of "freedom" and the source of human progress was seen by them as leading to a state of "anarchy," immediately undesirable in itself and tending in the long run to dissolve the social bonds that held society together.

I am not about to deny that there has been a strong "individualist" strain in modern thought reaching its acme of influence in the nineteenth century, nor that this strain of thought was reflected—as cause and consequence—in significant kinds of social behaviour by important social actors in the modern world. What I wish to caution against is the logical leap that has been made: from viewing individualism as *one* important social reality, to viewing it as *the* important social reality of the modern world, of bourgeois civilization, of the capitalist world-economy. It has simply not been so.

The basic problem resides in our imagery about how capitalism works. Because capitalism requires the free flow of the factors of production—of labour, capital and commodities—we assume that it requires, or at least that capitalists desire, a *completely* free flow, whereas in fact it requires and capitalists desire a *partially* free flow. Because capitalism operates via market mechanisms, based on the "law" of supply and demand, we assume that it requires, or capitalists desire, a perfectly competitive market, whereas it requires and capitalists desire markets than can be both utilized and circumvented at the same time, an economy that places competition and monopoly side by side in an appropriate mix. Because capitalism is a system that rewards individualist behaviour, we assume that it requires, or capitalists desire, that everyone act on individualist motivations, whereas in fact it requires and capitalists desire that both bourgeois and proletarians incorporate a heavy dosage of anti-individualist social orientation into their mentalities. Because capitalism is a system which has been built on the juridical foundation of property rights, we assume that it requires and capitalists desire that property be sacrosanct and that private property rights extend into ever more realms of social interaction, whereas in reality the whole history of capitalism has been one of a steady decline, not an extension, of property rights. Because capitalism is a system in which capitalists have always argued for the right to make economic decisions on purely economic grounds, we assume that this means they are in fact allergic to political interference in their decisions, whereas they have always and consistently sought to utilize the state machineries and welcomed the concept of political primacy.

ENDLESS ACCUMULATION

In short, what has been wrong with our concept of the bourgeois is our inverted (if not perverse) reading of the historical reality of capitalism. If capitalism is anything, it is a system based on the logic of the *endless* accumulation of capital. It is this endlessness that has been celebrated or chastised as its Promethean spirit.[16] It is this endlessness which, for Emile Durkheim, had anomie as its enduring counterpart.[17] It is from this endlessness that Erich Fromm insisted we all seek to escape.[18]

When Max Weber sought to analyse the necessary link between the

Protestant ethic and the spirit of capitalism, he described the social implications of the Calvinist theology of predestination.[19] If God were omnipotent, and if only a minority could be saved, human beings could do nothing to ensure that they would be among this minority, since if they could, they would thereby determine God's will and He would not then be omnipotent. [Weber pointed out, however, that this was all very well logically, but it was impossible psycho-logically.] Psychologically, one might deduce from this logic that any behaviour is permissible, since it is all predestined. Or one might become totally depressed and hence inactive, since all behaviour is futile in terms of the only legitimate objective, salvation. Weber argued that a logic that is in conflict with a psycho-logic cannot survive, and must be bent. Thus it was with Calvinism. To the principle of predestination the Calvinists added the possibility of foreknowledge, or at least of negative foreknowledge. While we could not influence God's behaviour by our deeds, certain kinds of negative or sinful behaviour served as signs of the absence of grace. Psychologically, now all was well. We were urged to behave in a proper manner since, if we did not, that was a sure sign that God had forsaken us.

I should like to make an analysis parallel to that of Weber, distinguishing between the logic and psycho-logic of the capitalist ethos. If the object of the exercise is the endless accumulation of capital, eternal hard work and self-denial are always logically *de rigueur*. There is an iron law of profits as well as an iron law of wages. A penny spent on self-indulgence is a penny removed from the process of investment and therefore of the further accumulation of capital. But although the iron law of profits is logically tight, it is psycho-logically impossible. What is the point of being a capitalist, an entrepreneur, a bourgeois if there is no personal reward whatsoever? Obviously, there would be no point, and no one would do it. Still, logically, this is what is demanded. Well, of course, then the logic has to be bent, or the system would never work. And it has clearly been working for some time now.

Just as the combination omnipotence-predestination was modified (and ultimately undermined) by foreknowledge, so the combination accumulation-savings was modified (and ultimately undermined) by rent. Rent, as we know, was presented by the classical economists (including by Marx, the last of the classical economists) as the veritable antithesis of profit. It is no such thing; it is its avatar. The classical economists saw an historical evolution from rent towards profit, which translated into our historical evolution from rent towards profit, which translated into our historical myth that the bourgeoisie overthrew the aristocracy. In fact, however, this is wrong in two ways. The temporal sequence is short-run and not long-run, and it runs in the other direction. Every capitalist seeks to transform profit into rent. This translates into the following statement: the primary objective of every "bourgeois" is to become an "aristocrat." This is a short-run sequence, not a statement about the *longue durée*.

What is "rent?" In narrowly economic terms, rent is the income that derives from control of some concrete spatio-temporal reality which cannot be said to have been in some sense the creation of the owner or the result of his own work (even his work as an entrepreneur). If I am lucky enough to own land near a fording point in a river and I charge a toll to pass through my land, I am receiving a rent. If I allow others to work on my land for their own account or to live in my building, and I receive from them a payment, I am called a rentier. Indeed in eighteenth-century France, rentiers were defined in documents as "bourgeois living nobly on their revenues," that is, avoiding business or the professions.[20]

Now, in each of these cases it is not quite true that I have done nothing to acquire the advantage that has led to the rent. I have had the foresight, or the luck, to have acquired property rights of some kind which is what permits me legally to obtain the rent. The "work" that underlay the acquisition of these property rights has two features. It was done in the past, not the present. (Indeed it was often done in the distant past, that is, by an ancestor). And it required the sanctification by political authority, in the absence of which it could earn no money in the present. Thus rent = the past, and rent = political power.

Rent serves the existing property-owner. It does not serve the one who seeks, by dint of current work, to acquire property. Hence rent is always under challenge. And since rent is guaranteed politically, it is always under political challenge. The successful challenger, however, will as a consequence acquire property. As soon as he does, his interest dictates a defence of the legitimacy of rent.

Rent is a mechanism of increasing the rate of profit over the rate that one would obtain in a truly competitive market. Let us return to the example of the river crossing. Suppose we have a river such that there is only a single point narrow enough to permit the building of a bridge. There are various alternatives. The state could proclaim that all land is potentially private land and that the person who happens to own the two facing lots on the opposing shores at the narrowest point can build a private bridge and charge a private toll for crossing it. Given my premise that there is only one feasible point of crossing, this person would have a monopoly and could charge a heavy toll as a way of extracting a considerable portion of the surplus-value from all the commodity chains whose itinerary involved crossing the river. Alternatively, the state could proclaim the opposing shores public land, in which case one of two further ideal-typical possibilities present themselves. One, the state builds a bridge with public funds, charging no toll or a cost-liquidating toll, in which case no surplus-value would have been extracted from those commodity chains. Or two, the state announces that, the shores being public, they can be used by competing small boat-owners to transport goods across the river. In this case, the acute competition would reduce the price of such services to one yielding a very low rate of profit to the boat-owners, thus allowing a minimal extraction of surplus by them from the commodity chains traversing the river.

RENT AND MONOPOLY

Note how, in this example, rent seems to be the same thing, or nearly the same thing, as monopoly profit. A monopoly, as we know, means a situation in which, because of the absence of competition, the transactor can obtain a high profit, or one could say a high proportion of the surplus-value generated in the entire commodity chain of which the monopolized segment is a part. It is quite clear, in fact self-evident, that the nearer an enterprise is to monopolizing a spatio-temporally specific type of economic transaction, the higher the rate of profit. And the more truly competitive the market situation, the lower the rate of profit. Indeed this link between true competitiveness and low rates of profit is itself one of the historic ideological justifications for a system of free enterprise. It is a pity capitalism has never known widespread free enterprise. And it has never known widespread free enterprise precisely because capitalists seek profits, maximal profits, in order to accumulate capital, as much capital as possible. They are thereby not merely motivated but structurally forced to seek monopoly positions, something which pushes them to seek profit-maximization via the principal agency that can make it enduringly possible, the state.

So, you see, the world I am presenting is topsy-turvy. Capitalists do not want competition, but monopoly. They seek to accumulate capital not via profit but via rent. They want not to be bourgeois but to be aristocrats. And since historically—that is, from the sixteenth century to the present—we have had a deepening and a widening of the capitalist logic in the capitalist world-economy, there is more not less monopoly, there is more rent and less profit, there is more aristocracy and less bourgeoisie.

Ah, you will say, too much! Too clever by half! It does not seem to be a recognizable picture of the world we know nor a plausible interpretation of the historical past we have studied. And you will be right, because I have left out half the story. Capitalism is not a stasis; it is a historical system. It has developed by its inner logic and its inner contradictions. In another language, it has secular trends as well as cyclical rhythms. Let us therefore look at these secular trends, particularly with respect to our subject of enquiry, the bourgeois; or rather let us look at the secular process to which we have given the label of bourgeoisification. The process, I believe, works something like this.

The logic of capitalism calls for the abstemious puritan, the Scrooge who begrudges even Christmas. The psycho-logic of capitalism, where money is the measure of grace more even that of power, calls for the display of wealth and thus for "conspicuous consumption." The way the system operates to contain this contradiction is to translate the two thrusts into a generational sequence, the *Buddenbrooks* phenomenon. Wherever we have a concentration of successful entrepreneurs we have a concentration of *Buddenbrooks*-types. Ergo, the aristocratization of the bourgeoisie in the late seventeenth-century Holland, for example. When this is repeated as farce, we call it the betrayal of the historic role of the bourgeoisie—in twentieth-century Egypt, for example.

Nor has this only been a question of the bourgeois as consumer. His penchant for the aristocratic style can also be found in his original mode of operation as an entrepreneur. Until well into the nineteenth century (with lingering survivals today), the capitalist enterprise was constructed, in terms of labour relations, on the model of the medieval manor. The owner presented himself as a paternal figure, caring for his employees, housing them, offering them a sort of social security programme, and concerning himself not merely with their work behaviour but with their total moral behaviour. Over time, however, capital has tended to concentrate. This is the consequence of the search for monopoly, the elimination of one's competitors. It is a slow process because of all the counter-currents which are constantly destroying quasi-monopolies. Yet enterprise structures have gradually become larger and involved the separation of ownership and control—the end of paternalism, the rise of the corporation, and the emergence therefore of new middle classes. Where the "enterprises" are in fact state-owned rather than nominally private, as tends to be the case in weaker states in peripheral and especially semi-peripheral zones, the new middle classes take the form, in large part, of an administrative bourgeoisie. As this process goes on, the role of the legal owner becomes less and less central, eventually vestigial.

How should we conceptualize these new middle classes, the salaried bourgeoisies? They are clearly bourgeois along the axis of life-style or consumption, or (if you will) the fact of being the receivers of surplus-value. They are not bourgeois, or much less so, along the axis of capital, or property rights. That is to say, they are much less able than the "classic" bourgeoisie to turn profit into rent, to aristocratize themselves. They live off their advantages attained in the present, and not off privileges they have inherited from the past. Furthermore, they cannot translate present income (profit) into future income (rent). That is to say, they cannot one day represent the past off which their children will live. Not only do they live in the present, but so must their children and their children's children. This is what bourgeoisification is all about—the end of the possibility of aristocratization (that fondest dream of every classical propertied bourgeois), the end of constructing a past for the future, a condemnation to living in the present.

Reflect upon how extraordinarily parallel this is to what we have traditionally meant by proletarianization—parallel, not identical. A proletarian by common convention is a worker who is no longer either a peasant (that is, a petty land-controller) or an artisan (that is, a petty machine-controller). A proletarian is someone who has only his labour-power to offer in the market, and no resources (that is, no past) on which to fall back. He lives off what he earns in the present. The bourgeois I am describing also no longer controls capital (has therefore no past) and lives off what he earns in the present. There is, however, one striking difference with the proletarian. He lives much, much better. The difference seems to have nothing, or very little, to do any longer with control or the means of production. Yet somehow this bourgeois, product of bourgeoisification, obtains the surplus-value created by that proletarian, product of proletarianization. So if it is not control of the means of production, there must still be something this bourgeois controls which that proletarian does not.

"HUMAN CAPITAL"

Let us at this point note the recent emergence of another quasi-concept, that of human capital. Human capital is what these new-style bourgeois have in abundance, whereas our proletarian does not. And where do they acquire the human capital? The answer is well-known: in the educational systems, whose primary and self-proclaimed function is to train people to become members of the new middle classes, that is, to be the professionals, the technicians, the administrators of the private and public enterprises which are the functional economic building-pieces of our system.

Do the educational systems of the world actually create human capital, that is, train persons in specific difficult skills which merit economically some higher reward? One might perhaps make a case that the highest parts of our educational systems do something along this line (and even then only in part), but most of our educational system serves rather the function of socialization, of babysitting, and of filtering who will emerge as the new middle classes. How do they filter? Here as well we know the answer. Obviously, they filter by merit, in that no total idiot ever gets, say, the Ph.D. (or at least it is said to be rare). But since too many (not too few) people have merit (at least enough merit to be a member of the new middle classes), the triage has to be, when all is said and done, a bit arbitrary.

No one likes the luck of the draw. It is far too chancy. Most people will do anything they can to avoid arbitrary triage. They will use their influence, such as they have, to ensure winning the draw, that is, to ensure access to privilege. And those who have more current advantage have more influence. The one thing the new middle classes can offer their children, now that they can no longer bequeath a past (or at least are finding it increasingly difficult to do so), is privileged access to the "better" educational institutions.

It should come as no surprise that a key locus of political struggle is the rules of the educational game, defined in its broadest sense. For now we come back to the state. While it is true that the state is increasingly barred from awarding pastness, encrusting privilege and legitimating rent—that is, that property is becoming ever less important as capitalism proceeds on its historical trajectory—the state is by no means out of the picture. Instead of awarding pastness through honorifics, the state can award presentness through meritocracy. Finally, in our professional, salaried, non-propertied bourgeoisies we can have "careers open to talent," providing we remember that, since there is too much talent around, someone must decide who is talented and who is not. And this decision, when it is made among narrow ranges of difference, is a political decision.

We can summarize thus our picture. Over time, there has indeed been the development of a bourgeoisie within the framework of capitalism. The current version, however, bears little resemblance to the medieval merchant whose description gave rise to the name, and little resemblance either to the nineteenth-century capitalist industrialist whose description gave rise to the concept as it is generally defined today by the historical social sciences. We have been bemused by the accidental and deliberately distracted by the ideologies in play. It is nonetheless true that the bourgeois as receiver of surplus-value is the central actor of the capitalist drama. That is to say, the argument that capitalism is a unique kind of historical system in that it alone has kept the economic realm autonomous from the political seems to me a gigantic misstatement of reality, albeit a highly protective one.

This brings me to my last point, about the twenty-first century. The problem with this final avatar of bourgeois privilege, the meritocratic system—the problem, that is, from the point of view of the bourgeoisie—is that it is the least (not the most) defensible, because its basis is the thinnest. The oppressed may swallow being ruled by and giving reward to those who are to the manor born. But being ruled by and giving reward to people whose only asserted claim (and that a dubious one) is that they are smarter, that is too much to swallow. The veil can more readily be pierced; the exploitation becomes more transparent. The workers, having neither tsar nor paternal industrialist to calm their angers, are more ready to elaborate on a narrowly interest-based explanations of their exploitation and such misfortunes as befall them. This is what Bagehot and Schumpeter were talking about. Bagehot still hoped that Queen Victoria would do the trick. Schumpeter, coming later, from Vienna and not from London, teaching at Harvard and thus having seen it all, was far more pessimistic. He knew it could not last too long, once it was no longer possible for bourgeois to become aristocrats.

NOTES

1.   G. Matoré, *La vocabulaire et la société médiévale*, Paris 1985. p. 292.
2.   G. Duby, *Las trois ordres ou l'imaginaire du féodalisme*, Paris 1978.
3.   M. Canard, 'Essai de sémantique: Le mot "bourgeois"', *Revue de philosophie française et de littérature*, XXVII, p. 33.
4.   D. J. Roorda, 'The Ruling Classes in Holland in the Seventeenth Century', in J. S. Bromley and E. H. Kossman, eds., *Britain and the Netherlands*, II, Gröningen 1964, p. 119, and idem. 'Party and Faction,' *Acta Historica Neerlandica*, II, 1967, pp. 196–97.
5.   A. Berle and G. Means, *The Modern Corporation and Private Property*, New York 1912.
6.   See, for a notable example, C. Wright Mills, *White Collar*, New York 1951.
7.   See, for example, A. Gorz, *Stratégie ouvrière et néocapitalisme*, Paris 1964.
8.   F. Fanon, *The Wretched of the Earth*, New York 1964, pp. 121–65.
9.   K. Marx, F. Engels, *The Communist Manifesto* [1848]. New York 1948.
10. W. Bagehot, *The English Constitution* [1867], London 1964.
11. M. Weber, *Economy and Society* [1922], III, New York 1968, e. g. pp. 1403–05.
12. J. Schumpeter, *Capitalism, Socialism and Democracy*, New York 1942, Chapter 12.
13. R. Miliband, *The State in Capitalist Society*, London 1969; N. Poulantzas, *Political Power and Social Classes* [1968], NLB, London 1973; and see the debate in *New Left Review* 58, 59, 82 and 95.
14. E. P. Thompson, *The Making of the English Working Class*, revised edition, London 1968.
15. C. Morazé, *Les bourgeois conquérants*, Paris 1957.
16. D. Landes, *Prometheus Unbound*, Cambridge 1969.
17. E. Durkheim, *Suicide* [1897], Glencoe 1951.
18. E. Fromm, *Escape from Freedom*, New York 1941.
19. M. Weber, *The Protestant Ethic and the Spirit of Capitalism* [1904–05]. London 1930.
20. G. V. Taylor 'The Paris Bourse on the Eve of the Revolution,' *American Historial Review*, LXVII, 4 July, 1961, p. 954.
21. July 1961, p. 914. See also M. Vovelle and D. Roche, "Bourgeois, Rentiers and Property Owners. Elements for Defining a Social Category at the End of the Eighteenth Century," in J. Kaplow, ed., *New Perceptions and the French Revolution: Readings in Historical Sociology*, New York 1961, and R. Forster, 'The Middle Class in Western Europe: An Essay,' in J. Schneider, ed., *Wirtschaftskräften und Wirtschaftswege: Beitrage zur Wirtschaftsgeschichte*, 1978.

22—The Ideological Tensions of Capitalism: Universalism Versus Racism and Sexism

> Just as nationalism and ethnicity emerge side by side, I am arguing that universalism and racism/sexism as ideologies emerge side by side and form a necessary symbiotic pair. The modern world-system bases itself on both ideologies, seemingly in contradiction one with the other, at the same time. This explains the kinds of cleavages we get and the continuing epistemological ambiguity of the antinomy universalism/ particularism.

The modern world, we have long been told, is the first to reach beyond the bounds of narrow, local loyalties and to proclaim the universal brotherhood of man. Or so we were told up to the 1970s. Since that time, we have been made conscious that the very terminology of universalist doctrine, as for example the phrase *the brotherhood of man*, belies itself, since this phrase is masculine in gender, thereby implicitly excluding or relegating to a secondary sphere all who are female. It would be easy to multiply linguistic examples, all of which reveal an underlying tension between the continuing ideological legitimation of universalism in the modern world and the continuing reality (both material and ideological) of racism and sexism in this same world. It is this tension, or more precisely this contradiction, that I wish to discuss. For contradictions not only provide the dynamic force of historical systems; they also reveal their essential features.

It is one thing to ask whence universalist doctrine, and how widely it is shared; or to ask why racism and sexism exist and persist. It is quite another to enquire into the origins of the pairing of the two ideologies, indeed what one might argue has been the symbiotic relationship of these presumed opposites. We start with a seeming paradox. The major challenge to racism and sexism has been universalist beliefs, and the major challenge to universalism has been racist and sexist beliefs. We assume that the proponents of each set of beliefs are persons in opposite

344

camps. Only occasionally do we allow ourselves to notice that the enemy, as Pogo put it, is us; that most of us (perhaps all of us) find it perfectly possible to pursue both doctrines simultaneously. This is to be deplored no doubt; but it is also to be explained, and by more than the simple assertion of hypocrisy. For this paradox (or this hypocrisy) is enduring, widespread, and structural. It is no passing human failing.

In previous historical systems it was easier to be consistent. However much these previous systems varied in their structures and in their premises, they all had no hesitation in making some kind of moral and political distinction between the insider and the outsider, in which both the belief in the higher moral qualities of the insider and the sense of obligation by insiders to each other took precedence over any abstract concept about the human species, if such abstractions were asserted at all. Even the three monotheistic world religions—Judaism, Christianity, and Islam—made such distinctions between insiders and outsiders despite their hypothetical commitment to a single God presiding over a singular human species.

This essay discusses first the origins of modern universalist doctrines, then the sources of modern racism and sexism, and finally the realities of the combination of the two ideologies, both in terms of what gave rise to it and what has been its consequences.

There are two main ways of explaining the origins of universalism as an ideology of our present historical system. One is to see universalism as the culmination of an older intellectual tradition. The other is to see it as an ideology particularly appropriate to a capitalist world-economy. The two modes of explanation do not necessarily contradict each other. The argument that it is the outcome or the culmination of a long tradition has to do precisely with the trio of monotheistic religions. The crucial moral leap, it has been argued, occurred when humans (or some humans) ceased to believe in a tribal god and recognized the unicity of God and therefore implicity the unicity of humanity. To be sure, the argument continues, the three monotheistic religions pursued the logic of their position only part-way. Judaism carved out a special position for the people chosen of God and was reluctant to encourage membership by adoption. Christianity and Islam both lifted the barriers to entry into the group of the chosen, and indeed went in the other direction with proselytization. But both Christianity and Islam normally required an af-

firmative act of allegiance (which one could make as a formerly nonbe-
lieving adult by formal conversion) in order to gain full access to the
kingdom of God. Modern Enlightenment thought, it is said, simply took
this monotheistic logic one step further, deriving moral equality and human rights from human nature itself, a characteristic with which we are
all born and as a result of which our rights become entitlements rather
than earned privileges.

This is not incorrect history of ideas. We have several important po-
liticomoral documents of the late eighteenth century that reflect this Enlightenment ideology, documents that were given widespread credence
and adherence as a result of major political upheavals (the French Revolution, the decolonization of the Americas, etc.). Furthermore, we can
carry the ideological history forward. There were many de facto omissions in these ideological documents of the eighteenth century—and
most notably those of nonwhites and women. But as time went on, these
omissions and others have been rectified by explicitly including these
groups under the rubric of universalist doctrine. Today even those social
movements whose raison d'être is the implementation of racist or sexist
policies tend to pay at least lip service to the ideology of universalism,
thereby seeming to consider it somehow shameful to assert overtly what
they very clearly believe and think should govern political priorities. It is
not hard therefore to derive from the history of ideas a sort of secular
upward curve of the acceptance of universalist ideology, and based on
that curve, to make a claim about the existence of a sort of inevitable
world-historical process at work.

The claim however that, since universalism has only been seriously
pursued as a political doctrine in the modern world, its origins must be
sought in the particular socioeconomic framework of this world also
seems very strong. The capitalist world-economy is a system built on the
endless accumulation of capital. One of the prime mechanisms that
makes this possible is the commodification of everything. These commodities flow in a world market in the form of goods, of capital, and of
labor power. Presumably, the freer the flow, the greater the degree of
commodification. Consequently, anything that restrains the flow is hypothetically counterindicated.

Anything that prevents goods, capital, or labor power from being a
marketable commodity serves to restrain such flows. Anything that uses

criteria of evaluating goods, capital, or labor power other than their market value and then gives these other valuations priority makes the item to that extent nonmarketable, or at least less marketable. Hence, by a sort of impeccable logic, particularisms of any kind whatsoever are said to be incompatible with the logic of a capitalist system, or at least an obstacle to its optimal operation. It would follow then that, within a capitalist system, it is imperative to assert and carry out a universalist ideology as an essential element in the endless pursuit of the accumulation of capital. Thus it is that we talk of capitalist social relations as being a "universal solvent," working to reduce everything to a homogeneous commodity form denoted by a single measure of money.

This is said to have two principal consequences. It is said to permit the greatest possible efficiency in the production of goods. Specifically, in terms of labor power, if we have a "career open to talents" (one of the slogans born out of the French Revolution), we are likely to place the most competent persons in the occupational roles most suitable for them in the world division of labor. And we have indeed developed whole institutional mechanisms—the public school system, the civil service, antinepotism rules—that are designed to establish what today we call a "meritocratic" system.

Furthermore, it is said, not only is meritocracy economically efficient but it is also politically stabilizing. To the extent that there are inequalities in the distribution of reward in historical capitalism (as in prior historical systems), resentment of those who receive greater rewards by those who receive fewer is less intense, it is argued, because its justification is offered on the basis of merit and not on the basis of tradition. That is, it is thought that privilege earned by merit is somehow more acceptable, morally and politically, to most people than privilege earned by inheritance.

This is dubious political sociology. The exact opposite is true in fact. While privilege earned by inheritance has long been at least marginally acceptable to the oppressed on the basis of mystical or fatalistic beliefs in an eternal order, which belief at least offers them the comfort of certainty, privilege earned because one is possibly smarter and certainly better educated than someone else is extremely difficult to swallow, except by the few who are basically scrambling up the ladder. Nobody who is not a yuppie loves or admires a yuppie. Princes at least may seem to be kindly father figures. A yuppie is nothing but an overprivileged sibling. The meritocratic system is politically one of the least stable systems. And it is precisely because of this political fragility that racism and sexism enter the picture.

The presumed upward curve of universalist ideology has long been thought theoretically to be matched by a downward curve of the degree of inequality generated by race or gender, both as ideology and as fact. This, however, has simply not been the case empirically. We could even perhaps make the inverse argument, that the curves of race and gender inequalities have actually been going up in the modern world, or at least they have not been going down—certainly in fact, possibly even as ideology. To see why this might be so, we should look at what the ideologies of racism and sexism actually assert.

Racism is not simply a matter of having an attitude of disdain for or fear of someone of another group as defined by genetic criteria (such as skin color) or by social criteria (religious affiliation, cultural patterns, linguistic preference, etc.). Racism normally includes such disdain and fear, but it is far more than that. Disdain and fear are quite secondary to what defines the practice of racism in the capitalist world economy. Indeed, it could even be argued that disdain and fear of the other (xenophobia) is an aspect of racism that entails a contradiction.

Xenophobia in all prior historical systems had one primary behavioral consequence: the ejection of the "barbarian" from the physical locus of the community, the society, the in-group—death being the extreme version of ejection. Whenever we physically eject the other, we gain the "purity" of environment that we are presumably seeking, but we inevitably lose something at the same time. We lose the labor power of the person ejected and therefore that person's contribution to the creation of a surplus that we might be able to appropriate on a recurring basis. This represents a loss for any historical system, but it is a particularly serious one in the case of a system whose whole structure and logic is built around the endless accumulation of capital.

A capitalist system that is expanding (which is half the time) needs all the labor power it can find, since this labor is producing the goods through which more capital is produced, realized, and accumulated. Ejection out of the system is pointless. But if one wants to maximize the accumulation of capital, it is necessary simultaneously to minimize the cost of production (hence the costs of labor power) and minimize the costs of political disruption (hence minimize—not eliminate, because one cannot eliminate—the protests of the labor force). Racism is the magic formula that reconciles these objectives.

Let us look at one of the earliest and most famous discussions about racism as an ideology. When Europeans came to the New World, they encountered peoples whom they slaughtered in large numbers—either directly by the sword or indirectly by disease. A Spanish friar, Bartolomé de Las Casas, took up their cause, arguing that Indians had souls which needed to be saved. Let us pursue the implications of the Las Casas argument which won the formal assent of the church, and eventually of the states. Since Indians had souls, they were human beings, and the rules of natural law applied to them. Therefore, one was not morally permitted to slaughter them indiscriminately (eject them from the domain). One was obliged instead to seek to save their souls (convert them to the universalist value of Christianity). Since they would then be alive and presumably en route to conversion, they could be integrated into the work force—at the level of their skills, of course, which translated into meaning at the bottom level of the occupational and reward hierarchy.

Racism operationally has taken the form of what might be called the "ethnicization" of the work force, by which I mean that at all times there has existed an occupational-reward hierarchy that has tended to be correlated with some so-called social criteria. But while the pattern of ethnicization has been constant, the details have varied from place to place and time to time, according to what part of the human genetic and social pools were located in a particular time and place and what the hierarchical needs of the economy were at that time and place.

That is to say, racism has always combined claims based on continuity with the past (genetic and/or social) with a present-oriented flexibility in defining the exact boundaries of these reified entities we call races or ethno-national-religious groupings. The flexibility of claiming a link with the boundaries of the past combined with the constant redrawing of these boundaries in the present takes the form of the creation and constant re-creation of racial and/or ethno-national-religious groups or communities. They are always there, and always ranked hierarchically, but they are not always exactly the same. Some groups can be mobile in the ranking system; some groups can disappear or combine with others;

while still others break apart and new ones are born. But there are always some who are "niggers." If there are no Blacks or too few to play the role, one can invent "white niggers."

This kind of system—racism constant in form and in venom, but somewhat flexible in boundary lines—does three things extremely well. It allows one to expand or contract the numbers available in any particular space-time zone for the lowest paid, least rewarding economic roles, according to current needs. It gives rise to and constantly re-creates social communities that actually socialize children into playing the appropriate roles (although, of course, they also socialize them into forms of resistance). And it provides a nonmeritocratic basis to justify inequality. This last point is worth underlining. It is precisely because racism is anti-universalistic in doctrine that it helps to maintain capitalism as a system. It allows a far lower reward to a major segment of the work force than could ever be justified on the basis of merit.

But if capitalism as a system begets racism, does it need to beget sexism as well? Yes, because the two are in fact intimately linked. The ethnicization of the work force exists in order to permit very low wages for whole segments of the labor force. Such low wages are in fact only possible because the wage earners are located in household structures for which lifetime wage-income provides only a relatively small proportion of total household income. Such households require the extensive input of labor into so-called subsistence and petty market activities—in part by the adult male to be sure, but in much larger part by the adult female, plus the young and the aged of both sexes.

In such a system, this labor input in nonwage work "compensates" the lowness of the wage-income and therefore in fact represents an indirect subsidy to the employers of the wage laborers in those households. Sexism permits us not to think about it. Sexism is not just the enforcement of different, or even less appreciated, work roles for women, no more than racism is just xenophobia. As racism is meant to keep people inside the work system, not eject them from it, so sexism intends the same.

The way we induce women—and the young and the aged—to work to create surplus-value for the owners of capital, who do not even pay them a little bit, is by proclaiming that their work is really nonwork. We invent the "housewife" and assert that she is not "working," merely "keeping house." Thus, when governments calculate the percentage of the so-called active labor force who are employed, "housewives" are neither in the numerator nor in the denominator of the calculation. And with sexism automatically goes ageism. As we pretend that the housewife's work is not creating surplus-value, so we pretend that the multiple work inputs of the nonwaged young and aged do not do so either.

None of this reflects working reality. But it does all add up to an ideology which is extremely powerful, and which all fits together. The combination of universalism-meritocracy serving as the basis by which the cadres or middle strata can legitimate the system and racism-sexism serving to structure the majority of the work force works very well. But only to a point, and that for a simple reason—the two ideological patterns of the capitalist world-economy stand in open contradiction to each other. The delicately poised combination threatens always to get out of hand, as various groups start to push the logic of universalism on the one hand and of racism-sexism on the other too far.

We know what happens when racism-sexism goes too far. Racists may try to eject the out-group totally—swiftly, as in the case of the Nazi slaughter of the Jews; less swiftly, as in the pursuit of total apartheid. Taken to this extreme, these doctrines are irrational and, because they are irrational, they are resisted. They are resisted, of course, by the victims, but they are also resisted by powerful economic forces who object not to the racism but to the fact that its primary objective—an ethnicized but productive work force—has been forgotten.

We can also imagine what happens when universalism goes too far. Some people may seek to implement a truly egalitarian allocation of work roles and work rewards in which race (or its equivalent) and gender genuinely play no part. Unlike taking racism too far, there is no swift way one can take universalism too far, for one has to eliminate not merely the legal and institutional barriers to universalism but the internalized patterns of ethnicization, and this inevitably requires at the very least a generation. So it is rather easy to resist universalism's going too far. In the name of universalism itself, one merely has to denounce the so-called reverse racism wherever steps are taken to dismantle the institutionalized apparatus of racism and sexism.

What we see, therefore, is a system that operates by a tense link between the right dosage of universalism and racism-sexism. There are always efforts to push one side or the other of this equation "too far." The result is a sort of zigzag pattern. This could go on forever, except for one problem. Over time, the zigs and zags are getting bigger, not smaller. The thrust toward universalism is getting stronger. So is the thrust toward racism and sexism. The stakes go up. This is for two reasons.

On the one hand, there is the informational impact of the accumulation of historical experience, by all participants. On the other hand, there are the secular trends of the system itself. For the zigzag of universalism and racism-sexism is not the only zigzag in the system. There is also the zigzag of economic expansion and contraction, for example, with which the ideological zigzag of universalism and racism-sexism is partially correlated. The economic zigzag is getting sharper. Why that is so is another story. Yet as the general contradictions of the modern world-system force the locus of the search for a successor system, it is in fact located in the sharpening tension, the increased zigs and zags, between universalism and racism-sexism. It is not a question of which half of this antinomy will in some sense win out, since they are intimately and conceptually tied to each other. It is a question of whether and how we will invent new systems that will utilize neither the ideology of universalism nor the ideology of racism-sexism. That is our task, and it is not an easy one.

—*Part Five*

Resistance, Hope, and Deception

23—1968, Revolution in the World-System: Theses and Queries

The world revolution of 1968 has come to play a central role in my analysis of the modern world-system, as the crucial moment in which the hegemony of liberalism in the geoculture of the modern world-system was effectively challenged. This essay served as the basic document for a conference held in 1988 to celebrate and look back on 1968. I seek to lay out here clearly a series of theses and queries, which then can be used to go forward in an analysis of where the world-system is heading as a result.

Thesis 1: *1968 was a revolution in and of the world-system*

The revolution of 1968 was a revolution; it was a single revolution. It was marked by demonstrations, disorder, and violence in many parts of the world over a period of at least three years. Its origins, consequences, and lessons cannot be analyzed correctly by appealing to the particular circumstances of the local manifestations of this global phenomenon, however much the local factors conditioned the details of the political and social struggles in each locality.

As an event, 1968 has long since ended. However, it was one of the great, formative events in the history of our modern world-system, the kind we call watershed events. This means that the cultural-ideological realities of that world-system have been definitively changed by the event, itself the crystallization of certain long-existing structural trends within the operation of the system.

ORIGINS

Thesis 2: *The primary protest of 1968 was against U.S. hegemony in the world-system (and Soviet acquiescence in that hegemony)*

In 1968, the world was still in the midst of what has come to be called in France the "thirty glorious" years — the period of incredible expansion of the capitalist world-economy following the end of the Second World War. Or rather, 1968 immediately followed the first significant evidence of the beginning of a long world-economic stagnation, that is, the serious difficulties of the U.S. dollar in 1967 (difficulties that have never since ceased).

The period 1945–1967 had been one of unquestioned hegemony of the United States in the world-system, whose bedrock was the incredible superiority in productive efficiency of the United States in all fields in the aftermath of the Second World War. The United States translated this economic advantage into a worldwide political and cultural domination by undertaking four main policy initiatives in the post-1945 period. It constructed around itself an "alliance system" with western Europe (and Japan) characterized as the leadership of the "Free World," and invested in the economic reconstruction of these areas (the Marshall Plan, etc.). The United States sought thereby both to ensure the role of western Europe and Japan as major economic customers, and to guarantee their internal political stability and international political clientship.

Second, the United States entered into a stylized Cold War relationship with the U.S.S.R. based on reserving to the U.S.S.R. a small but important zone of political domination (eastern Europe). This so-called Yalta arrangement enabled both countries to present their relationship as an unlimited ideological confrontation, with the important proviso that no changes in the East-West line were to occur and no actual military confrontations were to ensue, especially in Europe.

Third, the United States sought to achieve a gradual, relatively bloodless decolonization of Asia and Africa, on the assumption that this could be arranged via so-called moderate leadership. This was made all the more urgent by the victory of the Chinese Communist Party in China, a victory (be it noted) that was achieved despite the counsels of the U.S.S.R. Moderation was defined as the absence of significant ideological links of this leadership with the U.S.S.R. and world Communism and, even more, the willingness of the decolonized states to participate in the existing set of international economic arrangements. This process of decolonization under the control of moderates was abetted by the occasional and judicious use of limited U.S. military force.

Fourth, the U.S. leadership sought to create a united front at home by minimizing internal class conflict, through economic concessions to the skilled, unionized, working class on the one hand, and through enlisting U.S. labor in the worldwide anti-Communist crusade on the other hand. It also sought to dampen potential race conflict by eliminating blatant discrimination in the political arena (end of segregation in the armed forces, constitutional invalidation of segregation in all arenas, Voting Rights Act). The United States encouraged its principal allies to work in parallel ways toward maximizing internal unity.

The result of all these policy initiatives by the United States was a system of hegemonic control that operated quite smoothly in the 1950s. It made possible the continuing expansion of the world-economy, with significant income benefits for "middle" strata throughout the world. It made possible the construction of the United Nations network of international agencies, which at that time reflected the political will of the United States and ensured a comparatively stable world political arena. It contributed to the "decolonization" of large parts of what came to be called the Third World with surprising rapidity. And it ensured that, in the West, generally, the 1950s was a period of relative political quietude.

Nonetheless, by the 1960s, this pattern of successful "hegemony" had begun to fray, in part because of its very success. The economic reconstruction of the U.S.'s strong allies became so great that they began to reassert some economic (and even some political) autonomy. This was one, albeit not the only, meaning of Gaullism, for example. The death of Stalin marked the end of a "monolithic" Soviet bloc. It was followed, as we know, by a (still ongoing) process of destalinization and desatellization, the two major turning-points of which were the Report of Kruschchev to the XXth Party Congress in 1956 and the Sino-Soviet split in 1960. The smoothness of the decolonization of the Third World was disturbed by two long and draining anti-colonial wars in Algeria and Vietnam (to which should be associated the long Cuban struggle). Finally, the political "concessions" of the 1950s to "minority groups" in the United States (and elsewhere in the Western world) accentuated expectations that were not in fact being met, either in the political or the economic arenas, and hence in actual practice stimulated rather than constrained further political mobilization.

The 1960s began with the tandem of Kennedy and Kruschchev, who in effect promised to do things better. Between them, they succeeded in lifting the heavy ideological lids that had so successfully held down the world in the 1950s, without however bringing about any fundamental reforms of the existing system. When they were removed from power, and replaced by the tandem Johnson-Brezhnev, the hopes of the early 1960s disappeared. However, the renewed ideological pressures that the powers attempted to reapply were now being placed on what was a more disabused world public opinion. This was the pre-revolutionary tinderbox in which opposition to U.S. hegemony, in all its multiple expressions, would explode in 1968 — in the U.S., in France, in Czechoslovakia, in Mexico, and elsewhere.

Thesis 3: *The secondary, but ultimately more passionate, protest of 1968 was against the "old left" antisystemic movements*

The nineteenth century saw the birth of two major varieties of antisystemic movements — the social and the national movements. The former emphasized the oppression of the proletariat by the bourgeoisie. The second emphasized the oppression of underdog peoples (and "minorities") by dominant groups. Both kinds of movements sought to achieve, in some broad sense, "equality." In fact, both kinds of movements used the three terms of the French revolutionary slogan of "liberty, equality, and fraternity" virtually interchangeably.

Both kinds of movements took concrete organizational form in one country after another, eventually almost everywhere, in the second half of the nineteenth and the first half of the twentieth century. Both kinds of movements came to emphasize the importance of obtaining state power as the indispensable intermediate achievement on the road to their ultimate objectives. The social movement, however, had an important worldwide split in the early twentieth century concerning the road to state power (parliamentary versus insurrectionary strategies).

By 1945, there existed three clear and separate networks of such movements on the world scene: the Third International Communist parties; the Second International social-democratic parties; the various nationalist (or national liberation) movements. The period 1945–1968 was a period of remarkable political achievement for these three networks of movements. Third International parties came to power, by one means or another, in a series of countries more or less contiguous to the U.S.S.R. (eastern Europe, China, North Korea). Second International parties (I use the term loosely, including in this category the Democratic Party in the United States as Roosevelt reshaped it) came to power (or at least achieved *droit de cité*, that is, the right of *alternance*) in the western world (western Europe, North America, Australasia). Nationalist or national liberation movements came to power in most formerly colonized areas in Asia, the Middle East, Africa, the Caribbean, and in somewhat different forms in long-independent Latin America.

The important point for the analysis of the revolution of 1968 was that the new movements that emerged then were led largely by young people who had grown up in a world where the traditional antisystemic movements in their countries were not in an early phase of mobilization but had already achieved their intermediate goal of state power. Hence these "old" movements could be judged not only on their promises but on their practices once in power. They were so judged, and to a considerable degree they were found wanting.

They were found wanting on two main grounds. First, they were found wanting in their efficacity in combatting the existing capitalist world-system and its current institutional incarnation, U.S. hegemony. Secondly, they were found wanting in the quality of life they had created in the "intermediate" state structures they presumably controlled. Thus it was that, in the words of one famous 1968 aphorism, they were no longer to be considered "part of the solution." Rather, they had become "part of the problem."

The anger of the U.S. SDS against "liberals," of the *soixante-huitards* against the PCF (not to speak of the socialists), of the German SDS against the SPD was all the more passionate because of their sense of fundamental betrayal. This was the real implication of that other 1968 aphorism: "Never trust anyone over the age of 30." It was less generational at the level of individuals than generational at the level of antisystemic organizations. I take it as no accident that the major outbreak in the Soviet bloc was in Czechoslovakia, a country with a particularly long and strong Third International tradition. The leaders of the Prague Spring fought their struggle in the name of "humanist Communism," that is, against the betrayal that Stalinism represented. I take it also as no accident that the major outbreak in the Third World was in Mexico, the country that had the oldest national liberation movement continuously in power, or that particularly important outbreaks occurred in Dakar and in Calcutta, two cities with very long nationalist traditions.

Not only was the revolution of 1968 directed, even if only secondarily, against the "old lefts" through the world, but these "old lefts" responded, as we know, in coin. The "old lefts" were first of all astonished at finding themselves under attack from the left (who us, who have such impeccable credentials?), and then deeply enraged at the adventurism that the "new lefts" represented in their eyes. As the "old lefts" responded with increasing impatience and hostility to the spreading "anarchism" of the "new lefts," the latter began to place greater and greater emphasis on the ideological centrality of their struggle with the "old lefts." This took the form of the multivariate "maoisms" that developed in the early 1970s in all parts of the world, including of course in China itself.

Thesis 4: *Counter-culture was part of revolutionary euphoria, but was not politically central to 1968*

What we came to call in the late 1960s "counter-culture" was a very visible component of the various movements that participated in the revolution of 1968. We generally mean by counter-culture behavior in daily life (sexuality, drugs, dress) and in the arts that is unconventional, non-"bourgeois," and Dionysiac. There was an enormous escalation in the quantity of such behavior directly associated with activism in the "movement." The Woodstock festival in the United States represented a kind of symbolic highpoint of such movement-related counter-culture.

But of course, a counter-culture was not a particularly new phenomenon. There had been for two centuries a "Bohemia" associated with youth and the arts. The relaxation of puritanical sexual mores had been a steady linear development throughout the twentieth century worldwide. Furthermore, "revolutions" had often previously been the occasion of counter-cultural affirmation. Here, however, two models of previous revolutions should be noted. In those revolutions that had been planned, organized, and involved long military struggle, revolutionary puritanism usually became an important element of discipline (as in the history of the Chinese Communist Party). Where, however, revolutionary circumstances included a large measure of spontaneous activity (as was the case in the Russian Revolution of 1917 or the triumph of Castro in Cuba), the spontaneity involved a breakdown in social constraints and hence was associated, at least initially, with counter-culture (for example, "free love" in post–1917 Russia). The revolution of 1968 had of course a particularly strong component of unplanned spontaneity and therefore, as the thesis says, counter-culture became part of the revolutionary euphoria.

Nonetheless, as we all learned in the 1970s, it is very easy to dissociate counter-culture from political (revolutionary) activity. Indeed, it is easy to turn counter-cultural trends into very profitable consumption-oriented life-styles (the transition from yippies to yuppies). While, therefore, the counter-culture of the new left was salient to most of these forces themselves, as it was to their enemies, in the final analysis it was a minor element in the picture. It may be one of the consequences of 1968 that Dionysiac life styles spread further. It was not one of its legacies. It is to the political legacies that we must now turn.

LEGACIES

Legacies of watershed-events are always complex phenomena. For one thing, they are always ambiguous. For another, they are always the object of a struggle by various heirs to claim the legacy, that is, the legitimacy of a tradition. Please note that there already exists a tradition of 1968. Traditions are rapidly created, and the "tradition" of the Revolution of 1968 was already functioning by the early 1970s. And in 1988 there are many celebrations, many books, and many attempts at recuperation as well. This should neither surprise us nor dismay us. World-historic events have lives of their own and they resist any kind of simple capture. 1968 is no different. Having thus warned you against myself, I shall nonetheless put before you what I think are the two principal legacies of 1968.

Thesis 5: *Revolutionary movements representing "minority" or underdog strata need no longer, and no longer do, take second place to revolutionary movements representing presumed "majority" groups*

1968 was the ideological tomb of the concept of the "leading role" of the industrial proletariat. This leading role had long been challenged, but never before so massively and so efficaciously. For in 1968 it was being challenged on the grounds that the industrial proletariat was and would always structurally remain just one component among others of the world's working class.

The historic attitude of both varieties of "old left" movements (the socialist and the nationalist) was that they represented the interests of the "primary" oppressed—either the "working class" of a given country or the "nation" whose national expression was unfulfilled. These movements took the view that the complaints of "other" groups who saw themselves as being treated unequally—the unfulfilled nationalities for socialist movements, the working class for nationalist movements, women for both kinds of movements, and any other group that could lay claim to social or political oppression—were at best secondary and at worst diversionary. The "old left" groups tended to argue for their own achievement, after which (they claimed) the secondary oppressions would disappear of themselves or at least be resolved by appropriate political action in the "post-revolutionary" era.

Needless to say, not everyone agreed with such reasoning. And the socialist and nationalist movements of the world often quarreled fiercely with each other over precisely this issue of priority of struggle. But none of the "old left" movements ever ceded theoretical ground on this issue of strategic priorities in the struggle for equality, although many individual movements made tactical and temporary concessions on such issues in the interests of creating or reinforcing particular political alliances.

As long as the "old left" movements were in their pre-revolutionary, mobilizing phases, the argument about what would or would not happen after their achievement of state power remained hypothetical. But once they were in state power, the practical consequences could be assessed on the basis of some evidence. By 1968, many such assessments had been made, and the opponents of the multiple "other" inequalities could argue, with some plausibility, that the achievement of power by "old left" groups had not in fact ended these "other" inequalities, or at least had not sufficiently changed the multiple group hierarchies that had previously existed.

At the same time, a century of struggle had begun to make clear two sociological realities that had great bearing on this debate. The first was that, contrary to prior theorizing, the trend of capitalist development was not to transform almost all the world's laboring strata into urban, male, adult, salaried factory workers, the ideal-type of the "proletarian" as traditionally conceived. The reality of capitalism was far more occupationally complex than that. This ideal-type "proletarian" had represented a minority of the world's laboring strata in 1850, of course. But it had then been thought this was merely transitional. However, such ideal-type "proletarians" remained a minority in 1950. And it was now clear that this particular occupational profile would probably remain a minority in 2050. Hence, to organize a movement around this group was to give priority—permanent and illegitimate priority—to the claims of one variety over other varieties of the world's laboring strata.

Analogously, it had become clear that "nationalities" were not just there in some form that could be objectively delineated. Nationalities were rather the product of a complex process of ongoing social creation, combining the achievement of consciousness (by themselves and by others) and socio-juridical labeling. It followed that for every nation there could and would be sub-nations in what threatened to be an unending cascade. It followed that each transformation of some "minority" into a "majority" created new "minorities." There could be no cut-off of this process, and hence no "automatic" resolution of the issue by the achievement of state power.

If the "proletariat" and the "oppressed nations" were not destined to transform themselves into uncontested majorities, but would forever remain one kind of "minority" alongside other kinds of "minorities," their claim to strategic priority in the antisystemic struggle would thereby be grievously undermined. 1968 accomplished precisely this undermining. Or rather, the revolution of 1968 crystallized the recognition of these realities in the worldwide political action of antisystemic movements.

After 1968, none of the "other" groups in struggle—neither women nor racial "minorities" nor sexual "minorities" nor the handicapped nor the "ecologists" (those who refused the acceptance, unquestioningly, of the imperatives of increased global production)—would ever again accept the legitimacy of "waiting" upon some other revolution. And since 1968, the "old left" movements have themselves become increasingly embarrassed about making, have indeed hesitated to continue to make, such demands for the "postponement" of claims until some presumed post-revolutionary epoch. It is easy enough to verify this change in atmosphere. A simple quantitative content analysis of the world's left press, comparing say 1985 and 1955, would indicate a dramatic increase of the space accorded to these "other" concerns that had once been considered "secondary."

Of course, there is more. The very language of our analyses has changed, has consciously and explicitly been changed. We worry about racism and sexism even in arenas once thought "harmless" (appellations, humor, etc.). And the structure of our organizational life has also changed. Whereas prior to 1968 it was generally considered a desideratum to unify all existing antisystemic movements into one movement, at least into one movement in each country, this form of unity is no longer an unquestioned desideratum. A multiplicity of organizations, each representing a different group or a different tonality, loosely linked in some kind of alliance, is now seen, at least by many, as a good in itself. What was a *pis aller* is now proclaimed as a "rainbow coalition" (a U.S. coinage that has spread).

The triumph of the Revolution of 1968 has been a triple triumph in terms of racism, sexism, and analogous evils. One result is that the legal situations (state policies) have changed. A second result is that the situations within the antisystemic movements have changed. A third result is that mentalities have changed. There is no need to be Polyannaish about this. The groups who were oppressed may still complain, with great legitimacy, that the changes that have occurred are inadequate, that the realities of sexism and racism and other forms of oppressive inequality are still very much with us. Furthermore, it is no doubt true that there has been "backlash" in all arenas, on all these issues. But it is pointless also not to recognize that the Revolution of 1968 marked, for all these inequalities, a historic turning-point.

Even if the states (or some of them) regress radically, the antisystemic movements will never be able to do so (or, if they do, they will thereby lose their legitimacy). This does not mean that there is no longer a debate about priorities among antisystemic movements. It means that the debate has become a debate about fundamental strategy, and that the "old left" movements (or tendencies) are no longer refusing to enter into such a debate.

Thesis 6: *The debate on the fundamental strategy of social transformation has been reopened among the antisystemic movements, and will be the key political debate of the coming twenty years*

There exists today, in a broad sense, six varieties of antisystemic movements. (a) In the Western countries, there are "old left" movements in the form of the trade-unions and segments of the traditional left parties—labor and social-democratic parties, to which one might perhaps add the Communist parties, although except for Italy these are weak and growing weaker. (b) In the same Western countries, there is a wide variety of new social movements—of women, "minorities," Greens, etc. (c) In the socialist bloc, there are the traditional Communist parties in power, among whom a strain of persistent antisystemic virus has never been extinguished, which gives rise to renewed (and "feverish") activity from time to time. The Gorbachev phenomenon, insofar as it appeals to "Leninism" against "Stalinism," can be taken as evidence of this. (d) In this same socialist bloc, a network is emerging of extra-party organizations quite disparate in nature, which seem increasingly to be taking on some of the flavor of Western new social movements. They have, however, the distinctive feature of an emphasis on the themes of human rights and anti-bureaucracy. (e) In the Third World, there are segments of those traditional national liberation movements still in power (as, for example, in Algeria, Nicaragua, and Mozambique) or heirs to such movements no longer in power (although "heritages" such as Nasserism in the Arab world tend to fritter). Of course, in countries with unfulfilled revolutions (such as South Africa or El Salvador), the movements, still necessarily in their mobilizing phase of struggle, have the strength and the characteristics of their predecessors in other states, when they were in that phase. (f) And finally, in these same Third World countries, there are new movements that reject some of the "universalist" themes of previous movements (seen as "Western" themes) and put forward "indigenist" forms of protest, often in religious clothing.

It seems clear that all six varieties of movements are far from uniformly antisystemic. But all six varieties have some significant antisystemic heritage, some continuing antisystemic resonance, and some further antisystemic potential. Furthermore, of course, the six varieties of movements are not entirely limited geographically to the various zones as I have indicated. One can find some trans-zone diffusion, but the geographical segregation of varieties holds true, broadly speaking, for the moment.

There are, I believe, three principal observations to make about the relation of these six varieties of (potentially, partially, historically) antisystemic movements to each other. First, at the time of the Revolution of 1968, the six varieties tended to be quite hostile to each other. This was particularly true of the relation of the "old" to the "new" variety in each zone, as we have already noted. But it was generally true more widely. That is, any one of the six varieties tended to be critical of, even hostile toward, all five other varieties. This initial, multifaced mutual hostility has tended to diminish greatly in the subsequent two decades. Today, one might speak of the six varieties of movements showing a hesitant (and still suspicious) tolerance toward each other, which is of course far short of being politically allied with each other.

Second, the six varieties of movements have begun tentatively to debate with each other about the strategy of social transformation. One principal issue is, of course, the desirability of seeking state power, the issue that has fundamentally divided the three "old" from the three "new" varieties of movements. Another, and derived, issue concerns the structure of organizational life. These are, to be sure, issues that had been widely debated in the 1850–1880 period, and at that time more or less resolved. They have now been reopened, and are being discussed again, now however in the light of the "real-existing" experience of state power.

Third, when and if this debate on global strategy will be resolved, even if the resolution takes the form of merging the six varieties of movements into one grand worldwide family, it does not follow that there will be a unified antisystemic strategy. It has long been the case, and will continue ever more to be so, that these movements have been strongly penetrated by persons, groups, and strata whose essential hope is not the achievement of an egalitarian, democratic world but the maintenance of an inegalitarian, undemocratic one, even if one necessarily different in structure from our existing capitalist world-economy (currently in its long structural crisis). That is to say, at the end of the debate among the movements, we shall most probably see a struggle within the possibly single family of movements between the proponents of an egalitarian, democratic world and their opponents.

LESSONS

What lessons are we to draw from the Revolution of 1968 and its aftermath? What lessons indeed are we to draw from more than a century of worldwide, organized antisystemic activity? Here I think the format of theses is not reasonable. I prefer to lay out the issues in the form of queries. These are queries, I hasten to add, that cannot find their answers in colloquia alone, or in the privacy of intellectual discussion. These are queries that can be answered fully only in the praxis of the multiple movements. But this praxis of course includes, as one part of it, the analyses and debates in public and in private, especially those conducted in a context of political commitment.

Query 1: *Is it possible to achieve significant political change without taking state power?*

I suppose the answer to this depends first of all on how one defines "significant." But the question is a real one nonetheless. If the Marxists won the political debate with the Anarchists in the nineteenth century, and the political nationalists won their parallel debate with the cultural nationalists, the explanation was the compelling force of one assertion that they made: Those with existing privilege will never cede it willingly, and will use their control of state violence to prevent significant change. It followed that ousting the privileged from state power was the prerequisite to significant change.

It seems quite clear that even today, in some countries (say, South Africa), there are governments representing privileged minorities that are resolutely unwilling to cede their privilege. In these countries it seems very implausible to suggest that any significant political change could occur in the absence of vigorous, and almost inevitably violent, political activity. South Africa is no doubt a quintessential instance of a state in which the majority of its citizens have never had *droit de cité* and have therefore never felt that the government was "theirs" in any sense whatsoever.

But today there is a large number of states in which the majority of the population believe that, in some sense, the government is "theirs." Most "post-revolutionary" regimes by and large enjoy this fundamental sense of popular support. This is no doubt true of the U.S.S.R. and of China, and of Algeria. But if of Algeria, is it not also true of India? And is this not true of Sweden, where fifty years of Social-Democratic regimes have "integrated" the working class into political life? And what about France, or Germany? One could go on. Each national case has its specificity. But it is surely clear that there is a very large number of states in which popular support for the state is widespread, and where therefore a struggle for the primary accession to state power has little resonance. It is probably not very useful to suggest therefore that some of these state structures are "post-revolutionary," implying that the others are "pre-revolutionary." Most of them are in the same boat in terms of degree of popular support (and popular cynicism). To repeat, this is not true in states where accession to state power by the majority still remains the primary political issue. But such states today are a minority.

Indeed, is not the prime issue in many states, and perhaps most especially in those that are self-consciously "post-revolutionary," the question of achieving the control by the "civil society" over the state? Is this not the heart of the internal political debate not only in the "socialist countries" but also in Latin America, and southern Europe, and Southeast Asia, and Black Africa? "More democracy is more socialism," says Mr. Gorbachev. But if so, what is the function of an antisystemic *movement* in the U.S.S.R.?

Query 2: *Are there forms of social power worth conquering other than "political" power?*

Obviously, there are other forms of social power—economic power, cultural power (Gramsci's "hegemony"), power over self (individual and "group" autonomy). And obviously, individuals, groups, and organizations constantly seek such kinds of power. But how does the effort to attain such power articulate with the *political* activity of antisystemic movements? In what sense will the achievement of more economic power, or more cultural power, or more power over self in fact contribute to a fundamental transformation of the world-system?

We are here before a question that has beset antisystemic movements since their outset. Is fundamental transformation the consequence of an accretion of improvements that, bit by bit and over time, create irreversible change? Or are such incremental achievements very largely a self-deception that in fact demobilize and hence preserve the realities of existing inequities? This is, of course, the "reformism-revolution" debate once again, which is larger than the constricted version of this debate symbolized by Eduard Bernstein versus Lenin.

That is to say, is there a meaningful *strategy* that can be constructed that involves the variegated pursuit of multiple forms of power? For this is what is suggested, at least implicitly, by a lot of the arguments of the new social movements that emerged in the wake of 1968.

Query 3: *Should antisystemic movements take the form of organizations?*

The creation of bureaucratic organizations as the instrument of social transformation was the great sociological invention of nineteenth-century political life. There was much debate about whether such organizations should be mass-based or cadre-based, legal or underground, one-issue or multi-issue, whether they should demand limited or total commitment of their members. But for over a century, there has been little doubt that organizations of some kind were indispensable.

The fact that Michels demonstrated a very long time ago that these organizations took on a life of their own that interfered quite directly with their ostensible *raisons d'être* did not seem to dampen very much the enthusiasm to create still more organizations. Even the spontaneous movements of 1968 became transformed into many such organizations. This no doubt had consequences that made many of the post-1968 generation very uncomfortable, as may be seen in the acerbic debates between Fundis and Realos in the German Green movement.

The tension between the political efficacity that organizations represent and the ideological and political dangers they incarnate is perhaps unresolvable. It is perhaps something with which we simply must live. It seems to me, however, that this is a question that has to be dealt with directly and debated thoroughly, lest we simply drift into two pointless factions of the "sectarians" and the "dropouts." The numbers of individuals throughout the world who are "ex-activists" and who are now "unaffiliated" but who wish in some way to be politically active has, I believe, grown very sharply in the wake of the post-1968 letdown. I do not think we should think of this as the "depoliticization" of the disillusioned, though some of it is that. It is rather the fear that organizational activity is only seemingly efficacious. But if so, what can replace it, if anything?

Query 4: *Is there any political basis on which antisystemic movements, West and East, North (both West & East) and South, can in reality join hands?*

The fact that there are *six* varieties of antisystemic movements, an "old" and a "new" variety in each of the three different zones, seems to me no passing accident. It reflects a deep difference of political realities in the three zones. Do there exist any unifying political concerns that could give rise to a common worldwide strategy? Is there any evidence that, even if this wasn't true in the period following 1945, it is beginning to be true in the 1980s, and might be even more true in the twenty-first century?

Here we need more than pieties and wishful thinking. There has never existed heretofore international (that is, interzonal) solidarity of any significance. And this fact has given rise to much bitterness. Three things seem to me important. One, the immediate day-to-day concerns of the populations of the three zones are today in many ways strikingly different. The movements that exist in these three zones reflect their differences. Second, many of the short-run objectives of movements in the three zones would, if achieved, have the effect of improving the situation for some persons in that zone at the expense of other persons in other zones. Third, no desirable transformation of the capitalist world-economy is possible in the absence of trans-zonal political cooperation by antisystemic movements.

This trans-zonal cooperation would have to be both strategic and tactical. It might be easier (albeit still not easy) to establish the bases of tactical cooperation. But strategic? It is probable that strategic collaboration can only be on the basis of a profound radicalization of the objectives.

For the great impediment to trans-zonal strategic collaboration is the incredible socioeconomic polarization of the existing world-system. But is there an objective (and not merely a voluntaristic) basis for such a radicalization?

Query 5: *What does the slogan, "liberty, equality, fraternity," really mean?*

The slogan of the French Revolution is familiar enough to us all. It seems to refer to three different phenomena, each located in the three realms into which we are accustomed to divide our social analyses: liberty in the political arena, equality in the economic arena, and fraternity in the socio-cultural arena. And we have become accustomed as well to debating their relative importance, particularly between liberty and equality.

The antinomy of liberty and equality seems to be absurd. I don't really understand myself how one can be "free" if there is inequality, since those who have more always have options that are not available to those who have less, and therefore the latter are less free. And similarly I don't really understand how there can be equality without liberty since, in the absence of liberty, some have more political power than others, and hence it follows that there is inequality. I am not suggesting a verbal game here but a rejection of the distinction. Liberty-equality is a single concept.

Can then fraternity be "folded into" this single concept of liberty-equality? I do not think so. I note first that fraternity, given our recent consciousness about sexist language, should now be banned as a term. Perhaps we can talk of comradeship. This brings us however to the heart of the issues raised by sexism and racism. What is their opposite? For a long time the lefts of the world preached one form or another of universalism, that is, of total "integration." The consciousness of the Revolution of 1968 has led to the assertion by those who most directly suffered from racism and sexism of the political, cultural, and psychological merits of building their own, that is separate, organizational and cultural structures. At a world level, this is sometimes called the "civilizational project."

It is correct to assert that the tensions between universalism and particularism are the product of the capitalist world-economy and are impossible to resolve within its framework. But that gives us insufficient guide for future goals or present tactics. It seems to me that the movements after 1968 have handled this issue the easy way, by swinging back and forth on a pendulum in their emphases. This leaves the issue intact as a permanent confusion and a permanent irritant. If we are to think of a trans-zonal strategy of transformation, it will have to include a fairly clear perspective on how to reconcile the thrust for homogeneity (implied in the very concept of a trans-zonal strategy) and the thrust for heterogeneity (implied in the concept of liberty-equality).

Query 6: *Is there a meaningful way in which we can have plenty (or even enough) without productivism?*

The search for the conquest of nature and the Saint Simonian moral emphasis on productive labor have long been ideological pillars not only of the capitalist world-economy but also of its antisystemic movements. To be sure, many have worried about excessive growth, and waste, and resource depletion. But, as with other such rejections of dominant values, how far can we, should we, draw the implications of the critiques?

Once again, it is easy to say that jobs versus ecology is a dilemma produced by the current system and inherent in it. But once again, this tells us little about long-term objectives or short-term tactics. And once again, this is an issue that has profoundly divided the antisystemic movements within zones, and even more across the zones.

CONCLUDING NOTE

One of the principal implicit complaints of the Revolution of 1968 was that the enormous social effort of antisystemic movements over the prior one hundred years had yielded so little global benefit. In effect, the revolutionaries were saying, we are not really farther along than our grandparents were, in terms of transforming the world.

The criticism was a harsh one, no doubt a salutary one, but also an unfair one. The conditions of the world-system revolution of 1968 were entirely different from those of the world-systemic revolution of 1848. From 1848 to 1968, it is hard to see, retrospectively, how the antisystemic movements could have acted other than they did. Their strategy was probably the only one realistically available to them, and their failures may have been inscribed in the structural constraints within which they necessarily worked. Their efforts and their devotion were prodigious. And the dangers they averted, the reforms they imposed probably offset the misdeeds they committed and the degree to which their mode of struggle reinforced the very system against which they were struggling.

What is important, however, is not to be a Monday morning quarterback of the world's antisystemic movements. The real importance of the Revolution of 1968 is less its critique of the past than the questions it raised about the future. Even if the past strategy of the "old left" movements had been the best possible strategy for the time, the question still remained whether it was a useful strategy as of 1968. Here the case of the new movements was a far stronger one.

The new movements however have not offered a fully coherent alternative strategy. A coherent alternative strategy is still today to be worked out. It will possibly take ten to twenty more years to do so. This is not a cause for discouragement; it is rather the occasion for hard collective intellectual and political work.

24—Social Science and the Communist Interlude, or Interpretations of Contemporary History

It is widely argued that the collapse of the Communisms in 1989 was a more important moment of cultural and political change than the world revolution of 1968. I do not agree. I try here to place what I call the Communist interlude, 1917–1989, into historical context. I gave this paper first as a talk at a meeting in Cracow in Poland in 1996 called to discuss "building an open society" in East-Central Europe.

A Communist interlude? Between what and what? And first of all, when? I shall consider it to be the period between November 1917 (the so-called Great October Revolution) and 1991, the year of the dissolution of the Communist Party of the Soviet Union in August, and of the USSR itself in December. This is the period in which there were states governed by Communist, or Marxist-Leninist, parties in Russia and its empire and in east-central Europe. To be sure, there are still today a few states in Asia that consider themselves to be governed by Marxist-Leninist parties, to wit, China, the Democratic Republic of Korea, Vietnam, and Laos. And there is Cuba. But the era in which there was a "socialist bloc of states" in any meaningful sense is over. So in my view is the era in which Marxism-Leninism is an ideology that commands significant support.

So we are talking of an interlude in the elementary sense that there was a point of time prior to the era in which there was a coherent bloc of states asserting that they were governed by Marxist-Leninist ideology and that today we are living in a period posterior to that era. Of course, its shadow was there before 1917. Marx and Engels had asserted in the *Manifesto* already in 1848 that "a spectre is haunting Europe, the spectre of Communism." And, in many ways, this spectre is still haunting Europe. Only Europe? Let us discuss that.

374

What was the spectre before 1917? What was it between 1917 and 1991? What is it today? I think it is not too difficult to come to an agreement on what the spectre was before 1917. It was the spectre that somehow the "people" — seen as a largely undereducated, uncultivated, and unsophisticated mass of persons — would rise up in some disorderly manner, destroy and confiscate property, and redistribute it more or less, putting into power persons who would govern without respect for talent or initiative. And in the process, they would destroy what was seen as valuable in a country's traditions, including of course its religious traditions.

This was not a totally delusionary fear. There is a scene in the movie version of Pasternak's *Doctor Zhivago* when Dr. Zhivago, returning from the front shortly after the revolution to his relatively palatial home in Moscow, is greeted not merely by his family but by the very large collective of persons who have occupied his home as their new residence. His own family has been relegated to a single room in the vast house. Zhivago, representing the essential idealistic Russian intellectual, is asked somewhat aggressively what he thinks of this new reality, and he replies, "This is a better arrangement, comrades, more just." To the end of his quite eventful life, Dr. Zhivago continues to believe that it is better, even if the reader/viewer is left to have more ambiguous sentiments.

We know the political and social history of nineteenth-century Europe fairly well. Let me summarize it. After the French Revolution, there was widespread and increasing acceptance in Europe of two concepts that would have been considered strange by most persons before the French Revolution. The first was that political change was an absolutely normal and expectable phenomenon. The second was that sovereignty, national sovereignty, resided not in rulers or legislatures but in something called the "people." These were not only new ideas; they were radical ideas, disturbing to most persons of property and power.

This new set of values that transcended particular states, what I call the emerging geoculture of the world-system, was accompanied by important changes in the demographic and social structuring of most European states. The rate of urbanization increased, and the percentage of wage labor increased. This sudden geographic concentration of sizable numbers of urban wageworkers in European cities, whose living conditions were generally abysmal, created a new political force composed of persons who were largely excluded from the benefits of economic growth: they suffered economically, were excluded socially, and had no say in the political processes, either at the national or the local levels. When Marx and Engels said, "Workers of the world, unite; you have nothing to lose but your chains," they were both referring to and addressing this group.

Two things happened in Europe between 1848 and 1917 that affected this situation. First, the political leaders of the different states began to effectuate a program of reform, *rational* reform, designed to respond to the plaints of this group, palliate their miseries, and appease their sense of alienation. Such programs were put into effect within most European states, albeit at different paces and at different moments. (I include in my definition of Europe the principal White settler states: the United States, Canada, Australia, and New Zealand.)

The programs of reform had three main components. The first was suffrage, which was introduced cautiously but steadily expanded in coverage: sooner or later all adult males (and then women as well) were accorded the right to vote. The second reform was remedial workplace legislation plus redistributive benefits, what we would later call the "welfare state." The third reform, if reform is the right word, was the creation of national identities, largely via compulsory primary education and universal military service (for males).

The three elements together—political participation via the ballot, the intervention of the state to reduce the polarizing consequences of ungoverned market relations, and a transclass unifying national loyalty—comprise the underpinnings, and indeed in actuality the definition, of the liberal state, which by 1914 had become the pan-European normal and partial practice. After 1848, the pre-1848 differences between so-called liberal and so-called conservative political forces diminished radically as they tended to come together on the merits of a reform program, although of course there continued to be debate about the pace of reform and about the degree to which it was useful to preserve the veneration of traditional symbols and authorities.

This same period saw the emergence in Europe of what is sometimes called the social movement, composed on the one hand of the trade unions and on the other hand of socialist or labor parties. Most, although not all, of these political parties considered themselves to be "Marxist," though what this really meant has been a continuing matter of dispute, then and since. The strongest among these parties, and the "model" party for itself and for most of the others, was the German Social-Democratic Party.

The German Social-Democratic Party, like most of the other parties, was faced with one major practical question: Should it participate in parliamentary elections? (With the subsequent question, Should its members participate in governments?) In the end, the overwhelming majority of the parties and of the militants of parties answered yes to these questions. The reasoning was rather simple. They could thereby do some immediate good on behalf of their constituencies. Eventually, with extended suffrage and sufficient political education, the majority would vote them into total power, and once in power, they could legislate the end of capitalism and the installation of a socialist society. There were some premises that underpinned this reasoning. One was the enlightenment view of human rationality: all persons will act in their own rational interest, provided they have the chance and the education to perceive it correctly. The second was that progress was inevitable, and that therefore history was on the side of the socialist cause.

This line of reasoning by the socialist parties of Europe in the pre-1914 period transformed them in practice from a revolutionary force, if they ever were one, into merely a somewhat more impatient version of centrist liberalism. Although many of the parties still talked a language of "revolution," they no longer really conceived of revolution as involving insurrection or even the use of force. Revolution had become rather the expectation of some dramatic political happening, say a 60 percent victory at the polls. Since at the time socialist parties were still doing quite poorly at the polls on the whole, prospective victory at the polls still bore the psychological flavor of revolution.

Enter Lenin, or rather enter the Bolshevik faction of the Russian Social-Democratic Party. The Bolshevik analysis had two main elements. First, the Bolsheviks said that the theorizing and praxis of the European social-democratic parties were not at all revolutionary but constituted at best a variant of liberalism. Second, they said that, whatever the justification for such "revisionism" might be elsewhere, it was irrelevant to Russian reality, since Russia was not a liberal state, and there was therefore no possibility that socialists could vote themselves into socialism. One has to say that these two assessments seem in retrospect absolutely correct.

The Bolsheviks drew from this analysis a crucial conclusion: Russia would never become socialist (and implicitly neither would any other state) without an insurrectionary process that involved seizing control of the state apparatus. Therefore, Russia's "proletariat" (the approved subject of history), which was in fact still numerically small, had to do this by organizing itself into a tightly structured cadre party that would plan and organize the "revolution." The "small" size of the urban industrial proletariat was more important to the implicit, not explicit, theorizing than Lenin and his colleagues admitted. For what we in effect got here was a theory of how to be a socialist party in a country that was neither wealthy nor highly industrialized, and was therefore not a part of the core zone of the capitalist world-economy.

The leaders of the October Revolution considered themselves to have led the first proletarian revolution of modern history. It is more realistic to say that they led one of the first, and possibly the most dramatic, of the national liberation uprisings in the periphery and semiperiphery of the world-system. What made this particular national liberation uprising different, however, from the others were two things: it was led by a cadre party that affected a universalist ideology and therefore proceeded to create a worldwide political structure under its direct control; and the revolution occurred in the particular country outside the core zone that was the strongest among them industrially and militarily. The whole history of the Communist interlude of 1917–91 derived from these two facts.

A party that proclaims itself a vanguard party, and then proceeds to achieve state power, cannot but be a dictatorial party. If one defines oneself as vanguard, then one is necessarily right. And if history is on the side of socialism, then the vanguard party is logically fulfilling the world's destiny by enforcing its will on everyone else, including those persons of whom it is supposed to be the vanguard, in this case, the industrial proletariat. Indeed, it would be remiss in its duty were it to act differently. If, in addition, only one of these parties in the entire world had state power, which was essentially the case between 1917 and 1945, then if one were to organize an international cadre structure, it does seem natural and plausible that the party of the state in power would become the leading party. In any case, this party had the material and political means to insist on this role against any opposition that arose. Thus it seems not unfair to state that the one-party regime of the USSR and its de facto control of the Comintern were almost inevitable consequences of the theory of the vanguard party. And with it came, if not quite inevitably then at least with high probability, what actually happened: purges, gulags, and an Iron Curtain.

No doubt the clear and continuous hostility of the rest of the world to the Communist regime in Russia played a big role in these developments. But it is surely specious to attribute these developments to that hostility, since Leninist theory predicted the hostility and therefore the hostility represented part of the constants of external reality with which the regime always knew it had to deal.

The hostility was to be expected. The internal structuring of the regime was to be expected. What was perhaps less to be expected was the geopolitics of the Soviet regime. There were four successive geopolitical decisions taken by the Bolsheviks that marked turning-points, and these do not seem to me to have been necessarily the only route that the Soviet regime could have taken.

The first was the reassembling of the Russian empire. In 1917, the Russian imperial forces were in military disarray, and vast segments of the Russian population were calling out for "bread and peace." This was the social situation within which the tsar was forced to abdicate, and in which, after a brief period, the Bolsheviks could launch their attack on the Winter Palace and seize state power.

At first, the Bolsheviks seemed to be indifferent to the fate of the Russian empire as such. After all, they were internationalist socialists, who were committed to a belief in the evils of nationalism, of imperialism, and of tsarism. They "let go" both Finland and Poland. One can be cynical and say that they were merely casting ballast overboard at a difficult moment. I think rather that it was a kind of immediate, almost instinctive, reaction in accord with their ideological prejudices.

What happened then was rational reflection. The Bolsheviks found themselves in a militarily difficult civil war. They were afraid that "letting go" meant the creation of actively hostile regimes on their borders. They wanted to win the civil war, and they decided that this required reconquest of the empire. It turned out to be too late for Finland and Poland, but not for the Ukraine and the Caucasus. And thus it was that, of the three great multinational empires that existed in Europe at the time of the First World War—the Austro-Hungarian, the Ottoman, and the Russian—only the Russian empire was to survive, at least until 1991. And thus it was that the first Marxist-Leninist regime became a Russian imperial regime, the successor to the tsarist empire.

The second turning-point was the Congress of the Peoples of the East in Baku in 1921. Faced with the reality that the long-awaited German revolution was not going to happen, the Bolsheviks turned inward and eastward. They turned inward insofar as they now proclaimed a new doctrine, that of building socialism in one country. And they turned eastward insofar as Baku shifted the world-systemic emphasis of the Bolsheviks from a revolution of the proletariat in highly industrialized countries to an anti-imperialist struggle in the colonial and semicolonial countries of the world. Both seemed sensible as pragmatic shifts. Both had enormous consequences for the taming of Leninism as a world revolutionary ideology.

To turn inward meant to concentrate upon the reconsolidation of the Russian state and empire as state structures and to put forward a program of economic catching up, via industrialization, with the countries of the core zone. To turn eastward was to admit implicitly (not yet explicitly) the virtual impossibility of a workers' insurrection in the core zone. It was also to join in the struggle for Wilson's self-determination of nations (under the more colorful banner of anti-imperialism). These shifts in objectives made the Soviet regime far less unpalatable to the political leadership of Western countries than its previous stance, and laid the basis for a possible geopolitical entente.

This led logically to the next turning-point, which came the very next year, 1922, in Rapallo, when Germany and Soviet Russia both reentered the world political scene as major players by agreeing to resume diplomatic and economic relations and to renounce all war claims on each other, thereby effectively circumventing the different kinds of ostracism each was suffering at the hands of France, Great Britain, and the United States. From that point on, the USSR was committed to a full integration in the interstate system. It joined the League of Nations in 1933 (and would have done so sooner, if permitted), allied itself with the West in the Second World War, cofounded the United Nations, and never ceased in the post-1945 world to seek recognition by everyone (and first of all, by the United States) as one of the world's two "great powers." Such efforts, as Charles de Gaulle was repeatedly to point out, might be hard to explain in terms of the ideology of Marxism-Leninism but were perfectly expectable as the policies of a great military power operating within the framework of the existing world-system.

And it was then not surprising that we saw the fourth turning-point, the often-neglected but ideologically significant dissolution of the Comintern in 1943. To dissolve the Comintern was first of all to recognize formally what had been a reality for a long time, the abandonment of the original Bolshevik project of proletarian revolutions in the most "advanced" countries. This seems obvious. What was less obvious is that this represented the abandonment of the Baku objectives as well, or at least in their original form.

Baku extolled the merits of anti-imperialist national liberation movements in the "East." But by 1943 the leaders of the USSR were no longer really interested in revolutions anywhere, unless they entirely controlled those revolutions. The Soviet leadership was not stupid, and it realized that movements that came to power through long national struggles were unlikely to surrender their integrity to someone in Moscow. Who would then? There was only one possible answer—movements that came to power because of and under the watchful eye of Russia's Red Army. Thus was born the Soviet policy toward the only part of the world of which this could possibly be true, at least at the time, east-central Europe. In the period 1944–47, the USSR was determined to place in power subservient Communist regimes in all areas where the Red Army found itself at the end of the Second World War, essentially Europe east of the Elbe. I say essentially because immediately there are three exceptions: Greece, Yugoslavia, and Albania. But we know what happened there. The Red Army was located in none of these three countries in 1945. In Greece, Stalin abandoned the Greek Communist Party dramatically. And both Yugoslavia and Albania, which had Marxist-Leninist regimes that had come to power through their own insurrectionary efforts, would openly break with the USSR. As for Asia, Stalin's foot-dragging was obvious to the world, not least of all to the Chinese Communist Party, which also broke dramatically with the USSR as soon as it could. Mao's meeting with Nixon is the direct outcome of this fourth Soviet turning-point.

After four turning-points, what was left? Not much of the old spectre of Communism. What was left was something quite different. The USSR was the second-strongest military power in the world. It was in fact strong enough to make a deal with the United States, which was the strongest power, and by far, that allowed it to carve out a zone of exclusive influence, from the Elbe to the Yalu, but not beyond. The deal was that this zone was its to control and that its free rein there would be respected by the United States, provided only that the USSR really stayed inside that zone. The deal was consecrated at Yalta and was essentially respected by the Western powers and the Soviet Union right up to 1991. In this, the Soviets played the game as the direct heirs of the tsars, performing their geopolitical role better.

Economically, the USSR had set out on the classic road to catching up, via industrialization. It did fairly well, considering all its handicaps and the costs of the destruction of the Second World War. If one looks at the 1945–70 figures, they are impressive on a world comparative scale. The USSR forced its satellite countries to pursue the same path, which made less sense for some of them, but these countries too did fairly well at first. But the economics were naive, not because they didn't leave enough place for private enterprise but because they assumed that steady "catching up" was a plausible policy and industrialization was the wave of the economic future. In any case, as we know, the USSR as well as the east-central European countries began to do badly in economic terms in the 1970s and 1980s and eventually collapsed. This was of course a period in which much of the world was also doing badly, and much of what happened in these countries was part of a larger pattern. The point, however, is that, from the point of view of people living in these countries, the economic failures were a sort of last straw, especially given the official propaganda that the greatest proof of the merits of Marxism-Leninism lay in what it could do immediately to improve the economic situation.

It was the last straw because the internal political situation in all these countries was one that virtually no one liked. Democratic political participation was nonexistent. If the worst of the terrorism was over by the mid-1950s, arbitrary imprisonment and control by the secret police were still the normal, ongoing reality of life. And nationalism was allowed no expression. This mattered perhaps least in Russia, where the reality was that Russians were on top of this political world, even if they were not allowed to say so. But for everyone else, Russian dominance was intolerable. Finally, the one-party system meant that, in all these countries, there was a very privileged stratum, the Nomenklatura, whose existence made the ideological claim of the Bolsheviks to represent egalitarianism seem a mockery.

There were always very many people in all these countries who in no sense shared the original Bolshevik objectives. What made the whole system collapse in the end, however, was that large numbers of those who did share these objectives became as hostile to the regimes as the others—perhaps even more hostile. The spectre that haunted the world from 1917 to 1991 had become transformed into a monstrous caricature of the spectre that had haunted Europe from 1848 to 1917. The old spectre exuded optimism, justice, morality, which were its strengths. The second spectre came to exude stagnation, betrayal, and ugly oppression. Is there a third spectre on the horizon?

The first spectre was one not for Russia or east-central Europe but rather for Europe (and the world). The second spectre was one for the whole world. And the third spectre will surely be that for the whole world again. But can we call it the spectre of Communism? Certainly not in the 1917–1991 use of the term. And only up to a point in the 1848–1917 usage of the term. But the spectre is nonetheless awesome and is not unrelated to the continuing problem of the modern world, its combination of great material and technological advance and extraordinary polarization of the world's populations.

In the ex-Communist world, many see themselves as having gone "back to normalcy." But this is no more realistic a possibility than it was when President Warren Harding launched that slogan for the United States in 1920. The United States could never go back to the pre-1914 world, and Russia and its ex-satellites cannot go back to the pre-1945 or pre-1917 world, neither in detail nor in spirit. The world has moved decisively on. And while most persons in the ex-Communist world are immensely relieved that the Communist interlude is behind them, it is not at all sure that they, or the rest of us, have moved into a safer or more hopeful or more livable world.

For one thing, the world of the next fifty years promises to be a far more violent one than the Cold War world out of which we have come.

The Cold War was highly choreographed, highly constrained by the concern of both the United States and the Soviet Union that there be no nuclear war between them, and just as important by the fact that the two countries had between them the necessary power to ensure that such a war would not break out. But this situation has changed radically. Russia's military strength, while still great, is considerably weakened. But so, it must be said, is that of the United States, if less so. In particular, the United States no longer has three elements that ensured its military strength previously: the money, popular willingness within the United States to bear the losses of military action, and political control over western Europe and Japan.

The results are already clear. It is extremely difficult to contain escalating local violence (Bosnia, Rwanda, Burundi, and so on). It will be virtually impossible over the next twenty-five years to contain weapons proliferation, and we should anticipate a significant increase in the number of states that have nuclear weapons at their disposition, as well as biological and chemical weapons. Furthermore, given, on the one hand, the relative weakening of U.S. power and the emergence of a triadic division among the strongest states and, on the other hand, a continuing economic North-South polarization in the world-system, we should expect the likelihood that there will be more deliberate South-North military provocations (of the Saddam Hussein variety). Such provocations will be increasingly difficult to handle politically, and if several occur simultaneously, it is doubtful that the North will be able to stem the tide. The U.S. military has already moved into a mode of preparing to handle *two* situations at the same time. But if there are three?

The second new element is South-North migration (which includes eastern Europe–western Europe migration). I say it is new, but of course such migration has been a feature of the capitalist world-economy for five hundred years now. Three things, however, have changed. The first is the technology of transport, which makes the process far easier. The second is the extensiveness of the global economic *and demographic* polarization, which makes the global push far more intensive. The third is the spread of democratic ideology, which undermines the political ability of wealthy states to resist the tide.

What will happen? It seems clear in the short run. In the wealthy states, we shall see the growth of right-wing movements that focus their rhetoric around keeping migrants out. We shall see the erection of more and more legal and physical barriers to migration. We shall nonetheless see a rise in the real rate of migration, legal and illegal—in part because the cost of real barriers is too high, in part because of the extensive collusion of employers who wish to utilize such migrant labor.

The middle-run consequences are also clear. There will come to be a statistically significant group of migrant families (including often the second-generation families) who will be poorly paid, not socially integrated, and almost certainly without political rights. These persons will constitute essentially the bottom stratum of the working class in each country. If this is the case, we shall be back to the pre-1848 situation in western Europe—an underclass concentrated in urban areas without rights and with very strong complaints, and this time clearly identifiable ethnically. It was this situation that led to the first spectre of which Marx and Engels spoke.

There is, however, now another difference with 1848. The world-system was riding a wave of enormous optimism about the future in the nineteenth century, and indeed up to about twenty years ago. We lived in an era in which everyone was sure that history was on the side of progress. Such faith had one enormous political consequence: it was incredibly stabilizing. It created patience, since it assured everyone that things would be better one day, one day soon, for at least one's children. It was what made the liberal state plausible and acceptable as a political structure. Today the world has lost that faith, and having lost it the world has lost its essential stabilizer.

It is this loss of faith in inevitable reform that accounts for the great turn against the state, which we see everywhere today. No one ever really liked the state, but the great majority had permitted its powers to grow ever greater because they saw the state as the mediator of reform. But if it cannot play this function, then why suffer the state? But if we don't have a strong state, who will provide daily security? The answer is we must then provide it ourselves, for ourselves. And this puts the world collectively back to the period of the beginning of the modern world-system. It was to get out of the necessity of constructing our own local security that we engaged in the construction of the modern state-system.

And one last, not so small, change. It is called democratization. Everyone speaks of it, and I believe it is really occurring. But democratization will not diminish, but add to, the great disorder. For, to most people, democratization translates primarily as the demand for three things as equal rights: a reasonable income (a job and later a pension), access to education for one's children, and adequate medical facilities. To the extent that there is democratization, people insist not merely on having these three, but on regularly raising the minimal acceptable threshold for each. But having these three, at the level that people are demanding each day, is incredibly expensive, even for the wealthy countries, not to speak of for Russia, China, India. The only way *everyone* can really have more of these is to have a radically different system of distribution of the world's resources than we have today.

So what shall we call this third spectre? The spectre of disintegration of the state structures, in which people no longer have confidence? The spectre of democratization, and the demand for a radically different system of distribution? The next twenty-five to fifty years will be a long political debate about how to handle this new spectre. It is not possible to predict the outcome of this worldwide political debate, which will be a worldwide political struggle. What is clear is that the responsibility of social scientists is to help in clarifying the historical choices that are before us.

25—America and the World: Today, Yesterday, and Tomorrow

In 1991, I was invited by the University of Vermont to participate in the bicentennial of its founding, which occurred in the year that Vermont joined the United States. I used the occasion to return to my origins and to assess the historical trajectory of the United States within the modern world-system.

G od, it seems, has distributed his blessing to the United States thrice: in the present, in the past, and in the future. I say it seems so, because the ways of God are mysterious, and we cannot pretend to be sure we understand them. The blessings of which I speak are these: in the present, prosperity; in the past, liberty; in the future, equality.

Each of these blessings has always involved measuring the United States of America by the yardstick of the world. Despite the long U.S. history of seeing itself as remote from the world, and removed especially from Europe, its self-definition has always been in fact in terms of the world. And the rest of the world has in turn always kept the United States in the forefront of its attention for some two hundred years now.

The problem with God's blessings is that they have a price. And the price we are willing to pay is always a call upon our righteousness. Each blessing has been accompanied by its contradictions. And it is not always obvious that those who received the blessings were those who paid its price. As we move from today into tomorrow, it is time once again to count our blessings, assess our sins, and behold our reckoning sheet.

TODAY

The today of which I speak began in 1945 and came to an end in 1990. In this period, in precisely this period and no longer, the United States has been the hegemonic power of our world-system. The origin of this hegemony has been in our prosperity; its consequence has been our prosper-

387

ity; the sign of our hegemony has been our prosperity. What did we do to merit this singular and rare privilege? Were we born great? Did we achieve greatness? Was greatness thrust upon us?

The present began in 1945. The world had just emerged from a long and terrible world war. Its battlefield had been the whole Eurasian land-mass, reaching from the island in the west (Great Britain) to the islands in the east (Japan, the Philippines, and the Pacific Islands) and from the northern zones of Eurasia to northern Africa, southeast Asia, and Melanesia in the south. Throughout this vast zone there had been im-mense devastation of human life and of the physical stock that was the basis of world production. Some areas were more devastated than oth-ers, but almost no part of this vast zone escaped free and clear. Indeed, the only major industrial zone in the world whose equipment and na-tional infrastructure were intact was North America. The factories of the United States were not only unbombed but had been brought to new levels of efficiency by wartime planning and mobilization.

Since the United States had entered the war with productive machin-ery that was already a match (at least) for all others in the world, the war-time destruction of the others created a gap in productive capacity and efficiency that was enormous. It was this gap that created the possibility for U.S. enterprises to flourish in the twenty-five years to come as they had never done before. And it was this gap that ensured that the only way these enterprises could flourish was by permitting a significant increase in the real wages of the workers of these enterprises. And it was this rise in real wages—translated into the ownership of homes, automobiles, and household durables, along with a vast expansion of educational oppor-tunity (and in particular of college education)—that constituted the prosperity that Americans knew and that amazed the world.

Prosperity is above all things an opportunity, an opportunity to en-joy, an opportunity to create, an opportunity to share. But prosperity is also a burden. And the first burden that prosperity imposes is the pres-sure to maintain it. Who wishes to give up the good things of life? There has always existed a minority of ascetics and another minority consti-tuted of those willing to divest themselves of privilege out of shame or guilt. But for most people, to renounce the good life is a mark of saint-hood or madness and, however admirable, is not for them. The United

States as a country in the period 1945–1990 acted normally. The country was prosperous and sought to maintain that prosperity.

Our country, its leaders but also its citizens, pursued as an obvious national goal not happiness (the perhaps utopian and romantic image that Thomas Jefferson inscribed in our Declaration of Independence) but prosperity. What did it take for the United States to maintain the prosperity it had in hand? Seen from the perspective of the immediate post-1945 years, the United States needed three things: customers for its immense industrial park; world order such that commerce could be pursued at lowest cost; and assurances that the production processes would not be interrupted.

None of the three seemed too easy to achieve in 1945. The very destructiveness of the world war that gave the United States its incredible edge had simultaneously impoverished many of the wealthier areas of the world. There was hunger in Europe and Asia, and its peoples could scarcely afford Detroit's automobiles. The ending of the war left unresolved large numbers of "national" issues, not only in Europe and northern Asia, but in many countries outside the war zones, in countries we came later to call the Third World. Social peace seemed remote. And, in the United States, Americans were poised to resume their own disruptive social conflicts of the 1930s, which had been adjourned but scarcely resolved by wartime political unity.

The United States moved, with less hesitancy than it had anticipated, to do what was necessary to eliminate these threats to its prosperity and its hopes for still greater prosperity. The United States invoked its idealism in the service of its national interests. It believed in itself and in its goodness and sought to serve the world and lead the world as it thought just and wise. In the process, the United States obtained the applause of many and incurred the wrath of others. It felt hurt by the wrath and warmed by the applause, but above all it felt impelled to pursue the path it had designed for itself and that it considered to be the path of righteousness.

The United States tends to look back upon the postwar world and celebrate four great achievements, for which it gives itself a large part of the credit. The first is the reconstruction of the devastated Eurasian landmass, and its reinsertion in the ongoing productive activity of the world-economy. The second is the maintenance of peace in the world-system, the simultaneous prevention of nuclear war and military aggression. The third is the largely peaceful decolonization of the ex-colonial world, accompanied by significant aid for economic development. The fourth is the integration of the American working class into economic well-being and full political participation, along with the ending of racial segregation and discrimination in the United States.

When, just after the Second World War, Henry Luce proclaimed that this was "the American century," it was to the expectation of just such accomplishments that he was pointing. This had indeed been the American century. These achievements were real. But each had its price and each had unanticipated consequences. The correct balance-sheet is far more complex morally and analytically than we are wont to admit.

It is of course true that the United States sought to aid in the reconstruction of the Eurasian landmass. It offered immediate relief in 1945, collectively through UNRRA and individually through CARE packages. It moved soon thereafter to more substantial, long-term measures, most notably through the Marshall Plan. A great deal of money and political energy was invested in the years between 1945 and 1960 in this reconstruction of western Europe and Japan. The objects of these initiatives were clear: to rebuild the destroyed factories and infrastructure; to re-create functioning market systems with stable currencies well integrated into international division of labor; and to ensure sufficient employment opportunities. Nor did the United States limit itself to direct economic assistance. It also sought to encourage the creation of inter-European structures that would prevent the revival of the protectionist barriers that were associated with the tensions of the interwar period.

To be sure, this was not simply altruistic. The United States needed a significant sector of foreign customers for its productive enterprises if they were to produce efficiently and profitably. A rebuilt western Europe and Japan would provide exactly the necessary base. Furthermore, Americans needed reliable allies who would take their political cues from the United States in the world arena, and the western European states, along with Japan, were the most likely countries to play this role. This alliance was institutionalized not only in the form of NATO and the U.S.-Japan Defense Treaty, but even more in the close continuing political coordination of these countries under U.S. "leadership." The net result was that, at least in the beginning, all the major decisions of international life were being taken in Washington, with the largely un-questioning acquiescence and support of a set of powerful clientstates.

The only serious obstacle the United States perceived in the world political arena was the Soviet Union, which seemed to be pursuing quite disparate, even opposite, political objectives. The U.S.S.R. was at one and the same time the only other significant military power in the post-1945 world and the political center of the world Communist movement, ostensibly dedicated to world revolution.

When we discuss relations between the United States and the Soviet Union in the postwar period, we tend to use two code words to express U.S. policy: Yalta and containment. They seem to be rather different. Yalta has acquired the flavor of a cynical deal, if not of a Western "sell-out." Containment symbolizes, by contrast, U.S. determination to stop Soviet expansion. However, in reality, Yalta and containment were not two separate, even less opposing, policies. They were one and the same thing. The deal was containment. Like most deals, it was basically of-fered by the stronger (the U.S.) to the weaker (the U.S.S.R.) and ac-cepted by both because it served their mutual interests.

The war ended with Soviet troops occupying the eastern half of Eu-rope and U.S. troops in the western half. The boundary was the river Elbe, or the line from Stettin to Trieste, as Churchill was to describe in 1946 the location of what we designated the "Iron Curtain." On the sur-face, the deal merely provided for the military status quo and peace in Europe, with the U.S. and the U.S.S.R. free to make what political ar-rangements they preferred within their respective zones. This military status quo—call it Yalta or call it containment—has been scrupulously respected by both sides from 1945 to 1990. It will one day be called the "Great American Peace" and looked back upon nostalgically as a golden era.

The deal had, however, three codicils that are less often discussed. The first codicil had to do with the functioning of the world-economy. The Soviet zone was neither to ask for nor to receive U.S. assistance in reconstruction. They were permitted to, indeed required to, withdraw into a quasi-autarkic shell. The advantages to the United States were sev-eral. The costs of reconstruction of the Soviet zone threatened to be enormous, and the United States already had more than enough on its plate to assist western Europe and Japan. Furthermore, it was not at all clear that even a reconstructed U.S.S.R. (and China) could provide a rapidly available significant market for U.S. exports, certainly nothing like what western Europe and Japan might offer. The investment in reconstruction would have therefore been insufficiently remunerative. Yalta represented a net economic gain for the United States in the short run.

The second codicil was in the ideological arena. Each side was allowed, indeed encouraged, to raise the decibels of mutual condemnation. John Foster Dulles intoned, and Stalin agreed, that neutralism was to be considered "immoral." The struggle between the so-called Communist and Free Worlds permitted a tight internal control within each camp: anti-Communist McCarthyism in the West, and spy trials and purges in the East. What was really being controlled—both in the West and in the East—was the "left," in the sense of all those elements who wished to put into question radically the existing world order, the capitalist world-economy that was reviving and flourishing under U.S. hegemony with the collusion of what may be called its subimperialist agent, the Soviet Union.

The third codicil was that nothing in the extra-European world—what we later came to call the Third World, and more recently the South—was to be allowed to call into question the Great American Peace in Europe, and its institutional underpinning, the Yalta-containment doctrine. Both sides were pledged to this, and ultimately respected it. But it was a difficult codicil to interpret, and turned out to be even more difficult to enforce.

In 1945, the United States did not anticipate that the Third World would be as tempestuous as it in fact became. The United States approached the problems of the Third World with a Wilsonian worldview but languidly. It was in favor of the self-determination of nations; it was in favor of improvement in their economic well-being. But it did not consider the matter to be urgent. (Nor, despite the rhetoric, did the Soviet Union.) In general, the United States gave priority to its relations with the Soviet Union and with western Europe. The European states were still in 1945 the colonial powers in Africa, a good part of Asia, and the Caribbean, and were determined to pursue any changes at their own pace and in their own style. They were therefore far less acquiescent to U.S. interference in their colonial realm than they were to U.S. interference in other arenas, even in their domestic affairs. (The U.S.S.R., be it noted, had similar problems with western European Communist parties.)

European footdragging and Soviet hesitancy meant that the U.S. initial position was one of minimal involvement in the ongoing political struggles of the Third World. But in fact western Europe turned out to be politically far weaker in the colonial world than they'd anticipated, and the U.S.S.R. was forced to be more activist than it had hoped because of pressures on it to be consistent with its Leninist ideological rhetoric. So the United States was forced as well into a somewhat more activist role. President Truman proclaimed "Point Four"—the doctrine of aid for economic development. It was only the last of the points in his speech, but it is the one we remember. The United States began to put quite gentle pressure on west European countries to speed up the process of decolonization and to accept full political independence as a legitimate outcome of the process. And it began to cultivate "moderate" nationalist leaders. The definition of "moderate" seems very clear in retrospect. A "moderate" nationalist movement was one that, while seeking political independence, was ready to accept (even expand) the integration of the country into the production processes of the world-economy, including the possibility of trans-national investment. In any case, the United States perceived its policy as one of maintaining and fulfilling its historic commitment to anti-colonialism deriving from its own origins as a nation.

Finally, there was no neglect of the home front. We often forget today how conflict-ridden the United States was in the 1930s. At that time, we were engaged in a full-fledged and vituperative debate about our role in world affairs: isolationism versus interventionism. There was also an acute class struggle between capital and labor. One of the folk heroes of the postwar period, Walter Reuther, was having his head bashed in on a Detroit bridge during the sitdown strikes of 1937. In the South, the Ku Klux Klan was very strong and Negroes were still being lynched. The wartime years were years of social truce, but many feared the resumption of the social conflict within the United States with the ending of the war. It would be difficult to be a hegemonic power, however, if the country was to remain as disunited as it had been in the 1930s. And it would be hard to take full profit from U.S. economic advantage, if production were to be constantly disrupted by strikes and labor conflict.

Yet within a very short time the United States seemed to put its house in order. Isolationism was buried with the symbolic but very significant conversion of Senator Vanderberg, who launched the idea of "bipartisan foreign policy" for a United States that was now ready "to assume its responsibilities" in the world arena. The great General Motors strike of 1945, led by the same Walter Reuther, came to a happy ending with a compromise that was to set the pattern for 25 years to come for all the unionized major industries: significant wage increases, combined with a no-strike pledge, a rise in productivity, and price rises for the final product. And two fundamental steps were taken to end the post-Reconstruction patterns of legalized segregation of Black and White: President Truman's integration of the armed forces in 1948; and the Supreme Court's 1954 unanimous ruling in Brown vs. the Board of Education (reversing Plessy vs. Ferguson) that segregation was unconstitutional. The United States was very proud of itself and the Voice of America was not reluctant to boast of our practical commitment to freedom.

By 1960, it seemed that the United States was achieving its objectives admirably. The new prosperity was visible. Suburbia was flourishing. Higher educational and health care facilities had expanded enormously. A truly national air-and-road network had been constructed. Western Europe and Japan were back on their feet. The U.S.S.R. was well contained. The U.S. labor movement, purged of its left wing, was a recognized component of the Washington establishment. And 1960 was the Year of Africa, the year in which sixteen African states, formerly colonies of four different European states, proclaimed their independence and joined the United Nations. The election of John F. Kennedy that year seemed the apotheosis of the new American reality. Power had passed, he said, to a new generation, born in this century, and therefore he implied fully rid of old hesitations and inadequacies, fully committed to a world of permanent prosperity and presumably of expanding freedom.

It was precisely at this point, however, that the price of prosperity began to come clear, its unanticipated consequences to be felt, and its institutional structures if not to crumble at least to shake and even tremble. Along with U.S. prosperity and even world prosperity came the realization of the growing gap, internationally and within the United States between rich and poor, core and periphery, the included and the excluded. In the 1960s the gap was only relative; in the 1970s and even more in the 1980s it became absolute. But even a relative gap, perhaps especially a relative gap, spelled trouble. The trouble was worldwide.

The trouble in western Europe and Japan seemed relatively innocent at first. By the 1960s, these countries were "catching up" with the United States—first of all in productivity; then, with some lag, in standard of living. By the 1980s, they exceeded the United States in productivity and had come to equal it in standard of living. This might be called an "innocent" form of trouble, since it bred a quiet form of rejection of U.S. hegemony, a form of rejection that was all the more efficacious precisely because it was quiet and self-confident about the future. To be sure, our allies were restrained by their gratitude; nonetheless, bit by bit, they tried to emerge from their political tutelage to assert their separate roles in the world-system. The United States had to utilize all its institutional and ideological strength to hold its allies in check, and this succeeded in part up to the end of the 1980s.

Elsewhere, however, the rebellions were less "innocent." Most persons in the eastern European countries refused to accept the legitimacy of the Yalta arrangements, both on the left and on the right. The initial Cold War ideological tightness could not hold, either in the United States or in the Soviet Union. The U.S. Senate censured McCarthy in 1954, and Khrushchev at the XXth Party Congress of the CPSU revealed and denounced Stalin's crimes. The peoples of eastern Europe took advantage of every loosening of the ideological cement to try, in various ways, to regain a freedom of action they were denied, most notably in 1956 in Poland and Hungary, in 1968 in Czechoslovakia, and in 1980 again in Poland. Since all these political uprisings were directed not against the United States but in the immediate sense against the Soviet Union, the United States felt free not to intervene in any way. Thus it remained faithful to its arrangements with the Soviet Union, and the latter was free to take the measures necessary to repress the uprisings.

It is in the Third World that events came to be most out of control, and right from the beginning. Stalin pressed the Chinese Communists to come to an arrangement with the Kuomintang. They ignored him, and marched into Shanghai in 1949. The real worry for the United States was not that China would now be a Soviet puppet, but that it would not be. The fear turned out to be justified. Within a year, U.S. troops would find themselves involved in a long, costly military operation in Korea merely to preserve the status quo. First the French, then the Americans were drawn into an even longer, even more costly war, which they would eventually lose at the military level. The languid scenario for the Middle East—conservative Arab states and Israel, all safely pro-Western—was upset by the rise of Nasser and Nasserism, which would be echoed in various forms from North Africa to Iraq. Algeria's war of independence would topple the Fourth French Republic and bring to power in France the figure least sympathetic to U.S. tutelage, Charles de Gaulle. And in Latin America, the long-standing political turmoil took a new more radical form with the arrival of Castro in power in Cuba.

Since these uprisings of the Third World were in fact directed primarily not against the Soviet Union but against the United States (unlike those in eastern Europe), the United States felt free to intervene. And intervene it did, with some vigor. If one looks at the balance-sheet over 45 years, one can say that at the military level the United States won some and lost some, and that at the political level it seemed to win some and lose some. The U.S.'s main strength was at the economic level, in its ability to punish states it deemed hostile (Vietnam, Cuba, Nicaragua). What is, I think, crucial to note is that globally, in all these affairs, the U.S.S.R. played a minor role. On the one hand, the movements in the Third World were engaged in defiance to the U.S. world order, and the U.S.S.R. was part of that world order. The impetus was local. The Great American Peace did not serve, in their views, the interests of the peoples of the Third World. On the other hand, while these uprisings forced the United States to pay much more military and political attention to the Third World than anyone ever dreamed conceivable in 1945, the fact is that none of the movements singly, nor even all of them collectively, was able to dismantle the Great American Peace or immediately threaten American prosperity. The price for the United States nonetheless became higher and higher.

There was a price to pay at home as well. It came from two sources. The first was the cost of maintaining order in the Third World. The most spectacular instance was the Vietnam War. The cost in lives and the cost in financial stability of the government were both high. But ultimately the highest cost was the cost in legitimacy of the state. Watergate would never have forced a president to resign had not the Presidency itself been already undermined by Vietnam.

The second source was the cost of relative deprivation. It was precisely the integration of trade-unions into the political establishment and the ending of legal segregation combined with the real increase in the incomes of skilled workers and the middle classes that brought to the fore the degree to which there were exclusions. The United States had moved from its pre-1945 situation when only a minority were prosperous to its post-1945 one where the majority felt prosperous, or at least moderately so. This was a trigger to action for the excluded, action that took the form of new consciousness—most notably Black (and later other minority groups') consciousness and womens' consciousness.

It was 1968 that brought all these challenges together into one big melting pot—resentment of U.S. imperialism, resentment of Soviet subimperialism and collusion with the United States, resentment of the integration of Old Left movements into the system reducing the presumed opposition to complicity, resentment of exclusions of oppressed minority strata and of women (extended subsequently to all sorts of other exclusions—the handicapped, the gays, the indigenous populations, etc.). The worldwide explosion of 1968—in the United States and western Europe, in Czechoslovakia and China, in Mexico and India—went on for three years more or less until the raging fires were brought under control by the forces sustaining the world-system. The fire was reduced to embers, but in the process it had gravely damaged the ideological supports of the Great American Peace. It would now only be a matter of time that this peace would come to an end.

The Great American Peace found its origin in American economic strength. It found its reward in American prosperity. It would not be undermined by its success. Starting from about 1967, the reconstruction of western Europe and Japan had reached a point that these countries not only were competitive with the United States but the total of world production thereby achieved brought on a long downturn in the world-economy in which we have been living ever since and that began to erode American prosperity. From 1967 to 1990, the United States sought to stem the tide of decline. It held out for 20-odd years until it all became too much. There were two modes of stemming the tide. One was the "low posture" of Nixon, Ford, and Carter. It stumbled on Iran. The second was the fake machismo of Reagan and Bush. It stumbled on Iraq.

The "low-posture" solution to the threatened loss of U.S. hegemony had three main pillars: Trilateralism, the OPEC oil rise, and the post-Vietnam syndrome. Trilateralism was an attempt to keep western Europe and Japan from achieving political autonomy by offering them the olive branch of a junior partnership in decision-making. Trilateralism succeeded to the degree that it forestalled any significant falling-out of the OECD countries on military policies, political strategies, and world financial arrangements. The west Europeans and the Japanese continued to respect U.S. leadership in form. But in reality, and without rhetoric, they pursued unremittingly the improvement of their relative position in world productive processes, knowing that eventually the U.S. hegemonic position would inevitably crumble for lack of an economic base.

The OPEC oil rise, under the leadership of the U.S.'s chief agents in the affair (Saudi Arabia and the Shah of Iran), was designed primarily to pump world surplus capital into a central fund that would then be recycled to Third World and socialist countries largely in the form of loans to states, providing short-run stability in these states and artificially sustaining the world market for industrial production. A secondary advantage of the OPEC oil rise was supposed to be that it created greater difficulties for western Europe and Japan than for the United States and hence slowed them down competitively. A tertiary consequence was that, by stimulating inflation in the OECD countries but especially in the United States, it reduced real wages. During the 1970s the effect of the OPEC oil rise on the world-economy had the consequences desired. It did indeed work to slow down the decline of U.S. economic advantage.

The third aspect of the "low posture" response was the post-Vietnam syndrome, which was not a reaction against Nixon but a fulfillment of his strategy: the opening to China and the withdrawal from Indochina, both of which were inevitably followed by such developments as the Clark Amendment on Angola and the belated withdrawal of support to Somoza in Nicaragua and to the Shah in Iran. Even the Soviet invasion of Afghanistan furthered this development, because it mired down Soviet political energies in an impossible situation, disabled them from gaining advantage in the Islamic world, and gave the United States an excuse to fan the ideological fires once again in a flagging western Europe.

What the United States obviously did not count on was that the movement led by the Ayatollah Khomeini was of an entirely different stripe from the movements of national liberation the Third World had known in the postwar period. The Chinese Communist Party and the Vietminh, the Nasserists and the Algerian FLN, Cuba's 26th of July Movement and Angola's MPLA were all opposed to U.S. hegemony and the existing world-system but operated nonetheless within the basic framework of its eighteenth-century Enlightenment *Weltanschauung*. They were against the system but also of the system. That is why, in the end, once in power, they could all be incorporated into its ongoing structures without too much difficulty.

Khomeini would have none of that. He knew Satan when he saw him. The No. 1 Satan was the United States, the No. 2 the Soviet Union, and he would play by no rules of the game that served either of their interests. The United States did not know how to handle such fundamental otherness, which is why Khomeini could so profoundly humiliate the United States, and thereby undermine its hegemony even more effectively than the 1968 world revolution of the new lefts and the excluded. Khomeini brought down Carter and the "low posture."

The United States then played its last card—Reagan's fake machismo. The enemy, said Reagan, is less Khomeini than Carter (and implicitly Nixon and Ford). The solution was to puff power. To our allies, no more Trilateral fluff but reideologization. The allies responded by continuing their own "low posture" vis-à-vis the United States. To the Third World, invade Grenada, bomb Libya (once), and eventually depose our renegade agent in Panama, Noriega. The Third World responded by forcing the United States out of Lebanon by suicide-bombing 200 Marines. To the folks at home, cut real wages not by inflation but by union-busting (starting with the air traffic controllers), by reallocation of national income to the wealthy, and by an acute recession that would transfer many middle-income earners to low-income jobs. Faced with the debt crisis in the world-economy (the direct consequence of the OPEC oil rise scam), engage in military Keynesianism in the United States to be financed by selling off the U.S. patrimony to our allies via a monumental U.S. debt burden that could not but deflate U.S. currency in the long run. And of course denounce the Evil Empire.

Ronald Reagan may believe he intimidated the U.S.S.R. into producing Gorbachev. But Gorbachev emerged in the U.S.S.R. because Ronald Reagan demonstrated that the U.S. was no longer strong enough to sustain the special arrangement with the U.S.S.R. The U.S.S.R. was now forced to be on its own, and on its own, without a Cold War deal, it was in desperately bad shape. Its economy, which could keep its head above water and even show significant growth during the great expansion of the world-economy in the 1950s and 1960s, was too inflexibly structured to cope with the great stagnation of the world-economy of the 1970s and 1980s. Its ideological steam had totally evaporated. Leninist developmentalism had proved as inefficacious as all the other varieties of developmentalism — socialist or free-market — have in the last fifty years.

Gorbachev pursued the only policy that was available for the U.S.S.R. (or perhaps one should better say Russia), if it were to maintain significant power in the twenty-first century. He needed to terminate the drain on Soviet resources of its pseudo-empire. He thus sought to force the pace of liquidating the military façade of the Cold War (now that its political utility was over) by a quasi-unilateral disarmament (withdrawal from Afghanistan, dismantling of missiles, etc.) thereby forcing the United States to follow suit. He needed as well to divest himself of an ever-more restive imperial burden in eastern Europe. The eastern Europeans were of course happy to oblige. They had wanted nothing more for at least twenty-five years. But the miracle of 1989 was made possible not because the United States changed its traditional position but because the Soviet Union did. And the U.S.S.R. changed its position not because of the U.S. strength but because of U.S. weakness. Gorbachev's third task is to restore the U.S.S.R. to a viable internal structure, including dealing with the now-released nationalisms. Here he may well have failed, but it is still too early to be sure that he cannot hold the U.S.S.R. together.

The miracle of 1989 (continued by the failed coup in the U.S.S.R. in 1991) was no doubt a blessing for the peoples of the eastern and central Europe, including the peoples of the U.S.S.R. It will not be an unmixed blessing, but at the very least it opens the possibility of renewal. But it was not a blessing for the U.S. The United States has not won the Cold War but lost the Cold War, because the Cold War was not a game to be won but rather a minuet to be danced. By transforming it at least into a game, there was a victory, but the victory was Pyrrhic. The end of the

Cold War in effect eliminated the last major prop the U.S. hegemony and U.S. prosperity, the Soviet shield.

The result was Iraq and the Persian Gulf crisis. Iraq did not suddenly discover its claims upon Kuwait. It had been making these claims for thirty years at least. Why did it choose this moment in time to invade? The immediate motivation seems quite clear. Iraq, like a hundred other countries, was suffering from the catastrophic consequences of the OPEC oil scam and the subsequent debt crisis. This was particularly aggravated in its case by the costly and futile Iran-Iraq war, in which Iraq was strongly abetted by a coalition, less strange that it appears, of the U.S., France, Saudi Arabia, and the U.S.S.R., intended to sap the strength of Khomeini's Iran. In 1990, Iraq was determined not to sink, and seizing Kuwaiti oil revenue (and incidentally liquidating a goodly part of its world debt) seemed a solution.

But how did Saddam Hussein dare? I do not believe he miscalculated. I think he calculated very well. He was playing "va banque." He had two strong cards. Card No. 1 was the knowledge that the U.S.S.R. would *not* be on his side. Had he thought to invade Kuwait five years earlier, the invasion would have rapidly provoked a U.S.-U.S.S.R. confrontation involving the likelihood of nuclear destruction, and hence just as rapidly followed the usual path of a U.S.-U.S.S.R. arrangement. Iraq would have had no choice but to back down, like Cuba in 1962. Iraq could invade because it had been liberated from Soviet constraint.

The second liberation was regional. In the wake of the new Gorbachev diplomacy, the U.S. and the U.S.S.R. entered into a process of resolving so-called regional conflicts, that is, no longer sustaining confrontational conflicts in the four regions where they had been most vigorously sustained in the 1970s and 1980s: Indochina, southern Africa, Central America, and the Middle East. In the first three areas, negotiations are ongoing. Only in the Middle East had these negotiations broken down. When it was clear that Israeli-P.L.O. negotiations were blocked and that the United States did not have the political power to force Israel to continue them, Iraq moved from the wings to the center of the stage. As long as negotiations had been ongoing, Saddam Hussein could do nothing, since he couldn't risk being blamed by the Palestinians and the Arab world for scuttling the negotiations. But once the Israelis scuttled them, Saddam Hussein could pose as the liberator of the Palestinians.

There was one final element in Iraq's calculations. The United States would lose no matter what. If the U.S. did nothing, Saddam Hussein was on his way to becoming the Bismarck of the Arab world. And if the U.S. reacted as it did in fact react, and built a military coalition against Iraq centered on the direct use of U.S. troops, Saddam Hussein might fall (this is why the game was "va banque") but the U.S. could not win. The war was unavoidable from day one, because neither Hussein nor Bush could accept any outcome other than military combat. Iraq of course lost disastrously in military terms, and it lost immensely in the destruction of lives and infrastructure. But it is still too early to argue that it lost in fact politically.

The United States proved to the world that it was indeed the strongest military power in the world. But, be it noted, for the first time since 1945 it was called upon to demonstrate it, by an act of deliberate military provocation. To win in such circumstances is already to lose in part. For if one challenger can dare, a second careful challenger may start to prepare himself. Even Joe Louis grew tired.

The demonstration of U.S. military strength has underlined its economic weakness. It has been widely noticed that the U.S. war effort was financed by others, because the U.S. could not finance it. The United States has loudly shouted that it is now the world's diplomatic broker. However, it plays this role not as a respected elder but rather as a power that wields a big stick, but that also has economic feet of clay.

To be a broker is only an advantage if one can produce lasting results. The United States was thus forced to begin itself in the Middle East a second game of "va banque." If it can bring about significant accord between Israel and the PLO, everyone will applaud. But this is a result that seems unlikely. If, in the coming 2–3 years, we collapse into more wars in the Middle East, possibly now with nuclear weapons, the United States will bear the brunt of the blame, its conservative Arab allies will collapse, and Europe will be called in to salvage a possibly unsalvageable situation. If all of this happens, may not Saddam Hussein still be around to crow? Nothing positive for U.S. power in the world has emerged from the Persian Gulf War.

The Iran crisis of 1980 and the Iraq crisis of 1990 were quite different.

They were two alternate models of Third World reaction to the Great American Peace. The Iran reaction used the way of fundamental rejection of Western values. The Iraq reaction was quite different. The regime in Iraq was Baathist, and the Baath is the most secularized movement in the Arab world. The Iraq reaction was in the end a military reaction, the attempt to construct large Third World states based on enough modern military strength to impose a new *rapport de forces* between North and South. These are the two faces of the future. The "low posture" of the United States was laid low by Khomeini. Its "fake machismo" has been laid low by Saddam Hussein.

The heyday of U.S. prosperity is now over. The scaffolding is being dismantled. The bases are crumbling. How shall we assess the era of U.S. hegemony, 1945–1990? On the one hand, it was the Great American Peace and an era of great material prosperity. It was also, by comparative historical standards, an era of tolerance, at least for the most part, despite the many conflicts, or perhaps because of the form the conflicts took. But it was built on too many exclusions to survive. And it is now over.

We are now entering into America's future, about which we have cause to be both despairing and very hopeful. But we cannot know which ways the winds will be blowing until first we look at America's past.

YESTERDAY

When shall we begin our story of America's past? I shall start the story somewhat unconventionally in 1791 on the basis of two important events—the adoption of the Bill of Rights, and the admission of the Republic of Vermont to the Union.

There is no greater symbol and concrete foundation to American liberty than the Bill of Rights. We hail it rightfully. We tend to forget that it was adopted in 1791, as the first ten amendments to the Constitution. That is, one important fact is that these clauses were not in the original Constitution, as written in 1787. This is because there was strong opposition to them. Happily, in the end, those who opposed these provisions lost the battle. But it is salutary to remember that the U.S. commitment to basic human rights was far from self-evident to the Founding Fathers.

We know of course that the Constitution sanctioned slavery as well and excluded the Native Americans from the polity. It was a Constitution that was the product of White settlers, many of whom but not all of whom wanted to ensconce basic human rights in their political structure, at least for themselves.

The admission of Vermont points to further ambivalences. Vermont, as we know, was not one of the Thirteen Colonies which proclaimed the Declaration of Independence, for Vermont proclaimed itself an autonomous entity only in 1777, was not recommended for recognition as such by the Continental Congress until 1784, and was not in fact admitted until 1791, when New York withdrew its objections. This struggle for recognition illustrates the many ambiguities of the U.S. war of independence. While the Thirteen Colonies were struggling for their independence from Great Britain, Vermont was struggling for its independence against New York (and to a lesser extent New Hampshire). Its attitude to the British was complex. Although Vermont was most often on the side of the Continental Congress, various of its leaders were at various moments of time from 1776 up to 1791 in quasi-negotiations with Great Britain.

What was the quarrel about? On the one hand, human rights. When Vermont adopted its state constitution in 1777, it was the first of these United States to abolish slavery and to provide for universal manhood suffrage at age 21. Vermont was in the avant-garde then, and seems to have tried ever since to remain there. Vermont's constitution was indeed in sharp contrast to the oligarchic constitution New York had adopted the year before, with its severely restricted franchise in a state where slavery was still important and would not be abolished until 1827.

But on the other hand, it was merely a quarrel between multiple groups of land speculators in which no particular moral virtue attached to any. If New York state blocked Vermont's admission to the American structures from 1777 to 1791, it was to defend the interests of its land speculators. And if it was to withdraw its objections in 1791, it was because Kentucky had posed its application for admission to the Union, and New York, counting votes in the Senate, wanted Vermont as a "northern" state there to counterbalance another "southern" state. In this way, 1791 prefigured 1861.

In what sense, and for whom, was America the "land of liberty"? It is normal that there were a multitude of motives that impelled different groups to participate in the war of independence. Plantation owners, large merchants, urban wage-workers, and small farmers had disparate interests. Only some of their motivations had to do with human rights or greater equality. Many were far more interested in safeguarding their property rights, against both British taxation and American radicalism. Furthermore, the right to expropriate Native Americans and chase them from their lands was precisely one of the rights the White settlers were afraid the British were too reluctant to sustain.

Nonetheless, the American Revolution was a revolution in the name of liberty. And the authors of the Declaration of Independence proclaimed it to the world. It was after all a revolution; that is, it did reaffirm in a most vigorous fashion not only that "all men are created equal" but that governments were instituted among men to secure "life, liberty, and the pursuit of happiness," and that, should any government ever become "destructive of these ends," it became "the right of the people to alter or abolish it." Revolution therefore was not only legitimate but obligatory, even if "prudence . . . will dictate that governments long established should not be changed for light and transient causes. . . ."

The new United States of America, born out of revolt against the mother country, legitimated by a written constitution that laid claim to being a consciously-constructed social compact that created a government with "the consent of the governed," fortified by a Bill of Rights that spelled out protections against this very government, seemed to itself and to the European world a beacon of hope, rationalism, and human possibility. The liberty it preached seemed to be triple: the freedom of the individual vis-à-vis the state and any and all social institutions (most notably, the freedom of speech), the freedom of the group against other more powerful groups (most notably, the freedom of religion), and the freedom of the people as a whole against outside control (independence).

These rights were not unknown elsewhere at the time, but they seemed more secure and more extensive in the United States than anywhere else, especially once the French Revolution seemed to go awry and ended by 1815 in a Restoration. Furthermore, to Europeans who felt oppressed in their own countries, the United States beckoned as the land of individual opportunity, actually carrying out the French Revolutionary motto of "la carrière ouverte aux talents." An open land, a vastly underpopulated land, it wanted immigrants and offered their children instant citizenship (*jus soli*). The United States was vast, fresh, and above all new (unweighed down by feudal history).

Or so we said, then and ever since. And so it has been believed, here and elsewhere, then and ever since. And this was largely true, provided we remember it was true for Whites only, primarily for White males, and for a long time only for Western European Protestant White males. This political primacy of European Whites was not peculiar to the United States. The point is that, despite its proclamations of universalist freedoms, the United States was no different in this regard. For this privileged group, the United States throughout its history has had very much to offer. The boundaries expanded; the so-called frontier was settled; the migrants were assimilated; and the country kept itself, as George Washington adjured it, free from "the insidious wiles of foreign influence. . . ." The United States was thus not only a land of opportunity but also a land of refuge.

In a very famous phrase, Abraham Lincoln in 1858 said "I believe this government cannot endure permanently half slave and half free." In retrospect, was he right? Despite the Emancipation Proclamation, despite the 13th, 14th, and 15th Amendments to the Constitution, despite even Brown vs. the Board of Education, have we not long endured being half slave and half free? Has there been any moment in our history where it was not possible to say that some, even many have suffered or were deprived merely because of the color of their skin or other like irrelevancies?

We must take a cold, hard look at our history and ask whether the very real liberty of half the population was not at the price of the very real lack of liberty of the other half? Was slavery (defined loosely) merely an anachronism that it has been our historical destiny to overcome, or was it a structural foundation and integral concomitant of the American dream? Was the American dilemma an inconsistency to be surmounted by wisdom and rationality or a building-block of our system?

The fact is that, at the moment we moved from our past to our present, as of 1945 that is, our record was glorious in some regards but utterly dismal in others. There was petty apartheid not merely in the South but in most of the great cities and great universities of the North. It was not until the 1970s that we were ready even to admit and discuss widely this dismal side of the record. And even today, much of the discussion is obscurantist.

Already the ancient Greeks had developed a system of liberty and equal political participation for the citizens and slavery for the (foreign) helots. We have developed our own political imagery from a contrast between tyranny, or despotism, or an absolutist monarchy and a republican democracy or a democratic republic. We forget that one of the historic founts of our political tradition, the Magna Carta of 1215, was a document that was imposed on the King of England by his lords and barons to guarantee their rights vis-à-vis him, not the rights of the serfs.

We think of a despotic system as one in which one man, or a very few at the top, can rule over and exploit all the others. But in fact, a very few at the top are limited in their political capacity to extract too much from the bottom, nor do they need all that much to sustain themselves very comfortably indeed. As we expand the size of this group at the top, as we make this group at the top more equal in their political rights vis-à-vis each other, it is not only possible to extract more from the bottom, but one needs to extract more in order to feed the needs of those at the top. A political structure with complete liberty for the top half can be the most oppressive form conceivable for the bottom half. And in many ways the most stable. Perhaps a country half slave, half free can long long endure.

The very possibility of individual upward mobility, which the United States as a country has pioneered and institutionalized and which the rest of the world has been borrowing, is one of the most efficacious instruments in maintaining the society as half slave half free. Upward mobility justifies the reality of social polarization. It minimizes the unrest by removing many potential leaders of protest from the bottom half while holding out the mirage of potential promotion to those left behind. It transforms the search for betterment into competition with others. And whenever one stratum has more or less moved up, there is always another to enter at the bottom.

It does however have one downside. The ideology of liberty and of potential betterment is a universalist doctrine. And although it may require that half be slave for the other half to be free, it promotes unease. Hence Myrdal could speak of an American dilemma. And our history bears him out. For we have struggled mightily with the devil. And having sinned, we have always feared God's wrath. The combination of *hybris* and profound Calvinist guilt has been the daily bread of Americans of all origins and faiths for all of our history.

In a sense then our past, from 1791 (or 1776 or 1607) to 1945, was one long prelude to our present. We proclaimed liberty throughout the land. We worked hard to transform nature and to become the economic giant of 1945. We used our liberty to achieve our prosperity. And in so doing, we set an example for the world. Of course, it was an impossible example. If our country was half slave half free, so was the world. If the price of freedom was slavery, if the price of prosperity was misery, if the price of inclusion was exclusion, how could everyone achieve what America stood for? How even could all Americans have it? That was our historical dilemma, our historical fate, our historical prison.

It is said that the earliest formal protest against slavery was made by the Germantown Mennonites in 1688 who asked: "Have these poor negers not as much right to fight for their freedom, as you have to keep them slaves?" Of course, all those who did not have their full share of liberty in these United States have always answered yes to the Mennonites. They had the right, and fought for it as best they could. Whenever they fought especially hard, they received some concession. But the concessions have never antedated the demands, and have never been more generous than politically required.

The blessing of liberty has been a true blessing; but it has also been a moral burden, because it has always been, and up to now has always had to be, a blessing only for some, even if the some were many, or (once again I repeat) probably especially when the some were many.

So thus we crossed the Sinai from 1791 to 1945 without "entangling alliances" and secure in the path of the Lord, to arrive in the land of milk and honey from 1945 to 1990. Will we now be expelled from the promised land?

TOMORROW

Is decline so terrible? Perhaps it is the greatest blessing of all. Once again, it was Abraham Lincoln who sounded the moral note: "As I would not be a slave, so I would not be a master." We have been masters of the world, perhaps benign and beneficent masters (or so say some of us), but masters nonetheless. That day is over. Is it so bad? As masters, we have been loved but also hated. We have loved ourselves but also hated ourselves. Can we now arrive at a more equilibrated vision? Perhaps, but not yet, I fear. I believe we are coming to the third part of our historical trajectory, perhaps the bumpiest, most exhilarating, and most terrible of all.

We are not the first hegemonic power to have declined. Great Britain did. The United Provinces did. And Venice did, at least within the context of the Mediterranean world-economy. And all these declines were slow and materially relatively uncomfortable. There is a lot of fat in a hegemonic power, and one can live off that fat for 50–100 years. No doubt one cannot be too extravagant, but we are not, as a nation, going to be consigned to some dustbin.

For one thing, we shall remain for quite some time the strongest military power in the world, despite the fact that we have become too weak to prevent upstarts like Iraq from forcing us to battle, or at least too weak to do it at anything but a very high political cost. And although our economy is faltering, and the dollar crumbling, no doubt we shall do quite well in the next major expansion of the world-economy, which will probably occur within five to ten years. Even as the junior partner of an eventual Japan-American economic cartel, the returns in global revenue would be high. And politically the United States will remain a heavyweight power, even if it becomes only one among several.

But psychologically the decline will be terrible. The nation has been on a high, and we must come down from it. It took us thirty years to learn how to perform gracefully and effectively the responsibilities of world leadership. It will no doubt take at least thirty years to learn to accept gracefully and effectively the lesser roles to which we shall now be consigned.

And since there will be less global current income, the question will immediately and urgently arise as to who will bear the burden of the decline, even a small decline, in our standard of living? We are seeing the difficulties already in our current debates over who is to pay for the enormous waste and ripoff of the S & L disaster, and who is to pay for reducing the debt burden. As our ecological sensitivities grow apace, and they will no doubt continue to do so, who will pay to repair Exxon spills in Alaska, Love Canals, and the far greater dangerous rubbish piles we shall doubtless be uncovering in the decades to come? It has indeed been voodoo economics, and not just in Reagan's time. There is nothing more sobering than having a big fat bill one just cannot pay and finding that your credit has become exhausted. For credit is creditability, and U.S. economic creditability is slipping away fast. No doubt, we shall live off our fat, and even off some Euro-Japanese charity given in fond memory of the Great American Peace and all our marvels then, but this will be even more humiliating in the long run than Khomeini imprisoning a whole American embassy.

What will we do then, we as a nation? There are fundamentally two paths open to us. There is the uptight path of violent social conflict, in which the restive underclasses are held down forcefully with brutality and prejudice—a sort of neo-fascist path. And there is the path of national solidarity, the common reaction to a shared social stress, in which we shall move beyond the blessings of liberty and prosperity to the blessing of equality, perhaps a less than perfect equality but a real one nonetheless, one with no major exclusions.

I shall take the optimistic road of relegating the neo-fascist path to the box of low likelihood. I do not believe it impossible, but there is quite a lot in our national traditions that militates against the success of neo-fascist movements. Furthermore, I do not think we will be quite desperate enough to take the leap, for it would be a leap, down this road. I think rather we are going to see a realization of more equality than we have ever dreamed possible, and more equality than any other country knows. This will be the third of God's blessings. And like the other two, it will have its price and its unanticipated consequences.

The reason we shall move remarkably forward in the domain of equality of life chances and life rewards in the next thirty years is very straightforward. It will be the direct consequence of our two previous blessings: liberty and prosperity. Because of our long-standing ideological and institutional commitment to liberty, however imperfect in execution, we have developed political structures that are remarkably susceptible to truly democratic decision-making provided there is the will and the capacity to organize politically. If one takes the four major arenas of unequal allocation—by gender, by race and ethnicity, by age, and by class—it is clear that those who receive less than their fair share add up to a majority of the voters, provided they define matters in this way.

That is where the era of prosperity comes in. It was precisely the realization of a prosperous America that underlined the gaps and the exclusions and, in the language that was developed in that era, created "consciousness." The first explosion of that consciousness was in 1968. It was but a rehearsal for the second explosion of consciousness that may be expected in the coming decade. This consciousness will provide the will. And the prosperity has provided the capacity. In no country in the world today are the disadvantaged strata so materially strong, strong enough in any case to finance their political struggle. And finally the inevitable cutbacks will provide the incentive. The fuse will be ignited.

Congress will not know what hits it. The demands will come from all sides and simultaneously. And very quickly, in my view, the United States may move from being the leader of conservative, status quo, free-market economics on the world scene to being perhaps the most social-welfare-oriented state in the world, the one with the most advanced redistributive structures. If it were not that everyone is telling us these days that socialism is a dead idea, it might even be thought—let us whisper the unspeakable—that the U.S. will become a quasi-socialist state. Who knows? Maybe the Republican Party might even take the lead, as Disraeli and Bismark did in the nineteenth century. Some may be horrified by this prospect, and some elated, but let us hesitate a moment before expressing our emotions.

I shall make two further presumptions. One is that our traditions of liberty will not be in any way hurt by this new egalitarianism, that the Supreme Court will further extend the definition of our civil liberties, that state police power will not grow at the expense of individual rights, and that cultural and political diversity will prosper. The second presumption is that this new egalitarianism will not have a negative impact on our productive efficiencies. We will, for reasons discussed previously, probably have a lower GNP per capita, but the new egalitarianism will be the response not the cause. And in any case the GNP per capita will still be high.

Will we then have arrived at Utopia? Surely not. For the price will be very high, and the unanticipated consequences frightening. The fundamental cost will be exclusion. As we eliminate exclusions within the state, we will accentuate them on the world level. Perhaps the United States will for the first time cease to be half slave half free. But thereby the world will become even more sharply half slave and half free. If from 1945–1990, in order to sustain half our population instead of 10 percent of our population at a high income level we had to increase the extraction from the other 50 percent, imagine what it will require to sustain 90 percent of our population at reasonably high income levels. It will require even more exploitation, and essentially this will have to be exploitation of peoples of the Third World.

Twenty years down the road, it is not hard to guess what would happen. In the first place, the pressure to come to America will be greater than it has ever been in all our history. If the United States looked attractive in the nineteenth century, and even more in the post-1945 period, think of how it would look in the twenty-first century if my double prediction—a fairly well-off, highly egalitarian country and a very economically-polarized world-system—were to be correct. Both the push and pull of migration would reach a maximum point. How could the United States stop unauthorized migration in the millions, even tens of millions? The answer is, it could not.

Meanwhile, those who do not emigrate but remain at home in the South, excluded ever more effectively from the prosperity of the North—not only North America but Europe and Northern Asia—will surely begin, in one area after another, to follow the example either of Iran or Iraq. The United States will not wish to do nothing about it (nor indeed will Europe or Japan) because of the plausible fear that this would create a global fireball. Remember, nuclear weapons are being secretly developed, may already have been fully developed, in at least Brazil and Argentina, Israel and Iraq, South Africa and Pakistan, and soon many others. During the Great American Peace, we feared a nuclear holocaust when in fact the likelihood was very low because of the U.S.-Soviet deal. The chance of nuclear wars, perhaps only regional but that is terrible enough, is far more real in the next fifty years.

Faced with the threat of massive unauthorized immigration and regional nuclear wars in the South, what will the United States do? Chances are that a quasi-socialist America would become a fortress America. Trying to isolate itself from the hopelessness and costs of Third World wars, it might turn to protecting its wealth and its patrimony. Failing to stem the tide of migration, it might turn toward creating a dike between the entitlements of citizens and those of non-citizens. Within no time, the United States could find itself in a position where the bottom 30, even 50 percent of its wage-labor force were non-citizens, with no suffrage and limited access to social welfare. Were that to happen, we would have reversed the clock by 150–200 years. The whole story of the United States and the western world from say 1800–1950 was the extension of political, economic, and social rights to the working classes. But if that gets defined as citizens only, then we are back at the starting-point, with a large part of the resident population excluded from political, economic, and social rights.

Nor will our problems stop there. We will discover, we are discovering, that the fastest, least expensive route to an ecologically clean United States is to dump the garbage elsewhere—in the Third World, in the high seas, even in space. Of course this only postpones our own problems for fifty years, and at the price of increasing the problems of others during those fifty years as well as later. But, back against the wall, is it not extremely tempting to postpone problems for fifty years? In fifty years, most of today's adult voters will be dead.

Thus, America's third blessing, equality, will at best have bought America time for 25–50 years. Somewhere down the line, in 2025 or 2050, the day of reckoning will arrive. And the United States (but not it alone) will face the same kind of choice then that it has today, but on a world scale. Either the world-system will move toward a repressive restructuring or it will move toward an egalitarian restructuring. But the latter will require a far greater reallocation of existing distribution than an egalitarian redistribution merely within the United States of today.

Of course, at this point, we are talking of the demise of our existing world-system and its replacement by something fundamentally different. And it is intrinsically impossible to predict what will be the outcome. We will be at a bifurcation point and the random fluctuations will be immense in effect. All that we can do is be lucid and be active. For our own activity will be part of those fluctuations and will have a profound effect on the outcome.

I have tried to make clear my vision of the coming fifty years: on one side, an increasingly wealthy North, a relatively internally-egalitarian North (for its citizens), and a United States no longer in the lead eco-

nomically or even geopolitically but in the lead in terms of social equality; on the other side, an increasingly disadvantaged South, ready to use
its military power, which shall increase to disrupt the world-system, often turning against all the values the West has cherished, with a large part
of its population trying the route of individual migration to the North,
and creating thereby the South within the North.

Some will say this is a pessimistic vision. I respond that it is not only
realistic; it is also optimistic. For it leaves wide open the door of will. In
the demise of our current world-system we can indeed create a far better
one. It is simply in no way historically inevitable that we do so. We must
seize the chance and struggle for salvation. Part of my realism is to assert
that the United States cannot achieve salvation alone. It tried this from
1791 to 1945. It tried this in other ways from 1990 to say 2025. But unless
it realizes that there is no salvation that is not the salvation of all humankind, neither it nor the rest of the world will surmount the structural crisis of our world-system.

CODA ON AMERICAN EXCEPTIONALISM

America has always believed that it is exceptional. And I may have
played into this belief by focusing my analysis around God's three successive blessings to America. However, not only is America not exceptional, but even American exceptionalism is not exceptional. We are not
the only country in modern history whose thinkers have sought to prove
that their country is historically unique, different from the mass of other
countries in the world. I have met French exceptionalists and I have met
Russian exceptionalists. There are Indian and Japanese, Italian and Portuguese, Jewish and Greek, English and Hungarian exceptionalists. Chinese and Egyptian exceptionalism is a veritable mark of national
character. And Polish exceptionalism is the match of any other. Exceptionalism is the marrow in the bones of almost all the civilizations our
world has produced.

I asserted that the American spirit has long been a combination of *hybris* and Calvinist guilt. Perhaps we might remember that what the
Greeks meant by *hybris* is the pretension of humans to be gods; and that
the strong point of Calvinist theology has always been that, if we believe
God to be omnipotent, it follows logically that we cannot pretend that

anything is predestined, since if it were it would thereby limit the power of God.

Perhaps the new Jerusalem is neither here nor in Jerusalem nor anywhere else. Perhaps the promised land is simply our earth, our home, our world. Perhaps the only people God chose is humankind. Perhaps we can redeem ourselves if we try.

26—The Agonies of Liberalism: What Hope Progress?

I have a somewhat uncommon definition of liberalism, which I insist has been an ideology and a movement of rational centrist reformism, and which I also insist has now seen the passing of its historical moment. In the 1990s I have written a number of essays to argue this theme, and to ask the question, what hope then for progress?

We meet on a triple anniversary: the 25th anniversary of the founding of Kyoto Seika University in 1968; the 25th anniversary of the world revolution of 1968; the 52nd anniversary of the exact day (at least on the US calendar) of the bombing of Pearl Harbor by the Japanese fleet. Let me begin by noting what I think each of these anniversaries represents.[1]

The founding of Kyoto Seika University is a symbol of a major development in the history of our world-system: the extraordinary quantitative expansion of university structures in the 1950s and 1960s.[2] In a sense, this period was the culmination of the Enlightenment promise of progress through education. In itself, this was a wonderful thing, and we celebrate it here today. But, as with many wonderful things, it had its complications and its costs. One complication was that the expansion of higher education produced large numbers of graduates who insisted on jobs and incomes commensurate with their status, and there came to be some difficulty in answering this demand, at least as promptly and as fully as it was made. The cost was the social cost of providing this expanded higher education, which was only one part of the cost of providing welfare in general for the significantly expanding middle strata of the world-system. This increased cost of social welfare would begin to lay a heavy burden on state treasuries, and in 1993 we were discussing throughout the world the fiscal crises of the states.

This brings us to the second anniversary, that of the world revolution of 1968. This world revolution started in most countries (but not all) within the universities. One of the issues that served as tinder for the fire was no doubt the sudden anxiety of these prospective graduates about their job prospects. But, of course, this narrowly egoistic factor was not the principal focus of the revolutionary explosion. Rather it was merely one more symptom of the generic problem, concern with the real content of the whole set of promises contained in the Enlightenment scenario of progress—promises that, on the surface, had seemed to have been realized in the period after 1945.

And this brings us to the third anniversary, the attack on Pearl Harbor. It was this attack that brought the U.S. into the Second World War as a formal participant. In fact, however, the war was not a war primarily between Japan and the U.S. Japan, if you will pardon my saying so, was a second-rank player in this global drama, and its attack was a minor intervening event in a long-standing struggle. The war was primarily a war between Germany and the U.S., and had been de facto a continuous war since 1914. It was a "thirty years' war" between the two principal contenders for succession to Great Britain as the hegemonic power of the world-system. As we know, the U.S. would win this war and become hegemonic, and thereupon would be the one to preside over this world-wide surface triumph of Enlightenment promises.

Hence, I shall organize my remarks in terms of this set of themes which in fact we mark by these anniversaries. I shall discuss first the era of hope and struggle for Enlightenment ideals, 1789–1945. Then I shall seek to analyse the era of Enlightenment hopes to be realized, but falsely realized, 1945–89. Thirdly, I shall come to our present era, the "Black Period" that began in 1989 and will go on for possibly as much as a half-century. Finally, I shall talk of the choices before us—now, and also soon.

THE FUNCTION OF LIBERALISM

The first great political expression of the Enlightenment, in all its ambiguities, was of course the French Revolution. What the French Revolution was about has itself become one of the great ambiguities of our era. The bicentennial in France in 1989 was the occasion of a very major attempt to substitute a new interpretation of this great happening for the long-dominant "social interpretation," now asserted to be outmoded.[3]

The French Revolution itself was the end point of a long process, not in France alone but in the entire capitalist world-economy as a historical system. For, by 1789, a goodly part of the globe had been located inside this historical system for three centuries already. And during those three centuries, most of its key institutions had been established and consolidated: the axial division of labour, with a significant transfer of surplus-value from peripheral zones to core zones; the primacy of reward to those operating in the interests of the endless accumulation of capital; the interstate system composed of so-called sovereign states, which however were constrained by the framework and the "rules" of this interstate system; and the ever-growing polarization of this world-system, one that was not merely economic but social, and was on the verge of becoming demographic as well.

What this world-system of historical capitalism still lacked, however, was a legitimating geoculture. The basic doctrines were being forced by the theoreticians of the Enlightenment in the eighteenth century (and indeed earlier), but they were to be socially institutionalized only with the French Revolution. For what the French Revolution did was to unleash public support for, indeed clamour for, the acceptance of two new world-views: that political change was normal and not exceptional; and that sovereignty resided in the "people," and not in a sovereign. In 1815, Napoleon, heir and world protagonist of the French Revolution, was defeated, and there followed a presumed "Restoration" in France (and wherever else the *anciens régimes* had been displaced). But the Restoration did not really, could no longer really, undo the widespread acceptance of these world-views. It was to deal with this new situation that the trinity of nineteenth-century ideologies—conservatism, liberalism, and socialism—came into being, providing the language of subsequent political debates within the capitalist world-economy.[4]

Of the three ideologies, however, it was liberalism that emerged triumphant, and as early as what might be thought of as the first world revolution of this system, the revolution of 1848.[5] For it was liberalism that was best able to provide a viable geoculture for the capitalist world-economy, one that would legitimate the other institutions both in the eyes of the cadres of the system and, to a significant degree, in the eyes of the mass of the populations, the so-called ordinary people.

Once people thought that political change was normal and that they in principle constituted the sovereign (that is to say, the decider of political change), anything was possible. And this of course was precisely the problem that faced those who were powerful and privileged within the framework of the capitalist world-economy. The immediate focus of their fears was to some extent the small but growing group of urban industrial workers. But, as the French Revolution had amply demonstrated, rural non-industrial workers could be quite as troublesome or fearsome from the perspective of the powerful and privileged. How were these "dangerous classes" to be kept from taking these norms too seriously, and thereupon interfering with the process of capital accumulation by undermining the basic structures of the system? This was the political dilemma that was posed acutely to the governing classes in the first half of the nineteenth century.

One obvious answer was repression. And repression was amply used. The lesson of the world revolution of 1848, however, was that simple repression was not ultimately very efficacious; that it provoked the dangerous classes, worsening tempers, rather than calming them. It came to be realized that repression, to be effective, had to be combined with concessions. On the other hand, the putative revolutionaries of the first half of the nineteenth century had also learned a lesson. Spontaneous uprisings were not very efficacious either, since they were more or less easily put down. Threats of popular insurrection had to be combined with conscious long-term political organization, if they were to speed up significant change.

In effect, liberalism offered itself as the immediate solution to the political difficulties of both Right and Left. To the Right, it preached concessions; to the Left, it preached political organization. To both, it preached patience: in the long run, more will be gained (for all) by a *via media*. Liberalism was centrism incarnate, and its siren was alluring. For it was not a mere passive centrism that it preached, but an active strategy. Liberals put their faith in one key premise of Enlightenment thought: that rational thought and action were the path to salvation, that is, to progress. Men (it was rarely a question of including women) were naturally rational, were potentially rational, were ultimately rational.

It followed that "normal political change" ought to follow the path indicated by those who were most rational—that is, most educated, most skilled, therefore most wise. These men could design the best paths of political change to pursue; that is, these men could indicate the necessary reforms to undertake and enact. Rational reformism was the organizing concept of liberalism, which therefore dictated the seemingly erratic position of liberals concerning the relation of the individual to the state. Liberals could simultaneously argue that the individual ought not to be constrained by state (collective) dictates and that state action was necessary to minimize injustice to the individual. They could thus be in favour of laissez-faire and factory laws at the same time. For what mattered to liberals was neither laissez-faire nor factory laws per se, but rather measured deliberate progress toward the good society, which could be achieved best, perhaps only, via rational reformism.

This doctrine of rational reformism proved in practice to be extraordinarily attractive. It seemed to answer everyone's needs. For those of conservative bent, it seemed as though it might be the way to dampen the revolutionary instincts of the dangerous classes. Some rights to suffrage here, a little bit of welfare-state provisions there, plus some unifying of the classes under a common nationalist identity—all this added up, by the end of the nineteenth century, to a formula that appeased the working classes, while maintaining the essential elements of the capitalist system. The powerful and the privileged lost nothing that was of fundamental importance to them, and they slept more peacefully at night (fewer revolutionaries at their windows).

For those of a radical bent, on the other hand, rational reformism seemed to offer a useful halfway house. It provided some fundamental change here and now, without ever eliminating the hope *and expectation* of more fundamental change later. It provided above all, to living men, something in their lifetime. And these living men then slept more peacefully at night (fewer policemen at their windows).

I do not wish to minimize a hundred and fifty years or so of continuous political struggle—some of it violent, much of it passionate, most of it consequential, and almost all of it serious. I do however wish to put this struggle in perspective. Ultimately, the struggle was fought within rules established by liberal ideology. And when a major group arose, the fascists, who rejected those rules fundamentally, they were put down and eliminated—with difficulty, no doubt; but they were put down.

There is one other thing we must say about liberalism. We have asserted it was not fundamentally anti-statist, since its real priority was rational reformism. But, if not anti-statist, liberalism was fundamentally anti-democratic. Liberalism was always an aristocratic doctrine; it preached the "rule of the best." To be sure, liberals did not define the "best" primarily by birth status but rather by educational achievement. The best were thus not the hereditary nobility, but the beneficiaries of meritocracy. But the best were always a group smaller than the whole. Liberals wanted rule by the best, aristocracy, precisely in order not to have rule by the whole of the people, democracy. Democracy was the objective of the radicals, not of the liberals; or at least it was the objective of those who were truly radical, truly antisystemic. It was to prevent this group from prevailing that liberalism was put forward as an ideology. And when they spoke to those of conservative bent who were resistant to proposed reforms, liberals always asserted that only rational reformism would bar the coming of democracy, an argument that ultimately would be heard sympathetically by all intelligent conservatives.

Finally, we must note a significant difference between the second half of the nineteenth century and the first half of the twentieth century. In the second half of the nineteenth century, the main protagonists of the demands of the dangerous classes were still the urban working classes of Europe and North America. The liberal agenda worked splendidly with them. They were offered universal (male) suffrage, the beginning of a welfare state, and national identity. But national identity against whom? Against their neighbours to be sure; but more importantly and pro-foundly, against the non-White world. Imperialism and racism were part of the package offered by liberals to the European/North American working classes under the guise of "rational reformism."

Meanwhile, however, the "dangerous classes" of the non-European world were stirring politically—from Mexico to Afghanistan, from Egypt to China, from Persia to India. When Japan defeated Russia in 1905, it was regarded in this entire zone as the beginning of the "roll-back" of European expansion. It was a loud warning signal to the "liber-als," who were of course primarily Europeans and North Americans, that now "normal political change" and "sovereignty" were claims that the peoples of the entire world, and not just the European working classes, were making.

Hence, liberals turned their attention to extending the concept of rational reformism to the level of the world-system as a whole. This was the message of Woodrow Wilson and his insistence on the "self-determination of nations," a doctrine that was the global equivalent of universal suffrage. This was the message of Franklin Roosevelt and the "four freedoms" proclaimed as a war aim during the Second World War, which was later to be translated by President Truman into "Point Four," the opening shot of the post-1945 project of the "economic development of underdeveloped countries," a doctrine that was the global equivalent of the welfare state.[6]

The objectives of liberalism and of democracy were once again, however, in conflict. In the nineteenth century, the proclaimed universalism of liberalism had been made compatible with racism by "externalizing" the objects of racism (outside the boundaries of the "nation") while "internalizing" the de facto beneficiaries of universal ideals, the "citizenry." The question was whether global liberalism of the twentieth century could be as successful in containing the "dangerous classes" located in what came to be called the Third World or the South, as a national-level liberalism in Europe and North America had been in containing their national "dangerous classes." The problem of course was that, at a world level, there was no place to which one could "externalize" racism. The contradictions of liberalism were coming home to roost.

TRIUMPH AND DISASTER

Still, in 1945, this was far from evident. The victory of the Allies over the Axis powers seemed to be the triumph of global liberalism (in alliance with the USSR) over the fascist challenge. The fact that the last act of the war was the dropping of two atomic bombs by the U.S. on the only non-White Axis power, Japan, was scarcely discussed in the U.S. (or indeed in Europe) as perhaps reflecting some contradiction of liberalism. The reaction, needless to say, was not the same in Japan. But Japan had lost the war, and its voice was not taken seriously at this point.

The U.S. was by now by far and away the strongest economic force in the world-economy. And, with the atomic bomb, it was the strongest military force, despite the size of the Soviet armed forces. It would within five years be able to organize the world-system politically by means of a four-fold programme: i) an arrangement with the USSR guaranteeing it control over a corner of the world in return for remaining in its corner (not of course rhetorically, but in terms of real policy); ii) an alliance system with both western Europe and Japan, which served economic, political, and rhetorical objectives as well as military ones; iii) a modulated, moderate programme to arrive at the "decolonization" of the colonial empires; iv) a programme of internal integration within the US, amplifying the categories of real "citizenship," and sealed with a unifying ideology of anti-Communism.

This programme worked, and worked remarkably well, for some twenty-five years, that is, precisely up to our turning point of 1968. How then shall we evaluate those extraordinary years, 1945-68? Were they a period of progress and of the triumph of liberal values? The answer has to be: very much yes, but also very much no. The most obvious indicator of "progress" was material. The economic expansion of the world-economy was extraordinary, the largest in the history of the capitalist system. And it seemed to occur everywhere—West and East, North and South. To be sure, there was greater benefit to North than to South, and the gaps (both absolute and relative) grew in most cases.[7] Since, however, there was real growth and high employment in most places, the era had a rosy glow. This was all the more so in that along with growth went greatly increased expenditures on welfare, as I've already mentioned, and in particular expenditures on education and health.

Secondly, there was peace once again in Europe. Peace in Europe, but not of course in Asia, where two long, wearing wars were fought—in Korea and Indochina. And not of course in many other parts of the non-European world. The conflicts in Korea and Vietnam were not however the same. Rather the Korean conflict is to be paired with the Berlin Blockade, the two occurring in fact almost in conjunction. Germany and Korea were the two great partitions of 1945. Each country was divided between the military-political spheres of the U.S. on the one side and the USSR on the other. In the spirit of Yalta, the lines of division were supposed to remain intact, whatever the nationalist (and ideological) sentiments of Germans and Koreans.

In 1949-52, the firmness of these lines was put to the test. After much tension (and in the case of Korea enormous loss of life) the outcome was in fact the maintenance of boundary status quo ante, more or less. Thus, in a real sense, the Berlin Blockade and the Korean War concluded the process of the institutionalization of Yalta. The second outcome of these two conflicts was the further social integration of each camp, institutionalized by the establishment of strong alliance systems: NATO and the

U.S.–Japan Defence Pact on the one side, the Warsaw Pact and the Soviet–Chinese accords on the other. Furthermore, the two conflicts served as direct stimulus of a major expansion in the world-economy, fuelled heavily as it was by military expenditures. European recovery and Japanese growth were two immediate major beneficiaries of this expansion.

The war in Vietnam was of a quite different type from that in Korea. It was the emblematic site (but far from the only one) of the struggle of national liberation movements throughout the non-European world. While the Korean War and the Berlin Blockade were part and parcel of the Cold War world regime, the Vietnamese struggle (as the Algerian and many others) was a protest against the constraints and structure of this Cold War world regime. They were therefore in this elementary and immediate sense the product of antisystemic movements. This was quite different from the struggles in Germany and Korea, where the two sides were never at peace but only at truce; that is, for each, peace was *faute de mieux*. The wars of national liberation were, on the contrary, one-sided. None of the national liberation movements wanted wars with Europe/North America; they wanted to be left alone to pursue their own paths. It was Europe/North America that was unwilling to leave them alone, until eventually forced to do so. The national liberation movements were thus protesting against the powerful, but they were doing so in the name of fulfilling the liberal agenda of the self-determination of nations, and the economic development of underdeveloped countries.

That brings us to the third great accomplishment of the extraordinary years, 1945–1968: the worldwide triumph of the antisystemic forces. It is only an apparent paradox that the very moment of the apogee of U.S. hegemony in the world-system and the global legitimation of liberal ideology was also the moment when all those movements whose structures and strategies had been formed in the period 1848–1945 as antisystemic movements came to power. The so-called Old Left in its three historic variants—Communists, Social-Democrats, and national liberation movements—all achieved state power, each in different geographic zones. Communist parties were in power from the Elbe to the Yalu, covering one-third of the world. National liberation movements were in power in most of Asia, Africa, and the Caribbean (and their equivalents in much of Latin America and the Middle East). And Social-Democratic movements (or their equivalents) had come to power, at least rotating power, in most of western Europe, North America, and Australasia. Japan was perhaps the only significant exception to this global triumph of the Old Left.

Was this a paradox? Was this the result of the juggernaut of social progress, the inevitable triumph of popular forces? Or was this a massive cooptation of these popular forces? And is there a way to distinguish intellectually and politically between these two propositions? These were the questions that were beginning to create unease in the 1960s. Whereas the economic expansion with its clear benefits in living standards around the world, relative peace in large zones of the world, and the seeming triumph of popular movements all lent themselves to positive and optimistic appraisals of world developments, a closer look at the real situation revealed major negatives.

The Cold War world regime was one not of the expansion of human freedom but of great internal repression by all the states, whose justification was the presumed seriousness of the highly choreographed geopolitical tensions. The Communist world had purge trials, gulags, and iron curtains. The Third World had one-party regimes and dissenters in prison or exile. And McCarthyism (and its equivalents in the other OECD countries), if less overtly brutal, was quite as effective in enforcing conformity and breaking careers, where necessary. Public discourse everywhere was allowed only within clearly delimited parameters.

Furthermore, in material terms, the Cold War regime was one of growing inequality, both internationally and nationally. And while antisystemic movements often moved against old inequalities, they were not shy about creating new ones. The *nomenklaturas* of the Communist regimes had their parallels in the Third World and in Social-Democratic regimes in the OECD countries.

In addition, it was quite clear that these inequalities were not randomly distributed. They were correlated with status-group (whether coded as race, religion, or ethnicity), and this correlation held both at the world level and within all states. And they were of course, correlated with gender and age-group, as well as with a number of other social characteristics. In short, there were groups left out, many such groups, groups adding up to considerably more than half of the world's population.

It was thus the realization of long-standing hopes in the years between 1945 and 1968, hopes that came to be thought of as falsely realized, which underlay and accounted for the world revolution of 1968. That revolution was directed first of all against the whole historical system — against the U.S. as the hegemonic power of this system, against the economic and military structures that constituted the pillars of the system. But the revolution was directed just as much, if not more, against the Old Left — against the antisystemic movements considered insufficiently antisystemic: against the USSR as the collusive partner of its ostensible ideological foe, the U.S.; against the trade unions and other workers' organizations who were seen as narrowly economistic, defending the interests primarily of particular status-groups.

Meanwhile, the defenders of the existing structures were denouncing what they regarded as the anti-rationalism of the revolutionaries of 1968. But, in fact, liberal ideology had hoisted itself by its own petard. Having insisted for over a century that the function of the social sciences was to advance the boundaries of rational analysis (as a necessary prerequisite of rational reformism), they had succeeded only too well. As Fredric Jameson points out:

> [M]uch of contemporary theory or philosophy . . . has involved a prodigious expansion in what we consider to be rational or meaningful behaviour. My sense is that, particularly after the diffusion of psychoanalysis but also with the gradual evaporation of "otherness" on a shrinking globe and in a media-suffused society, very little remains that can be considered "irrational" in the older sense of "incomprehensible" . . . Whether such an enormously expanded concept of Reason then has any further normative value . . . in a situation in which its opposite, the irrational, has shrunk to virtual nonexistence, is another and an interesting question.[8]

For if virtually everything had become rational, what special legitimacy was there any longer in the particular paradigms of Establishment social science? What special merit was there in the specific political programmes of the dominant elites? And most devastating of all, what special capacities did the specialists have to offer that ordinary people did not have, did dominant groups have that oppressed groups did not have? The revolutionaries of 1968 had spotted this logical hole in the defensive armour of the liberal ideologues (and in its not-so-different variant of official Marxist ideology) and jumped into the breach.

As a political movement, the world revolution of 1968 was no more than a brushfire. It flamed up ferociously, and then (within three years) it was extinguished. Its embers—in the form of multiple, competing pseudo-Maoist sects—survived another five to ten years, but by the end of the 1970s, all these groups had become obscure historical footnotes. Nonetheless, the geocultural impact of 1968 was decisive, for the world revolution of 1968 marked the end of an era, the era of the automatic centrality of liberalism, not merely as the dominant world ideology, but as the only one that could claim to be unremittingly rational and hence scientifically legitimate. The world revolution of 1968 returned liberalism to where it had been in the period 1815–48, merely one competing political strategy among others. Both conservatism and radicalism/ socialism were in that sense liberated from the magnetic field force of liberalism that had kept them in check from 1848 to 1968.

The process of demoting liberalism from its role as a geocultural norm to mere competitor in the global marketplace of ideas was completed in the two decades that followed 1968. The material glow of the 1945–68 period disappeared during the long Kondratieff-B downturn that set in. This is not to say that everyone suffered equally. Third World countries suffered first and worst. The OPEC oil rises were a first mode of trying to limit the damage. A large part of the world surplus was funnelled through the oil-producing states to OECD banks. The immediate beneficiaries were three groups: the oil-producing states who took a rent; the states (in the Third World and the Communist worlds) who received loans from OECD banks with which to restore their balance of payments; the OECD states who thereby could still maintain exports. This first attempt collapsed by 1968 in the so-called debt crisis. The second mode of trying to limit the damage was Reagan's military Keynesianism, which fuelled the speculative boom of the 1980s in the US. This collapsed in the late 1980s, pulling the USSR down with it. The third attempt was that of Japan plus the East Asian dragons and some surrounding states to benefit from the necessary and inevitable production relocations of a Kondratieff-B period. We are witnessing the limits of this effort in the early 1990s.

The net result of twenty-five years of economic struggle was a worldwide disillusionment with the promise of developmentalism, a keystone in the offerings of global liberalism. No doubt east and southeast Asia has been spared this sense of disillusion thus far, though this may be merely a time lag. Elsewhere however the consequences have been great, and particularly negative for the Old Left—first the national liberation movements, then the Communist parties (leading to the collapse of the Communist regimes of eastern Europe in 1989), and finally the Social-Democratic parties. These collapses have been celebrated by liberals as their triumph. It has rather been their graveyard. For liberals find themselves back in the pre-1848 situation of a pressing demand for democracy—for far more than the limited package of parliamentary institutions, multi-party systems, and elementary civil rights; this time for the real thing, a genuine egalitarian sharing of power. And this latter demand was historically the bugbear of liberalism, to counter which liberalism had offered its package of limited compromises combined with seductive optimism about the future. To the extent that today there is no longer a widespread faith in rational reformism via state action, liberalism has lost its principal politico-culture defence against the dangerous classes.

THE COLLAPSE OF LEGITIMACY

Thus it is we have arrived at the present era, what I think of as the Black Period before us, which can be said to have begun symbolically in 1989 (the continuation of 1968)[9] and will go on for at least twenty-five to fifty years.

I have emphasized thus far the ideological shield that dominant forces had constructed against the claims put forward insistently by the "dangerous classes" since 1789. I have argued that this shield was liberal ideology, and that it operated both directly and, even more insidiously, via an edulcorated socialist/progressive variant which had traded the essence of antisystemic claims for a substitute of limited value. And finally I have argued that this ideological shield was largely destroyed by the world revolution of 1968, of which the collapse of the communisms in 1989 was the final act.

Why however did this ideological shield collapse after a hundred and fifty years of such efficacious functioning? The answer to that question lies not in some sudden insight by the oppressed into the falsity of ideological claims. The awareness of the speciousness of liberalism had been known from the outset and asserted frequently with vigour throughout the nineteenth and twentieth centuries. Nonetheless the movements of the socialist tradition did not conduct themselves in ways that were consistent with their rhetorical critiques of liberalism. Quite the opposite, for the most part!

The reason is not hard to find. The social base of these movements — movements which all claimed grandly to speak in the name of the mass of humanity — was in fact a narrow bank of the world's population, the less well-off segment of the "modernist" sector of the world-economy as it was structured between say 1750 and 1950. These included the skilled and semiskilled urbanized working classes, the intelligentsias of the world, and the more skilled and educated groups in those rural areas in which the functioning of the capitalist world-economy was more immediately visible. This added up to a significant number, but not at all to the majority of the world's population.

The Old Left was a world movement supported by a minority, a powerful minority, an oppressed minority, but nonetheless a numerical minority of the world's population. And this demographic reality limited its real political options. Under the circumstances, it did the only thing it could. It opted for being a spur to speed up the liberal programme of rational reformism, and in this it succeeded very well. The benefits it brought to its protagonists were real, if only partial. But, as the revolutionaries of 1968 proclaimed, a lot of people had been left out of the equation. The Old Left had talked a universalist language, but had practised a particularist politics.

The reason that these ideological blinkers of specious universalism were tossed aside in 1968/1989 was that the underlying social reality had changed. The capitalist world-economy had pursued the logic of its ceaseless accumulation of capital so unremittingly that it was approaching its theoretical ideal, the commodification of everything. We can see this reflected in multiple new sociological realities: the extent of the mechanization of production; the elimination of spatial constraints in the exchange of commodities and information; the deruralization of the world; the near-exhaustion of the ecosystem; the high degree of monetarization of the work-process; and consumerism (that is, the enormously expanded commodification of consumption).[10]

All these developments are well-known, and are indeed the subject of continuous discussions in world media of communication. But consider what this means from the point of view of the endless accumulation of capital. It means first of all, most of all, an enormous limitation on the rate at which capital can be accumulated. And the reasons are fundamentally socio-political. There are three central factors. The first is a factor long recognized by analysts, but whose full realization is only being reached now. The urbanization of the world and the increase in both education and communications have engendered a degree of worldwide political awareness which both renders political mobilization easy and makes it difficult to obscure the degree of socio-economic disparities and the role of governments in maintaining them. Such political awareness is reinforced by the delegitimization of any irrational sources of authority. In short, more people than ever demand the equalization of reward and refuse to tolerate a basic condition of capital accumulation, low remuneration for labour. This is manifested both in the significant worldwide rise in the level of "historical" wages, and in the very high and still growing demand on governments to redistribute basis welfare (in particular, health and education) and to ensure steady income.

The second factor is the greatly increased cost to governments of subsidizing profit via the construction of infrastructure and permitting the externalization of costs by the enterprises. This is what journalists refer to as the ecological crisis, the crisis of rising health costs, the crisis of the high costs of big science, and so on. The states cannot at one and the same time continue to expand subsidies to private enterprise and expand welfare commitments to the citizenry. One or the other must give to an important degree. With a more aware citizenry, this essentially class struggle promises to be monumental.

And the third strain is the result of the fact that the political awareness is now worldwide. Both the global and the state-level disparities are racial/ethnic/religious in distribution. Hence, the combined result of political awareness and the fiscal crises of the states will be a massive struggle that will take the form of civil warfare, both global and state-level.

The multiple strains will have as their first victim the legitimacy of the state structures and therefore their ability to maintain order. As they lose this ability, there are economic as well as security costs, which in turn will render more acute the strains, and that in turn will further weaken the legitimacy of the state structures. This is not the future; it is the present. We see it in the enormously increased feeling of insecurity—concern about crime, concern about random violence, concern about the impossibility of securing justice in court systems, concern about the brutality of police forces—that has multiplied manyfold during the last ten to fifteen years. I am not contending that these phenomena are new, or even necessarily much more extensive than earlier. But they are perceived as new or worse by most people, and certainly as far more extensive. And the major result of such perceptions is the delegitimization of state structures.

This kind of escalating, self-reinforcing disorder cannot go on for ever. But it can go on for twenty-five to fifty years. And it is a form of chaos in the system, caused by the exhaustion of the systemic safety-valves, or to put it another way by the fact that contradictions of the system have come to the point that none of the mechanisms for restoring the normal functioning of the system can work effectively any longer.

NEW FRONTS OF STRUGGLE

But out of chaos will come a new order, and this then brings us to the last issue: the choices before us—now and also soon. Because it is a time of chaos, it does not mean that during the next twenty-five to fifty years we will not see in operation the major basic processes of the capitalist world-economy. People and firms will continue to seek to accumulate capital in all the familiar ways. Capitalists will seek support from state structures as they have done in the past. States will compete with other states to be major loci of the accumulation of capital. The capitalist world-economy will probably enter into a new period of expansion, which will further commodify economic processes worldwide and further polarize effective distribution of reward.

What will be different in the next twenty-five to fifty years will be far less the operations of the world market than the operations of the world's political and cultural structures. Basically, the states will steadily lose their legitimation and therefore find it difficult to ensure minimum security, internally or among themselves. On the geocultural scene, there will be no dominant common discourse, and even the forms of cultural debate will be a matter of debate. There will be little agreement on what constitutes rational or acceptable behaviour. The fact that there will be confusion, however, does not mean that there will be no purposive behaviour. Indeed, there will be multiple groups seeking to achieve clear, limited objectives, but many of these will be in acute direct conflict with each other. And there may be a few groups with long-term concepts of how to construct an alternative social order, even if their subjective clarity can have only have a poor fit with any objective probability that these concepts will in fact be useful heuristic guides to action. In short, everyone will be acting somewhat blindly even if they will not think they are so acting.

Nonetheless, we are condemned to act. Therefore, the first need that we have is to be clear about what has been deficient in our modern world-system, what it is that has made so large a percentage of the world's population angry about it, or at the least ambivalent as to its social merits. It seems quite clear to me that the major complaint has been the great inequalities of the system, which means the absence of democracy. This was no doubt true of virtually all known prior historical systems. What was different under capitalism is that its very success as a creator of material production seemed to eliminate all justification for the inequalities, whether manifested materially, politically, or socially. These inequalities seemed all the worse because they did not divide merely a very tiny group from everyone else, but as much as one-fifth or one-seventh of the world's population from all the rest. It is these two facts—the increase of total material wealth and the fact that more than a mere handful of people but far less than the majority could live well—that has so exasperated the sentiments of those who have been left out.

We can contribute nothing to a desirable resolution of this terminal chaos of our world-system unless we make it very clear that only a relatively egalitarian, fully democratic historical system is desirable. Concretely we must move actively and immediately on several fronts. One is the active undoing of the Eurocentric assumptions that have permeated the geoculture for at least two centuries now. Europeans have made great cultural contributions to our common human enterprise. But it is simply not true that, over ten thousand years, they have made much greater ones than other civilizational centres, and there is no reason to assume that the multiple loci of collective wisdom will be fewer in the millennium to come. The active replacement of the current Eurocentric bias

by a more sober and balanced sense of history and of its cultural evaluation will require acute and constant political and cultural struggle. It calls
not for new fanaticisms but for hard intellectual work, collectively and
individually.

We need in addition to take the concept of human rights and work
very hard to make it apply equally to us and to them, to citizen and to
alien. The right of communities to protect their cultural heritage is never
the right to protect their privilege. One major battleground will be in the
rights of migrants. If indeed, as I foresee for the next twenty-five to fifty
years, a very large minority of the residents of North America, Europe,
and yes Japan, will in fact be recent migrants or the children of such migrants (whether or not the migration will have been done legally), then
we all need to struggle to make sure such migrants have truly equal access to economic, social, and yes political rights in the zone into which
they have migrated.

I know that there will be enormous political resistance to this on the
grounds of cultural purity and of accumulated property rights. The
statesmen of the North are already arguing that the North cannot assume
the economic burden of the entire world. Well, why not? The North's
wealth has in very large part been the result of a transfer of surplus-value
from the South. It is this very fact which, over several hundred years, has
led us to the crisis of the system. It is not a question of remedial charity,
but of rational reconstruction.

These battles will be political battles, but not necessarily battles at the
level of the state. Indeed, precisely because of the process of delegitimizing the states, many of these battles (perhaps most of them) will go on at
more local levels among the groups into which we are reorganizing ourselves. And since these battles will be local and complex among multiple
groups, a complex and flexible strategy of alliances will be essential, but
will be workable only if we keep in the front of our minds the egalitarian
objectives.

Finally, the struggle will be an intellectual one, in the reconceptualization of our scientific canons, in the search for more holistic and sophisticated methodologies, in the attempt to rid ourselves of the pious
and fallacious cant about the value-neutrality of scientific thought. Rationality is itself a value-judgement if it is anything, and nothing is or can

be rational except in the widest, most inclusive context of human social organization.

You may think that the programme I have outlined for judicious social and political action over the next twenty-five to fifty years is far too vague. But it is as concrete as one can be in the midst of a whirlpool. First, make sure to which shore you wish to swim. And second, make sure that your immediate efforts seem to be moving in that direction. If you want greater precision than that, you will not find it, and you will drown while you are looking for it.

NOTES

1. This lecture was given at the 25th anniversary of the founding of Kyoto Seika University, 7 December 1993.

2. See John W. Meyer et al., "The World Educational Revolution, 1950–1970," in J. W. Meyer and M. T. Hannan, eds, *National Development 1950–1970*, Chicago 1979.

3. For a magnificent and quite detailed account of the intellectual debates surrounding the bicentennial in France, see Steven Kaplan, *Adieu 89*, Paris 1993.

4. For an analysis of this process, see my "The French Revolution as a World-Historical Event," in *Unthinking Social Science: The Limit of Nineteenth-Century Paradigms*, Cambridge 1991.

5. The process by which liberalism gained center stage and made its two contestants, conservatism and socialism, into virtual adjuncts instead of opponents, is discussed in my "Three Ideologies or One? The Pseudo-Battle of Modernity," in I. Wallerstein, *After Liberalism* (New York: New Press, 1995, 72–92).

6. The nature of the promises made by liberalism at the world level and the ambiguity of the Leninist response to global liberalism are explored in my "The Concept of National Development, 1917–1989: Elegy and Requiem," in G. Marks and L. Diamond, eds, *Reexamining Democracy*, Newbury Park 1992.

7. See a summary of the date in John T. Passé-Smith, "The Persistence of the Gap: Taking Stock of Economic Growth in the Post-World War II Era," in M. A. Seligson and J. T. Passé-Smith, eds, *Development and Underdevelopment: The Political Economy of Inequality*, Boulder, CO 1993.

8. *Postmodernism, or the Cultural Logic of Late Capitalism*, Durham, NC 1991, p. 268.

9. See G. Arrighi, T. K. Hopkins, and I. Wallerstein, "1989, The Continuation of 1968," *Review*, vol. 15, no. 2, spring 1992.

10. These points are elaborated in my "Peace, Stability, and Legitimacy, 1990–2025/2050," in G. Lundestad, ed., *The Fall of Great Powers: Peace, Stability, and Legitimacy*, London 1994 (chapter 27 of this volume).

27—Peace, Stability, and Legitimacy, 1990–2025/2050

> The collapse of liberalism is being followed by a period of unstable chaotic fluctuations, a dark period, out of which the world will emerge into a new historical system of an uncertain kind. I attempt here to outline, as best one can, what we may expect over the next fifty years, and what are our historical choices.

The period from 1990 to 2025/2050 will most likely be short on peace, short on stability, and short on legitimacy. In part, this is because of the decline of the United States as the hegemonic power of the world-system. But in even larger part, it is because of the crisis in the world-system as a world-system.

Hegemony in the world-system means by definition that there is one power in a geopolitical position to impose a stable concatention of the social distribution of power. This implies a period of "peace," meaning primarily the absence of military struggle—not all military struggle, but military struggle among great powers. Such a period of hegemony requires, and at the same time engenders, "legitimacy," if by that is meant the feeling by major political actors (including amorphous groups such as "populations" of the various states) either that the social order is one of which they approve or that the world ("history") is moving steadily and rapidly in a direction they would approve of.

Such periods of real hegemony, wherein the ability of the hegemonic power to impose its will and its "order" on other major powers is without serious challenge, have been relatively short in the history of the modern world-system. In my view, there have been only three instances: the United Provinces in the mid-seventeenth century, the United Kingdom in the mid-nineteenth, and the United States in the mid-twentieth. Their hegemonies, defined in this way, lasted about twenty-five to fifty years in each case.[1]

When such periods have ended, that is, when the erstwhile hegemonic power became once again simply one major power among others (even if it continued to be for some time the strongest among them militarily), then quite obviously there ensued less stability, and correlatively less legitimacy. This implies less peace. In this sense the present period following U.S. hegemony is essentially no different from that which followed British hegemony in the mid-nineteenth century or Dutch in the mid-seventeenth.

But if this were all there were to describing the period 1990–2025, or 1990–2050, or 1990–?, then it would scarcely be worth discussing except as a matter of the technical management of a shaky world order (which is how too many politicians, diplomats, scholars, and journalists have indeed been discussing it).

There is, however, more, probably much more, to the dynamic of the coming half-century or so of great world disorder. The geopolitical realities of the interstate system do not rest exclusively, even primarily, on the military *rapport de forces* among that privileged subset of sovereign states we call great powers—those states that are large enough and wealthy enough to have the necessary revenue base to develop a serious military capability.

First of all, only some states are wealthy enough to have such a tax base, such wealth being more the source than the consequence of their military strength, though of course the process is one of circular reinforcement. And the wealth of these states relative to that of other states is a function both of their size and of the axial division of labor in the capitalist world-economy.

The capitalist world-economy is a system that involves a hierarchical inequality of distribution based on the concentration of certain kinds of production (relatively monopolized, and therefore high-profit, production) in certain limited zones, which thereupon and thereby become the loci of the greatest accumulation of capital. This concentration enables the reinforcement of the state structures, which in turn seek to guarantee the survival of the relative monopolies. But because monopolies are inherently fragile, there has been a constant, discontinuous, and limited but significant relocation of these centers of concentration all through the history of the modern world-system.

The mechanisms of change are the cyclical rhythms, of which two are the most consequential. The Kondratieff cycles are approximately fifty to sixty years in length. Their A-phases essentially reflect the length of time particular significant economic monopolies can be protected; their B-phases are the periods of the geographical relocation of production whose monopolies have been exhausted, as well as the period of struggle for control of the prospective new monopolies. The longer hegemonic cycles involve a struggle between *two* major states to become the successor to the previous hegemonic power by becoming the primary locus of the accumulation of capital. This is a long process, which eventually involves having the military strength to win a "thirty years' war." Once a new hegemony is instituted, its maintenance requires heavy financing, which eventually and inevitably leads to a relative decline of the current hegemonic power and a struggle for a successor.

This mode of a slow but certain repeated restructuring and recentering of the capitalist world-economy has been very efficacious. The rise and decline of great powers has been more or less the same kind of process as the rise and decline of enterprises: The monopolies hold for a long while, but they are ultimately undermined by the very measures taken to sustain them. The subsequent "bankruptcies" have been cleansing mechanisms, ridding the system of those powers whose dynamism is spent and replacing them with fresher blood. Through it all, the basic structures of the system have remained the same. Each monopoly of power held for a while but, just like economic monopolies, was undermined by the very measures taken to sustain it.

All systems (physical, biological, and social) depend on such cyclical rhythms to restore a minimal equilibrium. The capitalist world-economy has shown itself to be a hardy variety of historical system, and it has flourished rather exuberantly for some five hundred years now, a long time for an historical system. But systems have secular trends as well as cyclical rhythms, and the secular trends always exacerbate the contradictions (which all systems contain). There comes a point when the contradictions become so acute that they lead to larger and larger fluctuations. In the language of the new science, this means the onset of chaos (the sharp diminution of that which can be explained by deterministic equations), which in turn leads to bifurcations, whose occurrence is certain but whose shape is inherently unpredictable. Out of this a new systemic order emerges.

The question is whether the historical system in which we are living, the capitalist world-economy, has entered, or is entering into, such a time of "chaos." I propose to weigh the arguments, offer some guesses about the forms such "chaos" might take, and discuss what courses of action are open to us.

I propose not to discuss at length the elements I consider to be the "normal" reflections of a Kondratieff B-phase or of a hegemonic B-phase; I will merely summarize them very briefly.[2] I should, however, make clear that, although a hegemonic cycle is much longer than a Kondratieff cycle, the inflection point of a hegemonic cycle coincides with that of a Kondratieff cycle (but not, of course, every one). In this case, that point was around 1967–73.

The phenomena that are symptomatic of a normal Kondratieff B-phase are: the slowdown of growth in production, and probably a decline in per capita world production; a rise in rates of active waged work unemployment; a relative shift of loci of profits, from productive activity to gains from financial manipulations; a rise of state indebtedness; relocation of "older" industries to lower-wage zones; a rise in military expenditures, whose justification is not really military in nature but rather that of countercyclical demand creation; falling real wages in the formal economy; expansion of informal economy; a decline in low-cost food production; increased "illegalization" of interzonal migration.

The phenomena that are symptomatic of the beginning of hegemonic decline are: increased economic strength of "allied" major powers; currency instability; decline of authority in world financial markets with the rise of new loci of decision making; fiscal crises of the hegemonic state; decline of organizing (and stabilizing) world political polarization and tension (in this case, the Cold War); a decline of popular willingness to invest lives in the maintenance of hegemonic power.

All this, as I've said, seems to be to have been "normal" and historically expectable. What should now happen, in the "normal" cyclical process, is the rise of replacement structures. We should enter, within five to ten years, a new Kondratieff A-phase, based on new monopolized leading products, concentrated in new locations. Japan is the most obvious locus, Western Europe the second, the United States the third (but what may prove to be a poor third).

We should also now see a new competition for hegemony beginning. As the U.S. position crumbles, slowly but visibly, two successor applicants should flex their muscles. In the current situation, they could only be Japan and the European Community. Following the pattern of the two previous successions—England vs. France to succeed to the Dutch; and the United States vs. Germany to succeed to Great Britain—we should in theory expect, not immediately, but over the next fifty to seventy-five years, that the sea/air power, Japan, would transform the previous hegemonic power, the United States, into its junior partner, and begin to compete with the land-based power, the EC. Their struggle should culminate in a "thirty years' (world) war" and the putative triumph of Japan.

I should say right off that I do not expect this to happen, or rather not quite. I think both processes of reorganization—that of the worldwide system of production and that of the distribution worldwide of state power—have already begun, and in the direction of the "traditional" (or "normal" or previous) pattern. But I expect the process to be interrupted or diverted because of the entry into the picture of new processes or vectors.

To analyze this clearly, I think we need three separate time frames: the next few years; the following twenty-five to thirty years; the period after that.

The situation in which we find ourselves today in the 1990s is quite "normal." It is not yet one that I would call "chaotic"; rather it is the final acute subphase (or the culminating moment) of the current Kondratieff B-phase—comparable to 1932–39, or 1893–97, or 1842–49, or 1786–92, etc. The worldwide rates of unemployment are high, rates of profit low. There is great financial instability, reflecting acute and justified nervousness in the financial market about short-run fluctuations. Increased social unrest reflects the political inability of governments to offer plausible short-run solutions and therefore an inability to re-create a sense of security. Both scapegoating within states and beggaring-thy-neighbor among states become more politically attractive in situations where the usual adjustment remedies seem to provide little instant alleviation of pain.

In the course of this process, a large number of individual enterprises are reducing their activity or are being restructured or are going bankrupt, in many cases never to reopen. Particular groups of workers and particular entrepreneurs will thereby lose out permanently. While all states will suffer, the degree of suffering will vary enormously. At the end of the process, some states will have risen, and others will have fallen, in comparative economic strength.

At such moments, great powers are often paralyzed militarily because of a combination of internal political instability, financial difficulties (and therefore reluctance to bear military costs), and concentration on immediate economic dilemmas (which leads to popular isolationism). The world's response to the warfare that resulted when Yugoslavia collapsed is a typical instance of such paralysis. And this, I insist, is "normal" — that is, part of the expectable patterns of the operation of the capitalist world-economy.

Normally, we should then come into a time of recovery. After a shakedown of the waste (both of luxury consumerism and ecological carelessness) and inefficiencies (whether logrolling or featherbedding or bureaucratic rigidities) should come a new dynamic thrust, lean and mean, of new monopolized leading industries and newly created segments of world purchasers to augment the total effective demand—in short, renewed expansion of the world-economy en route to a new era of "prosperity."

The three nodes, as already suggested and as is widely acknowledged, will be the United States, Western Europe, and Japan. The first ten years or so of this next Kondratieff A-phase will no doubt see an acute competition of the three centers to gain the edge for their particular product variation. As Brian Arthur has been showing in his writings, which particular variant wins out has little or nothing to do with technical efficiency, and everything to do with power.[3] One might add persuasion to power, except that in this situation persuasion is largely a function of power.

The power of which we are speaking is primarily economic power, but it is backed by state power. Of course, this constitutes a self-reinforcing cycle: A little power leads to a little persuasion, which creates more power, and so on. It's a matter of one country's propelling itself into the lead and running with it. At some point, a threshold is passed. The "Beta" products lose out, and there are "VHS" monopolies. My bet is simple: Japan will have more "VHSs" than the EC, and U.S. entrepreneurs will make deals with Japanese entrepreneurs to get a cut of the pie.

What the U.S. entrepreneurs will get out of such arrangements, as they fully commit themselves in the years between, say, 2000 and 2010, is quite obvious—not being left out altogether. What Japan will get out of it is equally obvious, three things especially: (1) if the United States is a partner, it is not a competitor; (2) the United States will still be the strongest military power, and Japan for many reasons (recent history and its impact on internal politics and regional diplomacy, plus the economic advantages of low military expenditure) will prefer to rely on a U.S. military shield for a while yet; (3) the United States still has the best R&D structure in the world-economy, even if its advantage in this area too will eventually disappear. Japanese enterprises will reduce costs by taking advantage of this structure.

Faced with this grand economic alliance, the EC members will put aside all their minor quarrels, if they haven't long since done so. The EC is incorporating the EFTA countries, but will *not* incorporate the countries of east-central Europe (except perhaps in a limited free trade area, possibly akin to the relationship between Mexico and the United States in NAFTA).

Europe (that is, the EC) will constitute a second economic megalith and a serious competitor to the Japan-United States condominium. The rest of the world will relate to the two zones of this bipolar world in multiple ways. From the viewpoint of the economic centers of power, there will be three crucial factors to consider in determining how important these other countries are: the degree to which their industries will be essential to, or optional for, the operation of the key commodity chains; the degree to which particular countries will be essential to, or optimal for, the maintenance of adequate effective demand for the most profitable sectors of production; the degree to which particular countries will serve strategic needs (geomilitary location and/or power, key raw materials, etc.).

The two countries not yet significantly or sufficiently integrated into the two networks in creation, but which will be essential to include for all three of the above reasons, will be China for the Japan-United States condominium and Russia for the EC. In order for these two countries to be well integrated, they will have to maintain (or, in the case of Russia, first achieve) a certain level of internal stability and legitimacy. Whether they can do so, and perhaps be helped to do so by interested parties, is still an open question, but I believe the odds are moderately favorable.

Suppose this picture to be correct: the emergence of a bipolar world-economy with China part of the Japan-United States pole and Russia part of the Europe pole. Suppose also that there is a new, even very large, expansion of the world-economy from 2000 to 2025 or so, on the basis of new monopolized leading industries. What can we then expect? Would we have in effect a repeat of the period 1945–1967/73, the "trente glorieuses" of worldwide prosperity, relative peace, and above all, high optimism for the future? I do not think so.

There will be several differences that are evident. The first and most obvious to me is that we shall be in a bipolar, rather than a unipolar, world-system. To categorize the world-system between 1945 and 1990 as unipolar is not a view that is widely shared. It goes against the autodesignation of the world as one of a "cold war" between two superpowers. But since this cold war was based on an arrangement, made between two consenting antagonists, that the geopolitical balance would be essentially frozen; and since (despite all the public declarations of conflict) this geopolitical freeze was never significantly violated by either of the two antagonists; I prefer to think of it as a choreographed (and hence extremely limited) conflict. In reality, it was U.S. decision makers who were calling the shots, and their Soviet counterparts must have felt the weight of this reality time and time again.

By contrast, in the years 2000–2025, I do not expect that we will be able to say that either the Japan-United States condominium or the EC will be "calling the shots." Their economic and geopolitical real power will be too balanced. In so elementary and unimportant a matter as votes in interstate agencies, there will be no automatic, or even easy, majority. To be sure, there may be very few ideological elements to this competition. The base may be almost exclusively that of material self-interest. This will not necessarily make the conflict less acute; indeed, it will be harder to patch it over with mere symbols. As the conflict becomes less political in form, it may become more mafioso in form.

The second major difference derives from the fact that the world investment effort may be concentrated in China and Russia during the years 2000–2025 to a degree comparable to the concentration of investment in Western Europe and Japan in the years 1945–67/73. But this will mean that the amount that is left over for the rest of the world must be different in 2000–2025 than in 1945–67/73. In 1945–67/73, virtually the only "old" area where there was continued investment was the United

States. In 2000–2025, continued investment will have to cover the United States, Western Europe, and Japan (and indeed a few others such as Korea and Canada as well). The question, therefore, is, After one has invested in the "old" areas plus the "new" ones, how much will remain (even in small doses) for the rest of the world? The answer will surely be much less than in the period 1945–67/73.

This in turn will translate into a situation quite different for countries in the "South" (however defined). Whereas, in 1945–67/73, the South did benefit from the expansion of the world-economy, at least from its crumbs, in 2000–2025 it risks not getting even crumbs. Indeed, the current disinvestment (of the Kondratieff B-phase) in *most* parts of the South may be continued rather than reversed in the A-phase ahead. Yet the economic demands of the South will be not less but more. For one thing, the awareness of the prosperity of the core zones and the degree of the North-South gap is far greater today than it was fifty years ago.

The third difference has to do with demography. World population continues for the time being to follow the same basic pattern it has followed for some two centuries now. On the one hand, there is worldwide growth. It is fueled by the fact that, for the poorer five-sixths of the world's population, death rates have been declining (for technological reasons) while birth rates have not been or have not been declining as much (because of the absence of sufficient socioeconomic incentive). On the other hand, the percentage of world population of the wealthy regions of the world has been declining, despite the fact that the decline in their death rate has been far sharper than that of the less wealthy regions, because of the still greater lowering of their birth rate (primarily as a way of optimizing the socioeconomic position of middle-class families).

This combination has created a demographic gap paralleling (perhaps exceeding) the economic North-South gap. To be sure, this gap was there already in 1945–67/73. But it was less great then because of the still persisting cultural barriers in the North to limiting the birth rate. These barriers have now been largely swept aside, precisely during the 1945–67/73 period. The world demographic figures of 2000–2025 will reflect this far more acute disparity in social practices.

The response we can expect is truly massive pressure for migration from South to North. The push will clearly be there, not only from those prepared to take low-paid urban employment but a fortiori from the significantly growing numbers of educated persons from the South. There will also be a bigger pull than before, precisely because of the bipolar split in the core zones, as well as the consequent acute pressure this will cause employers to reduce labor costs by employing migrants (not only as low-skilled personnel but also as middle-level cadres).

There will of course be (there already is) an acute social reaction within the North—a call for more repressive legislation to limit entry and to limit the sociopolitical rights of those who do enter. The result may be the worst of all de facto compromises: an inability to prevent effectively the entry of migrants, combined with the capability to ensure second-class political status for them. This would imply that by 2025 or so, in North America, the EC, and (even) Japan, the population socially defined as being of "Southern" origin may well range from twenty-five to fifty percent, and much higher in certain subregions and within large urban centers. But since many (perhaps most) of these persons will not have voting rights (and perhaps only limited access at best to social welfare provisions), there will be a high correlation of those occupying the lowest-paid urban jobs (and urbanization will by then have reached new heights) with those who are being denied political (and social) rights. It was this kind of situation in Great Britain and France in the first half of the nineteenth century that led to well-founded fears that the so-called dangerous classes would pull the house down. At that time, the industrialized countries invented the liberal state to overcome just this danger, granting suffrage and offering the welfare state to appease the plebeians. In 2030, Western Europe/North America/Japan may find themselves in the same position as Great Britain and France were in in 1830. "The second time as farce"?

The fourth difference between the prosperity that reigned between 1945 and 1967/73 and what we can expect between the years 2000 and 2025 will have to do with the situation of the middle strata in the core zones. These were the great beneficiaries of the period 1945–67/73. Their numbers increased dramatically, both absolutely and relatively. Their standard of living went up dramatically as well. And the percentage of posts defined as "middle stratum" went up sharply as well. The middle strata became a major pillar of stability of the political systems, and they formed a very large pillar indeed. Furthermore the skilled workers, the economic stratum below them, came to dream of nothing more than to become part of these middle strata—via union-backed wage increases, higher education for their children, and government-aided improvement in living conditions.

Of course, the overall price for this expansion was a significant rise in costs of production, a secular inflation, and a serious squeeze on the accumulation of capital. The present Kondratieff B-phase is consequently spawning acute worries about "competitivity" and about the fiscal burdens of the state. This worry will not diminish, but will indeed increase, in an A-phase in which there are two acutely competing poles of growth. What one can expect therefore is a persistent effort to reduce, absolutely and relatively, the numbers of middle strata in the production processes (including the service industries). There will also be a continuation of the present attempt to reduce state budgets, an attempt that ultimately will threaten most of all these middle strata.

The political fallout of this cutback on middle strata will be very heavy. Educated, used to comfort, middle strata threatened with being *déclassé* will not take passively such a retrogression of status and income. We already saw their teeth during the world-wide revolution of 1968. To pacify them, economic concessions were made from 1970 to 1985. These countries are paying the price now, and these concessions will be difficult to renew, or, if renewed, will affect the economic struggle between the EC and the Japan-United States condominium. In any case, the capitalist world-economy will be faced with the immediate dilemma of either limiting capital accumulation or suffering the politico-economic revolt of erstwhile middle strata. It will be a bitter choice.

The fifth difference will be in the ecological constraints. Capitalist entrepreneurs have been living off the externalization of costs from the beginnings of this historical system. One major externalized cost has been the cost of renewing the ecological base of an ever-expanding global production. Since entrepreneurs did not renew the ecological base and there was also no (world) government ready to tax sufficiently for this purpose, the ecological base of the world-economy has been steadily reduced. The last and largest expansion of the world-economy, from 1945 to 1967/73, used up the remaining margin, which is what has given rise to the green movements and the planetary concern for the environment.

The expansion of 2000–2025 will therefore lack the necessary ecological base. One of three outcomes is possible. The expansion will be aborted, with the attendant political collapse of the world-system. The ecological base will be depleted more than it is physically possible for the earth to sustain, with attendant catastrophes such as global warming. Or the social costs of cleanup, limitation of use, and regeneration will be accepted seriously.

If the third, and functionally least immediately damaging, of the three is the collective path chosen, it would create an immediate strain on the operations of the world-system. Either the cleanup would be done at the expense of the South, thereby making still more acute the North-South disparity, and providing a very clearly focused source of North-South tension, or the costs would be disproportionately assumed by the North, which would necessarily involve a reduction of the North's level of prosperity. Furthermore, whichever path is taken, serious action on the environment will inevitably reduce the margin of global profit (despite the fact that environmental cleanup will itself become a source of capital accumulation). Given this second consideration, and given a context of acute competition between the Japan-United States condominium and the EC, we may expect considerable cheating and therefore inefficacy in the process of regeneration—in which case we are back to either the first or the second outcome.

The sixth difference will be in the reaching of two asymptotes in the secular trends of the world-system: geographical expansion and deruralization. The capitalist world-economy had already in theory expanded to include the entire globe by 1900. This was, however, true primarily of the reach of the interstate system. It became true of the reach of the production networks of the commodity chains only in the period 1945–67/73. It is now, however, true of both. The capitalist world-economy has equally been undergoing a process of deruralization (sometimes called, less exactly, proletarianization) for four hundred years, and for the last two hundred with increasing speed. The years 1945–67/63 saw a spectacular jump in this process—Western Europe, North America, and Japan becoming fully deruralized and the South partially but significantly so. It is probable this process will be completed in the period 2000–2025.

The ability of the capitalist world-economy to expand into new geographical zones has historically been a crucial element in maintaining its rate of profit and hence its accumulation of capital. This has been the essential counter to the creeping rise in the cost of labor engendered by the combined growth in both political and workplace power of the working classes. If now there are no longer new working strata which have not yet acquired either the political or the workplace power to increase the part of the surplus value they could retain available to be recruited, the result would be the same kind of squeeze on the accumulation of capital that is being caused by ecological exhaustion. Once geographical lines are reached, and populations deruralized, the difficulties entailed by the political process of cost reduction become so great that savings can't really be achieved. Real costs of production must rise globally, and therefore profits must decline.

There is a seventh difference between the coming Kondratieff A-phase and the last one; it has to do with the social structure and the political climate of the countries of the South. Since 1945, the proportion of the middle strata in the South has risen significantly. This wasn't hard, since it was extraordinarily small up to then. If it went from only five to ten percent of the population, then it has doubled in proportion and, given the population increase, quadrupled or sextupled in absolute numbers. Since this is fifty to seventy-five percent of the world's population, we are talking about a very large group. The cost of keeping them at the consumption level to which they feel minimally entitled will be impressively high.

In addition, these middle strata, or local cadres, were by and large quite busy with "decolonization" in the period 1945–67/73. This was obviously true of all those living in those parts of the South that were colonies as of 1945 (almost the whole of Africa, South and Southeast Asia, the Caribbean, and miscellaneous other areas). It was also almost as true of those living in the "semicolonies" (China, parts of the Middle East, Latin America, Eastern Europe), where various forms of "revolutionary" activity comparable in psychic tonality to decolonization were occurring. It is not necessary here to evaluate the quality or the existential meaning of all these movements. It is enough to observe two characteristics of all these movements: They consumed the energies of large numbers of people, especially of the middle strata. And these people were suffused with political optimism, which took a particular form, best summed up in the pithy saying of Kwame Nkrumah: "Seek ye first the political kingdom, and all things shall be added unto you." In practice this meant that the middle strata of the South (and the *potential* middle strata) were ready to be somewhat patient about their weak economic status: they felt sure that if they could achieve political power during a first thirty-year period or so, they or their children would find their economic reward in the subsequent thirty-year period.

In the period 2000–2025, not only will there be no "decolonization" to preoccupy these cadres and keep them optimistic but also their economic situation will almost certainly become worse, for the various reasons adduced above (concentration on China/Russia, expansion of numbers of cadres in the South, world-wide effort to cut back on middle strata). Some of these may escape (that is, migrate) to the North. This will only make the plight of those who remain more bitter.

The eighth and ultimately most serious difference between the last and the next Kondratieff A-phase is purely political: the rise of democratization and the decline of liberalism. For it must be remembered that democracy and liberalism are not twins but, for the most part, opposites. Liberalism was invented to counter democracy. The problem that gave birth to liberalism was how to contain the dangerous classes, first within the core, then within the world-system as a whole. The liberal solution was to grant limited access to political power and limited sharing of the economic surplus value, at levels that would not threaten the process of the ceaseless accumulation of capital or the state-system that sustained it.

The basic theme of the liberal state nationally and the liberal interstate system worldwide has been rational reformism, primarily via the state. The formula of the liberal state, as it was developed in the core states in the nineteenth century—universal suffrage plus the welfare state—worked marvelously well. In the twentieth century, a comparable formula was applied to the interstate system in the form of the self-determination of nations and the economic development of underdeveloped nations. It stumbled, however, over the inability to create a welfare state at the world level (as advocated, for example, by the Brand Commission). For this could not be done without impinging on the basic process of the capital accumulation of capital. The reason was rather simple: The formula applied within core states depended for its success on a hidden variable—the economic exploitation of the South, combined with anti-South racism. At the world level, this variable did not exist, logically could not exist.[4]

The consequences for the political climate are clear. The years 1945–67/73 were the apogee of global liberal reformism: decolonization, economic development, and, above all, optimism about the future prevailed everywhere—West, East, North, and South. However, in the subsequent Kondratieff B-phase, with decolonization completed, the expected economic development became in most areas a faint memory, and optimism dissolved. Furthermore, for all the reasons we have already discussed, we do not expect economic development to return to the fore in the South in the coming A-phase, and we believe optimism has thus been fatally undermined.

At the same time, the pressure for democratization has been steadily growing. Democracy is basically antiauthority and antiauthoritarian. It is the demand for equal say in the political process at all levels and equal participation in the socioeconomic reward system. The greatest constraint on this thrust has been liberalism, with its promise of inevitable steady betterment via rational reform. To democracy's demand for equality now, liberalism offered hope deferred. This has been a theme not merely of the enlightened (and more powerful) half of the world establishment but even of the traditional antisystemic movements (the "Old Left"). The pillar of liberalism was the hope it offered. To the degree that the dream withers (like "a raisin in the sun"), liberalism as an ideology collapses, and the dangerous classes become dangerous once more.

This, then is where we seem to be heading in the next A-phase, circa 2000–2025. Although it will appear to be a spectacularly expansive period in some ways, in others it will be very sour. This is why I expect little peace, little stability, and little legitimacy. The result will be the onset of "chaos," which is merely the widening of the normal fluctuations in the system, with cumulative effect.

I believe a series of things will occur, none of them new phenomena. What may be different will be the inability to limit their thrusts and thus bring the system back to some kind of equilibrium. The question is: To what degree will this lack of ability to limit the thrusts prevail?

(1) The ability of the states to maintain internal order will probably decline. The degree of internal order is always fluctuating, and B-phases are noto-

riously moments of difficulty; for the system as a whole, however, and over four to five hundred years, internal order has been steadily increasing. We may call this the phenomenon of the rise of "stateness."

Of course, over the last one hundred years, the imperial structures *within* the capitalist world-economy (Great Britain, Austria-Hungary, most recently the U.S.S.R./Russia) have all disintegrated. But the thing to notice is rather the historic construction of states, which created their citizenry out of all those located within their boundaries. Such was metropolitan Great Britain and France, the United States and Finland, Brazil and India. And such also was Lebanon and Somalia, Yugoslavia and Czechoslovakia. The breakup or collapse of the latter is quite different from the breakup of the "empires."

One may dismiss the breakdown of stateness in the peripheral zone as either expectable or geopolitically insignificant. But it goes against the secular trend, and the breakdown of order in too many states creates a serious strain on the functioning of the interstate system. It is however the prospect of the weakening of stateness in the core zones that is most threatening. And the undoing of the liberal institutional compromise, which we have argued is occurring, suggests that this is happening. The states are deluged with demands for both security and welfare that they are politically unable to meet. The result is the steady privatization of security and welfare, which moves us in a direction out of which we had been moving for five hundred years.

(2) The interstate system has also been growing more structured and regulated for several hundred years, from Westphalia to the Concert of Nations to the UN and its family. There has been a tacit assumption that we have been easing ourselves into a functional world government. In a spirit of euphoria, Bush proclaimed its imminence as a "new world order," but the disappearance of reformist optimism has on the contrary shaken an interstate system whose foundations were always relatively weak.

Nuclear proliferation is now as inevitable, and will be as rapid, as expanded South-North migration will be. Per se, it is not catastrophic. Medium-size powers are probably no less "trustworthy" than big ones. Indeed they may be all the more prudent in that they may fear retaliation even more. Still, to the extent that stateness declines and technology advances, the creeping escalation of local tactical nuclear warfare may be difficult to contain.

As ideology recedes as the explanation for interstate conflicts, the "neutrality" of a weak confederal United Nations becomes ever more suspect. The ability of the UN to "peacekeep," limited as it is, may decline rather than increase in such an atmosphere. The call for "humanitarian interference" may come to be seen as merely the twenty-first-century version of nineteenth-century Western imperialism, which also affected civilizational justifications. Might there be secessions, multiple secessions, from the nominally universal structures (following the line North Korea has suggested vis-à-vis the IAEA)? Might we see the construction of rival organizations? It is not to be ruled out.

(3) If the states (and the interstate system) come to be seen as losing efficacy, to where will people turn for protection? The answer is already clear—to "groups." The groups can have many labels—ethnic/religious/linguistic groups, gender or sexual preference groups, "minorities" of multiple characterizations. This too is nothing new. What is new is the degree to which such groups are seen as an *alternative* to citizenship and participation in a state that by definition houses many groups (even if unequally ranked).

It is a matter of trust. Whom shall we trust in a disorderly world, in a world of great economic uncertainty and disparity, in a world where the future is not at all guaranteed? Yesterday, the majority answered the states. This is what we mean by legitimacy, if not of the states that existed in the present, then at least of those states we could expect to create (postreform) in the near future! States had an expansive, developmental image; groups have a defensive, fearful image.

At the same time (and this is precisely the rub), these same groups are also the product of the phenomenon of democratization, of the sense that the states have failed because liberal reform was a mirage, since the "universalism" of the states involved in practice forgetting or repressing many of the weaker strata. Thus the groups are products not only of intensified fear and disappointments but also of egalitarian consciousness-raising, and thus are a very powerful rallying point. It is hard to imagine that their political role will soon diminish. But given their self-contradictory structure (egalitarian but inward-looking), the amplification of this role may be consequently quite chaotic.

(4) How then will we dampen the spread of South-South wars, minority-minority conflicts in the North, that are one kind of derivation of such "groupism"? And who is in the moral, or military, position to do such dampening. Who is ready to invest their resources in it, especially given the projection of an intensified and roughly balanced North-North competition (Japan-United States vs. EC)? Here and there, some efforts will be made. But for the most part, the world will look on, as it did in the Iran-Iraq war and as it is doing in former Yugoslavia or in the Caucasus, or indeed in the ghettos of the United States. This will be all the more true as the number of simultaneous South-South conflicts grow.

Even more serious, who will limit North-South little wars, not only initiated, but deliberately initiated, not by the North but by the South, as part of a long-term strategy of military confrontation? The Gulf War was the beginning, not the end, of this process. The United States won the war, it is said. But at what price? At the price of revealing its financial dependence on others to pay for even little wars? At the price of setting itself a very limited objective—that is, one far less than unconditional surrender? At the price of having the Pentagon discuss a future world military strategy of "win, hold, win"?

President Bush and the U.S. military gambled that they could get their limited victory without much expenditure of lives (or money). The gamble worked, but it may seem wise to the Pentagon not to push one's luck. Once again, it is hard to see how the United States, or even the combined military of the North, could handle several Persian Gulf "crises" at the same time. And, given the pattern of the world-economy and that of the evolving world social structure I have postulated for 2000–2025, who would be so bold as to argue that such multiple simultaneous Persian Gulf "crises" will not occur?

(5) There is one last factor of chaos we should not underestimate—a new Black Death. The etiology of the AIDS pandemic remains a subject of great controversy. No matter, since it may have launched a process: AIDS has promoted the revival of a new deadly TB whose spread will now be autonomous. What is next? The spread of this disease not only reverses a long-term pattern of the capitalist world-economy (parallel to reversing the pattern of the growth of stateness and the strengthening of the interstate system) but also contributes to the further breakdown of stateness both by adding to the burdens of the state machinery and by stimulating an atmosphere of mutual intolerance. This breakdown in turn feeds the spread of the new diseases.

The key thing to understand is that one cannot predict which variable will be most affected by the spread of pandemic diseases: It reduces food consumers but also food producers. It reduces the number of potential migrants, but it increases labor shortages and a need for migration. In every case, which variable will be more? We shall not know until it is over. This is simply one more instance of the indeterminacy of the outcome of bifurcations.

This, then, is the picture of the second time frame, the entry into a period of chaos. There is a third time frame, the outcome, the new order that is created. Here one can be most brief because it is the most uncertain. A chaotic situation is, in a seeming paradox, that which is most sensitive to deliberate human intervention. It is during periods of chaos, as opposed to periods of relative order (relatively determined order), that human intervention makes a significant difference.

Are there any potential intervenors of systemic, constructive vision? I see two. There are the visionaries of restored hierarchy and privilege, the keepers of the eternal flame of aristocracy. Individually powerful persons but lacking any collective structure—the "executive committee of the ruling class" has never held a meeting—they act (if not conjointly, then in tandem) during systemic crises because they perceive everything to be out of control. At that point, they proceed on the Lampedusan principle: "Everything must change in order that nothing change." What they will invent and offer the world is hard to know, but I have confidence in their intelligence and perspicacity. Some new historical system will be offered, and they may be able to push the world in its direction.

Against them are the visionaries of democracy/equality (two concepts I believe to be inseparable). They emerged in the period 1789–1989 in the form of the antisystemic movements (the three varieties of "Old Left"), and their organizational history was that of a gigantic tactical success and an equally gigantic strategic failure. In the long run, these movements served more to sustain than to undermine the system.

The question mark is whether a new family of antisystemic movements will now emerge, with a new strategy, one strong enough and supple enough to have a major impact in the period 2000–2025, such that the outcome will not be Lampedusan. They may fail to emerge at all, or to survive, or to be supple enough to win out.

After the bifurcation, after say 2050 or 2075, we can thus be sure of only a few things. We shall no longer be living in a capitalist world-economy. We shall be living instead in some new order or orders, some new historical system or systems. And therefore we shall probably know once again relative peace, stability, and legitimacy. But will it be a better peace, stability, and legitimacy than we have hitherto known, or a worse one? That is both unknowable and up to us.

NOTES

1. Immanuel Wallerstein, "The Three Instances of Hegemony in the History of the Capitalist World-Economy," (ch. 16 this volume).
2. Each of the points here summarized briefly has been elaborated at greater length in many essays written over the past fifteen years, a good collection of which is included in Immanuel Wallerstein, *Geopolitics and Geoculture: Essays in a Changing World-System* (Cambridge: Cambridge University Press, 1991).
3. See *inter alia* W. Brian Arthur, "Competing Technologies, Increasing Returns, and Lock-in by Historical Events," *Economic Journal* XLIX, no. 394 (Mar. 1989), 116–131; and W. Brian Arthur, Yu. M. Ermoliev and M. Kaniovski, "Path-Dependent Processes and the Emergence of Macro-Structure," *European Journal of Operations Research* XXX (1987), 292–303.
4. A more detailed exposition of this effort and its failure is expounded in "The Concept of National Development, 1917–1989: Elegy and Requiem" and "The Collapse of Liberalism," chapters 6 and 13 of *After Liberalism* (New York: New Press, 1995).

28—The End of What Modernity?

> Amidst so much proclamation that we are living in a post-modern era, I
> felt it necessary to look again at what modernity has been and is sup-
> posed to be. This is a history of perceptions of modernity, which points
> therefore to the political/moral choices that are before us.

When I went to college in the late 1940s, we learned about the
virtues and the realities of being modern. Today, almost a
half-century later, we are being told of the virtues and the realities of being post-modern. What happened to modernity that it is no
longer our salvation, but has become instead our demon? Is it the same
modernity of which we were speaking then and are speaking now? Of
which modernity are we at an end?

The *Oxford English Dictionary*, always a first place to look, tells us
that one meaning of "modern" is historiographical: "commonly applied
(in contradistinction to ancient and medieval) to the time subsequent to
the Middle Ages." The OED cites an author using "modern" in this
sense as early as 1585. Furthermore, the OED informs us that modern
also means "pertaining to or originating in the current age or period," in
which case "post-modern" is an oxymoron, which one should, I think,
deconstruct.

Some 50 years ago, "modern" had two clear connotations. One was
positive and forward-looking. "Modern" signified the most advanced
technology. The term was situated in a conceptual framework of the presumed endlessness of technological progress, and therefore of constant
innovation. This modernity was in consequence a fleeting modernity—
what is modern today will be outdated tomorrow. This modernity was
quite material in form: airplanes, air-conditioning, television, comput-
ers. The appeal of this kind of modernity has still not exhausted itself.
There may no doubt be millions of children of the new age who assert
that they reject this eternal quest for speed and for control of the environment as something that is unhealthy, indeed nefarious. But there are
billions—billions, not millions—of persons in Asia and Africa, in Eastern Europe and Latin America, in the slums and ghettos of Western

Europe and North America, who yearn to enjoy fully this kind of modernity.

There was in addition, however, a second major connotation to the concept of modern, one that was more oppositional than affirmative. One could characterize this other connotation less as forward-looking than as militant (and also self-satisfied), less material than ideological. To be modern signified to be anti-medieval, in an antinomy in which the concept "medieval" incarnated narrow-mindedness, dogmatism, and above all the constraints of authority. It was Voltaire shouting "Ecrasez l'infâme." It was Milton in *Paradise Lost* virtually celebrating Lucifer. It was all the classical "Revolutions"—the English, the American, the French to be sure, but also the Russian and the Chinese. In the United States, it was the doctrine of the separation of church and state, the first Ten Amendments to the Constitution, the Emancipation Proclamation, Clarence Darrow at the Scopes trial, Brown vs. the Board of Education, and Roe vs. Wade.

It was in short the presumptive triumph of human freedom against the forces of evil and ignorance. It was a trajectory as inevitably progressive as that of technological advance. But it was not a triumph of humanity over nature; it was rather a triumph of humanity over itself, or over those with privilege. Its path was not one of intellectual discovery but of social conflict. This modernity was not the modernity of technology, of Prometheus unbound, of boundless wealth; it was rather the modernity of liberation, of substantive democracy (the rule of the people as opposed to that of the aristocracy, the rule of the best), of human fulfillment, and yes of moderation. This modernity of liberation was not a fleeting modernity, but an eternal modernity. Once achieved, it was never to be yielded.

The two stories, the two discourses, the two quests, the two modernities were quite different, even contrary one to the other. They were also, however, historically deeply intertwined one with the other, such that there has resulted deep confusion, uncertain results, and much disappointment and disillusionment. This symbiotic pair has formed the central cultural contradiction of our modern world-system, the system of historical capitalism. And this contradiction has never been as acute as it is today, leading to moral as well as to institutional crisis.

Let us trace the history of this confusing symbiosis of the two modernities—the modernity of technology and the modernity of liberation—over the history of our modern world-system. I divide my story into three parts: the 300–350 years that run between the origins of our modern world-system in the middle of the fifteenth century to the end of the eighteenth century; the nineteenth and most of the twentieth centuries, or to use two symbolic dates for this second period, the era from 1789 to 1968; the post-1968 period.

The modern world-system has never been fully comfortable with the idea of modernity, but for different reasons in each of the three periods. During the first period, only part of the globe (primarily most of Europe and the Americas) constituted the historical system, which we may call a capitalist world-economy. This is a designation we may indeed use for the system for that era, primarily because the system already had in place the three defining features of a capitalist world-economy: there existed a single axial division of labor within its boundaries, with a polarization between core-like and peripheral economic activities; the principal political structures, the states were linked together within and constrained by an interstate system whose boundaries matched those of the axial division of labor; those who pursued the ceaseless accumulation of capital prevailed in the middle run over those who did not.

Nonetheless, the geoculture of this capitalist world-economy was not yet firmly in place in this first period. Indeed, this was a period in which, for the parts of the world located within the capitalist world-economy, there were no clear geocultural norms. There existed no social consensus, even a minimal one, about such fundamental issues as whether the states should be secular; in whom the moral location of sovereignty was invested; the legitimacy of partial corporate autonomy for intellectuals; or the social permissibility of multiple religions. These are all familiar stories. They seem to be stories of those with power and privilege seeking to contain the forces of progress, in a situation in which the former still controlled the principal political and social institutions.

The crucial thing to note is that, during this long period, those who defended the modernity of technology and those who defended the modernity of liberation tended to have the same powerful political enemies. The two modernities seemed to be in tandem, and few could have used a language that made a distinction between the two. Galileo, forced to submit to the Church, but muttering (probably apocryphally) *Eppur si muove*, was seen as fighting both for technological progress and for human liberation. One way of resuming Enlightenment thought might be to say that it constituted a belief in the identity of the modernity of technology and the modernity of liberation.

If cultural contradiction there was, it was that the capitalist world-economy was functioning economically and politically within a framework that lacked the necessary geoculture to sustain it and reinforce it. The overall system was thus maladapted to its own dynamic thrusts. It may be thought of as uncoordinated, or as struggling against itself. The continuing dilemma of the system was geocultural. It required a major adjustment if the capitalist world-economy was to thrive and expand in the way its internal logic required.

It was the French Revolution that forced the issue, not merely for France but for the modern world-system as a whole. The French Revolution was not an isolated event. It might rather be thought of as the eye of a hurricane. It was bounded (preceded and succeeded) by the decolonization of the Americas—the settler decolonizations of British North America, Hispanic America, and Brazil; the slave revolution of Haiti; and the abortive Native American uprisings such as Túpac Amarú in Peru. The French Revolution connected with and stimulated struggles for liberation of various kinds and nascent nationalisms throughout Europe and around its edges—from Ireland to Russia, from Spain to Egypt. It did this not only by evoking in these countries resonances of sympathy for French revolutionary doctrines but also by provoking reactions against French (that is, Napoleonic) imperialism that were couched in the name of these very same French revolutionary doctrines.

Above all, the French Revolution made it apparent, in some ways for the first time, that the modernity of technology and the modernity of liberation were not at all identical. Indeed, it might be said that those who wanted primarily the modernity of technology suddenly took fright at the strength of the advocates of the modernity of liberation.

In 1815, Napoleon was defeated. There was a "Restoration" in France. The European powers established a Concert of Nations that, at least for some, was supposed to guarantee a reactionary status quo. But this was in fact to prove impossible. And in the years between 1815 and 1848, a geoculture was elaborated that was designed instead to promote the modernity of technology while simultaneously containing the modernity of liberation.

Given the symbiotic relationship of the two modernities, it was not an easy task to obtain this partial unyoking of the two modernities. Yet it was accomplished, and it thereby created a lasting geocultural basis for legitimating the operations of the capitalist world-economy. At least it succeeded for 150 years or so. The key to the operation was the elaboration of the ideology of liberalism, and its acceptance as the emblematic ideology of the capitalist world-economy.

Ideologies themselves were an innovation emerging out of the new cultural situation created by the French Revolution.[1] What those who thought in 1815 that they were reestablishing order and tradition discovered was that in fact it was too late: a sea-change in mentalities had occurred, and it was historically irreversible. Two radically new ideas had become very widely accepted as almost self-evident. The first was that political change was a normal occurrence, rather than an exceptional one. The second was that sovereignty lay in an entity called the "people."

Both concepts were explosive. To be sure, the Holy Alliance rejected both these ideas totally. However, the British Tory government, the government of the new hegemonic power in the world-system, was far more equivocal, as was the Restoration monarchy of Louis XVIII in France. Conservative in instinct, but intelligent in the exercise of power, these two governments were equivocal because they were aware of the strength of the typhoon in public opinion, and they decided to bend with it rather than risk a break.

Thus emerged the ideologies, which were quite simply the long-run political strategies designed to cope with the new beliefs in the normality of political change and the moral sovereignty of the people. Three principal ideologies emerged. The first was conservatism, the ideology of those who were most dismayed by the new ideas and thought them morally wrong, that is, those who rejected modernity as nefarious.

Liberalism arose in turn in response to conservatism as the doctrine of the defenders of modernity who sought to achieve its full flourishing — methodically, with a minimum of sharp disruption, and with a maximum of controlled manipulation. As the U.S. Supreme Court said in 1954 when it outlawed segregation, they believed that the changes should proceed "with all deliberate speed," which as we know really means "not too fast, but then again not too slow." The liberals were totally committed to the modernity of technology, but they were rather queasy about the modernity of liberation. Liberation for the technicians, they thought, was a splendid idea; liberation for ordinary people, however, presented dangers.

The third great ideology of the nineteenth century, socialism, emerged last. Like the liberals, socialists accepted the inevitability and desirability of progress. Unlike the liberals, they were suspicious of top-down reform. They were impatient for the full benefits of modernity — the modernity of technology to be sure, but even more the modernity of liberation. They suspected, quite correctly, that the liberals intended "liberalism" to be limited both in its scope of application and in the persons to whom it was intended to apply.

In the emerging triad of ideologies, the liberals situated themselves in the political center. While liberals sought to remove the state, particularly the monarchical state, from many arenas of decision-making, they were always equally insistent on putting the state into the center of rational reformism. In Great Britain, for example, the repeal of the Corn Laws was no doubt the culmination of a long effort to remove the state from the business of protecting internal markets against foreign competition. But in the very same decade the very same parliament passed the Factory Acts, the beginning (not the end) of a long effort to get the state into the business of regulating conditions of work and employment.

Liberalism, far from being a doctrine that was anti-state in essence, became the central justification for the strengthening of the efficacy of the state machinery.[2] This was because liberals saw the state as essential to achieving their central objective — furthering the modernity of technology while simultaneously judiciously appeasing the "dangerous classes." They hoped thereby to check the precipitate implications of the concept of the sovereignty of the "people" that were derived from a modernity of liberation.

In the nineteenth-century core zones of the capitalist world-economy, liberal ideology translated itself into three principal political objectives — suffrage, the welfare state, and national identity — the combination of which liberals hoped would achieve the objective of appeasing these "dangerous classes" while nonetheless ensuring the modernity of technology.

The debate over the suffrage was a continuous one throughout the century and beyond. In practice, there was a steady upward curve of expansion of the eligibility to vote, in most places in this order: first to smaller property-holders, then to propertyless males, then to younger persons, then to women. The liberal gamble was that previously excluded persons, once they received the vote, would accept the idea that the periodic vote represented their full claim to political rights, and that therefore they would then drop any other more radical ideas about effective participation in collective decision-making.

The debate over the welfare state, really a debate about the redistribution of surplus-value, was also a continuous one and also showed a steady upward curve of concessions, at least until the 1980s when it started to recede for the first time. What the welfare state essentially involved was a social wage, where a portion (a growing portion) of the income of wage-workers came not directly from employers' wage packets but indirectly via governmental agencies. This system partially delinked income from employment, enabled some slight equalization of wages across skill levels and wage-rents; and shifted part of the negotiations between capital and labor to the political arena wherein, with the suffrage, workers had somewhat more leverage. The welfare state did, however, less for workers at the bottom end of the wage-scale than it did for a middle stratum, whose size was growing and whose political centrality was becoming the strong underpinning of centrist governments committed to the active reinforcement of liberal ideology.

Neither the suffrage nor the welfare state nor even the pair would have been enough to tame the dangerous classes without adding a third crucial variable that ensured that these dangerous classes would not inspect too closely how great were the concessions of the suffrage and the welfare state. This third variable was the creation of national identity. In 1845, Benjamin Disraeli, Earl of Beaconsfield, future "enlightened Conservative" Prime Minister of Great Britain, published a novel entitled *Sybil, or the Two Nations*. In his "Advertisement," Disraeli tells us that the subject is "the Condition of the People," something apparently so terrible in that year that, in order not to be accused by readers of exaggeration, he "found the absolute necessity of suppressing much that is genuine." It is a novel that incorporated in the plot the then powerful Chartist movement. The novel is about the "Two Nations of England, the Rich and the Poor" who, it is suggested, derive from two ethnic groups, the Normans and the Saxons.[3]

Disraeli, in the concluding pages, is quite harsh about the limited relevance to the "people" of formal political reform, that is, of classical liberalism. His text reads:

> The written history of our country for the last ten reigns has been a mere phantasma, giving the origin and consequence of public transactions a character and colour in every respect dissimilar to their natural form and hue. In this mighty mystery all thoughts and things have assumed an aspect and title contrary to their real quality and style: Oligarchy has been called Liberty; an exclusive Priesthood has been christened a National church; Sovereignty has been the title of something that has had no dominion, while absolute power has been wielded by those who profess themselves the servants of the People. In the selfish strife of factions, two great existences have been blotted out of the history of England, the Monarch and the Multitude; as the power of the Crown has diminished, the privileges of the People have disappeared; till at length the sceptre has become a pageant, and its subject has degenerated again into a serf.
>
> But Time, that brings all things, has brought also to the mind of England some suspicion that the idols they have so long worshipped, and the oracles that have so long deluded them, are not the true ones. There is a whisper rising in this country that Loyalty is not a phrase, Faith not a delusion, and Popular Liberty something more diffusive and substantial than the profane exercise of the sacred rights of sovereignty by political classes.[4]

If Great Britain (and France, and indeed all countries) were "two nations," the Rich and the Poor, Disraeli's solution clearly was to make them into one—one in sentiment, one in loyalty, one in self-abnegation. This "oneness" we call national identity. The great program of liberalism was not to make states out of nations, but to create nations out of states. That is to say, the strategy was to take those who were located within the boundaries of the state—formerly the "subjects" of the king-sovereign, now the sovereign "people"—and make them into "citizens," all identifying with their state.

In practice this was accomplished by various institutional requirements. The first consisted of establishing clear legal definitions of membership in the polity: The rules varied, but always tended to exclude (with lesser or greater rigor) new arrivals in the state ("migrants") while usually including all those who were considered "normally" resident.

The unity of this latter group was then usually reinforced by moving towards linguistic uniformity: a single language within the state; and quite often just as important, a language different from that of neighboring states. This was accomplished by requiring all state activities to be conducted in a single language, by sustaining the activity of scholarly unification of the language (e.g., national academies controlling dictionaries), and by forcing the acquisition of this language on linguistic minorities.

The great unifying institutions of the people were the educational system and the armed forces. In at least all the core countries, elementary education became compulsory, and in very many so did military training. The schools and the armies taught languages, civic duties, and nationalist loyalty. Within a century, states that had been two "nations" — the Rich and the Poor, the Normans and the Saxons — became one nation in self-regard, in this particular case the "English."

One should not miss one final crucial element in the task of creating national identify — racism. Racism unites the race deemed superior. It unites it within the state at the expense of some minorities to be excluded from full or partial citizenship rights. But it unites the "nation" of the nation-state vis-à-vis the rest of the world; not only vis-à-vis neighbors, but even more vis-à-vis the peripheral zones. In the nineteenth century, the states of the core became nation-states concomitant with becoming imperial states, who established colonies in the name of a "civilizing mission."

What this liberal package of suffrage, the welfare state, and national identity offered above all to the dangerous classes of the core states was hope — hope that the gradual but steady reforms promised by liberal politicians and technocrats would *eventually* mean betterment for the dangerous classes, an equalization of recompense, a disappearance of Disraeli's "two nations." The hope was offered directly to be sure, but it was also offered in more subtle ways. It was offered in the form of a theory of history that posited as inevitable this amelioration of conditions, under the heading of the irresistible drive to human liberty. This was the so-called Whig interpretation of history. However the politico-cultural struggle had been seen in the sixteenth to eighteenth centuries by people at the time, the two struggles — for the modernity of technology and the modernity of liberation — were definitely defined in the nineteenth century retrospectively as a single struggle centered around the social hero of the individual. This was the heart of this Whig interpreta-tion of history. This retrospective interpretation was itself part, indeed a major part, of the process of imposing a dominant geoculture in the nine-teenth century for the capitalist world-economy.

Hence, precisely at the moment in historical time when, in the eyes of the dominant strata, the two modernities came more than ever to seem to be divergent and even in conflict one with the other, the official ideology (the dominant geoculture) proclaimed the two to be identical. The dominant strata undertook a major educational campaign (via the school system and the armed forces) to persuade their internal dangerous classes of this identity of object. The intent was to convince the danger-ous classes to mute their claims for the modernity of liberation, and to invest their energies instead in the modernity of technology.

At an ideological level, this was what the class struggles of the nine-teenth century was about. And to the degree that workers' and socialist movements came to accept the centrality and even the primacy of the modernity of technology, they lost the class struggle. They exchanged their loyalty to the states for very modest (albeit real) concessions in the achievement of the modernity of liberation. And by the time the First World War had arrived, all sense of the primacy of the struggle for the modernity of liberation had indeed been muted, as the workers of each European country rallied round the sacred flag and national honor.

The First World War marked the triumph of liberal ideology in the European-North American core of the world-system. But it also marked the point at which the core-periphery political cleavage in the world-system came to the fore. The European powers had barely realized their final world conquests of the last third of the nineteenth century when the rollback of the West began.

Throughout East Asia, southern Asia, and the Middle East (with later prolongations in Africa, and resonances in nominally-independent Latin America), national liberation movements began to emerge—in multiple guises, and with varying degrees of success. In the period from 1900 to 1917, various forms of nationalist uprising and revolution oc-curred in Mexico and China; in Ireland and India; in the Balkans and Turkey; in Afghanistan, Persia, and the Arab world. New "dangerous classes" had now raised their heads, waving the banner of the modernity of liberation. It was not that they were opposed to the modernity of technology. It was that they thought that their own hope for technological modernity would be a function of first achieving liberation.

The years from 1914 to 1945 were marked by one long struggle in the core, primarily between Germany and the United States, for hegemony in the world-system, a struggle in which, as we know, the United States triumphed. But the same years, and beyond, were a period of far more fundamental North-South struggle. Once again, the dominant strata (located in the North) tried to persuade the new dangerous classes of the identity of the two modernities. Woodrow Wilson offered the self-determination of nations and Presidents Roosevelt/Truman/Kennedy offered the economic development of the under-developed nations, the structural equivalents on a world scale of universal suffrage, and the welfare state at the national level within the core zone.

The concessions were indeed modest. The dominant strata also offered "identity" in the form of the unity of the free world against the Communist world. But this form of identity was greeted with enormous suspicion by the so-called Third World (that is, the peripheral and semi-peripheral zones *minus* those in the so-called Soviet bloc). The Third World considered the so-called Second World as in fact part of their zone and therefore objectively in the same camp. Faced however with the realities of U.S. power combined with the symbolic (but for the most part only symbolic) oppositional role of the Soviet Union, the Third World by and large opted for non-alignment, which meant that they never came to "identify" with the core zone in the way that the working classes in the core had come to identify with the dominant strata in a shared nationalism and racism. The liberal geoculture was working less well on a world scale in the twentieth century than it had on a national scale in the core zones in the nineteenth.

Still, liberalism was not yet at bay. Wilsonian liberalism was able to seduce and to tame Leninist socialism in ways parallel to how European liberalism had seduced and tamed social-democracy in the nineteenth century.[5] The Leninist program became not world revolution, but anti-imperialism with socialist construction, which on inspection turned out to be mere rhetorical variants on the Wilsonian/Rooseveltian concepts of the self-determination of nations and the economic development of underdeveloped countries. In Leninist reality, the modernity of technology had once again taken priority over the modernity of liberation. And just like the dominant liberals, the supposedly oppositional Leninists argued that the two modernities were in fact identical. And, with the aid of the Leninists, the liberals of the North began to make headway in persuading the national liberation movements of the South as well of this identity of the two modernities.

Precisely 25 years ago, in 1968, this convenient conceptual blurring of the two modernities was loudly and vigorously challenged by a world-wide revolution that took the form primarily, but not at all exclusively, of student uprisings. In the United States and in France, in Czechoslovakia and in China, in Mexico and in Tunisia, in Germany and in Japan, there were insurrections (and sometimes deaths), which, however different lo-cally, all essentially shared the same fundamental themes: The moder-nity of liberation is all, and has not been achieved. The modernity of technology is a deceptive trap. Liberals of all varieties—liberal liberals, conservative liberals, and above all socialist liberals (that is, the Old Left)—are not to be trusted, are indeed the prime obstacle to liberation.[6]

I myself was caught up in the centerpiece of the U.S. struggles, that of Columbia University,[7] and I have two overwhelming memories of that "revolution." One is the sense of genuine elation of the students in the buildings who were discovering through the practice of collective libera-tion what they experienced as a process of personal liberation. The sec-ond was the deep fear this release of liberatory sentiment evoked amongst most of the professorate and the administration, and most espe-cially among those who considered themselves apostles of liberalism and modernity, who saw in this upsurge an irrational rejection of the obvious benefits of the modernity of technology.

The world revolution of 1968 flamed up and then subsided, or rather was suppressed. By 1970 it was more or less over everywhere. Yet it had a profound impact on the geoculture. For 1968 shook the dominance of the liberal ideology in the geoculture of the world-system. It thereby re-opened the questions that the triumph of liberalism in the nineteenth century had closed out or relegated to the margins of public debate. Both the world right and the world left moved away once again from the liberal center. The so-called new conservatism was in many ways the old con-servatism of the first half of the nineteenth century resurrected. And the new left was in many ways similarly the resurrection of the radicalism of the early nineteenth century, which I remind you was at that time still symbolized by the term "democracy," a term later to be appropriated by centrist ideologues.

Liberalism did not disappear in 1968; it did, however, lose its role as the defining ideology of the geoculture. The 1970s saw the ideological spectrum return to that of a real triad, undoing the blurring of the three ideologies that had occurred when they had become de facto simply three variants of liberalism between say 1850 and the 1960s. The debate seemed to turn back 150 years or so. Except that the world had moved on, in two senses: The modernity of technology had transformed the world social structure in ways that threatened to destabilize the social and economic underpinnings of the capitalist world-economy. And the ideological history of the world-system was now a memory that affected the current ability of the dominant strata to maintain political stability in the world-system.

Let us look at the second change first. Some of you may be surprised that I place so much emphasis on 1968 as a turning-point. You may think: Is not 1989, the symbolic year of the collapse of the Communisms, a more significant date in the history of the modern world-system? Did 1989 not in fact represent the collapse of the socialist challenge to capitalism, and therefore the final achievement of the objective of liberal ideology, the taming of the dangerous classes, the universal acceptance of the virtues of the modernity of technology? Well, no, precisely not! I come to tell you that 1989 was the continuation of 1968, and that 1989 marked not the triumph of liberalism and therefore the permanence of capitalism but quite the opposite, the collapse of liberalism and an enormous political defeat for those who would sustain the capitalist world-economy.

What happened economically in the 1970s and 1980s was that, as a result of a Kondratieff-B downturn or stagnation in the world-economy, state budgets almost everywhere were particularly strained in the peripheral and semiperipheral zones of the world-economy. This was not true of an extended East Asian zone in the 1980s, but in such downturns there is always one relatively small zone that does well precisely because of the overall downturn, and the East Asian growth of the 1980s in no way refutes the general pattern.

Such downturns have of course happened repeatedly in the history of the modern world-system. However, the political consequences of this particular Kondratieff-B phase were more severe than any previous one, just because the previous A-phase, 1945–1970, seemingly marked the worldwide political triumph of the movements of national liberation and other antisystemic movements. In other words, just because liberalism had seemed to pay off so well worldwide in 1945–1970 (self-determination with economic development), the let-down of the 1970s and 1980s was all the more severe. It was hope betrayed and illusions shattered, particularly but not only in the peripheral and semiperipheral zones. The slogans of 1968 came to seem all the more plausible. Rational reformism (a fortiori when it had been clothed in "revolutionary" rhetoric) seemed a bitter deception.

In country after country of the so-called Third World, the populaces turned against the movements of the Old Left and charged fraud. The populaces may not have been sure what to substitute—a riot here, a religious fundamentalism there, an anti-politics in a third place—but they were sure that the pseudo-radicalism of the Old Left was in fact a phony liberalism that paid off only for a small elite. In one way or another the populaces of those countries sought to oust these elites. They had lost faith in their states as the agents of a modernity of liberation. Let us be clear: they had not lost their desire for liberation, merely their faith in the old strategy of achieving it.

The collapse of the Communisms in 1989–91 then was merely the last in a long series, the discovery that even the most radical rhetoric was no guarantor of the modernity of liberation, and probably a poor guarantor of the modernity of technology.[8] Of course, in desperation and temporarily, these populaces accepted the slogans of the revitalized world right, the mythology of the "free market" (of a kind, be it said, not to be found even in the United States of western Europe), but this was a passing mirage. We are already seeing the political rebound in Lithuania, in Poland, in Hungary, and elsewhere.

It is, however, also true that neither in Eastern Europe nor anywhere else in the world is it likely that people ever again will believe in the Leninist version of the promises of rational reformism (under the appellation of socialist revolution). This is of course a disaster for world capitalism. For the belief in Leninism had served for 50 years at least as the major *constraining* force on the dangerous classes in the world-system. Leninism in practice had been a very conservative influence, preaching the inevitable triumph of the people (and hence implicitly patience). The protective cloak of Leninism has now been lost to the dominant strata in the modern world-system.[9] The dangerous classes may now become truly dangerous once again. Politically, the world-system has become unstable.

At the very same time, the socioeconomic underpinnings of the world-system have been seriously weakening. Let me just mention four such trends, which do not exhaust the list of structural transformations. First, there is a serious depletion of the world pool of available cheap labor. For four centuries now, urban wage laborers have been able repeatedly to use their bargaining power to raise the portion of surplus-value they can obtain for their labor. Capitalists have nonetheless been able to counter the negative effect this has on the rate of profit by expanding, just as repeatedly, the labor pool and thereby bringing into the wage labor market new groups of previously non-waged laborers who were initially ready to accept very low wages. The final geographical expansion of the capitalist world-economy in the late nineteenth century to include the entire globe has forced an acceleration of the process of deruralization of the world labor force, a process that is far advanced and may be substantially completed in the near future.[10] This inevitably means a sharp increase in worldwide labor costs as a percentage of the total cost of worldwide production.

A second structural problem is the squeeze on the middle strata. They have been correctly perceived as a political pillar of the existing world-system. But their demands, on both employers and the states, have been expanding steadily, and the worldwide cost of sustaining a vastly expanded middle stratum at even higher *per personam* levels is becoming too much to bear for both enterprises and state treasuries. This is what is behind the multiple attempts of the last decade to roll back the welfare state. But of two things one. Either these costs are not rolled back, in which case both states and enterprises will be in grave trouble and frequent bankruptcy. Or they will be rolled back, in which case there will be significant political disaffection among precisely the strata that have provided the strongest support for the present world-system.

A third structural problem is the ecological crunch, which poses for the world-system an acute economic problem. The accumulation of capital has for five centuries now been based on the ability of enterprises to externalize costs. This has essentially meant the overutilization of world resources at great collective cost but at virtually no cost to the enterprises. But at a certain point the resources are used up, and the negative toxicity reaches a level that it is not possible to continue. Today we find we are required to invest heavily in cleanup, and we shall have to cut back in usage not to repeat the problem. But it is equally true, as enterprises have been shouting, that such actions will lower the global rate of profit.

Finally, the demographic gap doubling the economic gap between North and South is accelerating rather than diminishing. This is creating an incredibly strong pressure for South to North migratory movement, which in turn is generating an equally strong anti-liberal political reaction in the North. It is easy to predict what will happen. Despite increased barriers, illegal immigration will rise everywhere in the North, as will know-nothing movements. The internal demographic balances of states in the North will change radically and acute social conflict can be expected.

Thus, it is that today and for the next 40–50 years, the world-system is finding itself in acute moral and institutional crisis. To return to our opening discourse on the two modernities, what is happening is that there is at last a clear and overt tension between the modernity of technology and the modernity of liberation. Between 1500 and 1800, the two modernities seemed to be in tandem. Between 1789 and 1968, their latent conflict was kept in check by the successful attempt of liberal ideology to pretend that the two modernities were identical. But since 1968, the mask is off. They are in open struggle with each other.

There are two principal cultural signs of this recognition of the conflict of the two modernities. One is the "new science," the science of complexity. Suddenly, in the last ten years, a very large number of physical scientists and mathematicians have turned against the Newtonian-Baconian-Cartesian ideology that has claimed for 500 years at least to be the only possible expression of science. With the triumph of liberal ideology in the nineteenth century, Newtonian science had become enshrined as universal truth.

The new scientists have challenged not the validity of Newtonian science but its universality. Essentially they have argued that the laws of Newtonian science are those of a limited special case of reality, and that to understand reality scientifically one must greatly expand our framework of reference and our tools of analysis. Hence, today, we hear the new buzz words of chaos, bifurcations, fuzzy logic, fractals, and most fundamentally the arrow of time. The natural world and all its phenomena have been historicized.[11] The new science is distinctly *not* linear. But the modernity of technology was erected on the pillar of linearity. Hence the new science raises the most fundamental questions about the modernity of technology, at least in the form it has been expounded classically.

The other cultural sign that recognizes the conflict of the two modernities is the movement, primarily in the humanities and the social sciences, of "post-modernity." Post-modernity, I hope I have made clear, is not *post*-modern at all. It is a mode of rejecting the modernity of technology on behalf of the modernity of liberation. If it has been stated in this bizarre form, it is because the post-modernists have been seeking a way to break out of the linguistic hold liberal ideology has had on our discourse. Post-modernity as an explanatory concept is confusing. Post-modernity as an annunciatory doctrine is no doubt prescient. For we are indeed moving in the direction of another historical system. The modern world-system is coming to an end. It will however require at least another 50 years of terminal crisis, that is of "chaos," before we can hope to emerge into a new social order.

Our task of today, and for the next 50 years, is the task of utopistics. It is the task of imagining and struggling to create this new social order. For it is by no means assured that the end of one inegalitarian historical system will result in a better one. The struggle is quite open. We need today to define the concrete institutions through which human liberation can finally be expressed. We have lived through its pretended expression in our existing world-system, in which liberal ideology tried to persuade us of a reality that the liberals were in fact struggling against, the reality of increasing equality and democracy. And we have lived through the disillusionment of failed antisystemic movements, movements that were themselves as much part of the problem as of the solution.

We must engage in an enormous worldwide multilogue, for the solutions are by no means evident. And those who wish to continue the present under other guises are very powerful. The end of what modernity? Let it be the end of false modernity, and the onset, for the first time, of a true modernity of liberation.

ACKNOWLEDGMENT

I gave this as an Address to the President's Forum, "The End of Modernity," Bucknell University, Sept. 30, 1993.

NOTES

1. See the more detailed argument in my "The French Revolution as a World-Historical Event," in *Unthinking Social Science: The Limits of Nineteenth-Century Paradigms* (Cambridge Polity Press, 1991), 7–22.

2. This argument is elaborated in my "Liberalism and the Legitimation of Nation-States: An Historical Interpretation," *Social Justice* 19/1 (Spring 1992): 22–33.

3. Benjamin Disraeli, Earl of Beaconsfield, *Sybil, or the Two Nations* (London: John Lane, The Bodley Head, 1927 [Orig. ed. 1845]).

4. Ibid., 641.

5. See my "The Concept of National Development, 1917–1989," in G. Marks and L. Diamond, editors, *Reexamining Democracy* (Newbury Park: Sage, 1992), 79–89.

6. For a fuller analysis of the world revolution of 1968, see my "1968, Revolution in the World-System," in *Geopolitics and Geoculture: Essays in the Changing World-System* (Cambridge: Cambridge University Press, 1991), 65–83. [Ch. 23 this volume]

7. For an excellent account, see Jerry L. Avorn, et al., *Up Against the Ivy Wall: A History of the Columbia Crisis* (New York: Atheneum, 1968).

8. For a step-by-step analysis of how 1989 grew out of 1968, see G. Arrighi, T. K. Hopkins, and I. Wallerstein, "1989, The Continuation of 1968," *Review* 15/2 (Spring 1992): 221–242.

9. See my longer explication of this in "The Collapse of Liberalism," in R. Miliband and L. Panitch, editors, *Socialist Register 1992* (London: Merlin Press, 1992), 96–110.

10. See R. Kasaba and F. Tabak, "The Restructuring of World Agriculture, 1873–1990," in P. McMichael, editor, *Food and Agricultural Systems in the World-Economy* (Westport, CT.: Greenwood Press, 1995), 79–93.

11. For the implications of this for social analysis, see the special issue, "The 'New Science' and the Historical Social Sciences," *Review* 15/1 (Winter 1992).